Education, Social Justice and Inter-agency Working

The idea of joined-up policy and inter-agency working is central to contemporary education and wider social policy agendas. This book explores policy and practice in a range of areas where education and other agencies including health, social and employment services and housing interact.

The contributors investigate why joined-up policy has risen to the top of the current political agenda and how this connects with the promotion of 'Third Way' policies which seek to challenge social exclusion. They address the extent to which partnership or joined-up policy is capable of achieving social change, examining the subject in a range of contexts, conditions and countries.

The collection draws together papers exploring the significance of newly unfolding initiatives with others which explore longer established areas of education and social policy. International comparisons are drawn with European, US, Australian and Japanese perspectives, and the significance for future policy and practice is drawn.

Essential reading for scholars and professionals working in the area of Education and Social Policy, this book will also be of great interest to all those interested in promoting social justice for adults and children experiencing the effects of exclusion.

Sheila Riddell obtained her PhD on 'Gender and option choice' from the University of Bristol in 1988. Since then she has taught and researched in Scotland, and she is now Director of the Strathclyde Centre for Disability Research at the University of Glasgow. **Lyn Tett** is currently Head of the Department of Higher Education and Lifelong Learning, Moray House Institute of Education, University of Edinburgh. She has researched and written extensively in the area of adult literacy and has recently edited (together with J. Crowther and M. Hamilton) *Powerful Literacies*, published by NIAVCE in 2001.

Routledge Research in Education

Education, Social Justice and Inter-agency Working

Joined-up or fractured policy?

Edited by Sheila Riddell and Lyn Tett

London and New York

First published 2001
by Routledge
11 New Fetter Lane, London EC4P 4EE

Simultaneously published in the USA and Canada
by Routledge
29 West 35th Street, New York, NY 10001

Routledge is an imprint of the Taylor & Francis Group

Typeset in Baskerville by Taylor & Francis Books Ltd
Printed and bound in Great Britain by Biddles Ltd,
Guildford and King's Lynn

British Library Cataloguing in Publication Data
A catalogue record for this book is available from the British Library

Library of Congress Cataloging in Publication Data
Education, social justice, and inter-agency working :
joined-up or fractured policy/edited by Sheila Riddell and Lyn Tett
Includes bibliographical references and index.
1. Socially handicapped children–Services for. 2. Socially handicapped
children–Education. 3. Socially handicapped youth–Services for.
4. Socially handicapped youth–Education. 5. Social work with the socially
handicapped. 6. School social work. 7. Social work with the socially
handicapped–Great Britain. I. Riddell, Sheila. II. Tett, Lyn.

HV713 .E38   2001
362.7–dc21   2001019759

ISBN 0–415–24922–8

Contents

Illustrations

Tables

Figures

Contributors

Stephen Baron is Professor in Urban Education at the University of Glasgow. He has researched issues of community and education since the 1970s and is currently part of the team evaluating the City of Glasgow's pilot reorganisation of its schools into 'Learning Communities'. He is currently completing the text of *Community and Control: Surveillance, Containment and the State* for Pearson Education.

William Lowe Boyd is Distinguished Professor of Education at the Pennsylvania State University, and Professor-in-Charge of the Graduate Program in Educational Administration. A specialist in educational administration and education policy and politics, he has published over 120 articles and has co-edited thirteen books. He has served as president of the Politics of Education Association, is an officer of the American Educational Research Association, and has been a Visiting Fulbright Scholar in Australia and England. As a researcher for the National Center on School Leadership, the National Center on Education in the Inner Cities, and the Mid-Atlantic Regional Laboratory for Student Success, he has studied school effectiveness and efforts to achieve co-ordinated, school-linked services for at-risk children and their families.

Jill Clark is Senior Research Associate in the Department of Education, University of Newcastle. Her background is in criminology and she has undertaken a wide range of research into issues of education and disadvantage. She is currently evaluating community education programmes in an inner-city setting.

Robert L. Crowson is a Professor of Educational Administration and Policy with the Peabody College of Vanderbilt University. His PhD was earned at the University of Chicago. Crowson has specialised in the study of large-city school administration, particularly the urban principalship, school–community relations, co-ordinated children's services and the politics/organisation of city schools. He has served as a Senior Research Fellow with the National Center on School Leadership and the National Center for Education in the Inner Cities. His most recent book (in press) is focused upon issues in community development and school reform.

Alan Dyson is Professor of Special Needs Education in the Department of Education, University of Newcastle. He is Co-Director of the Special Needs Research Centre, where he has undertaken a good deal of research on policy-related issues. However, his interests extend beyond special needs education to wider issues of social and educational inclusion. His current research is in school–community relations in areas of social housing. He has a substantial background as a teacher in urban schools.

Richard Hatcher is a Senior Lecturer in the Faculty of Education at the University of Central England, Birmingham, UK. He has written widely on education policy and on issues of equality.

Hiroyuki Kasama is an Associate Professor in Early Childhood Education at the Kushiro campus of the Hokkaido University of Education, Japan. He was a research fellow in Moray House Institute of Education, University of Edinburgh, from 1999 to 2000, where his research focused on parental education as community education and the differences between early years education in Japan and Scotland.

Helen Kay is now Research Officer with Children in Scotland (the national membership agency for organisations and professionals working with children and their families) and was a research fellow in Moray House Institute of Education, University of Edinburgh, from 1997 to 1998.

Andrew Kendrick is a Senior Lecturer in the Department of Social Work at Dundee University. He completed a PhD in Social Anthropology at the London School of Economics in 1984. Since then he has carried out research on a range of child-care issues, including decision-making in child care, residential child care, and inter-agency work with children and young people in difficulty.

Dominique Leblond is a Senior Lecturer in the Department of Education at University Paris XII, France. She has written articles on education in a comparative perspective, with a particular focus on recent French and British policies.

Jane Lightfoot is a Research Fellow at the Social Policy Research Unit, University of York. Her research interests include the health-related support needs of pupils in mainstream schools who have a chronic illness or physical disability, and communication between health and education staff. She is also involved in researching the participation of children and young people in local health services development.

Gwynedd Lloyd is a Senior Lecturer in the Faculty of Education, University of Edinburgh. Her current research interests include exclusion from school, emotional and behavioural difficulties, gender and deviance, and ADHD, including issues around the use of medication.

Ian Martin is Senior Lecturer in the Department of Community Education, Moray House Institute of Education, University of Edinburgh.

Jane Martin now works for the Improvement and Development Agency, London, and was a research fellow in the School of Education, University of Birmingham.

Alan Millward is Reader in Special Needs Education in the Department of Education, University of Newcastle, where he is also Co-Director of the Special Needs Research Centre. He has conducted research on policy-related issues, particularly in relation to social and educational inclusion. His current research is in school–community relations in areas of social housing.

Enid Mordaunt is a Research Fellow in the Department of Social Policy at the University of Edinburgh. After a career in the education service, she now researches in the field of the inspection and regulation of public services, most notably OFSTED, Social Services Inspectorate, HM Inspectorate of Probation and HM Inspectorate of Prisons. Her work on administrative justice and complaint resolution in public services is currently examining the level and nature of procedural justice in SEN complaints to the Commissioners for Local Administration in England and Scotland.

Suzanne Mukherjee was a Research Fellow at the Social Policy Research Unit, University of York, between 1996 and 2001. Here she undertook research into support for children who have a chronic illness or physical disability, and was involved in implementing research findings in practice. Suzanne is currently based in the Department of Health Studies, University of York, where she is researching the impact of inflammatory bowel disease on parents and their children.

Pamela Munn is Professor of Curriculum Research and Associate Dean, Moray House Institute of Education, University of Edinburgh. She has a long-standing interest in a range of topics, including parental involvement in school governance and factors contributing to school ethos.

Sally Power is Professor of Education and Assistant Dean of Research at the Institute of Education, University of London. Her research interests include sociology of education policy, and she currently directs a major ESRC-funded project on Education Action Zones.

Stewart Ranson is Professor of Education, School of Education, University of Birmingham.

Sheila Riddell obtained her PhD on 'Gender and option choice' from the University of Bristol in 1988. Since then, she has taught and researched in Scotland, and is now Director of the Strathclyde Centre for Disability Research at the University of Glasgow. Sheila Riddell recently chaired a Scottish Executive Advisory Committee on the Education of Children with Severe Low Incidence Disabilities. Her research is currently focused on education, training and employment of disabled people. She has researched and written extensively on aspects of special educational needs policy and practice in the context of transitions to adulthood for disabled young people, mainstream and special school provision, assessment and recording/statementing and the use of Individualised Educational Programmes.

Jane Salisbury is co-ordinator of postgraduate studies at the School of Social Sciences, University of Wales, Cardiff, where she lectures in education policy, qualitative research methods and post-16 education and training. She has published papers on classroom ethnography, vocational education and training and the sociology of work. Some of her recent work has focused on educational reform and gender equality in Wales.

Robert Semmens is now senior lecturer at Melbourne University's Youth Research Centre. He began his career as a secondary teacher and student counsellor before a period of six years managing institutional facilities and community programmes for young offenders. He then entered teacher training as a lecturer at Melbourne State College, first to train teachers in the area of special education and integration, and more recently to teach at graduate and undergraduate levels in the area of social issues affecting student performance at school. Bob completed his PhD in 1986 on 'Curriculum aims in a youth training centre', based on data collected at the Malmsbury Youth Training Centre. Since then he has evaluated education and training programmes at Barwon Prison and Fairlea Women's Prison, and the delivery of correctional education and training programmes across Australia, as well as several projects related to school discipline and other mainstream schooling issues for disaffected students.

Patricia Sloper is a Senior Research Fellow and Leader of the Children and Families Team at the Social Policy Research Unit, University of York. She has long-standing research interests in the needs and experiences of chronically ill and disabled children and their families. The Children and Families Team's work focuses on support related to illness or disability in children and younger adults, multi-agency working, accessing the views of children, and ways of promoting research findings in practice.

Emer Smyth is Senior Research Officer with the Economic and Social Research Institute, Dublin. Her research interests centre on education and school-to-work transitions. She has recently published a study of school effectiveness in the secondary sector in Ireland, *Do Schools Differ?* (Oak Tree Press/ESRI 1999).

Joan Stead is a Research Fellow in the Faculty of Education, University of Edinburgh. She has recently carried out research into school inclusion/exclusion for Show and Gypsy Travellers, and refugee pupils. Research interests also include education for citizenship, social justice and qualitative methodology.

Lyn Tett is currently Head of the Department of Higher Education and Lifelong Learning, Moray House Institute of Education, University of Edinburgh. She has researched and written extensively in the areas of adult literacy and participation in higher education by socially excluded groups. She has a particular interest in the factors, such as class, gender and disability, that lead to the exclusion of adults from post-compulsory education and of the action that might be taken to promote social inclusion.

E. Kay M. Tisdall presently holds a joint post as Policy and Research Manager, Children in Scotland (the national membership agency for organisations and professionals working with children and their families) and Lecturer in Social Policy, University of Edinburgh. She convenes an interdisciplinary MSc in Childhood Studies at the university, that brings together academic disciplines to consider theories, policies and consultation with children and young people.

Alastair Wilson joined the Strathclyde Centre for Disability Research as a Research Fellow in 1997. Since then he has carried out research projects on strategies to counter the social exclusion of children in six European countries and the Employment Service's work preparation programme in Scotland. He also worked as Research Fellow on the ESRC funded project *The Meaning of the Learning Society for Adults with Learning Difficulties* and contributed to a review of social exclusion in relation to disabled people in Glasgow, funded by the Joseph Rowntree Foundation.

Acknowledgements

Both Sheila and Lyn would like to acknowledge the ongoing support of family and colleagues.

Lyn would like to thank the staff and students of the Department of Community Education, University of Edinburgh for their support, inspiration and enthusiasm that has kept her going through the 'dark times as well as the good times'.

Sheila would like to say a big thank you to Pauline Banks, Alastair Wilson, Charlotte Pearson, Deborah Hopkins, Nicola Cogan and Brian Sweeney at the Strathclyde Centre for Disability Research for their hard work and commitment. A particular thank you to Jean McPartland, who manages to stay calm in the face of impossible deadlines.

1 Education, social justice and inter-agency working

Joined-up or fractured policy?

Sheila Riddell and Lyn Tett

Introduction

The theme of inter-agency working and partnership, sometimes referred to by the shorthand term 'joined-up government', is at the centre of New Labour's vision of the modernised welfare state. The need to make policy connections appears to be regarded as particularly critical in relation to those at the social margins, for whom the liaison of education, social work, health, social security and employment services is regarded as critical. This edited collection explores policy and practice in a range of areas where education and other agencies interact.

In this introductory chapter, we frame some of the questions which are addressed by the papers which follow. The first question which concerns us is why joined-up policy has risen to the top of the political agenda at this point in time. How does it connect with other aspects of New Labour's political agenda, in particular the promotion of the 'Third Way' policies which reflect the dominance of global capitalism while seeking to mitigate some of its excesses and challenge social exclusion? Further questions arise about whose interests are served by the pursuit of joined-up policy, in particular when such policies are focused so tightly on those at the social margins.

A further question which bubbles to the surface throughout the book is the extent to which partnership, inter-agency working or joined-up policy is capable of achieving social change. The government has set itself the goal of moving towards greater social justice, with clear performance indicators and pre-defined milestones and long-term targets. Partnership is seen as a way of achieving greater social inclusion, but questions remain about whether this is actually the case and what evidence is available to support this belief. Furthermore, if partnership is seen as an alternative to forms of welfare based on internal and external markets, then what evidence is there that it leads to 'better' social outcomes, whether these are expressed in terms of social justice or greater effectiveness and efficiency?

The final question concerns the conditions which make for successful partnership working. Does the involvement of a range of professional agencies, parents and the voluntary sector make complicated decisions easier or easy decisions more complicated? In the following paragraphs, we flesh out some of the issues associated with each of these questions.

Policy goals associated with inter-agency working

The modernisation of welfare and the pursuit of social justice

During the late 1970s, a consensus arose that public services were wasteful, inefficient and geared towards serving the needs of self-interested professionals rather than the general public. Prime Minister James Callaghan in his 1976 Ruskin College speech raised these points in relation to education, and in 1979 the incoming Conservative government placed the reform of the public sector at the forefront of its political agenda. Informed by theorists of the right, such as von Hayek, the Conservatives committed themselves to 'rolling back the welfare state' to release individual initiative and entrepreneurialism (Deakin 1994). Quasi-markets were promoted, based on the creation of internal markets and the requirement that public sector organisations compete with those in the voluntary and private sectors to run public services. Coupled with the marketisation of the public sector was the rise of the audit culture (Power 1987) which required service purchasers to specify service standards, expressed as clear deliverables and performance indicators, to be achieved by service providers. The impact of the new managerialism on the public sector has been widely discussed (e.g. Clarke and Newman 1997; Clarke *et al.* 2000). At its worst, new managerialism was seen to foster a dull conformity whereby all policy goals were expressed as quantifiable targets and only those things which were readily measurable were valued. It should be noted, however, that new managerialism has been enthusiastically adopted by New Labour, and social justice goals are expressed in terms of targets, milestones and performance indicators.

Just as new managerialism may be seen as a continuous element within Conservative and New Labour policy, so the desire to transform the welfare state has been placed at the heart of New Labour's political project. However, whereas the Conservatives routinely portrayed state welfare as fostering cultures of dependency and inefficiency, New Labour has depicted the reform of welfare as inextricably connected with the pursuit of social justice. Joined-up policy is seen to lie at the heart of the new intelligent welfare state. Thus, in the 1994 Report of the Commission on Social Justice, the following key points are emphasised:

- Social justice cannot be achieved through the social security system alone; employment, education and housing are at least as important as tax and benefit policy in promoting financial independence.
- The welfare state must be shaped by the changing nature of people's lives, rather than people's lives being changed to fit in with the changing nature of the welfare state; the welfare state must be personalised and flexible, designed to promote individual choice and personal autonomy.

Since New Labour was elected in 1997, joined-up government in the interests of social justice has been actively pursued (see Chapter 2, by Sally Power, for discussion of social justice in the context of Education Action Zones). The rhetoric of partnership runs throughout both the UK and Scottish governments' policy documents on social justice. For example, the report of the Scottish Taskforce on Poverty states:

> Achieving our ambitious targets can only happen through partnership with colleagues across the UK. We share a common commitment to delivering social justice. A belief that we are stronger together and weaker apart as people, as communities and as nations ... The targets in the Scottish Social Justice Report can only be delivered through focus, leadership and 'new directions' in the allocation and use of public, private and voluntary sector resources.
>
> (Scottish Executive 1999b: 2)

Part of the social justice strategy is the Modernising Government programme, with the major goal of delivering public services to meet the needs of citizens, not the convenience of service providers (Scottish Executive 1999b). The development of person-centred services involves the breaking down of the old vertical hierarchies, such as the historical division between the UK Benefits Agency and Employment Service, which have recently been merged. The Report of the Scottish Taskforce on Poverty also recommends the pooling of departmental budgets to fund particular community initiatives and, in some cases, the transfer of resources from particular agencies to fund new patterns of welfare delivery. For example, it is envisaged that £140 million will be transferred from health boards to local authority social work departments and the voluntary sector in Scotland to provide care in the community for people previously in long-stay hospitals.

Joined-up policy and social justice

As discussed above, New Labour has identified joined-up government as the key to achieving greater social justice. At this point we consider the definition of social justice employed by the government, which often remains implicit rather than explicit. A number of commentators such as Driver and Martell (1998) have suggested that the key difference between Old and New Labour was the former's emphasis on equality of outcome compared with the latter's emphasis on equality of opportunity. This distinction is clearly evident in New Labour's blueprint, the Report of the Commission on Social Justice published in 1994. This report outlined three possible futures for Britain. The first, favoured by New Labour, was characterised as the Investors' Britain, whereby greater social justice is achieved not by the traditional 'tax and spend' policies of the left but by 'redistributing opportunities as well as income' (Commission on Social Justice 1994: 95). Contrasted with this is the Deregulators' Britain, whereby the free market is allowed to run untrammelled, producing great wealth for some but insecurity and poverty for those at the social margins, ultimately leading to social destabilisation. The third possible future is described as the Levellers' Britain, where the focus is on achieving greater economic equality. Both high and low wages would be strictly regulated, so that the gap between high and low earners would shrink. The downside of this scenario is that businesses and entrepreneurs might leave the UK and economic growth would slow, producing a 'poorer but kinder' Britain. The policy of reducing inequality of opportunity rather than outcome is reflected in many New Labour welfare policies, yet some contradictions remain unresolved. In particular, the growth of poverty during the 1980s and 1990s is identified as a major source of social injustice to be tackled. The means of tackling this, it is suggested, is by some redistribution to the poorest through benefits and fiscal policy, but, more importantly, through widening opportunities. However, no mechanisms are suggested to check the growing wealth of the richest in society, leaving open the possibility that measures to redistribute opportunity and (more modestly) income will be outstripped by moves to increase the amount of wealth controlled by the social elite.

As noted above, inter-departmental working accompanied by targeting resources on the poorest in society is seen as one of the central means of tackling social exclusion. However, as noted by Fraser (1997) and Power (Chapter 2), a major problem in such an approach, described by Fraser as the politics of distribution, is that it may damage the social esteem, or 'recognition' of the groups identified as the chief policy beneficiaries. Children with special educational needs or those in Education Action Zones or New Community Schools are beneficiaries of differential funding mechanisms. However, there is a danger that parents of children in schools which are not receiving enhanced funding may feel disadvantaged and resent the groups they feel have been singled out for special treatment. Since social justice reflects the politics of both (re)distribution and recognition, there are clearly problems if the social status of certain groups is undermined by the very policies designed to widen opportunities. It is possible, for example, that if inter-agency working is seen as a policy targeted at poor communities, there is a danger that both the communities receiving such interventions and this mode of service delivery may become stigmatised (see Power's chapter on Education Action Zones and Lloyd *et al.*'s chapter on alternatives to exclusion). On the other hand, efforts to 'roll out' educational interventions, such as early intervention or New Community Schools, to the wider population, while removing any stigma inevitably involves a reduction in the scale of resources targeted at the poorest communities, thereby possibly reducing the redistributive effects. Clearly, debates over whether social justice policies should focus on equal outcomes or equal opportunities, and the extent to which strategies should focus on (re)distribution or recognition, are likely to continue. While New Labour's approach is castigated as hopelessly timid by some, its rejoinder would be that the old 'tax and spend' approach was not spectacularly successful either. The more cautious approach adopted has led to a Labour government being elected for two successive terms of office for the first time.

Social capital and joined-up policy

New Labour has framed its social justice policies in terms of fighting social exclusion and promoting social inclusion, reflected in the establishment of the Social Exclusion Unit as part of the Cabinet Office in England and the creation of the Social Inclusion Network in Scotland. In conceptualising social exclusion, the government has sought to shift away from a sole focus on material deprivation towards a recognition of the salience of wider social and cultural factors. Thus, while it is recognised that poverty is likely to produce social alienation, it is also recognised that unless ways are found of hooking individuals and communities into positive social networks based on trust and reciprocity, money spent on alleviating material disadvantage may be wasted. Drawing on the work of Etzioni (1993) and Putnam (2000), social capital features increasingly prominently in New Labour thinking. The privileged position of the concept of social capital is almost certainly due to its compatibility with Third Way policies more generally. Work by researchers such as Wilkinson (1999) suggests that highly unequal societies are inefficient, since the erosion of social capital leads to high rates of mortality and morbidity and a host of other social problems, including crime and violence. Investment in social capital, on the other hand, promotes social justice but also is essential to the reproduction of human capital and economic growth. Partnership between public, private and voluntary sector agencies, individual service users and communities, is seen as the way of promoting social capital and lies at the heart of many recent educational initiatives not only in the UK, but also, as illustrated by chapters in this book, in other European countries, the USA and Australia. The nurturance of social capital is dependent not only on the breaking down of old departmental boundaries, but also on the development of new roles for services users and professionals, discussed in the following sections.

Joined-up policy and user empowerment

The idea that service users should play a significant role in shaping the type of services available and their mode of delivery is, of course, not a new one, but the notion of service users as partners has been used for a range of ideological purposes. In the area of special educational needs, for instance, the idea that parents might work in partnership with professionals was emphasised in the Warnock Report (DES 1978), but, as noted by Mordaunt (Chapter 8), professionals have been very reluctant to relinquish power to parents and policy changes have been pursued at different rates throughout the UK, with greater parental rights being guaranteed in England than in Scotland. The right of disabled children to contribute to important decisions about their education (Tisdall, Chapter 12) has been even slower to be recognised in practice.

Within the wider sphere of education, the promotion of parents as educational consumers was used by the previous Conservative administration to advance the marketisation of education. By giving parents the power of choice of school, it was believed that 'good' schools would expand and flourish, while 'failing' schools would wither and be closed down. The reality of this policy was, of course, somewhat different, with schools in socially disadvantaged areas experiencing falling rolls and reduced funding, but tending to survive while offering their remaining pupils an increasingly impoverished educational experience. Other measures, such as the establishment of school boards in Scotland and governing bodies in England, were ostensibly to give parents a stronger say in the running of their school, although the extent to which such measures actually resulted in a redistribution of power is contested (Vincent 2000). Vincent suggests a further model of parental involvement, that of parent as citizen. Parent-Centred Organisations, Vincent suggests, while being 'limited, fragile and partial in their scope and their impact', nonetheless 'go some way towards the creation of a language and several arenas in which (at least some) parents acting as citizens can participate in shaping educational opportunities for all children' (Vincent 2000: xiii). In addition to the chapters by Mordaunt and Tisdall, an international comparison of partnership with parents is provided by Kasama and Tett (Chapter 14). By exploring different experiences in Japan and Scotland, the authors highlight the different uses of partnership in the two countries and the different types of empowerment (or lack of it) which result.

Joined-up policy and the new professionals

Just as service users are construed differently within the modernised welfare state, so the casting aside of departmental boundaries and the deregulation of services creates new roles for professionals. Within the post-war welfare state, each professional group worked within clear boundaries, operating according to specific working practices and with clear routes of accountability. Within the new welfare state, the boundary between public, private and voluntary sector workers and those employed by particular departments is increasingly blurred. Workers are cast in the role of social entrepreneurs, crossing departmental boundaries in order to undertake a particular task, whether this is engaging with parents in pre-school education (Smyth, this volume), working in one of the models of full-service schools (Semmens; Boyd and Crowson; Hatcher and Leblond; Power; and Baron, all this volume) or finding jobs or educational placements for young unemployed people (Salisbury; Riddell and Wilson, this volume). The idea of the free-ranging worker adopting an extremely flexible and innovative working practice has been developed most fully in the context of New Deal programmes. In order to move individuals destined for long-term unemployment back into the labour market, job brokers have been instructed to use any means at their disposal to persuade employers to find work for individuals and to support individuals in holding down a job or a training programme placement. The rolling out of the New Deal for Disabled People, jointly managed by the DSS and DfEE and moving into delivery mode in late 2001, is based on principles of social entrepreneurialism, with job brokers managing the relationship between prospective employers and employees. The underlying theory is that social capital can be drawn upon and further developed by calling on employers' sense of community responsibility in creating jobs or lifelong learning opportunities for disabled people and other groups at risk of social exclusion.

However, as Salisbury and Riddell and Wilson make clear in Chapters 15 and 16, relationships on the ground may be less straightforward and outcomes not as rosy as sometimes depicted. In the FE college setting described by Salisbury, lecturers found the flexibility demanded of New Deal difficult to accommodate within the more rigid time-frames and programmes they were used to operating. In the pilot New Deal for Disabled People (NDDP) described by Riddell and Wilson, placements were sometimes unsatisfactory due to lack of time for in-depth profiling and the shortage of job opportunities. The case studies of disabled people make clear that even those counted as success stories within the NDDP had a somewhat shallow toe-hold within the labour market and were likely to be the most vulnerable to redundancy.

Can inter-agency working achieve change?

The present UK administrations at Westminster and Holyrood are committed to developing 'evidence-based policy' and acknowledge that in many areas inadequate social information is available. As past of the Modernising Government programme, for example, the Scottish Executive is embarking on a major exercise to improve the quality of its statistical information to inform its social inclusion agenda. An example of this is the gathering of small area statistics, for example, linked to patterns of expenditure and indices of social disadvantage. It has been found, for instance, that about £100 million of public money is spent in Greater Easterhouse, in the west of Scotland, each year. It is planned to put in place systems to find out which groups of the population are recipients of this money and what benefits are evident in relation to reducing social exclusion. A theme running throughout this book is that, despite the rhetoric of evidence-based policy, in reality policy is often based on political whim or a hunch that an idea culled from one particular setting may work in another. Clear examples of this are evident in the development of the New Community Schools initiative in Scotland, described by Baron in Chapter 6, and the range of pre-school initiatives in six European countries described by Smyth (Chapter 13). Smyth's analysis suggests that when evaluation does take place, it is sometimes poorly conceived, being tacked on to an initiative rather than being an integral part of the project design. This is partly to do with political imperatives, where politicians need to introduce new initiatives almost immediately on being elected. Given the complexity of many social problems, research may suggest the need for cautious expectations rather than promises of rapid social change favoured by some politicians. Evidence of the effectiveness of *Zones d'Education Prioritaires* described by Hatcher and Leblond in Chapter 3 indicates at best uncertainty about the efficacy of the full-service schooling idea in France. This may explain why UK politicians were not anxious to draw on French findings in planning Education Action Zones. Overall, there is remarkably little evidence relating to the question of whether inter-agency working is likely to achieve social change, in particular the regeneration of social capital and the elimination of social exclusion, which appears to be its prime aim.

What conditions are necessary to underpin successful partnerships?

It is clear that joined-up working has a number of costs, not least in terms of the number of professionals from different agencies who may be required to sit round a table in order to produce a children's services plan or community care plan, involving social work, education, health and the voluntary sector. This time cost is likely to be exacerbated in countries like Scotland, where the thirty-two local authorities do not map neatly on to the fifteen health boards, requiring duplication of personnel from a particular agency at many meetings. However, it is evident that, where joined-up working operates effectively, considerable savings are likely to accrue to the Treasury. For example, where New Deal programmes are effective in moving people from benefits and into employment, there are likely to be major benefits savings.

In its current thinking about the conditions underpinning successful partnership, the UK government appears to be emphasising 'partnership with a purpose'. Thus in the NHS Plan for Scotland (Scottish Executive Health Department 2001), the types of partnership working required under the internal market, where Health Boards and Trusts spent much time in internal negotiation, are dismissed as inefficient. Unified Health Boards have been created , with a mission to develop closer working relationships with local authorities, social work departments and housing departments. In particular, the Plan states a commitment to the improvement of services for children with special needs delivered 'at home ... or in schools rather than in other institutions ... The emphasis must be on joined-up thinking and joined-up action, both nationally and locally, to deliver innovative services that promote inclusion' (Scottish Executive Health Department 2001: 61).

Despite the emphasis on fitness for purpose in partnership working, it is evident that this ideal is not always achieved. For example, Lightfoot *et al.* (Chapter 9) illuminate the statutory and practical difficulties in managing the health needs of children in school. Given that increasing numbers of children with specific health needs are being included in mainstream schools, there is a pressing need for clear understandings about the locus of responsibility for the administration of medication and indemnity arrangements. Such arrangements, however, appear not to be in place either in Scotland (Scottish Executive 1999b) or in England. Mordaunt and Tisdall (Chapters 8 and 12) also illustrate the cultural divisions between different groups of professionals providing services to disabled children in schools. Other areas targeted for joined-up approaches will require even more radical adjustments of professional cultures. These include the amalgamation of the Benefits Agency and the Employment Service to provide a joined-up approach to assisting unemployed people, and the current Department of Health/Department of Work and Pensions initiative on job retention and rehabilitation, which is intended to co-ordinate the activities of health, employment and education personnel in assisting people who experience illness or sudden trauma back into the labour market rather than on to incapacity benefits.

Overall, for inter-agency approaches to work well, there needs to be a clear underlying rationale. However, this in itself is not enough, since deep-rooted cultural differences between professional groups, vested interests in maintaining departmental boundaries and statutory restrictions may undermine efforts to engage in partnership working.

The structure of the book

Chapters 2 to 7 focus on various attempts to build closer links between schools and their communities and to provide a range of social services within an educational setting to facilitate rapid intervention. Sally Power discusses one of New Labour's flagship initiatives to tackle social exclusion in education. The Education Action Zones Initiative exemplifies key aspects of 'joined-up-ness', that is a desire to understand and tackle the complex nature of social and educational exclusion, a recognition of the need to draw together different sectors and sources of welfare and a blurring of the conventional boundary between state and civil society. The points she makes about the problems and possibilities of joined-up action in Education Action Zones are reflected in subsequent chapters on full-service schools in Australia (Semmens) and the USA (Boyd and Crowson), in *Zones d'Education Prioritaires* (Hatcher and Leblond) and in New Community Schools in Scotland (Baron) and the former model of Scottish community schools (Tett *et al.*). Power points out, first, that local initiatives inevitably encourage inter-agency working at a local level but may ignore the higher-level difficulties in partnership arrangements. Second, she notes that the emphasis on social entrepreneurship means that funds are distributed on a competitive basis, which may in itself damage inter-agency working. Third, she notes that while social deprivation is acknowledged as the fundamental cause of social exclusion, educational solutions are proposed which leave the basic problem unchallenged. Hatcher and Leblond compare Education Action Zones with *Zones d'Education Prioritaires*, commenting on the curious failure of European governments to learn lessons from each other's social experiments. In this case, the overwhelming lesson appears to be that while a third of ZEP schools may have succeeded in reducing educational inequality, in a fifth of such schools educational inequality appears to have increased compared with non-ZEP schools. Hatcher and Leblond also draw attention to the danger that additional funding of some schools may damage the social status of those who attend, since they may simultaneously be stigmatised as socially disadvantaged and regarded as over-privileged.

Boyd and Crowson in Chapter 4 provide fascinating insights into the early development of the full-service schooling programme in the United States. They draw attention to the radical notion underpinning the full-service schools movement that, rather than simply conceptualising schools as in need of reform, a more positive approach was to work out how such institutions might themselves play an active role in neighbourhood regeneration by galvanising community groups, children and parents into social capital generation. They draw attention to the challenges for the school improvement movement posed by New Community Schools, in particular the need to look beyond pedagogic practices within the classroom to the community beyond. The limitations on the social change potential of schools is explored and, like other contributors, Boyd and Crowson note that in areas of deep poverty, public and private investment, not just engagement with the community, is of paramount importance. Finally, Boyd and Crowson allude to one of the paradoxes of full-service schools. If the anti-educational values of the local community are identified as, in part, the cause of low educational achievement, then stronger engagement with the local community might actually serve to further depress, rather than enhance, educational outcomes. Bob Semmens picks up this latter theme and notes that one of the problems with full-service schools in Australia has been that they have, on occasion, robbed individuals and communities of their sense of agency, both a cause and an effect of the erosion of social capital. This raises the question of whether such initiatives should be controlled by professionals or by communities themselves. Unless full-service schools can help pupils to understand their future citizenship roles, there is a danger that they will fail and pharmacological solutions will be sought to control pupil behaviour.

The final two chapters in this section, by Baron and Tett *et al.*, provide a commentary on New Community Schools in Scotland and their antecedent in the form of traditional community schools. Baron (Chapter 6) concludes, like Semmens, that at their worst New Community Schools may represent a 'swarming of disciplinary mechanisms' (Vincent and Tomlinson 1997), with the new professionals acting to disempower people who are already socially marginalised. Chapter 7 by Tett *et al.*, on the old community schools in Scotland, highlights difficulties in attaining fruitful partnerships between schools and community education. Whereas the mission of community education is to reach into and draw from communities, schools see their core business in terms of teaching and learning within classrooms. The project of engagement in community development and democratic renewal is not on the agenda for the vast majority of schools, and current metrics of attainment in external examinations and national tests do not encourage such thinking. Tett *et al.* point out that lessons from this research have not informed the development of New Community Schools, so that existing problems are likely to be replicated.

The following group of chapters explores the development of partnership arrangements for particular groups of children and in relation to education and a range of other agencies, including health, social work and housing. Mordaunt explores the different forms which partnership working has taken in England and Scotland for children with special educational needs. While parental rights have been strengthened in statute in England, in Scotland the power of professionals has remained relatively unchallenged. While, as pointed out by Tisdall, the Standards in Scotland's Schools etc. (Scotland) Act 2000 places an onus on education authorities to foster partnership with parents, educational psychologists in Scotland are lobbying to alter the provisions of the 1980 Education (Scotland) Act (as amended) to record the special educational needs of children who have greater difficulties in learning than other children of their age. If such changes do indeed take place, as various ministerial pronouncements have suggested, then parents of the 2 per cent of children with the most significant special educational needs will have even fewer rights than their counterparts in England. Such discrepancies highlight the growing disparities in social policy which are likely to occur in different parts of the UK as devolution bites. Differences in policy across the UK are also alluded to by Lloyd *et al.* (Chapter 11), who note that while statistics suggest permanent exclusions in Scotland are much lower than in England, this may well be a product of the way the statistics have been gathered than any real disparity. Lloyd and her colleagues outline findings from a research project assessing alternatives to exclusion involving close interaction between social work and education. They point out that superficially the outcomes of this intervention appear to be very positive, but closer analysis suggests that many of the pupils who appear to have been 'saved' from exclusion are no longer in mainstream education and are therefore likely to leave school with few qualifications. The alternatives to the exclusions initiative are plagued by short-term funding, which means that projects have little time to embed and their long-term effects cannot be properly assessed. In addition, confusion remains over the specific responsibilities of particular agencies. Smyth's analysis of pre-school intervention in six European countries (Chapter 13) shows that there is a welfare/education dichotomy, with a priority given to either care or education, present throughout Europe. She also shows that for disadvantaged children, the focus is on supplementary care-type programmes rather than addressing their needs in mainstream educational provision. Finally, she shows again the lack of reliable evaluation data on which policies are based, and this data is perhaps the most telling point to emerge from her analysis.

Chapters 9 and 10, by Lightfoot *et al.* on health and Clark *et al.* on housing, illuminate the way in which grass-roots attempts to build co-operative working practices between different agencies may be hindered by the lack of a macro framework to facilitate such developments. Lightfoot *et al.* point out that while it may be possible to arrange joint working practices to be put in place for children with Statements of Need, for children who are not identified in this way finding an appropriate health contact is like 'stabbing in the dark'. While the new SEN and Disability Act 2001 requires 'reasonable adjustments' to be made to avoid 'substantial disadvantage', unless better codes for joint working at national and local levels are developed, this statutory requirement is likely to remain a pious hope. Clarke *et al.* point out the legacy of the marketisation of the public sector for children's education, which produced a double jeopardy for children on the poorest estates. They note that 'right to buy' policies meant that better council houses in more salubrious areas tended to be bought by their occupiers, who in turn often chose to send their children to schools outwith the estate. If the population of social housing estates has become residualised, they comment, the problems of schools in these areas are doubly residualised as more aware parents remove their children to neighbouring schools. Even schools not identified as 'failing' have experienced destabilisation as their population has changed. Implicit in this chapter is the need for congruence within different sectors of education policy. There is little point in investing money in Education Action Zones or New Community Schools initiatives if other parts of social policy are increasing social and educational segregation.

The final three chapters all focus in different ways on the range of roles ascribed to professionals and service users in different social policy and national contexts. Kasama and Tett's comparison of parents' relationship to schooling in Scotland and Japan (Chapter 14) alerts us to the deep historical and cultural influences on parents' approaches to education. Such differences are not only likely to occur in different countries, but are also likely to affect the expectations of minority ethnic groups within a particular country, as the experiences of Japanese parents in Scotland makes clear. Whereas these parents were aware of being more readily included in social aspects of Scottish primary schools, they were dismayed by the schools' tendency to be secretive about what they were teaching and how the children were performing.

Chapters 15 and 16, by Salisbury and Riddell and Wilson, focus on the relationship between lifelong learning and inter-agency working. The New Deal exemplifies key elements of individualised services provided by new professionals acting as social entrepreneurs in the modern welfare state, yet huge uncertainties over roles and responsibilities existed between service users and providers. Were the young people in Further Education and the disabled people on work placement conscripts or volunteers? Were the Personal Advisers who worked with them enforcing the discipline of education and work, or were they enablers and counsellors? Finally, how did the role of Personal Advisers, intended to transgress departmental boundaries, fit in with those of lecturers in Further Education and trainers in voluntary sector agencies, whose roles were much more clearly defined?

We hope that this collection of papers leaves the reader with many questions to ponder. In particular, questions remain as to whether the current focus on joined-up policy reflects growing anxieties about the ability of governments to make meaningful interventions in people's lives through the management of welfare. Alternatively, as Clarke and Newman (1997) have suggested, demands for inter-agency working may reflect the failure of governments to resolve structural problems, particularly in relation to the global economy and the distribution of wealth, which results in problems being passed down the line for those at the grass roots, who have least power in the system, to resolve. Coupled with this is the question of whether the new roles assigned to workers and service users in the modernised welfare state may be seen as empowering or, as we suggested above, the further 'swarming of disciplinary mechanisms'.

References

Clarke, J. and Newman, E. (1997) *The Managerial State*, London: Sage.

Clarke, J., Gewirtz, S. and McLaughlin, E. (eds) (2000) *New Managerialism: New Welfare*, London: Open University Press.

Commission on Social Justice (1994) *Social Justice: Strategies for National Renewal*, London: Vintage.

Deakin, N. (1994) *The Politics of Welfare: Continuities and Change*, Brighton: Harvester Wheatsheaf.

Driver, S. and Martell, L. (1998) *New Labour: Politics After Thatcherism*, Cambridge: Polity Press.

Etzioni, A. (1993) *The Spirit of Community*, London: Fontana.

Fraser, N. (1997) 'From redistribution to recognition? Dilemmas of justice in a post-socialist age' in N. Fraser (ed.) *Justice Interruptus*, New York: Routledge.

Power, M. (1987) *The Audit Society: Rituals of Verification*, Oxford: Oxford University Press.

Putnam, R.D. (2000) *Bowling Alone: The Collapse and Revival of American Community*, New York: Simon and Schuster.

Scottish Executive (1999a) *Report of the Advisory Committee into Severe Low Incidence Disabilities (The Riddell Report)*, Edinburgh: Scottish Executive.

——(1999b) *Social Justice … A Scotland Where Everyone Matters*, Edinburgh: Scottish Executive.

Scottish Executive Health Department (2001) *Our National Health: A Plan for Action, A Plan for Change*, Edinburgh: Scottish Executive.

Vincent, C. (2000) *Including Parents? Education, Citizenship and Parental Agency*, Buckingham: Open University Press.

Vincent, C. and Tomlinson, S. (1997) 'Home–school relationships: "the swarming of disciplinary mechanisms"?' *British Educational Research Journal*, 23(3): 361–77.

Wilkinson, R. (1999) 'The social environment', in D. Gordon, M. Shaw, D. Dorling and G. Davey Smith (eds) *Inequalities in Health: The Evidence Presented to the Inquiry into Inequalities in Health Chaired by Sir Donald Acheson*, Bristol: Policy Press.

2 'Joined-up thinking'?

Inter-agency partnerships in Education Action Zones

Sally Power

Introduction

In June 1998, twenty-five Education Action Zones (EAZs) were announced as the 'standard bearers in a new crusade uniting business, schools, local education authorities and parents to modernise education in areas of social deprivation' (DfEE 1998). Many claims have been made about the policy which has been identified as a 'forerunner for the future delivery of public services in the next century' (Byers, cited by Rafferty 1998: 4). Some of these claims centre on experimentation, some on standards. Others concentrate on the potential of zones to involve public–private partnerships, while others see in them the possibility of a new more inclusive politics of education. In this chapter, though, I want to concentrate in particular on the extent to which zones embody the New Labour preference for 'joined-up thinking'.

The post-war welfare state

The legislative and administrative arrangements of the British welfare system that developed in the post-war years can be characterised in terms of divisions – divisions between areas of responsibility and divisions between central and local government. At central government level, welfare policy and provision is divided up between departments which historically have had little interaction. National policies are then interpreted and implemented at local level, where the division between different areas remains sharply demarcated. The picture is further complicated by a lack of congruence between boundaries. Although boroughs in the larger urban areas share administrative boundaries for some areas of responsibilities, those in the shire counties do not. There are currently, for instance, 150 local education authorities (LEAs) and 354 housing authorities in England. Health authority boundaries are different again.

It has increasingly been recognised that the bureaucratic nature and specialised division of labour in the welfare state make it insufficiently responsive to the multifarious needs of families in crisis. This was very evident in some research we undertook for Shelter (Power *et al.* 1995) on policy and provision relating to the education of children living in temporary accommodation. The research revealed that demarcated and fragmented responsibility hindered awareness of the scale of difficulties created by homelessness and led to inadequate and inconsistent provision of services. Indeed, the traditional demarcation of different areas of welfare provision has been seen as a contributory factor in the marginalisation of welfare recipients (Becker 1997). Fragmentation of provision makes it difficult for policy-makers and service providers to perceive the multiple effects of their policies on 'whole' persons and households. This in turn appears to make it easier to 'pass off' responsibility to other sectors and influences the kind of provision homeless families receive.

It was the bureaucratic and insufficiently flexible nature of services that was partly behind the neo-liberal attack on the welfare state. During the Thatcher and Major years, there was a fundamental reorientation to the politics of welfare marked by successive attempts to 'roll back the state'. Before the Thatcher years, welfare provision had been premised on the notion that social disadvantage could be ameliorated through more intervention, more money and more expert help. Thatcherism, and the associated new right agenda, turned these assumptions upside down. The welfare state became part of the problem, not the solution. It was seen to have contributed to an inefficient and ineffective monopoly. What was needed was a welfare 'market' which would change supposed beneficiaries from passive recipients to consumer-clients who would select what they needed from a range of services and providers.

Whether the market could ever have delivered this promise in the longer term is open to question. Certainly, in the shorter term there was little evidence of welfare consumer empowerment. Neo-liberals might argue that this is hardly surprising, given the culture shift among both providers and recipients that would be required. But even so, there was little to suggest that new right welfare policies broke with the past in terms of demarcated provision and bureaucratic structure. The Thatcher and Major governments may have applied the same kind of policies (specifically quasi-markets) to different areas of welfare, but they did little to create new cross-linkages. Indeed, it is possible to argue that the concentration on institutional limitations actually *strengthened* demarcations between welfare areas. Thus, it became fashionable to treat the solution to educational problems as largely to be found within the educational arena (Whitty 1997) – a position which severely underplayed the long-established research evidence connecting educational achievement to socio-economic background.

Something of the same blindness is evident in New Labour's education policies. In particular, the argument that poverty should not be used as an *excuse* for under-achievement has been taken to mean that poverty is not an *explanation* for under-achievement (Whitty *et al.* 1999). As with the Conservatives, institutional-level factors are seen as being of paramount importance. However, New Labour's education policies are more than just a continuation of the new right (Power and Whitty 1999). There is little doubt that New Labour has, as Giddens recommends, taken on some of the right's criticisms of the welfare state in seeing it as 'essentially undemocratic, depending as it does upon a top-down distribution of benefits ... bureaucratic, alienating and inefficient' (Giddens 1998: 112–13). But rather than reduce, or even remove, the state's responsibility for public welfare, New Labour has tried to restructure provision.

New Labour, the welfare state and joined-up thinking

One way in which New Labour is attempting to reconceptualise welfare provision is through what has become fashionably known as 'joined-up thinking'. This lies behind the concept of 'social exclusion', which has gained such political currency over the last couple of years, being based on an understanding of the interconnected nature of social problems and the inadequacy of fragmented approaches to these problems. However, there are broad and narrow versions of what it is that should be 'joined up'. At the current time, Education Action Zones, despite their early promise, tend to embody the rather narrower versions of 'joined-up-ness'. In this chapter, I want to argue that we need to look at 'joined-up-ness' in its broader sense and that, unless the broader view is taken, any integration of welfare provision is likely to be superficial and ultimately ineffective.

I want to claim that 'joined-up-ness', as it is presented in some Labour policy pronouncements and visions of new welfare settlements presented by the 'Third Way' advocates (e.g. Giddens 1998), has at least three dimensions:

- understanding of the complex nature of social and educational exclusion;
- recognition of the need to draw together different sectors and sources of welfare;
- blurring of the conventional boundary between state and civil society.

Although there are inconsistencies within the government's approach, it seems to me that, in its more radical form, this kind of joined-up thinking has the potential to make some kind of difference provided that it can be translated and practised at the local level.

The complex nature of social and educational exclusion

One way in which New Labour differs from the new right is the acknowledgement that growing inequalities, more fashionably referred to as social exclusion, are a *social* not just a personal problem. In contrast to Margaret Thatcher's now famous assertion that 'there is no such thing as society', New Labour recognises that inequality cannot be accounted for in terms of individual or family pathologies. It also recognises the 'joined-up' nature of societal well-being. Social exclusion therefore damages more than just those who are socially excluded – it is damaging at all levels of society.[1]

Social exclusion is also seen to be something that is not one-dimensional. Under 'old left' politics, social disadvantage was generally seen as a product of material disadvantage. However, under New Labour there is an acknowledgement of the cultural dimensions of disadvantage. Blair has commented in this connection that 'It's a very modern problem, and one that is more harmful to the individual, more damaging to self-esteem, more corrosive for society as a whole, more likely to be passed down from generation to generation, than material poverty' (Blair 1997a).

The notion of exclusion, therefore, emphasises the political–economic and the cultural–valuational dimensions of exclusion. Increasing social *in*clusion, at its most basic level, involves an appeal to both the politics of redistribution and the politics of recognition (Fraser 1997). Relatedly, it can be linked to currently fashionable 'social capital' theories (see Gamarnikow and Green 1999) which hold that strengthening the mutuality of communities and enhancing trust can promote both greater social *and* economic well-being.

The integration of different sectors and sources of welfare

Acknowledgement of the multifaceted nature of exclusion requires moving beyond one-dimensional and fragmented forms of welfare provision. As the Prime Minister argued at the launch of the Social Exclusion Unit in 1997:

> all too often governments in the past have tried to slice problems up into separate packages ... in many areas dozens of agencies and professions are working in parallel, often doing good things, but sometimes working at cross purposes with far too little co-ordination and co-operation ... Joined-up problems demand joined-up solutions.
>
> (Blair 1997a)

It is important to note that integration of remedies relates not just to cross-sector public welfare provision, but also to joining up public, private and voluntary sector providers. In common with other aspects of Third Way policy, the new welfare system requires a new 'synergy' between public and private (Giddens 1998) and an expanded role for voluntary and other third sector organisations.

Breaking down demarcation between state and civil society

Perhaps most radically, though, joined-up thinking would seem to involve breaking down the conventional boundaries between state and civil society. If the old left saw the solutions in terms of increasing state involvement and the new right saw the solution in terms of promoting consumer rights, the new approach is apparently for the state and civil society to operate 'in partnership'.

In connection with the socially excluded, for instance, Giddens (1998: 120) talks of the need for 'positive welfare' which would break down the stigma of being a welfare recipient – but without re-invoking the unworkable idea of welfare consumer: 'In the positive welfare society, the contract between individual and government shifts, since autonomy and the development of self – the medium of expanding individual responsibility – become the prime focus.'

If the old left emphasised 'rights' and the new right concentrated on 'responsibilities', New Labour talks of the importance of balancing the two. In this connection, 'social entrepreneurship' (e.g. Blair 1997b; Leadbetter 1997) and 'volunteering' are increasingly seen as the way forward – particularly through the development of civic associations and networks at the local level.

Joined-up thinking and the EAZ policy

Although it is hard to see a strong New Labour commitment to 'joined-up' thinking within the overall programme of education reform (Power and Whitty 1999; Mortimore and Whitty 1999), there are certainly strong elements of 'joined-up-ness' in the Education Action Zones policy.

The policy is underpinned by recognition of the relationship between socio-economic deprivation and poor educational attainment.[2] Indeed, it is important to note that, at least in the early phases, the policy had two twin objectives – reducing educational under-achievement *and*, in parallel, reducing social deprivation. Acknowledgement of the interconnected nature of the problems to be addressed is also evident in the fact that the policy involves elements of redistribution and recognition (see Power and Gewirtz 2001). The EAZ policy also recognises the need to draw together different agencies. Indeed, the preference for 'integrated' solutions lies behind the increasing amount of area-based initiatives introduced by New Labour. In addition to EAZs, there are Health Action Zones (HAZs), 'employment' zones, Sure Start, New Deal for Communities and targeted Social Regeneration Budget (SRB) funds. These have initiated a whole new welfare vocabulary. In Education Action Zones we have 'wrap-around' school services and 'one-stop shops' for health and social services.

The EAZ policy is built upon the concept of partnership – not just between different sectors of public providers but between private, voluntary and public sectors. It was a condition of application that zones be organised around such partnerships and that central government funds should be supplemented by contributions (either in cash or in kind) from private and voluntary bodies.

The rhetoric of the policy also emphasises the communal nature of the enterprise. The ideas of communities 'working together' is reflected in the new decision-making fora which, at least in theory, might be seen to embody those 'experiments with democracy' (Giddens 1998; Halpin 1999). In addition, drawing parents into the educative process itself can be seen to dissolve the stigmatising distinctions between 'lay' and 'professional' expertise and between welfare provider and welfare recipient, which underlay much of the welfare state.

Joined-up thinking in three Education Action Zones

In the next section I will consider in more detail whether the broad vision of 'joined-up-ness' is manifest within EAZ policy at the local level. In order to do this I shall look at the proposals outlined in three successful bids – referred to here as Kenningham, Norbridge and Nairton. There are, of course, problems in using bids to interpret implementation at the local level. The bids were put together quickly and comparison with early action plans reveals that some strategies have subsequently changed. Moreover, it needs to be remembered that gaining zone status was a competitive process and successful bids were likely to be those that 'spoke the same language' as New Labour. However, applications and action plans overplay rather than underestimate the extent of integration. Research on the early experiences of EAZs suggests that inter-agency working is currently even more limited in practice than it is in the proposals (Power *et al.* 2000).

The complex nature of social and educational exclusion

To some extent, the zone applications *do* reflect a broader understanding of the nature of social and educational exclusion. They are very explicit about the scale of poverty and social deprivation in their respective areas. Presumably as part of the strategy to attract funds, each bid begins by outlining where their zone stands on various indices of social disadvantage. Kenningham, for instance, has 'considerable social and economic deprivation'. Tables are used to illustrate various levels that place it in the top 10 per cent nationally of most deprived areas. Norbridge, like Kenningham, provides plenty of statistics to show its rank in the top ten most deprived wards – drawing attention to 'pronounced deprivation and ill health and average life-expectancy is among shortest in the country'. Nairton claims to be *the* most deprived area in the country, citing not only high levels of poverty and disease, but also environmental deprivation: 'a lack of high-quality community, leisure and retail facilities. There is relatively little green space and the immediate environment of many of the schools is stark and uninspiring.'

And it is not the case that the poor in these areas are presented as the 'feckless' and/or 'workshy' depicted by some Conservative politicians during the 1970s and 1980s. In his analysis of a similar initiative, Educational Priority Areas (EPAs), Halsey (1972) identified three alternative explanations of the sources of poverty commonly put forward: inadequate socialisation by the family; inadequate socialisation by other socialisation agencies such as schools; or lack of opportunity in the social structure. Unlike the EPAs, most of the zone applications take the more radical position and locate the source of poverty within the changing structure of employment opportunities. Kenningham, for instance, refers to 'the disrupting effects of Kenningham's slow industrial decline over many years'.

While zone bids identify the problem within the diminishing opportunities of the changing economic structure, they do not take on economistic explanations alone. To varying degrees, they also recognise the cultural dimensions of disadvantage – although the problems are often located in the community rather than in the wider society. The Kenningham bid, for instance, refers to 'pockets of intense neighbourhood antagonism and aggression'. Nairton recognises that 'Many parents have had a poor experience of education and this is sometimes reflected in an anti-school culture. Schools are alienated from communities. Education is not valued. Schools and teachers are not respected.'

In talking about the cultural dimensions of disadvantage, the bids shift from a more radical understanding of social exclusion to a narrower explanation for educational under-achievement. In particular, the notion of the dysfunctional family is present in varying degrees throughout all three of the zone bids we looked at. Norbridge refers to 'generally low levels of literacy and in many cases low levels of basic skills and often a lack of parental support or inadequate parenting skills'. Nairton is even more explicit in its attribution of blame:

> many parents do little to ensure their children attend school punctually and regularly, that they complete homework and that they subscribe to basic norms of behaviour. There are frequent incidents of poor and abusive parental behaviour towards school staff. Sometimes this involves violence … Many parents and families are unable to handle conflict within the norms of acceptable behaviour … There is a very high incidence of poor pupil behaviour often associated with poor parental behaviour.

This statement strongly embodies the sentiments identified by Halsey (1972) as indicative of explanations of poverty that were based on inadequate family socialisation. Here, families were accused of 'failing to provide the early training in literacy, numeracy, and acceptance of work and achievement habits which constitute the normal upbringing of a middle class child' (Halsey 1972: 19).

So that while understandings of social exclusion and educational achievement are 'joined up' to some extent, there are significant gaps in the reasoning that are likely to create significant problems for the effectiveness of any provision. Perhaps because each zone application has to lay strong claims to 'social need' in order to compete for funds, and perhaps because of the pathologising of pupils and families, the zones are in danger of creating a perception of these localities that is entirely negative.

In this connection, it is worth bearing in mind Smith's (1987: 30) analysis of the demise of EPAs. He argues that lack of coherence over the conceptualisation of disadvantage led to the 'internal collapse' of the policy. In particular, he argues that the tendency to emphasise the 'worst' features of EPAs led to a perception that disadvantage was attributable to familial and individual pathologies rather than broader structural processes. He warns that the discourse surrounding the earlier reforms clearly did not refer to '*our* neighbourhood, *our* housing or *our* children'. Thus, through experimenting with 'other people's children', the EAZ policy is also in danger of compounding the division between 'welfare receivers' and 'welfare providers'.

The implications of these gaps in 'joined-up' thinking become evident in the next section, which looks at how these different understandings of social exclusion and educational under-achievement connect, or fail to connect, with zone strategies.

Drawing together different sectors and sources of welfare

All the bids outline the need for a multi-agency approach to solving their area's problems. Kenningham asserts that:

> There are currently many educational and welfare organisations working in the area. Their efforts however lack co-ordination and proper funding. We believe that with co-operation a significant impact could be made on the standards of learning in our community.

Two of the zones also fall within Health Action Zones, and increasingly draw from other sources of government funding.[3] Norbridge will bring these together through establishing collaborative arrangements which 'will be charged with addressing the skills and knowledge gaps and share know-how and resources in developing the new joint focus agenda ... to develop a more integrated approach and find new ways of tackling social exclusion'.

Nairton similarly asserts that 'Clearly any response to the problems faced by the schools in the zone has to be a multi-agency response involving a range of services provided by the council and other organisations.'

Not only do the zones commit themselves to inter-agency working, they also, as we noted earlier, have to draw in non-public-sector partners. The precise nature of these partnership arrangements varies from zone to zone – as does the kind of organisation involved. In terms of sector involvement, the breakdown of our three zones' partners is shown in Table 2.1.[4]

While all the bids make an explicit commitment to cross-agency provision and draw together representatives from public, private and voluntary sectors, there is less explication of just how these forms of integration are to effect any change. Perhaps not surprisingly, given the speed at which the bids had to be prepared, there is very little detail or substance about the mechanisms of integration. But even allowing for this, there is something of a mismatch between the claims of 'joined-up-ness' and the nature and kinds of partnerships envisaged.

There is a remarkable absence of representation of welfare providers other than those in education. In terms of the public sector, for instance, *all* core partners are in the educational sphere. Nairton has some health sector involvement, and, as we have seen, Norbridge has promised collaboration between the EAZ and the HAZ. But there are no details about how this is to be achieved. Although Kenningham does not have other welfare providers as partners, it is the only one of the three to propose having other public sector service providers represented on the forum. In addition to the usual people – representatives of teachers, governors, community (e.g. church) and business – Kenningham also intends to involve the local medical centre, social services, youth and leisure services and the local policy. Although such representation does not ensure

Table 2.1   Breakdown of partners in the three zones in terms of sector involvement

*Kenningham (4 **main partners**, 8 others)*

Public	Private	Voluntary
LEA	Local airport	**Education–business partnership**
Local TEC	4 local engineering firms	Educational organisation
Local FE college		Urban regeneration project
Local university		

*Norbridge (5 **main partners**, 7 others)*

Public	Private	Voluntary
LEA	**Multinational (MN) retailer**	**Education–business partnership**
Local TEC	**MN communications firm**	Literacy project
Local university	Building society	
Local FE college	Insurance company	
	Solicitors	
	Local business	

*Nairton (12 **main partners**, 26 others)*

Public	Private	Voluntary
LEA	**MN communications firm**	**Business partnership**
Local FE college	**MN IT firm**	**2 education–business partnership**
Local teachers' organisation	**MN business consultants**	**Local partnership project**
3 universities	Educational service suppliers	Youth charity
Sixth form college	**Teacher recruitment firm**	Crime charity
Local TEC	Property consultants	Local community association
Careers guidance	MN construction firm	Teacher training supporter
Governors' forum	Industrial trainers	2 local dioceses
Local health authority	Local transport provider	Association of parent governors
Community health services	Supply teacher agency	Industry training board
Police		Liveried 'company'
		Community renewal

collaboration, it is probably a necessary condition. Again, harking back to our Shelter research, lack of awareness and provision of adequate services was most marked in authorities with no formal inter-departmental liaison procedures. Neither Nairton nor Norbridge seems to have any structured means of representation or consultation. Liaison is mentioned, but there is no evidence of formal mechanisms designed to ensure it.

If we look at the private and voluntary sector organisations, they are nearly all concentrated on areas involving the provision of educational services or work-related training. The various contributions (where they are indicated) from the business sector are almost inevitably 'in kind'. Those from the 'voluntary sector' are more likely to involve cash, but only where it comes from education–business partnerships.

The composition of the partnerships and the nature of their contributions, combined with the concentration on family failings, mean that the remedies which the zones propose seem somewhat out of alignment with their own diagnoses of the kind of difficulties they face.

As mentioned earlier, each of the areas made strong claims for extra funds on the basis of the disadvantages created by continued economic decline and the resultant material and environmental deprivation. But all of the 'solutions' seem to centre on family, or perhaps more accurately, maternal deprivation.

Kenningham is also the only one which clearly identifies any specific cross-area initiatives outside the sphere of education – the construction of a residential foyer for young people who need secure low-cost housing to continue their post-16 education. Aspects to do with mental health do appear in the bids, but again they are based on a deficit model of zone pupils and parents. Norbridge, for instance, wants to develop an 'early intervention strategy to give parents awareness and skills to support and encourage their children's learning'.

Cross-sector involvement in Norbridge and Nairton in particular is more connected with blurring the boundaries between home and school.

Breaking down demarcation between state and civil society

It could be argued that blurring of boundaries between home and school represents one way of revitalising civil society. The zones talk of working in partnership with parents – of giving them an increased role in their children's education and of increasing participation in the zone generally. Themes of social entrepreneurship and volunteering are evident. Let us look at these proposals in more detail:

Kenningham proposes to:

- extend the role of the educational welfare officer;
- undertake family support outreach work – to involve parents with their children in pre-school play and learning;
- befriend parents and bringing them together around pre-school projects to raise morale and ambition;
- befriend parents of 'difficult 11- to 13-year-olds';
- run parenting courses in local primary schools;
- train parents as classroom assistants;
- have twilight, weekend and summer school provision;

- use adult volunteers (parents and post-16 student volunteers) to befriend parents.

Norbridge will provide:

- access to enhanced ICT facilities for parents 'to develop strong Intranet links and community involvement, using ICT to motivate parents and develop the learning culture of the parents within the area so that they feel empowered to aid both their own and their children's learning';
- 'parental learning ... to develop good learning habits for parents and children. The zone would actively promote parents' self-esteem and belief that they can succeed';
- 'out of hours learning ... extended hours for study support'.

Nairton will provide:

- support outside the school day;
- an extended adult basic skills programme targeted at parents;
- parenting classes with input from different agencies;
- schools to be developed as IT learning centres for adults with access in the evening and at weekends, study support programmes for pupils before and after schools;
- Saturday schools, extensive summer school programme;
- pastoral strategy for parents and pupils;
- the development of multi-agency rapid response teams (including a specialist behaviour management team) to isolate or eliminate disruptive behaviour;
- common procedures for dealing with aggressive parents and publicity of the council's hard line on tackling incidents of violent or threatening behaviour;
- a zone-wide model for behaviour management and standard minimum expectations in relation to pupil behaviour.

The blurring of the boundary between home and school has several aspects. One is a 'deinstitutionalisation' of learning. In part this is in response to the new ICTs, but it also represents a commitment on the part of zones to take learning out of the classroom. There is also a move away from the conventional school day. All the zones offer 'extended' learning opportunities. Parents too are to be involved as 'partners' – special classes will be made available to them and they will be 'befriended' and encouraged to act as volunteers.

Although such initiatives show some sort of 'joined-up thinking', they do not connect with the material conditions within which zone populations live – nor with parents' experiences of education. As the bids have made clear, many zone parents are seen to be antagonistic to schools. It is hard to see how offering them a closer relationship with an institution to which they feel no allegiance is likely to be successful.

It might be argued that the fuller incorporation of parents within their children's education breaks down the boundary between welfare providers and welfare recipients, but it is equally possible to argue that this kind of approach merely represents an extension of professional control. Far from being a mutual (even if unbalanced) interchange of ideas and experience, the zones have no ambiguity as to who it is that needs to learn. The provision of 'parenting classes', 'family counselling' and 'behaviour management' to address educational achievement and social exclusion leaves little doubt that the source of their disadvantage lies within the family. Such provision certainly deflects attention away from economic and institutionally based explanations. Overemphasising parental responsibilities may bring about a situation in which the balance between rights and responsibilities shifts too far in favour of the latter (Lister 1990).

But even putting aside the deficit notions upon which such provisions are based, the kind of befriending and volunteering proposed within the zones overlooks the material circumstances of the poor, and of poor women in particular. As Ward (1986, cited in Lister 1990) argues, 'being poor takes up an enormous amount of time and energy'. The scarcity of time is likely to be an additional stumbling block to any new form of political association – although it has to be said that these opportunities looked fairly limited anyway (see Power and Gewirtz 2001).

In short, one aspect that appears less joined-up in the detail than in the overall vision is the relationship between the 'poor' and 'society'. The interconnectedness of societal well-being may be evident in government-level rhetoric, but it has not been translated to the local level. Within these proposals, there is a strong sense of division between those who will provide and those who will receive.

Discussion

This chapter began by arguing that 'joined-up thinking' has the potential to make meaningful change – especially when there are broad visions of what it is to be joined up. There are, however, a number of problems with 'joined-up thinking' to which we should be alert. One is that the logic of 'joined-up thinking' leads to an increasing number of area-based interventions – because it is at the local level that it is easiest to bring together different sectors and partners working together. Moreover, because of the partnership approach and the emphasis on 'social entrepreneurship', funds are increasingly allocated on a competitive basis. In addition, because 'joined-up thinking' requires a multi-dimensional approach, receiving funds for one project automatically improves the chances of receiving funds for other connected projects. Thus, even apart from variations in the capabilities of local agencies to bid successfully, the logic of 'joined-up thinking' is likely to exacerbate differences in funding between localities. A mixed economy of schooling, developed on a local basis and dependent on the amount of local capital available, is likely to reinforce variations even between disadvantaged areas. As Giddens (1998: 78) himself concedes, one of the dangers of 'downward democratisation' is the extent to which it can exacerbate fragmentation and inequality of provision across communities.

But even in those areas which have been successful in gaining funds – such as the ones referred to in this chapter – there is little to suggest at this point that zones will be able to break down the culture of departmental segregation between welfare areas. There is a lack of coherence about what needs to be 'joined up' at the local level. In part this is because of the nature of the bidding culture and the speed of application. But the bids also reflect a continued allegiance to 'old' compartmentalised perceptions of social exclusion and educational under-achievement. Social deprivation is acknowledged as a factor in poor attainment, but because of either the limited amount of funds or the dominant nature of the partnership arrangements, it is educational solutions that are proposed. Moreover, in the main, these remedies concerned with social exclusion are directed at the family rather than at the institution.

Zones may further help to blur the boundaries between public, private and voluntary sectors – but it needs to be noted that current private and voluntary sector involvement is not yet mould-breaking, either in policy or in practice (Power *et al.* 2000). The partnerships largely draw on expertise and resources in the areas of education and training and are therefore rarely able to address any of the cited problems of economic and environmental deprivation.

Not only is cross-sector involvement quite limited, but it is also based on a pathologised perspective of the family. Seeking educational answers to social problems has long been shown to be an inadequate approach that can serve to further pathologise the disadvantaged. The counterproductive effects of 'partial' solutions are outlined by Fraser:

> Although the approach aims to redress economic injustice, it leaves intact the deep structures that generate class disadvantage. Thus, it must make surface reallocations again and again. The result is to mark the most disadvantaged class as inherently deficient and insatiable, as always needing more and more. In time such a class can even come to appear privileged, the recipient of special treatment and undeserved largesse. Thus, an approach aimed at redressing injustices of distribution can end up creating injustices of recognition.
>
> (Fraser 1997: 25)

The blurring of the boundary between home and school rather than empowering parents seems set to bring them more closely under professional control. A confident and involved citizenry is unlikely to be realised by psychotherapeutic approaches to the problems of poverty and cultural deprivation. For these to be addressed, more sophisticated 'joined-up' thinking needs to be undertaken that more closely matches the remedies with the causes.

Notes

1   Giddens (1998) provides an interesting analysis of the implications for social exclusion at the 'top' of the social hierarchy.
2   There is, of course, considerable inconsistency in New Labour's position here. As I have noted earlier, it is frequently claimed that poverty cannot be used to 'excuse' poor school performance.
3   Some areas seem to be much more adept at engaging with the New Labour 'bidding culture'. In addition, once funds start to arrive the logic of the 'joined-up' approach tends to mean that more funds follow to help promote a 'multi-pronged' attack on social exclusion.
4   The difficulties in categorising many of these organisations, particularly those that relate to various education–training partnerships, are perhaps indicative of the extent to which the boundary between the public and the private is already blurred.

References

Becker, S. (1997) *Responding to Poverty: The Politics of Cash and Care*, London: Longman.

Blair, T. (1997a) Speech given at Stockwell Park School, Lambeth, at launch of Social Exclusion Unit, 8 December.

——(1997b) Speech given at Aylesbury Estate, Southwark, 2 June.

DfEE (1998) '£75 million boosts radical education action zones to raise standards', Press Release, 23 June.

Fraser, N. (1997) 'From redistribution to recognition? Dilemmas of justice in a "postsocialist" age', in N. Fraser, *Justice Interruptus*, New York: Routledge.

Gamarnikow, E. and Green, T. (1999) 'Developing social capital: dilemmas, possibilities and limitations in education', in A. Hayton (ed.) *Tackling Disaffection and Social Exclusion: Education Perspectives and Policies*, London: Kogan Page.

Giddens, A. (1998) *The Third Way: The Renewal of Social Democracy*, Cambridge: Polity Press.

Halpin, D. (1999) 'Democracy, inclusive schooling and the politics of education', *International Journal of Inclusive Education*, 3(3): 225–38.

Halsey, A.H. (ed.) (1972) *Educational Priority: Vol. 1 EPA Problems and Policies*, London: Her Majesty's Stationery Office.

Leadbetter, J. (1997) *The Rise of the Social Entrepreneur*, London: Demos.

Lister, R. (1990) *The Exclusive Society: Citizenship and the Poor*, London: Child Poverty Action Group.

Mortimore, P. and Whitty, G. (1999) 'School improvement: a remedy for social exclusion?', in A. Hayton (ed.) *Tackling Disaffection and Social Exclusion: Education Perspectives and Policies*, London: Kogan Page.

Power, S. and Gewirtz, S. (2001) 'Reading Education Action Zones', *Journal of Education Policy*, 16(1): 39–51.

Power, S. and Whitty, G. (1999) 'New Labour's education policy: first, second or Third Way?' *Journal of Education Policy*, 14(5): 535–46.

Power, S., Whitty, G. and Youdell, D. (1995) *No Place to Learn: Homelessness and Education*, London: Shelter.

Power, S., Whitty, G., Gewirtz, S., Halpin, D. and Dickson, M. (2000) 'Paving a Third Way? A policy trajectory analysis of education action zones', Interim Report to the ESRC.

Rafferty, F. (1998) 'Action zones will pilot new ideas', *Times Educational Supplement*, 6 February: 4.

Smith, G. (1987) 'Whatever happened to Educational Priority Areas', *Oxford Review Of Education*, 13(1): 23–38.

Whitty, G. (1997) 'Social theory and education policy: the legacy of Karl Mannheim', *British Journal of Sociology of Education*, 18(2): 149–63.

Whitty, G., Power, S. and Halpin, D. (1998) *Devolution and Choice in Education*, Buckingham: Open University Press.

Whitty, G., Power, S, Gamarnikow, E., Aggleton, P., Tyrer, P. and Youdell, D. (1999) 'Health, housing and education: tackling multiple disadvantage', in A. Hayton (ed.) *Tackling Disaffection and Social Exclusion: Education Perspectives and Policies*, London: Kogan Page.

3 Education Action Zones and *Zones d'Education Prioritaires*

Richard Hatcher and Dominique Leblond

Introduction

In 1998 the British 'New Labour' government launched the first twenty-five Education Action Zones (EAZs), a new policy initiative aimed at raising standards of achievement in schools in socially disadvantaged areas. A second group of forty-eight zones was approved in 1999. There are now seventy-three zones. Each usually comprises two secondary schools and their associated primary schools, totalling between a dozen and twenty schools altogether. Recently the government has announced the launch of a further fourteen small EAZs, each containing one secondary school and its local primary schools. Up to fifty small EAZs are planned. By 2001 it is anticipated that 10 per cent of all schools will be in EAZs.[1] At present, all the zones are in England: there are none in Wales, Scotland or Northern Ireland.

Coincidentally, in 1998 the French Socialist Party-led government of the 'plural left' announced the relaunch of its policy of *Zones d'Education Prioritaires* (ZEPs). ZEPs were first proposed in 1981 and launched in 1982. Like EAZs, their purpose is to improve educational achievement in socially disadvantaged areas. A relaunch of the policy took place in 1991, and a second relaunch in 1998, by which time there were 571 ZEPs, containing 11.1 per cent of nursery, primary and lower secondary schools (*collèges*) (*Le Monde de l'éducation*, February 2000: 23). One of the new elements in the 1998 relaunch was the creation of *Réseaux d'Education Prioritaires* (Education Priority Networks), which are similar to ZEPs except that the criteria for disadvantage are less stringent and there is no additional salary paid to teachers working in them. The notion of 'network' is intended to signify an inclusive rather than a segregative orientation. REPs may include existing ZEP schools. In 1999, after the relaunch, there was a total of 865 ZEPs and REPs, containing one in five of all pupils and a higher proportion in some areas (e.g. Paris had 14 ZEPs, but it has now transformed them into 14 ZEPs and 20 REPs, which together take a third of all Paris primary school pupils and one in four secondary pupils). ZEPs and REPs are roughly comparable in size to EAZs; another element of the 1998 relaunch was a reduction in the size of the largest ZEPs. (For convenience we will use the term ZEPs to include REPs as well.)

A number of European countries have made use of zonal policies to tackle areas of social disadvantage in education (Gille 1993), including Education Priority Areas in the UK – a short-lived experiment introduced following the Plowden Report in 1967. But the policy of ZEPs is by far the most ambitious in its scale and duration. It is curious that no reference to the French experience is made in the British government's EAZ policy documentation. The reason is unclear: is it a case of unacknowledged policy borrowing, or do the British government and its advisers regard ZEPs as a policy from which they cannot learn anything (too 'old Labour'?), or are they are perhaps unaware of it (though that seems difficult to believe)? We don't know which of these is more worrying. Reference to ZEPs is also noticeably absent from the British academic literature on education policy and 'school improvement' – its points of reference are largely restricted to the English-speaking world. (Conversely, reference to Plowden's EPAs is seldom made in the French literature.)

The aim of this chapter is to make an initial contribution to a comparative policy analysis of these education zone developments.[2] Though we set the scene with a brief overview of the rationales for zones in England and France, our focus here is on one dimension of the zones: their character as local partnerships. A consideration of other central aspects of zones, in particular issues of teaching and learning, is beyond the scope of this chapter.

Why zones?

Why have education zones become central to education policy in both France and England? In France, the rationale for the proposing of ZEPs in 1981 arose out of the perceived failure of the comprehensive school – the *collège unique*. The *collège* had democratised access to secondary education but had not reduced social inequality in terms of pupil attainment. ZEPs were devised as a form of positive discrimination explicitly intended to tackle this. As the government circular of 1 July 1981 makes explicit, the proposed initiative

> only has meaning if it is inscribed in a policy of struggle against social inequality. Its priority aim is to contribute to correcting this inequality, by the selective reinforcement of educational action in the zones and in the social milieux where the level of educational failure is highest.
>
> (quoted in Bouveau 1997: 49)

EAZs were first proposed in England with a similar aim. In his foreword to *Excellence in Schools* (DfEE 1997: 3), the Labour government's first major policy document on education after it was elected, David Blunkett, the Secretary of State for Education, stated that one of the government's principal objectives was 'to eliminate, and never excuse, under-achievement in the most deprived parts of our country'. However, in France the optimism of the early 1980s has been tempered today by a recognition of the limited extent to which schools can compensate for wider social inequalities, and it is noticeable that in

England subsequent EAZ objectives and outcome targets are posed in terms of raising standards of achievement but not in terms of reducing relative inequalities.

Education zones in both countries enable social disadvantage in schooling to be tackled through a combination of two strategies: the targeting of extra money and the mobilising of local action.

Targeting extra money

Both EAZs and ZEPs attract additional funding. ZEPs enable additional resources to be targeted on areas of high social deprivation: '*donner plus à ceux qui ont moins* (to give more to those who have less)'. ZEPs spend on average an additional 10 per cent per pupil (Cédelle 2000). However, this may still be less than the amount spent on pupils in areas where prosperous municipalities fund schools more generously than the average. Charlot (1998a) speaks of *negative* discrimination in some ZEPs, where, for example, class sizes are larger than they are in some non-ZEP areas or where the number of places in nursery classes for 2-year-olds is less than the national average. In addition, public money is supplemented by regular voluntary donations by parents through the *coopérative scolaire*, which subsidise books, visits, etc. The amounts raised vary widely according to the social milieu of the school.

EAZs receive their additional funding on a flat rate basis, in the form of £750,000 a year allocated directly by government, on top of the normal funding provided by the local education authority (LEA). The additional government grant is conditional on the zone itself finding a further £250,000 from the private sector. This is a mode of funding which is unique to EAZs in England and has no parallel in France. The newly announced small EAZs will receive £250,000 a year. They are encouraged to seek business sponsorship, which will be matched by government up to an additional £50,000 a year.

As with France, disparities in funding between LEAs, as well as the level of parental donations, can mean that the average spent on pupils in schools in some EAZs is less than that in some non-EAZ areas. A further point is worth noting: teachers in ZEPs, but not in EAZs, receive a supplement to their salaries, approximately 600 francs a month (together with additional seniority which benefits subsequent career development).

It is difficult to compare the levels of resourcing between EAZs and ZEPs. Figures for the amount spent on pupils in EAZs are not available. According to the 1998 OECD report on spending per secondary pupil, the UK spends £2,680 as against the EU average of £3,145 (*Times Educational Supplement*, 14 April 2000). There is variation among EAZs, but to take one zone as an example, the additional funding it receives is the equivalent of approximately £150 per pupil. As a percentage of £2,680, £150 is approximately an extra 5 per cent, compared to the ZEP figure of 10 per cent.

Mobilising local action

In 1982 Alain Savary, the Minister of Education and author of the ZEP policy, appealed for a general mobilisation at the local level around education on the grounds that 'The state can do nothing by itself' ('*L'état ne peut rien à lui seul*', Lettre aux enseignants, 6 September 1982). ZEPs were situated in the context of local urban development policy, the DSQ (Développement Social de Quartiers). In this context, the ZEPs would open up the opportunity for a range of actors at the local level, in addition to opportunities for teachers to contribute to raising achievement at school level. This, it was argued, would be both more democratic, in the sense of enabling people to have a direct influence in activities which affect their lives, and more efficient in terms of raising standards of achievement. This rationale continues to underpin the ZEP policy and has been restated recently in the major government report entitled *Les déterminants de la réussite scolaire en ZEP* (*The determinants of educational success in ZEPs*), written by two national school inspectors, Catherine Moisan and Jacky Simon, and published in September 1997. The Moisan–Simon Report was the basis of the relaunch of the ZEPs the following year.

- Social origin is a powerful determinant of the school success of children.
- The concentration of economically, socially and culturally disadvantaged people in certain districts or establishments increases this inequality.
- The system can and must compensate for this inequality in terms of resources (give more to those who have less) and strategies (projects, teaching strategies, evaluation).
- This policy will not be fruitful unless it is run in such a way that the projects and actions rest on a local diagnosis of the difficulties. The designation of the zones, the allocation of resources and the examination of projects relates to the academic or departmental level, not the national.
- The school cannot fight alone against the range of difficulties, it has to work in a coherent way with its partners.

(Moisan and Simon 1997: 4)

In the UK, the creation of local partnerships to improve education was the key point made in the one short paragraph of rationale for EAZs in *Excellence in Schools* (DfEE 1997). Only later was the commitment to target additional funding to the zones adopted.

We want to develop new and imaginative ways of helping schools to achieve our overall objectives. That will require effort from all concerned, and particularly parents and the local community. The initiative will only succeed on the basis of active partnerships, taking careful account of the distinctive characteristics of the areas concerned.

(DfEE 1997: 39)

In the subsequent document *Meet the Challenge* (DfEE 1998a), a booklet published by the DfEE as an invitation to submit bids for the second phase of zones, EAZs are described as being 'at the forefront of the Government's plans ... to raise standards and tackle disadvantage' (DfEE 1998a: 3). In answer to the question 'Why are Education Action Zones needed?' it refers to the problems of low educational achievement coupled with high levels of truancy, exclusions of pupils from school and youth crime.

> Experience has demonstrated that conventional solutions to these problems have not always been successful. Evidence also indicates that standards rise fastest where schools themselves, with the support of parents and the local community, take responsibility for improvement.
>
> *(ibid.)*

> Education Action Zones will give local partnerships the freedom and the resources to propose collaborative and innovative strategies that would be difficult to put into practice at the level of the individual school. They can also develop proposals which draw on the support and ideas of the local community.
>
> (DfEE 1998a: 4)

However, the case rests on assertion: no reference is given for the experience and evidence invoked. The sub-text, familiar from numerous statements by government spokespeople, is that LEAs cannot be relied on – they are regarded as often being part of the problem rather than the solution – and that the private sector has a unique and indispensable role as a catalyst for modernising the school system.

How successful are the zones?

Interestingly, in spite of the apparently separate development of the two policy discourses, the ZEP and EAZ agendas share a number of common themes even if they are operationalised differently: a focus on teaching and learning ('*recentrer sur les apprentissages*' is a key theme of the relaunched ZEP policy); individual pupil support; a stress on literacy education; extra-school educational activities; partnership between home and school; and inter-agency partnership. How successful have these strategies been?

In the UK, the DfEE has claimed that the first group of EAZs are already showing improvements in raising pupil attainment, though it might be thought too early to make judgements about the success of the EAZs (Publicnet 2000). It needs to be remembered that raising standards is not the same as reducing inequality. Standards of attainment of all pupils may improve while the equality gap between different social groups remains the same or even widens, and this has been the case in the UK in recent years (Gillborn and Mirza 2000). EAZs should be judged by their success not only in raising standards but also, and principally, in reducing social inequality in education.

How successful are the ZEPs in reducing social inequality in education? In France a balance-sheet can be drawn of a policy in place now for nearly two decades. Social class differences in educational outcomes in French education, as in British, are substantial. For example, the government's target of 80 per cent reaching the level of the '*bac*' (i.e. completing the course – not necessarily passing the exam) is already attained in middle-class areas, while the figure in socially disadvantaged areas is 30 per cent. The overall picture of the ZEPs is that they have not succeeded in narrowing the gap with non-ZEP schools. However, that conclusion immediately needs to be qualified in two ways because there is some evidence of success. First, during the period since the ZEPs were launched, social inequality in France has widened but educational inequality has remained the same. It can be argued that the ZEPs have therefore had some success in preventing the gap widening, whereas it has widened in Britain (Bouveau and Rochex 1997). Second, there is considerable variation in the effectiveness of ZEPs. In some ZEPs, educational inequality has been reduced. According to Gerard Chauveau, a leading researcher into ZEPs, attainment in one in three ZEP colleges has improved in relation to non-ZEP colleges, but in one in five attainment has worsened relatively (cited in Baumard 2000).

The new public management and education

EAZs and ZEPs are not unique developments in the public sectors in France or England. They exemplify a widespread new approach to the public sector which is powerfully reshaping the management and provision of public services across the world, promulgated by international organisations such as the OECD.

> [A]n OECD ... study of public sector reforms criticised old-style bureaucratic structures which were 'highly centralised, rule-bound and inflexible' and which emphasised 'process rather than results', inhibited efficiency and effectiveness and were not able to respond rapidly enough to the demands of change.
>
> (Taylor *et al.* 1997: 79)

The OECD approves

> the creation of a 'performance-oriented' and 'less centralised' public sector with the following characteristics: a focus on results and efficiency and effectiveness, decentralised management environments, flexibility to explore alternatives to public provision of services, establishment of productivity targets and a competitive environment between public sector organisations, along with the strengthening of strategic capacities at the centre of the organisation.
>
> (Taylor *et al.* 1997: 82)

This new model of public sector provision has provided the general policy orientation for the European Union in the field of school education, but taking different forms in different countries in accord with national specificities (Green *et al.* 1999). Under the Conservative governments of Thatcher and Major it was adopted in a particularly market-orientated form, presented as a 'rolling back of the state' to clear the ground for market forces to operate. Under the Labour government there is less reliance on market forces as the principal dynamic of reform of the school system, and more on the role of the state driving reform from the centre and intervening at the local level to manage decentralisation.

The influence of the new model of public sector management can also be identified in France. Even if, not having had the advantage of a Thatcher government, the process is less advanced, the tradition of the 'school of the republic' is being eroded. Françoise Lorcerie contrasts the old 'juridical' model of administration, characterised by unilateralism, regularity, impersonality and conformity, with the new public management. She speaks of

> the managerial transformation of administration, of which the key themes are: responsibilisation, autonomy, participation, evaluation. The crucial orientation is given by the word efficiency. Above all it's a question of promoting in a pragmatic way the modes of functioning which enable the objectives assigned to the public service to be achieved.
>
> (Lorcerie 1999: 83)

Bernard Charlot (1994) places the new public management in the wider context of the changing role of the state in relation to the economy in France and Western societies in general. Increased global competition means that productivity has to be raised through new technology, flexible work methods, improved product quality, diversification and decentralised decision-making. This affects schools in two ways. One is the demand to raise the education standards of the future worker, consumer and citizen – symbolised by the slogan of 80 per cent to achieve the *baccalauréat*. The other is the application of business management methods to the school system in the interests of efficiency. A similar argument has been made about British education policy (see, for example, Hatcher 1998a).

The political characterisation of the 'new public management' is a matter of debate. Does it represent an opportunity to reinvigorate and strengthen public service institutions by promoting local democratic participation and improving the quality of provision? Or is it a neo-liberal project to undermine the public sector and open it up to market relations in the form of business interests and local consumerism? It is in the context of that debate that we will discuss education zones.

Territorialisation, contracts and partnership

Education zones embody three key elements of the new public management: decentralisation to the local level (*territorialisation*, to use the French term), contractualisation and partnership. Here we draw on the analysis of Dominique Glasman:

> The policy of contractualisation is, in the provision of public service and its 'modernisation', indissociable from territorialisation and partnership ... Faced with the growing complexity of problems and the diversity of local situations, the State gives up imposing from above a way of doing things which is applicable everywhere, and delegates to the local actors the responsibility of finding arrangements in order to respond in particular to the effects of the social 'crisis'. The State is not absent, since its decentralised services are often carried out fully by the 'actors' thus assembled, but the other 'actors' are invited to 'participate' fully, including financially. All the actors are charged with coming together, on a relevant territorial basis, and finding, 'in partnership', the solutions to the problems they all encounter. According to this policy, the way to dynamise the social world is to adopt a local perspective. In this perspective, the policy of contractualisation is the means to mobilise the local actors, and the 'contract' serves to establish the agreement. That is to say that the 'contract', the policy of contractualisation, is first to be considered in its political dimensions. It is a link between the State and the citizens or between the citizens themselves, and a mode of action of the institutions which are involved in the contracts.
>
> (Glasman 1999: 2)

We will discuss in turn how each of these three elements of the new public management – territorialisation, contractualisation and partnership – apply to the policies of ZEPs and EAZs.

Territorialisation – the significance of the local

The policy combination of geographically targeted additional resourcing and the encouragement of educational actions by local actors is common to both EAZs and ZEPs. But the difference in the national contexts gives decentralisation to the local a very different meaning in each country. In the British context, while some features of the EAZ policy have been controversial, the underlying themes of positive discrimination to counter educational disadvantage and of education as a partnership of school, parents and community are not in themselves contentious. On the contrary, they have been the conventional wisdom of British education since at least the 1960s, exemplified in the 1967 Plowden Report. Furthermore, the importance of the local is embedded in the system of elected local councils having the function of local education authorities (LEAs) with considerable power. Though their power has in recent years been eroded from above by greater central government control over the school system (including the national curriculum, national tests, and new inspection and funding mechanisms), and from below by the compulsory delegation of powers to schools (Local Management of Schools), LEAs still retain important responsi-

bilities relating to the provision of schools, the content and quality of educational provision and the employment of teachers. In these respects there is a
strong contrast with the French context.

In France the introduction of ZEPs has meant a new settlement of the local
and the national, particularly in the 1990s. In 1991, the *Plan de modernisation du
service public de l'éducation nationale* announced a new conception of the role of
central government: 'the time to manage everything, control everything, is over';
'in future the administration must initiate, stimulate, provide coherence, contract
out, evaluate'. It proposed 'to increase the spaces of responsibility at every level
of the system, giving to the various decision-makers the possibility of implementing real choices in the framework of broad national objectives' (quoted in
Charlot 1994: 36).

It is important to understand just how radical the ZEP policy is. It represents
a fundamental break with the republican tradition of the previous hundred years
of French education. In this tradition the functions of the school, to create the
future citizens of the republic and to provide equality of opportunity for merit,
were to be accomplished through uniform universal provision ensured by tight
centralised state control over the schools. There was no place for a recognition of
localism or particularism. The local authority (the *commune* or the *municipalité*) has
had little role in schooling apart from responsibility for the premises (though the
Paris *municipalité* employs teachers of art, music and physical education to work
in schools, and the elected regional tier of government can influence the provision of vocational tracks in *collèges* and *lycées*).

The ZEP initiative, particularly since its reforms in the 1990s, has created a
big debate in French education on the meaning of *territorialisation*. One of the key
points at issue concerns its implications for equality. The basis of the ZEP policy
is that social justice requires a responsiveness to local needs. The *Rapport de la
Commission Education–Formation du Xe Plan 1989–92* affirms:

> In the first place, the absolute necessity of a diversity of education in terms
> of the diversity of pupils. It is a recognised truth today that uniformity
> engenders inequality: a literal attachment to equality maintains inequality
> when it does not aggravate it.
>
> (quoted in Charlot 1994: 40)

From the recognition of local difference in need flows the necessity, it is
argued, of local differentiation of provision and therefore decentralisation of
power.

> You can't manage diversity and heterogeneity by means of national circulars
> published in Paris in the offices of the minister of education. The logic of diver-
> sity combines here with that of efficiency: both demand that power is delegated
> to the periphery, that recognition is given to a zone of autonomy of the
> actors, to those who confront daily concrete problems, in concrete situations.
>
> (Charlot 1994: 41)

However, while social justice requires that individual and group differences are recognised, not overridden in the name of uniformity, differentiation of provision does not in itself guarantee greater equality. It may be a means to reduce inequalities, but it may reinforce a logic of segregation and inequality. This is the question posed by differentiating educational practices within zones, and by the idea of zones themselves as a differentiated form of provision.

Contractualisation – central government and local partnerships

Territorialisation requires new forms of state regulation. Our starting-point for understanding the relation of education zones to central government is Clarke and Newman's discussion of the 'managerial state':

> We have witnessed striking changes in the organisational form of the state and the way state power works. Much analysis has framed these changes in terms of the retreat or withdrawal of the state … In this view, the state is now mainly conceived of as a combination of policy making and financing functions increasingly separated from service delivery. Nevertheless, we think it can be argued that far from being shifts towards a 'rolling back' of the state, these changes involve a 'rolling out' of state power but in new, dispersed, forms. These new forms both cross and reorganise the conventional boundaries of public and private (or state and non-state). Dispersal engages more agencies and agents into the field of state power, empowering them through its delegatory mechanisms and subjecting them through processes of regulation, surveillance and evaluation.
>
> (Clarke and Newman 1997: 30)

Thus in France the new approach validates the local in a way that is new in French education, but it represents a reworking rather than a displacement of centralised state control: 'the territorialisation of education policy is not a conquest by the local, but the result of a national policy: it has been willed, defined, organised and put into place by the State' (Charlot 1994: 27). ZEPs are subject to government control in two ways: by virtue of their structural position within the education administration, and through a specific set of contractual mechanisms.

First, the ZEPs are an integral part of the existing administrative structure of the French school system, in contrast with EAZs which have been deliberately constructed as a new form of local governance forming an additional layer to the existing school–LEA–central government structure. ZEPs are under the control of the *rectorats* of the *académies* (a regional administrative structure of which there are thirty in France). First of all, therefore, decentralisation means the reallocation of certain powers *within* the state apparatus, from the national to the regional level. It is the decision of the *rectorat* to designate and apply for national approval for zones, to fund them and to decide on their objectives.

Immediate responsibility for each ZEP belongs to an inspector within the *académie*. In the French system, responsibility for the appointment and promotion of teachers also lies with the inspectors, not with the head of the school, so the control exercised by the state educational administration over the ZEP is dominant and direct.

Second, this control is secured by a system of contracts with the ZEPs. They are of three types:

- *contrats de réussite* (CR) – actions to be taken to improve education;
- *contrats locaux d'accompagnement scolaire* (CLAS) – actions to supplement school education;
- *contrats éducatifs locaux* (CEL) – actions to provide an educational framework favourable to the global development of the personality of the child or young person.

(Glasman 1999: 10)

The groundwork for the contractual system was laid by the 1989 loi d'orientation introduced by Lionel Jospin, then Minister of Education, which stipulated that each zone had to have a *projet de zone*, an action plan based on approved objectives which served as a contract between the schools and the zone. The Jospin relaunch also connected the ZEPs to the local urban development plan, the DSQ. These were the major additions to the zone policy introduced in the first relaunch of the ZEP by Jospin in 1990. But in the view of Lorcerie it was the 1998 relaunch which marked the real adoption of the new managerial approach. 'The innovation introduced by the relaunch of the ZEPs is to extend the managerial perspective to affirmative action in the domain of schooling' (Lorcerie 1999: 82).

The political characterisation of contractualisation is ambivalent. It can be part of a neo-liberal project, providing the economic basis for market relationships between employers and employees, between members of a partnership, or between providers and consumers. But it can also be a way of strengthening public services by making them more effective, as an alternative to the market. 'One can see in the development of education contracts the sign, even the principal form, of the rise of the logic of the market. One can also see in it a way to reactivate the mission of the institution' (Glasman 1999: 9). However, even in the context of strengthening public services against the market, contracts can work in two ways, as authoritarian or participatory forms of management. In their authoritarian managerial form, the improvement of the public service is premised on the instrumentalisation of teachers and other workers on the ground, an amplification of controls and a restriction of their autonomy. In a more participatory form of management, aiming at the same improvement, contracts are based on their mobilisation, the recognition of their competences, their training and their commitment.

In France the key instrument is the *contrat de réussite* between the ZEP and the *académie*. Each contract is specific to each zone, time-limited and evaluated in terms of progress in academic achievement measured by national tests taken by the majority of children at ages 8 and 11.

> The *contrat de réussite* concerns the *Zones d'Education Prioritaires* and the *Réseaux d'Education Prioritaires*. Since the process of the relaunch of the ZEPs, which gave the opportunity for its introduction (1998), it designates the form under which a '*projet*' is both made official and made the object of a commitment to act; this commitment is undertaken both by the leaders of the ZEP or the REP and by the authorities of the *académie*. This entails providing the human or material resources judged necessary to lead a project to success, which the signatory 'actors on the ground' agree, for their part, to put into practice. The *contrat de réussite* supposes that the accent is put on the leadership, the support, the involvement of teams working on the ground, as well as on professional development and evaluation. Organisationally, the CR involves first and foremost the world of national education: the rector and inspectors of the *académie*, heads of schools, teachers, other education staff. But it can also mobilise other actors: social workers, local authority staff, health service workers, police, etc.
>
> (Glasman 1999: 17)

The *contrat de réussite* of each ZEP links together all the schools within it around a common set of objectives and actions. It provides the basis for this local *communauté éducative*, ensuring a commonality and continuity of educational experience and justifying the recent policy of the *académies* of refusing applications by parents to send their children to schools outside the area (*dérogations*).

EAZs are not an integral part of state education administration in the way that ZEPs are, as we will see below. But they are, like the ZEPs, controlled by contracts. The ZEP *contrat de réussite* is drawn up by the ZEP co-ordinator, inspectors, the education advisor (*conseilleur pédagogique*), representatives of support services, the heads of the schools, and one representative per school elected from the teaching staff of each school. This is a much more participatory model than that of the EAZs. In England teachers may or may not be involved in the decision as to whether or not a school participates in a bid to set up an EAZ. In some cases they are consulted and may even have the deciding voice; in others the decision is taken by the head teacher and the school governing body. But in any case, teachers are unlikely to be involved in, or even consulted about, decisions at the level of the precise targets for the zone. They have little or no representation on the zone decision-making bodies (see below). Yet they will be held responsible for the attainment of the targets set for the zone.

The initial form the contract takes is the bid to the DfEE for approval to establish a zone. If the EAZ bid is successful, a detailed annual Action Plan has to be submitted, spelling out the proposed actions, their anticipated outcomes and their costs. Frequent and detailed financial accounts also have to be submitted to the DfEE for approval. The DfEE stipulates that the bid has to include the 'main plans for improving performance, highlighting any particularly innovative strategies: … there must be measurable outcomes and you should consider identification and sharing of good practice, quality issues, and how to provide value for money' (DfEE 1998a: 23).

As an example of what is meant by measurable outcomes, we quote from the successful bid to set up one of the two EAZs in Birmingham:

Targets
1   At all key stages, to improve pupil attainment by 20 per cent over the 3 year period of the zone as measured by:

- the percentage of children scoring 4 and above in Literacy and Numeracy in Birmingham's Baseline assessments
- the percentage of children achieving Level 2 and above and Level 4 and above in the end of KS1 and KS2 assessments in English and Mathematics
- the percentage of students achieving Level 5 and above in the end of KS3 tests
- the percentage of students achieving 5 A–C and 5 A–E grades at GCSE and average point score per student.

2   To decrease exclusion rates by 20 per cent over the 3-year period
3   To improve attendance so that all schools reach a minimum of 90 per cent
4   To increase the hours schools are open for learning by 50 per cent over the 3-year period
5   Doubling the number of learning opportunities available in the zone over the 3-year period
6   Reduce the number of school leavers leaving without training or employment by 25 per cent
7   Increase the number of adults entering into accredited courses by 15 per cent
8   Double the number of volunteers in local education, health and community organisations.

(Birmingham City Council 1998: 26–7)

It is interesting to compare this with a ZEP *contrat de réussite*. We will take the *contrat de réussite* for 2000–3 for REP 5 in Paris as an example. The document contains a detailed evaluation of pupil attainment in 1999. It defines the three principal themes of the REP: learning in difference; learning to live together; developing collaboration among teachers across the zone. Each theme is translated into a number of objectives, tasks and actions. So, for example, one of the objectives of the first theme, 'learning in difference', is 'to give meaning to learning'; the tasks flowing from it are to develop mastery of the oral and written language, and a number of actions are proposed to achieve it. Nowhere are there any quantitative targets for pupil attainment or teacher performance. The monitoring and evaluation of progress provide the basis for a process of professional development and innovation in which quantified targets for improvement play no role.

The contrast with EAZs is striking. EAZ schools, and the zone itself, are subject to regular inspection by Ofsted (the government Office for Standards in Education). Schools which fail to meet their targets are subject to punitive measures or even closure, and zones which fail to meet their targets risk losing their funding. An additional source of pressure on teachers, and the main reason why the National Union of Teachers has a formal position of opposition to EAZs, is that zones are able to disapply the nationally agreed pay and conditions agreement for teachers in order to install 'more flexible approaches'. Although the government encourages them to do so, union opposition has so far deterred any zone from attempting it.

Partnerships

The idea of 'partnership' is central to current management discourse at every level, as Mayo notes:

> From the World Bank and the International Monetary Fund, and the Standing Conference of Local and Regional Authorities of Europe, through to voluntary and local community sector associations, partnerships are firmly on the agenda in the second half of the 1990s, along with community participation and community development.
>
> (Mayo 1997: 5)

Partnership is the key word in the vocabulary of zones, both in France and in England. We want to begin by drawing some points from the wider literature on partnership before applying them to education zones.

There is a tendency in official government literature about the merits of partnership to present an idealised model which assumes that achieving consensus among the participants is relatively unproblematic. In contrast, we would want to stress the conflictual character of co-ordinating different and unequal interest and identity groups, and therefore the crucial question of differential power relations. Thus, following Nevin and Shiner's (1995) work on local communities and partnership, we would want to distinguish between involvement and empowerment. We would also want to distinguish between strategic power and operational power: some partners may have the power to set the agenda, some only to participate in the implementation of agendas set by others. In other words, partnerships are characterised by processes of inclusion and exclusion. Just as some potential partners may be wholly or partially excluded, so others may be compulsorily included – projects which are presented as 'partnerships' are not necessarily entirely the product of voluntary collaboration. In the case of education zones, for example, teachers and parents (and in a sense pupils) are designated as 'partners' whether they desire it or not.

We would also want to make use of the distinction made by Mackintosh (1992) between three models of partnership – synergy, budget enlargement, and transformational. The transformational model 'assumes that there are benefits to be gained by exposing the different partners to the assumptions and working methods of other partners' (Mayo 1997: 5). For example, governments may promote partnerships bringing together public and private sector organisations with the aim that private sector organisations might become more socially aware, and public sector organisations may become more market-orientated. Thus, for Mackintosh, 'partnership becomes a mutual struggle for transformation' (1992: 216).

A further important distinction is made by Lowndes and Skelcher (1998) between partnership as an organisational form and modes of social co-ordination within partnerships. 'Partnerships are associated with a variety of forms of social co-ordination – including network, hierarchy and market' (Lowndes and Skelcher 1998: 314). Mayo (1997) notes the political ambivalence of the discourse of partnerships, invoked to serve market and public service agendas. Lowndes *et al.* (1997) describe several sets of attitudes towards partnerships. At one end of the spectrum of views are the enthusiasts, for whom networking and partnership have opened up local governance, leading to new approaches and more effective community participation. At the other are the opponents, for whom partnerships represent an attack on local democracy, a new unelected institutional landscape for public services. As the authors say, 'the spread of networks and partnerships can be seen as symptomatic of a political malaise, where unrepresentative groupings fill the "democratic deficit" in local politics' (Lowndes *et al.* 1997: 342).

Having established some points of reference in the debate about partnership, we turn now to examine zones as forms of partnership. We begin by noting a significant difference between ZEPs and EAZs in the organisational form of the partnership. In England, education policy has proceeded further down the road of decentralisation, differentiation, and local partnerships involving schools, local authorities, communities and other interests than has its French counterpart. In consequence, the concept of local education partnership has been translated into a more autonomous, formally structured and potentially inclusive organisational form in EAZs than in ZEPs.

In France, responsibility for the zone lies with the inspector, with the zone director, who is usually either the inspector or the principal of a *collège* in the ZEP appointed on a part-time basis by the *rectorat* of the *académie*, and a zone co-ordinator, often a seconded teacher. There is a *conseil de zone*, a zone council, comprising the above together with the heads and teacher representatives of all the schools, which is responsible for drawing up the *contrat de réussite* in accordance with the directives of the *académie*, and which may meet on a regular basis, but has only an advisory role. In contrast, EAZs have a zone director who is appointed by the decision-making body of the zone, the Action Forum. This is a statutory body, formally independent from both the government and the local education authority, which is supposed to comprise the various 'stakeholders' in the partnership. The composition of the membership of each Action Forum has to conform to DfEE guidelines and to be approved by the Secretary of State.

The formal organisational structure of EAZs is given considerable promi-
nence in government policy. According to the DfEE's handbook for Education
Action Zones (1998b: para 2.1.3), 'Both the title and the composition of the
Action Forum are intended to underscore the importance of a partnership
approach to achieving improvements across a community.' To what extent is this
claim borne out by an examination of EAZ Action Forums? We will take a
typical example. According to its published newsletter (quoted in Hatcher
1998b), the Salford and Trafford Action Forum has a membership of 48 or 49
and meets six times a year. It comprises:

18 representatives of school governing bodies (one from each school)
1–2 representative(s) of the Secretary of State
2 from Salford City Council
2 from Trafford MBC
4 from private sector (business executives/managers)
2 from Manchester TEC
1 from Careers Partnership
2 parent representatives from Salford and Trafford schools
2 teachers' association representatives
3 from the community and voluntary sector
1 from Salford University
2 from education and business partnerships
1 director from Salford and Trafford Health Authority
2 from the Further Education sector
1 from Salford Roman Catholic diocese
1 from Manchester Church of England diocese
1 from Greater Manchester Probation Service
1 from First Organisation
1 from Manchester Council for Community Relations.

The largest interest bloc is management at school level – 18 head teachers or
chairs of school governing bodies – and managers of other governmental agencies. Out of the 48 or 49 places on the Forum, only 2 are allocated to parents'
representatives. The 'community and voluntary sector' category is allocated 3
places, but this covers not just representatives of the local community but
representatives of charitable trusts and other semi-official agencies operating in
the area, and it may therefore virtually or entirely exclude local people representing the local community. Classroom teachers have no places allocated to
them as of right, though they may occupy the 2 places allocated to the
teachers' unions.

In practice much of the actual policy-making process of EAZs takes place not
in the Forum itself but in the much smaller and more frequent meetings of the
Executive Board (the title varies locally), whose composition is more exclusive
than the Forum. Continuing with the example of the Salford and Trafford EAZ
Executive Board, which meets monthly, it comprises:

4 head teachers
4 LEA representatives
1 from Manchester TEC
2 from private sector
1 from Health Authority
1 from FE.

Out of the 13 places, there are none at all for representatives of parents, the local community or classroom teachers.

The composition of the zone decision-making bodies reflects the power relations by which some groups are privileged and others marginalised. Those who are in practice at the centre of the educational partnership for pupil success – the teachers, the parents and the school students themselves – are largely or entirely excluded from the managerial partnership which controls the decision-making of the zone.

It also needs to be remembered that the power of one partner in the zone, the government, is not reflected in its numerical weight. The DfEE does not just steer the zones from a distance through its control over the contracts on which the zone is based: it has a direct involvement in the zone itself, not only in influencing key participants behind the scenes, but also by having a representative of the DfEE as a member of each Action Forum, with in effect a veto over decisions. In the British context this direct involvement of central government in education administration at the local level is quite exceptional. And as Lowndes *et al.* (1997: 341) point out, 'an agenda led by central government can detract from the local identification of needs and the local development of appropriate policies and organisational responses'.

The DfEE also exercises power over the zone through its recommended Code of Conduct for Action Forums (DfEE 1998b: Annex G), which recommends that a member of an AF should 'acknowledge that differences of opinion may arise in discussion of issues, but, when a majority decision of the forum prevails, it should be supported'; and should 'base his or her view on matters before the forum on an honest assessment of the available facts, unbiased by *partisan or representative* views' (our emphasis). The intended consequence is the prevention of the expression of views outside the Forum by the representatives of parents, community groups or classroom teachers who dissent from the in-built management-dominated Forum majority.

We turn now to examine the processes of inclusion and exclusion which characterise the relations between the partners in EAZs. In one of the first published research studies of the internal processes of EAZ partnerships, Ken Jones and Kate Bird (2000) describe the conflict between the agendas of key players striving to influence zone developments. They identify

> not the stable functioning of an established relationship, or even the conscious construction of new partnerships, but rather a process of partial displacement and recombination, wherein there was an attempt to decentre

some existing 'partners' in educational governance, to increase the importance of others and to install new ones.

(Jones and Bird 2000: 504)

We want to track some of these processes of inclusion and exclusion in the
ongoing construction of partnerships in EAZs and ZEPs. We begin with the
school.

Not only are school representatives – head teachers and chairs of school
governing bodies – numerically predominant in EAZ decision-making, but zone
agendas tend to be dominated by the schools' agendas. We quote from the
conclusion of the evaluation report of the first year of one of the zones in
Birmingham:

> There was general agreement that the zone was dominated by a schools
> agenda. This was seen as inevitable by many head teachers, a result of the
> identification of educational targets as a criterion of the success of the zone.
> However, it was seen by many outside the schools as divisive, marginalising
> or excluding parental, community and local agency interests from effective
> partnership in the governance of the zone. The conflict between different
> agendas, underpinned by the need to achieve differing and perhaps
> conflicting objectives, was a fundamental issue for the governance of the
> zone.
>
> (Rikowski *et al.* 2000: 125)

The dominance of school-based pupil performance targets over EAZ agendas
was reinforced by the widespread belief among educational professionals that
views based on their professional expertise were not a matter for negotiation, as
the Birmingham report reveals:

> Another problem was that some felt that the Action Forum was not the
> place where all key policy-decisions were discussed and taken. There was
> also a feeling that 'educational' discussions did not take place on the Forum
> as they should, indeed, some representatives of non-education agencies felt
> that education professionals on the Forum excluded or prevented discussion
> of certain issues they wished to discuss.
>
> (Rikowski *et al.* 2000: 127)

A similar phenomenon can be noted in France, often in the form of a corpo-
ratist defence of republican statism. The school wants to be the shaper of
society. 'It tends to fix itself its own objectives, its own methods, and does not
intend to make them the objects of possible negotiation with "partners" who are
not "competent" (in the legal as well as the technical sense)' (Glasman 1999: 9).

One of the principal areas of conflict this can generate is between the schools
and local authorities. In France, one of the principal partners in the ZEP is the
local authority, the *collectivité locale*. There are significant differences between the

roles of local authorities in France and England in relation to zones. In England, there are 149 local education authorities, in effect the education departments of local town and county councils. (London has no unitary education authority: it is divided into 33 separate LEAs.) They exercise overall responsibility for schools in their areas, but their powers were substantially reduced under the Conservative government with the introduction of school-based management as well as greater government control over schooling. The Labour government has tended to regard LEAs as in many respects obstacles to their modernising project, mired in a bureaucratic and often 'Old Labour' culture. EAZs represent a further step in their marginalisation. EAZs are a new form of local governance of a cluster of schools which is not controlled by or accountable to the LEA. Power is exercised by the Action Forum, the body representing the various partners in the zone, on which the LEA is represented but as only a numerically small minority of members. However, in practice the power exercised by LEAs in relation to EAZs may greatly exceed their numerical representation on the Action Forums, as a result of the still significant power of the LEA in relation to the schools in its area, and the absence of any comparable rival structure. Indeed, while the dynamic of EAZs is potentially towards undermining the power of LEAs, the government has had to rely on LEAs to play a leading role in establishing most of them.

According to Clarke and Stewart (1998), one of the principles of the 'new public management' is that the local authority must recognise the contribution of other organisations – public, private and voluntary – and see its task as enabling, rather than controlling, that contribution. They describe it as a shift in role from service provider to community leadership, which they regard as conforming to the dominant European model of community governance, in which local authorities have a power of general competence to represent the community governing itself, but in which services are provided by a plurality of providers, increasingly on a partnership basis. In France, school education has until recently proved the exception to this model. If the direction of change in the UK has been the deployment of zones as a structure of governance to sideline LEAs, the opposite is the case in France. According to Bouveau and Rochex (1997), a new and key feature of the relaunch of the ZEPs by Jospin in 1990, which created 544 zones, was that over half were closely integrated into local council urban development projects. Every town with an urban regeneration project inscribed its schools in ZEPs. The increased integration of ZEPs into the terrain of local government meant that local authorities sought increased influence over ZEP policy, for two reasons. One was a function of the increased local authority funding of education budgets in the 1990s, from 7 per cent in 1984 to 20 per cent in 1997 (Derouet 2000). But according to Glasman (1999) local councils want more influence over schooling not only because they fund it, but because they have to deal with the problems created by youth who fail at school, such as violence in the community: school is best placed to address the problems because it is the only institution they belong to. The perspective of the local authority may be very different from that of the school.

The 'contrat' provides at the same time the opportunity and the framework to open up a debate, in the heart of society, on the question of education, while enlarging the circle of protagonists deemed legitimate. Other actors than those of the school can lay claim to competence to educate (in both senses, pedagogic and juridical), refuse to limit their educational intervention to the legal prerogatives which are their own (in terms of the construction and maintenance of school premises, equipment, provision of staff, etc.) and reject even more strongly a monopoly which the school claims and of which in their eyes the effectiveness is far from being entirely satisfactory concerning its own mission: learning, socialisation, transmission of culture.

(quoted from *La Gazette des communes* (1998) in Glasman 1999: 10)

Glasman describes the resulting processes of resistance, accommodation and transformation which are taking place in the school:

Certainly, it is widely admitted today that it cannot fulfil its mission on its own. But when it appeals for collaboration, it is more in the expectation that it will ensure the conditions of education than in envisaging a new division of educational labour between the school and its 'partners' ... Nevertheless, in fact, this new division is being installed little by little, even in the heart of the school itself (municipal *animateurs* in sport, music, the plastic arts) or on its periphery (*accompagnement scolaire*). A close cooperation with the external 'partners' is, for some school professionals, a means of articulating the fundamental mission of the school ... considering that it can less than ever limit itself to cognitive learning but must concern itself with the 'globality' of the child, and that it must not remain isolated from what happens in its environment.

(Glasman 1999: 9)

However, while recognising and legitimising new actors in education, the 'contract' is also a way to circumscribe them. *La Communale* criticises 'the poverty of the concept of a "local educational project" which is reduced to a programme of peri- and extra-school activities' (quoted in Glasman 1999: 10). Local authorities want to be involved in the design of projects – their aims, methods, resources and roles. But the national policy documentation is unclear if local authorities should participate in the process of drawing up the contract itself: 'the legitimacy of the participation of local organisations, as well as the area of participation, is in fact an issue of debate or relation of forces' (*ibid.*: 11).

Parents and schools

Partnership between school and parents is a key concept of the zone policies in both France and England. It is important to distinguish two different conceptions of partnership in this context. One operates at the level of the individual pupil, and refers to the relationship between the teacher and the parent, the school and the home, as in some sense co-educators. For example, referring to EAZs, the DfEE publication *Meet the Challenge* says,

> A strong partnership between home and schools is vital, but some parents and schools find it hard to make this partnership work well. A lack of space and facilities at home sometimes makes homework difficult; and other demands on parents, pupils and schools alike can also put some pupils at a disadvantage when learning out of school. Further barriers to pupils' learning may arise if parents themselves have difficulties in basic skills or had an unhappy and unsuccessful time at school. Parents may also need help and support to tackle their child's attendance or behavioural problems.
>
> (DfEE 1998a: 15)

All EAZs have the promotion of the educational role of the parent as an objective. But at the heart of the concept of partnership between home and school is an ambivalence: while partnership is premised on the idea that the school cannot fulfil its functions alone, working-class parents and communities are often simultaneously valorised as partners and stigmatised as deficits. A recent study of EAZ bids concludes that a deficit model of working-class families pervades them, 'positioning families as deficient and dysfunctional in relation to education':

> It is ... rather worrying to discover in the EAZ bid documentation that EAZ families are regarded as fundamentally non-educogenic. Discussions of problematic families tend to focus rather stereotypically on single parents and benefit dependency, lack of parenting skills, and inadequate care and concern among parents for their children's education.
>
> (Gamarnikow and Green 1999: 13–14)

In the French context, Payet (1997) notes that ZEPs are saturated with a discourse of partnership with parents, while at the same time parents are constructed in relations of inclusion and exclusion. He contrasts schools' relationships with middle-class parents with those with working-class and especially immigrant families (p. 102). This problem is acknowledged by Moisan and Simon in their government report on ZEPs:

> It is clear that the relations between families and school constitute an essential determinant of children's success. When they are characterised by lack of involvement, by powerlessness expressed on both sides, and by a lack of understanding sometimes mixed with aggression, the obstacles for the children are immense. This issue is one of the most difficult and most conflictual in the ZEPs. In some schools they talked to us more about the parents than about the children.
>
> Education is a 'shared responsibility' between parents and school. But there is often a lack of understanding and sometimes conflict between the

principles of the two 'worlds'. Above all teachers have the feeling of themselves alone assuming this role: *'the families give us a blank cheque'. 'The parents,
when they are present, either don't want or don't know or can't do it.'* This develops
among teachers an understandable anxiety which becomes either scorn for
families or a desire 'to educate the parents'. It is significant that the objective of 'restoring parental authority' figures in many ZEP projects.

(Moisan and Simon 1997: 47)

The adoption by teachers of a deficit model of working-class families has
important consequences for how they teach them. A social-determinist view of
the possibility of working-class achievement in school leads to a *'misérabilist'*
professional perspective which contributes to reinforcing patterns of working-
class failure (Bouveau and Rochex 1997). But it also has important consequences
for the role which parents are enabled to play in local educational policy-
making, and here we turn from parents' involvement in partnership with the
school at the level of the individual child to the collective participation of
parents and other local community representatives in the partnership of the
zone itself.

In the French context, Glasman speaks of how the dominance of professional
education interests is accompanied by the marginalisation or exclusion of lay
interests: 'the filtering out of participants operates sometimes to the detriment of
the *associations* (local community organisations) and, more generally, to the detriment of the local inhabitants' (1999: 6). Speaking of parents, Glasman notes that
'The contracts strongly risk being negotiated without them, putting them on the
margins' (p. 12). In England, Gamarnikow and Green (1999) come to an identical conclusion in their analysis of EAZ bids: they are about developing
networks among professionals, not among lay members of communities. John
Yandell, a participant in the debate around the bid to set up a zone in Hackney,
London, provides a graphic example of

who is left out of this notion of partnership. The area around my school –
the area that was at the centre of the EAZ as originally conceived – is one in
which there are a large number of actually existing community organisations – African/Caribbean, Turkish/Kurdish, and many others. A
significant number of these organisations have a specific and explicit interest
in education. But in every version of the EAZ proposals that Hackney has
produced so far – and there have been at least five drafts – there has only
been one mention of one organisation that could in any sense be seen as
representative of a particular ethnic minority community.

(Yandell 1999: 15)

And for those parents and community members who do find places in EAZ
Action Forums, their position can be problematic, as the report on one of the
Birmingham zones concludes.

The predominance of professionals on the Action Forum left parents, already at a disadvantage in their day to day dealings with schools, vulnerable and out-numbered. There was concern about whether those parents who were on the Action Forum should be there as individuals or as effective representatives of the body of parents. There was also a relatively low level of representation of members of minority ethnic groups. Many representatives of agencies external to the schools felt that the community focus of the zone was not strong enough.

The situation was further complicated by the fact that there were very different views among teachers of what 'partnership' with parents and community should mean. Given that many parents were socially and educationally disadvantaged the promotion of an equal relationship with them on the Action Forum and in the day to day life of the school's home territory was doubly problematical. Enabling the voices of parents who are not actively involved in community groups to be heard was also an issue.

(Rikowski *et al.* 2000: 125)

In the English context, the involvement of parents as co-educators seems to be disassociated from, and given much greater importance than, their role as partners in zone decision-making. It echoes Nevin and Shiner's (1995) distinction between involvement and empowerment. In contrast, much greater importance in France is placed on their representative role. There are two main national federations of parents' groups which have statutory rights of representation and consultation on school councils and at higher levels. While there is no formal representation of parents on the ZEP council, the parent body is statutorily represented on school councils (in contrast to parent governors in the UK who explicitly do not have a representative function), and the weakness of this representative function in ZEP schools is regarded as a major problem by Moisan and Simon in their report:

the most serious problem resides in the absence of collective representation of parents. In practice, the federations of parents of pupils (FCPE and PEEP) are very weak in the ZEPs and the delegates (when they exist) represent no-one except themselves on the various councils, and furthermore they belong to the most advantaged fringes of the population ... The general case can be summed up thus: there are no associations of parents of popular milieux.

(Moisan and Simon 1997: 48)

However, a principal cause of the problem may well be the fact that the role of parents' representatives is restricted to specific and non-pedagogical issues. At school level, parents in England may have more informal involvement than that offered by formal representation in France.

Business

Finally, we come to perhaps the most striking difference between the two countries in terms of the partners in zones. One of the features of the EAZs is that they are required to have business 'partners' (Hatcher 1998b). In sharp contrast, in France business does not feature as a partner in the zones, and its role in relation to schooling is restricted to collaborative arrangements with vocational courses in vocational and/or technological *lycées*, and the provision of two weeks of workplace experience for all *collège* students.

EAZ business partners include major international companies such as ICI, Barclays Bank, Colgate Palmolive, John Laing Construction, Kelloggs, Tesco, McDonald's, Shell, Tate and Lyle, American Express, British Aerospace and Rolls-Royce. Particularly prominent are information technology companies, including some of the biggest names: IBM, Bull Information Services, British Telecom and Research Machines. They are joined by a new but expanding education business sector – companies such as Nord Anglia and Arthur Andersen – aiming to contract out education management and other services from schools and local authorities.

The EAZ policy assigns several roles to business. First, it is expected to provide money and resources. Zones receive an extra £750,000 a year from government. They are expected to find an additional £250,000 a year from their business 'partners' (often in kind: for example, supplying computers or management training or mentoring for pupils). The reasons behind this are several: it reduces state spending on education; it encourages schools to be entrepreneurial in seeking funding for themselves; and it brings schools and business closer together, with the aim of increasing the influence of business agendas. However, a recent survey by the National Union of Teachers has revealed that private sector donations have fallen far short of the target figure (*Times Educational Supplement*, 17 November 2000: 7).

A second role is to take part in managing the zone. The original intention expressed by the government was that some of the zones would be actually run by private companies, but so far none are. Nevertheless, private companies can play leading roles (for example, a senior manager from Shell is the chairperson of the Lambeth Zone in London) and exercise considerable influence because of the resources they command.

A third role is to influence the content of education. The partnership with business is intended to make schools more responsive to business agendas. Schools are encouraged to adopt a work-related curriculum and to develop employability skills which will be attractive to employers.

And finally, a fourth role is to apply business methods and expertise to the management of schools. As Michael Barber, Labour's chief education advisor, said at the launch of the EAZ policy in January 1998, 'Successful companies are uniquely able to manage change and innovation' (*Times Educational Supplement*, 7 January 1998). What this means in practice is illustrated by the programme of a conference in March 2000 of the Education Action Zone Network, designed to highlight good practice. Workshops at the conference included: 'What businesses can bring to EAZs'; 'Business links for ICT solutions', with RM; 'Business solutions to educational challenges', with British Aerospace; 'Classrooms in companies and companies in classrooms'; and 'Leadership challenge – how business solutions developed by Rolls-Royce are being used to bring about change in schools'. Though it was entitled a 'Partnership Conference', parents and local community groups did not feature.

Conclusion

The question we have posed throughout this chapter concerns the ambivalence of the zone project, in France and in England. Does it represent a reinvigoration of the school system as a public service, or a threat to it? Does it represent an authentic extension of local participatory democracy or does the rhetoric of partnership mask a new configuration of dominant interests and marginalised popular voices? Is it a positive step towards enhancing the ability of the school system as a public service to tackle the issue of social inequality in education, or does it in practice have little effect on, or even tend to reinforce, the very problem it claims to address?

The creation of education zones is a form of positive discrimination, intended to enable extra resources to be targeted and selected educational strategies to be applied in order to reduce social inequality in pupil attainment. It is too early to evaluate how successful EAZs are in reducing inequality, but the balance-sheet of ZEPs is that only one in three zones has achieved some reduction in social inequalities in schooling, and in one in five social inequality has actually increased compared with non-ZEP schools. Bernard Charlot has argued, in his contribution to the conference on the re-launch of the ZEPs which took place in Rouen in 1998, that the ZEP policy is tending to reinforce inequality rather than reduce it.

> The ZEPs were born in a spirit of positive discrimination, but little by little they have become diverted towards a logic of territorial differentiation. Today, social inequality is socio-geographical. To accept local educational differentiation ends up in fact ratifying social inequalities and favouring the creation of educational ghettos. Only a strong political discourse can prevent this diversion from positive discrimination towards territorial differentiation.
> (Charlot 1998a)

His argument is that territorialisation leads to the differentiation of schools along social class lines, as they adapt to the different social milieux they serve. ZEPs mark the establishment of a two-speed school system. For Charlot this represents a process of neo-liberalisation of schooling:

> we are present at the progressive and conflictual transformation of the public school into the liberal school. The State is disengaging itself, the school is entering little by little into the logic of 'civil society' and the market, it is more and more connected to the family and thus more and more permeated by social inequality. In the end, it will be the children of

the districts devastated by the economic crisis and their parents who will be the big losers in this change ...

This evolution operates in the name of pedagogic differentiation, '*ouverture*' etc., and gets support from a general movement of decentralisation which is supposed to liberate the creative forces of the locality.

(Charlot 1998b: 243–4)

There are two possible courses of action which flow from this analysis. One is, in the name of equality, to resist processes of decentralisation and diversification, and to insulate the school from local partnership insofar as it appeared to open the door to the dangers of adaptation to particularism and consumerism. This would be to return to the historical tradition of French education, with the attendant risk of restoring older modes of social reproduction. The alternative course of action is to try to ensure that a responsiveness to local communities and the construction of and participation in local education partnerships are geared to reducing social inequality in schooling, not sustaining it. This depends in part on the pedagogic strategies pursued. But it can also depend – and this is the concern of this chapter – on the extent to which local partnerships for educational equality are inclusive, democratic and participatory. How far is this true of the existing models of zone partnership in ZEPs and EAZs?

In both countries the establishment and ongoing construction of zone partnerships is characterised by processes of inclusion and exclusion, by dominance and subordination. First, in both countries one 'partner' above all, central government, dominates the local partnership, partly through the managerial mechanism of zone contracts based on government objectives. Government education objectives set the agendas of school management, and these come to dominate within the zones. Second, the process of horizontal dispersal of power at the local level distinguishes sharply between different categories of actors. In one category can be grouped state agencies other than the school – local government, health, social services, etc., together with non-governmental agencies operating in a semi-official capacity. These are central to the new model of local social partnership informing both ZEPs and EAZs. But that is not to say that the process of constructing that partnership is unproblematic. On the contrary, it often brings the school into conflict with other professional identities and roles. This is particularly the case, in contrasting ways in the two countries, with the relationship between zones and local authorities. In France the government's aim is to use zones to bring local authorities into a more prominent role in education, and change the schools accordingly. In England the government's intention is to use zones to change the schools, and this entails reducing the influence of LEAs.

A second category of actors comprises the private sector. Here there is a significant difference between EAZs, where the involvement of private companies is supposed to be central, and ZEPs, in which they have no place. The third category comprises teachers other than heads of schools, who in both countries are more likely to experience zone contracts as instruments of management than as agreements they have participated in negotiating.

The fourth category comprises parents. Whatever the rhetoric of partnership, their voices, especially those of working-class parents and ethnic minority communities, tend to be marginalised by exclusionary professionalist agendas, often sustained by deficit ideologies. Parents are more likely to be involved in zones in a perspective of enhancing their parenting competence than of empowering them as partners in zone decision-making. The conclusion drawn by Gamarnikow and Green in their analysis of EAZ bids seems to apply equally to ZEPs: 'this represents a potentially repressive agenda which is unlikely to disturb the status quo, let alone build a civil society of effective, ever-expanding partnerships and equalising of social and economic opportunities' (Gamarnikow and Green 1999: 19).

Comparisons between the school systems in France and England have often contrasted the centralised character of the one and the decentralised character of the other, deriving from their very different historical origins. The education zones in both countries exemplify the extent to which a process of convergence is taking place as social-democratic governments translate the neo-liberal model of public sector management into national contexts. In both countries the experience in practice of education zones poses the urgent question of genuine local democratic participation in our school systems.

Acknowledgements

This chapter arises out of our joint research into ZEPs in the Paris area, with funding from the Nuffield Foundation. One of us has also been involved in the baseline evaluation of the two Birmingham EAZs directed by Professor Stewart Ranson of Birmingham University, with Glenn Rikowski and Faith Webster of the University of Central England, Birmingham. The views expressed here are our own.

Correspondence

Richard Hatcher: Richard.Hatcher@uce.ac.uk
Dominique Leblond: Leblond@univ-paris12.fr

Notes

1   After this chapter was written there were significant developments in the British government's policy for EAZs. After unfavourable inspections of six zones by Ofsted (the Office for Standards in Education) the government quietly halted the expansion of EAZs (*Guardian*, 5 January 2001). The creation of small EAZs will continue as part of the Excellence in Cities programme, and eighty are expected to be approved by September 2001. In March 2001 the Ofsted report was made public. EAZs had significantly improved standards in primary schools (the main factor appears to be additional classroom assistants) but had had 'no significant impact' in secondary schools. The inspectors added that the zones had not been 'test-beds for genuinely innovative action' (quoted in the *Guardian*, 6 March 2001). David Blunkett, the

Education Secretary, speaking immediately after the publication of the report, admitted that the EAZ initiative had been 'over-hyped'. His explanation of the zones' lack of success was that 'We expected too much of people at the local level' (quoted in *Times Educational Supplement*, 9 March 2001: 10). We would contend that the real reason is exactly the opposite. The zones' lack of success is due in large part to the way in which the government has set up the zones, preventing, as we argue in this chapter, the effective participation of teachers, parents and communities.

2   In Britain the current government agenda for EAZs can be found on the DfEE's website (DfEE 2000). In France the recently revised policy for ZEPs was announced in the *Official Bulletin of National Education* of 16 July 1998, entitled *'Relance de l'éducation prioritaire: mise en place des réseaux d'éducation prioritaire et des contrats de réussite'* (quoted in Lorcerie 1999).

References

Baumard, M. (2000) 'Vingt ans plus tard, un lifting s'impose', *Le Monde de l'éducation*, February: 26.

Bentley, T. (1998) *Learning Beyond the Classroom*, London: Routledge.

Birmingham City Council (1998) 'Education Action Zones. Report of the Chief Education Officer', Education Committee, 9 June.

Bouveau, P. (1997) 'Les ZEP et la ville: l'évolution d'une politique scolaire', in A. van Zanten (ed.) *La scolarisation dans les milieux 'difficiles'*, Paris: INRP.

Bouveau, P. and Rochex, J.-Y. (1997) *Les ZEP, entre école et société*, Paris: Hachette.

Cédelle, L. (2000) 'Quand l'Etat donne "plus", que donne-t-elle?' *Le Monde de l'éducation*, February: 27.

Charlot, B. (1994) 'La territorialisation des politiques éducatives: une politique nationale', in B. Charlot (ed.) *L'école et le territoire*, Paris: Armand Colin.

——(1998a) *Quelle relance pour les ZEP?* Strasbourg: Académie de Strasbourg, http://crdp.cristal.net/cravie/charlot.html

——(1998b) 'Postface', in Y. Careil, *De l'école publique à l'école libérale*, Rennes: Presses Universitaires de Rennes.

Chauveau, G. and Rogovas-Chauveau, E. (1995) *A l'école des banlieues*, Paris: ESF.

Clarke, J. and Newman, J. (1997) *The Managerial State*, London: Sage.

Clarke, M. and Stewart, J. (1998) *Community Governance, Community Leadership and the New Local Government*, York: Joseph Rowntree Foundation.

Department for Education and Employment (DfEE) (1997) *Excellence in Schools*, London: DfEE.

——(1998a) *Meet the Challenge*, London: DfEE.

——(1998b) *The EAZ Handbook*, London: DfEE.

——(2000) *Meet the Challenge: Education Action Zones*, http://www.dfee.gov.uk/mc_eaz/summary.htm

Derouet, J. (2000) 'School autonomy in a society with multi-faceted political references: the search for new ways of coordinating action', *Journal of Education Policy*, 15(1): 61–9.

Gamarnikow, E. and Green, A.T. (1999) 'The Third Way and Social Capital: Education Action Zones and a new agenda for education, parents and community?' *International Studies in Sociology of Education*, 9(1): 3–22.

Gillborn, D. and Mirza, H.M. (2000) *Educational Inequality*, London: Ofsted.

Gille, A.-M. (1993) 'Les zones d'éducation prioritaires, une problematique européenne?' in Observatoire des Zones Prioritaires (ed.) *Memoires de ZEP pour l'Avenir*, Gennevilliers: OZP.

Glasman, D. (1997) 'La professionalisation des "accompagnateurs scolaires": une double contrainte?' in A. van Zanten (ed.) *La scolarisation dans les milieux 'difficiles'*, Paris: INRP.

——(1999) 'Reflexions sur les "contrats" en éducation', *Ville Ecole Intégration*, 117: 1–22, http://www.cndp.fr/vei/Vei/glasman117.htm

Green, A., Wolf, A. and Leney, T. (1999) *Convergence and Divergence in European Education and Training Systems*, London: Institute of Education.

Hatcher, R. (1998a) 'Labour, official school improvement and equality', *Journal of Education Policy*, 13(4): 485–99.

——(1998b) 'Profiting from schools: business and Education Action Zones', *Education and Social Justice*, 1(1): 9–16.

——(1999) 'Exclusion, consultation or empowerment? Developing popular democratic participation in decision-making in school education', *Education and Social Justice*, 2(1): 45–57.

Jones, K. and Bird, K. (2000) '"Partnership" as strategy: public–private relations in Education Action Zones', *British Educational Research Journal*, 26(4): 491–506.

Lorcerie, F. (1999) 'Le contrat de réussite dans la nouvelle relance des zones d'éducation prioritaires', *Education et Societés*, 1(3): 81–96.

Lowndes, V. and Skelcher, C. (1998) 'The dynamics of multi-organizational partnerships: an analysis of changing modes of governance', *Public Administration* 76, Summer: 313–33.

Lowndes, V., Nanton, P., McCabe, A. and Skelcher, C. (1997) 'Networks, partnerships and urban regeneration', *Local Economy*, 11(4): 333–42.

Mackintosh, M. (1992) 'Partnership: issues of policy and negotiation', *Local Economy*, 7(3): 210–24.

Mayo, M. (1997) 'Partnerships for regeneration and community development', *Critical Social Policy*, 52: 3–26.

Moisan, C. and Simon, J. (1997) *Les determinants de la réussite scolaire en ZEP*, Paris: Inspection générale de l'éducation nationale/Inspection générale de l'administration de l'éducation nationale.

Nevin, B. and Shiner, P. (1995) 'The left, urban policy and community empowerment: the first steps towards a new framework for urban regeneration', *Local Economy* 10(3): 204–17.

Payet, J.P. (1997) 'L'école et la construction de la citoyenneté', in A. van Zanten (ed.) *La scolarisation dans les milieux 'difficiles'*, Paris: INRP.

Publicnet (2000) 'Jury still out on Education Action Zones', 4 July, www.publicnet.co.uk/publicnet/00070401.htm

Rikowski, G., Webster, F., Ranson, S. and Hatcher, R. (2000) *Aston/Nechells Education Action Zone Base-Line Report*, Birmingham: University of Birmingham and University of Central England.

Taylor, S., Rizvi, F., Lingard, B. and Henry, M. (1997) *Educational Policy and the Politics of Change*, London: Routledge.

Yandell, J. (1999) 'Obstructing the highway: resisting EAZs in Hackney', *Education and Social Justice* 2(1): 13–17.

4 Coordinated school-linked services

The US experience

William Lowe Boyd and Robert L. Crowson

Introduction

The new institutional theories in the study of organizations discuss the power of 'contagion' in spreading innovations (Scott and Christensen 1995). Indeed, new ideas and accompanying changes can sometimes spread very rapidly, almost like epidemics, even within organizational sectors thought to be resistant to reform (Singh *et al.* 1991).

The rapid expansion of coordinated services efforts throughout the United States since the late 1980s represents an example of this. There were historical roots quite early in the twentieth century in the progressive era and particularly, later, in some of the Great Society interventions of the 1960s. However, the aggressive development of a system of coordinated services for children and families in need received its most solid foundation as recently as the late 1980s, in reports of some service-needs conferencing, the results of some early experimentation, and reports of the 'conditions' of children and families in poverty. Two of the most influential documents were *The Conditions of Children in California* (Kirst 1989) and *Joining Forces* (Levy and Copple 1989).

The spread of coordinated services programs, from the late 1980s on, was so rapid that by 1993 one of its foremost advocates, Sharon Lynn Kagan, was claiming that efforts were 'blossoming across the country from Maine to California' (Kagan and Neville 1993: 78). Such 'blossoming' had already received a solid boost, by this time, from state legislation in New Jersey (1988), Kentucky (1990), and California (1991), with each establishing statewide programmatic thrusts in the family services arena (see Smrekar and Mawhinney 1999).

In 1993 the authors of this chapter also published their first in a series of inquiries into implementation issues in the provision of school-based services (Crowson and Boyd 1993). Drawing on the available reports, handbooks, evaluations, and case-studies of the time, we observed that an array of 'institutional realities' presented a difficult, uphill climb for service-coordination. Among the problematic elements were matters of professional control and 'turf,' organizational disincentives to collaboration, legal and budgetary dilemmas, communications and confidentiality barriers, questions of governance and managerial support, and reconceptualizations of professional or organizational roles.

Throughout the 1990s, additional reports and analyses continued to document the deep administrative problems encountered by those attempting coordinated services (see Smrekar and Mawhinney 1999; Cibulka and Kritek 1996; Lawson and Hooper-Briar 1997). A substantial blow to the movement in the US occurred in 1994, when the Pew Charitable Trust announced the termination of its then-sizeable support of school-linked family centers. The Trust's decision came on the heels of some weak evaluation results (Cohen 1994).

Just a year later, an assessment of the New Futures initiative (by Julie White and Gary Wehlage), then funded by the Annie E. Casey Foundation, added fuel to the 'no-effects' fire. Among the most damaging of the findings was the observation that the outreach programs were invariably 'top-down' – ignoring family and community expressions of service needs, while depending instead upon professionally identified definitions of client 'need' (White and Wehlage 1995). None of this stopped or even slowed the movement. The notion of coordinated services continued to increase in popularity in the transition into the twenty-first century. Indeed, in the specialized arena of health services particularly, a survey in late 2000 reported an increase of more than ten times (over the past decade) in the number of school-based health clinics in operation across the United States (*Wall Street Journal*, 9 November 2000).

Amid the growth, however, the conception of the central 'problem' behind much of the services effort has evolved. There is now less talk of a dangerously fragmented delivery system, with (as a consequence) the need for a coordination of children's and family services. The result in the US has been a somewhat reduced focus upon inter-agency cooperation among professional service-providers.

There is also less attention at present on school-centered programs of family assistance – but, at the same time, the development of a much greater variety of forms and strategies for outreach – e.g., neighborhood-organization led programs, communities-of-faith efforts, private-sector interventions, and many more school-*linked* in place of school-*based* programs. Finally, much recent activity in the services movement has been directed toward efforts which bridge *pedagogically* between schools and families/communities – particularly with programs of after-school activities and after-school tutoring, adolescence-assistance and youth-development programs, summer-schooling, arts and music education, and family help through day-care (Behrman 1999; Jacobson 2000).

A new services paradigm in the United States

The changed conceptualization of 'the problem' in the US which has emerged finds its altered foundation in a larger ecology of community development activities above programs of family assistance. Although interest continues in inter-agency partnering, the focus increasingly is upon community action rather than the delivery of professionally dominated services to a poverty-area clientele.

Lizbeth Schorr (1997) has argued in this new-paradigm vein, claiming that the added delivery of professional services by themselves falls far short of the full scope of efforts needed to strengthen families and to improve learning opportunities in low-income neighborhoods. As Schorr (1997: 291) puts it, people increasingly recognize that educational success necessitates a key place for the school 'at the table where community reform is being organized.'

Some intellectual shifts of consequence in the movement toward a community development approach to family assistance include the following. First, the concept of social capital has grown in importance and application (see Driscoll and Kerchner 1999). Much influenced by the work of James Coleman (1988, 1990), social capital has (over time) become central to the rationale underlying coordinated services. The claim is that critical cultural resources and supports, as well as 'hard' resources through direct assistance, are passed from institutions to families in full-services programming. In community development, theorizing the idea of social capital is much more of a two-way street, however. The community itself is full of cultural resources, serves itself as a source of capital, and joins institutional service providers in a reciprocally 'productive' relationship between school and neighborhood (Driscoll and Kerchner 1999).

Second, and relatedly, the community development initiative reconceptualizes a point-of-departure in resolving the dilemma of school reform/improvement. Ideally, coordinated service efforts join matters of pedagogy with a program of family assistance, in a broadened appreciation of what-it-takes for children to succeed in school. Reconceptualized within a community development frame, the altered starting-point for reform is the neighborhood rather than the school. 'Going local' (Shuman 1998) and 'restoring a sense-of-place' (Driscoll and Kerchner 1999) are among the operative phrases here – finding the sources of successful inter-agency cooperation in the larger ecology of the community rather than in the narrower professionalism of the school and other 'providers.' On the other hand, Driscoll and Kerchner (1999: 397) caution that any effort 'to rebuild neighborhoods without a strategy for schooling can have only limited success.'

Third, without denying the power and importance of services (to children and families), the altered paradigm foresees a much larger program of highly economic outreach beyond professional, inter-agency partnering. A services agenda may be necessary but not sufficient – especially in deep-poverty circumstances with major 'infrastructure' needs in housing quality, employment opportunities, recreational outlets, law enforcement, etc. (see Littell and Wynn 1989; Haveman and Wolfe 1994). Matters of public and private investment, entrepreneuralism, regeneration, rebuilding, resourcefulness, incentives creation, market forces, and assisting self-help can all join in creating a community development climate that goes far beyond the narrow scope of activity captured in a purely services agenda.

In brief summary, a rapidly increasing interest in community development (as a revised strategy for improving educational opportunity and school performance) reconceptualizes the services relationship as a two-way street (school-to-neighborhood and neighborhood-to-school). This strategy also carries an image of much deeper roots in the culture and ecology of each neighborhood than has been the case in most services programming; and the revised strategy foresees a far wider group of 'actors' in helping to produce added opportunity than the usual array of agency-based professionals. The private and for-profit sector, faith-based institutions, youth organizations, community activists, and neighborhood establishments for the arts are all typical partners in efforts toward both revitalization and education in many US communities.

Services against development: some key issues

The full-service movement has encountered many well-documented difficulties in the ability of cooperating partners to share information, deal with turf issues, retrain and reorient participating professionals, mingle resources, merge or blend disciplinary perspectives, and 'involve' a neighborhood clientele meaningfully (see Crowson and Boyd 1993; White and Wehlage 1995; Cibulka and Kritek 1996; White and Hansen-Turton 1997; Smrekar and Mawhinney 1999). In comparison, however, the community development approach is by no means without its own set of dilemmas and political/administrative issues.

As an initial issue, there is a central question regarding basic assumptions of 'approach' in assistance to families. The development idea assumes that 'market' forces can be effectively introduced to low-income communities – that enterprising and investment, incentives and subsidies, employment and empowerment, rebuilding and repair can begin a transformation process that trickles down to much-improved opportunities for families and their children, to reformed and better-performing schools. Indeed, some strategists suggest an 'enterprising' role for the school itself – an active, linkages-establishing positioning of the school to assist in the market-based regeneration of its own neighborhood environment (Schorr 1997; Boyd *et al.* 1997; Driscoll and Kerchner 1999).

The how-to-approach question pits some sets of deeply rooted values against one another. As mentioned earlier, the 'services' approach has strong progressive-era roots, in the late-nineteenth and early-twentieth century development of the settlement-house movement and accompanying programs of outreach to improve children's health and family welfare (see Ravitch 2000). But there was also a larger agenda. Theda Skocpol (1992) writes that a significant element in the progressive-era beginnings of children's and family services was the effort to protect poor families *from* the ravages of the market. 'Healthy' homes and neighborhoods, and what's 'good' for families and children, were to be provided by a well-trained cadre of informed and committed persons as a hedge against the horrors of sweatshop industrialism.

A residue of distrust against 'the market' characterizes human-services professionalism to this date. The language of development (e.g., enterprising, incentive-structures, self-help, entrepreneurism, investment) is not typically the language of the serving professions. Professional service-providers are much more comfortable with a vocabulary of defining and meeting needs, offering assistance, diagnosis and support, and the 'service trajectory.' The choice of basic approach between bottom-up market-centeredness and a more top-down strategy of professional 'intervention' is not easily compromised.

Another unresolved, if not competing, value has to do with questions of control. Control issues have emerged as key constraints in much of the coordinated services programming, ranging from matters of turf protection, to just what is involved in 'partnering,' to who's in charge administratively (see Smylie *et al.* 1994). Beyond complaints that much of the services effort has been too heavily dominated by professionals (vs. the clientele), the community development approach moves a discussion of control much more deeply into the politics of empowerment.

Empowerment is a difficult construct to define adequately. A common assumption is that empowering actions typically include a transfer of some elements of control from stronger to weaker participants. Persons are *em*powered, by other folks; they are allowed in, invited to join the game. However, a deeper sense of just what empowerment is, and what control means, recognizes that power already resides within and controls are already in place – in the very culture of each community. There is not a 'transfer' of power necessary, just a recognition and acceptance.

'Culturalist' (or regime) interpretations of power see power as a key, structural element of each community's overall way of life, lodged in its essential values, institutions, special history, shared expectations, neighborhood relationships, etc. (see Elkin 1987; Stone 1989; Ramsay 1996). Communities are already empowered, although (and here's the key issue) their powers are not always sensed and used effectively by service providers, who may fear that to integrate professionalism with a community's values, concerns, and interests is to suffer a loss of control. Services can be supplied to families from a position of power-over, but community development tends to require a rather considerable amount of power-with.

A third issue separating services from development returns to a point-of-departure question, mentioned earlier. The services movement has the considerable strength of institutional ecology behind it; the development approach is centered instead upon the values of community ecology (see Tucker *et al.* 1992).

Institutional ecology brings a knowledge- and research-based domain of professional practice and technology to carefully diagnosed clientele needs, with diagnoses and consequent services that are usually quite similar across varieties of communities. The services provided – whether in health, welfare, guidance, employment, or educational arenas – are backed by 'best known' professional practice, undertaken by highly trained (indeed, usually 'certified') service providers. There is a consideration of special local needs and conditions, to be sure, but in the main, agency services look much the same whatever the community.

Alternatively, community development relates closely, as a movement, to a new fascination with uniqueness and 'going local' in American public education. In a way, this seems a bit out of place in an age of state and national standards, and high-stakes testing, as well as an age continuing to stress the provision of choice-of-school options to families through magnets, vouchers, and charter schools. Nevertheless, a back-to-the-neighborhood trend is very much in evidence, particularly around the somewhat nostalgic value of re-introducing a spirit of 'old time' culture into education, where there are close linkages and identities between each school and its nearby community.

The ecology of the community, from this perspective, has precedence over the more generalized ecology of the social service institution (see Bronfenbrenner 1979; Goodlad 1987). A 'sense of place' and the uniqueness of place are to drive the institutional environment, rather than the other way around. Using this paradigm, Driscoll and Kerchner (1999) define communities as 'zones of production', wherein, out of their own complex environments, questions of economic development, pedagogy, institutional investments, family welfare, empowerment, and togetherness can all be resolved 'upward' from the special qualities of each neighborhood rather than 'downward' from the generalized technologies of a service agency.

Implications for inter-agency cooperation

In brief recapitulation, the emerging context for inter-agency cooperation (in service provision in the US) finds less activity than earlier in school-centered programs of generalized assistance to families, and somewhat more interest today in direct pedagogical services to children (e.g., after-school tutoring). Additionally, there is also a movement away from fairly narrow services agendas toward a larger arena of community development activity, and a decided movement toward community-up initiatives in place of professionalism-down.

By no means, however, is there less regard than before for the local school. Indeed, an added embeddedness of the school in the culture of its community, and a leadership role for the school as part of an overall 'community of support' for families and children are both very much a part of the revised agenda (see Wehlage *et al.* 1989; Kagan and Neville 1993).

What are the implications in this new US scenario for inter-agency working and for matters of social inclusion/exclusion? A first, administrative implication is the need for a re-thinking of some key 'mental models' of school leadership. For long, a solid piece of the lore of the school principalship has been a balancing act in the school–community relationship, usually referred to as 'bridging and buffering' (see Hanson 1981; Ogawa 1994; Ogawa and White 1994). School administrators are taught to walk the tightrope of bridging to the community while simultaneously buffering the organization and its professionals from undue intrusion from the community.

The result, a number of scholars claim, has been the maintenance over the years of a sizeable 'gap' between schools and their communities (Deal and Peterson 1994; Smrekar 1996). The call now is for a new role that replaces bridging and buffering with a more outreach-oriented exercise of 'civic capacity' (Goldring and Hausman, in press). School administrators who exercise civic capacity reach out actively from their schools to help *build* or *develop* their respective communities. It is a concept, according to Goldring and Hausman (*ibid.*: 11), that 'goes way beyond notions of partnering or collaborating' into 'a new mental model of schooling.'

Relatedly, a second implication is the need for new attention as to just what it does mean to partner. Today's partnering, argue Seymour Sarason and Elizabeth Lorentz (1998), requires much more than just a bit of collaboration. It means meaningful 'boundary crossings,' where there is resource exchange, a true 'network' approach to shared objectives, and much more selflessness than is typical of most inter-agency relationships (Sarason and Lorentz 1998).

However, although the idea of partnering is currently in vogue in the client-services literature, the evidence is that even the maintaining-one's-turf collaboration that Sarason deplores is extraordinarily hard to do (see Smrekar and Mawhinney 1999). There has not, unfortunately, been the kind of basic research into what-it-takes to partner in the public domain that has been emerging from studies of successful for-profit collaboration. For example, notable corporate-sector studies of the chances-of-success effects of information-flow between partnering organizations (Gulati 1995), differences-in-organizational-rules effects (Ullman 1998) and actor social-similarity effects (Kraatz 1998) have not penetrated public-sector inquiry.

What *is* beginning to occur in the school–community relationship, however, is the type of partnership activity called for by White and Wehlage in 1995. The test for community services, they argued at that time, is far less a success in providing resources and services than it is a test in reshaping the priorities and practices of schools toward a closer understanding of, and of course partnership with, the family and neighborhood clientele (White and Wehlage 1995: 35).

Some recent studies of a new thrust in community-organizing toward school reform, by Dennis Shirley (1997), are illustrative of such reshaping, as is a study by Charis McGaughy (in press) of 'an amazing alignment' of participants in community development/educational-reform partnering in Akron, Ohio. This new partnering, by the way, is far more likely to be a network of community organizations with the schools (e.g., neighborhood banks, churches, businesses, youth centers, etc.) than it is likely to be an inter-agency 'service' relationship.

Two additional implications of the community development scenario combine to bring the movement deeply into questions of social justice. As early leaders in the drive to move school–community relations into a development mode, Weeres and Kerchner (1996) argued that the development (or neighborhood revitalization) strategy derives much of its strength from a sense of a 'larger picture' than that which drives the coordinated services effort. The notion that each neighborhood is a reflection of regeneration/renewal citywide is a key part of this strategy (see Judd and Parkinson 1990), as is the idea that public schooling, even at the neighborhood level, is also a fundamental part of the 'basic industry' of the entire city (Weeres and Kerchner 1996).

Nevertheless, although they are supporters of the movement, Halpern (1995) as well as Green and Brintnall (1994) warn that there has not been a great deal of potential for revitalization in the most deeply distressed of neighborhoods –

and therefore up-from-the-community makes little sense when most of the key resources in the lives of community residents continue to come from public supports, outside services, and transfer payments.

Indeed, a form of urban 'triage,' targeting those communities which already have investment and development well underway, rather than the deepest of poverty neighborhoods, is highlighted in some of the national policymaking behind this movement (US Department of Housing and Urban Development 1995). As James Traub (2000: 90) concludes: in the most incredibly adverse of urban environments, the 'idea of directly addressing that environment through jobs programs, housing, health care or the adoption of "a living wage" [still] survives only in the fringes of political discourse.'

A fifth, and closely related, implication of the new drive into community action is that questions around differences in culture (between school and community) reach new levels of importance and salience. In an earlier report of some field studies of coordinated-services experimentation (Crowson and Boyd 1996), we quoted an incident reported by Arvey and Tijerina (1992: 25) from their services work in an Hispanic neighborhood in Houston, Texas:

> One incident that really brought home the differences in the expectation of planners and the experience of the people affected was the first partnership luncheon. Our parent representative, a woman actively involved for the past five years in her children's school and a perceived leader among parents, had never before attended a 'luncheon.' She had no idea what was expected and felt very uncomfortable in attending.

Even seemingly small differences in terminology can reflect some vital 'discontinuities' of culture between the professional and his or her clientele, as noted by Ogbu (1974).

In a development relationship with the community far more than in an inter-agency services relationship, observe Torres and Miron (in press), one cannot work effectively without a very deep sense of neighborhood culture and its consequences. Not only a lack of understanding but preconceived notions of local cultures can be devastating. A deep appreciation of 'the dialectics of land-scape' (e.g., the strains produced by social class inequalities, by cultural isolation, and by varying workforce experiences) must be carefully considered in the drive toward development (Torres and Miron, in press). Development is far more diffi-cult and dangerous (with more potential for exclusion) than is the narrower role of 'serving.'

Conclusion

We have argued in this chapter that although the idea of coordinated, school-linked services continues to gain in appeal in the United States, its focus and its conceptual foundations are changing. Increasingly, community-based organiza-tions rather than the schools are displaying initiative in offering an array of after-school services (e.g., after-school child care, youth development programs, tutoring, successful parenting classes) (see, Behrman, 1999). These neighborhood organizations typically cover the institutional waterfront from local churches to city parks departments and libraries, Boys' and Girls' Clubs, YM or YWCAs, community organizers, and banks or local for-profit organizations.

As community institutions have displayed greater initiative, a larger and broader paradigm around inter-agency partnering has been emerging as well. A definition of 'the problem' has proceeded from community responsiveness through children's and family services to inter-agency cooperation in the regeneration of the community itself. Included in this paradigm shift is a realization that: (a) the idea of supplying 'social capital' to a community through a service agenda tends to undervalue and perhaps leave untapped the cultural and institutional strengths/resources that are already there; plus (b) the idea of rediscovering 'a sense of place' and a greater awareness of community-ecology, in service delivery and development, can offer help in bringing relationships more effectively into a 'two-way street' between professionals and their communities.

Overall, however, despite a changing source of developmental and even pedagogical initiatives in many communities, there is not yet widespread participation among educators and local schoolhouses in community development activity in the US (Boyd *et al.* 1997). Much of the energy to date, as mentioned earlier, is coming from individual and organizational actors lying outside of the professional field of public education. Bureaucratic and professional models of the school–community relationship have long dominated American thinking, while a more 'democratic' model (emphasizing opportunities for inclusion and parent/community governance) has thus far failed to gain widespread appeal (Boyd 1996; Slater and Boyd 1999).

There is much ground yet to be covered, in the US, in recapturing the 'old' nineteenth-century goal of community embeddedness for local schooling, outlined by Alan Peshkin (1997: 25) as a coming-together of school and community once again as 'shared places of enduring importance and collective memory.'

References

Arvey, H.H. and Tijerina, A. (1992) 'The school of the future: implementation issues in a school/community connection.' Paper presented at an invitational conference on school/community connections, 'Exploring Issues for Research and Practice,' Washington, D.C., National Center on Education in the Inner Cities, 23–4 October.

Behrman, R.E. (ed.) (1999, Fall) 'When school is out,' *The Future of Children*, 9(2): 4–20.

Boyd, W.L. (1996) 'Competing models of schools and communities: the struggle to reframe and reinvent their relationships.' Invited keynote address for a conference on 'Leading the Learning Community,' Australian Council for Educational Administration, Perth, Western Australia, 1 October.

Boyd, W.L., Crowson, R.L. and Gresson, A. (1997) 'Neighborhood initiatives, community agencies, and the public schools: a changing scene for the development and learning of children,' in M.C. Wang and M.C. Reynolds (eds) *Development and Learning of Children and Youth in Urban America*, Philadelphia: Temple University Center for Research in Human Development and Education, pp. 81–103.

Bronfenbrenner, U. (1979) *The Ecology of Human Development*, Cambridge, MA: Harvard University Press.

Cibulka, J. and Kritek, W. (eds) (1996) *Coordination among Schools, Families, and Communities: Prospects for Educational Reform*, Albany, NY: State University of New York Press.

Cohen, D.L. (1994) 'Demise of PEW project offers lessons to funders,' *Education Week*, 1 (1 June): 15.

Coleman, J. (1988) 'Social capital and the creation of human capital,' *American Journal of Sociology*, 94, Supplement: S95–S120.

——(1990) *Foundations of Social Theory*, Cambridge, MA and London, England: Belknap Press of Harvard University Press.

Crowson, R.L. and Boyd, W.L. (1993) 'Coordinated services for children: designing arks for storms and seas unknown,' *American Journal of Education*, 101(2): 140–79.

——(1996) 'Structures and strategies: toward an understanding of alternative models for coordinated children's services,' in J.G. Cibulka and W.J. Kritek (eds) *Coordination among Schools, Families, and Communities: Prospects for Educational Reform*, Albany, NY: State University of New York Press, pp. 137–69.

Deal, T.E. and Peterson, K.D. (1994) *The Leadership Paradox: Balancing Logic and Artistry in Schools*, San Francisco: Jossey-Bass.

Driscoll, M.E. and Kerchner, C.T. (1999) 'The implications of social capital for schools, communities, and cities,' in J. Murphy and K.S. Louis (eds) *Handbook of Research on Educational Administration*, second edition, San Francisco: Jossey-Bass, pp. 385–404.

Dryfoos, J. (1994) *Full-Service Schools: A Revolution in Health and Social Services for Children, Youth, and Families*, San Francisco: Jossey-Bass.

Elkin, S.L. (1987) *City and Regime in the American Republic*, Chicago: University of Chicago Press.

Goldring, E.B. and Hausman, C. (in press) 'Civic capacity and school principals: the missing links for community development,' in R. Crowson (ed.) *Community Development and School Reform*, Greenwich, CT: JAI Press.

Goodlad, J.I. (ed.) (1987) *The Ecology of School Renewal*, eighty-sixth yearbook of the National Society for the Study of Education (NSSE), Chicago: University of Chicago Press.

Green, R.E. and Brintnall, M. (1994) 'Conclusions and lessons learned,' in R.E. Green (ed.) *Enterprise Zones: New Directions in Economic Development*, Newbury Park, CA: Sage, pp. 241–57.

Gulati, R. (1995) 'Social structure and alliance formation patterns: a longitudinal analysis,' *Administrative Science Quarterly*, 40(4): 619–52.

Halpern, R. (1995) *Rebuilding the Inner City: A History of Neighborhood Initiatives to Address Poverty in the United States*, New York: Columbia University Press.

Hanson, E.M. (1981) *Educational Administration and Organizational Behavior*, Boston: Allyn and Bacon.

Haveman, R. and Wolfe, B. (1994) *Succeeding Generations: On the Effects of Investments in Children*, New York: Russell Sage Foundation.

Jacobson, L. (2000) 'New event making case for better after-school options,' *Education Week*, 20(6): 6.

Judd, D. and Parkinson, M. (eds) (1990) *Leadership and Urban Regeneration*, Newbury Park, CA: Sage.

Kagan, S.L. and Neville, P.R. (1993) *Integrating Services for Children and Families: Understanding the Past to Shape the Future*, New Haven: Yale University Press.

Kirst, M. (ed.) (1989) *The Conditions of Children in California*, Berkeley: Policy Analysis for California Education (PACE).

Kraatz, M.S. (1998), 'Learning by association? Interorganizational networks and adaptation to environmental change,' *Academy of Management Journal*, 41(6): 621–43.

Lawson, H. and Hooper-Briar, K. (1997) *Connecting the Dots: Progress Toward the Integration of School Reform, School-Linked Services, Parent Involvement and Community Schools*, Oxford, OH: Danforth Foundation and Miami University, the Institute for Educational Renewal.

Levy, J. and Copple, C. (1989) *Joining Forces: A Report From the First Year*, Alexandria, VA: National Association of State Boards of Education.

Littell, J. and Wynn, J. (1989) *The Availability and Use of Community Resources for Young Adolescents in an Inner-City and a Suburban Community*, Chicago: University of Chicago, Chapin Hall Center for Children.

McGaughy, C. (in press) 'The role of education in community development: the Akron Enterprise Community Initiative,' in R. Crowson (ed.) *Community Development and School Reform*, Greenwich, CT: JAI Press.

Ogawa, R.T. (1994) 'The institutional sources of education reform: the case of school-based management,' *American Educational Research Journal*, 31: 519–48.

Ogawa, R.T. and White, P.A. (1994) 'School-based management: an overview,' in S.A. Mohrman and P. Wohlstetter (eds) *School-Based Management: Organizing for High Performance*, San Francisco: Jossey-Bass, pp. 53–80.

Ogbu, J.U. (1974) *The Next Generation: An Ethnography of Education in an Urban Neighborhood*, New York: Academic Press.

Peshkin, A. (1997) *Places of Memory: Whiteman's Schools and Native American Communities*, Mahwah, NJ: Lawrence Erlbaum Associates.

Ramsay, M. (1996) *Community, Culture, and Economic Development: The Social Roots of Local Action*, Albany, NY: SUNY Press.

Ravitch, D. (2000) *Left Back: A Century of Failed School Reforms*, New York: Simon and Schuster.

Sarason, S.B. and Lorentz, E.M. (1998) *Crossing Boundaries: Collaboration, Coordination, and the Redefinition of Resources*, San Francisco: Jossey-Bass.

Schorr, L.B. (1997) *Common Purposes: Strengthening Families and Neighborhoods to Rebuild America*, New York: Anchor Books.

Scott, W.R. and Christensen, S. (eds) (1995) *The Institutional Construction of Organizations*, Thousand Oaks, CA: Sage.

Shirley, D. (1997) *Community Organizing for Urban School Reform*, Austin: University of Texas Press.

Shuman, M.H. (1998) *Going Local: Creating Self-Reliant Communities in a Global Age*, New York: Free Press.

Singh, J.V., Tucker, D.J. and Meinhard, A.G. (1991) 'Institutional change and ecological dynamics,' in W.W. Powell and P.J. DiMaggio (eds) *The New Institutionalism in Organizational Analysis*, Chicago: University of Chicago Press, pp. 390–422.

Skocpol, T. (1992) *Protecting Soldiers and Mothers*, Cambridge, MA: Harvard University Press.

Slater, R.O. and Boyd, W.L. (1999) 'Schools as polities,' in J. Murphy and K.S. Louis (eds) *Handbook of Research on Educational Administration*, second edition, San Francisco: Jossey-Bass, pp. 323–35.

Smrekar, C.E. (1996) *The Impact of School Choice and Community*, Albany, NY: State University of New York Press.

Smrekar, C.E. and Mawhinney, H.B. (1999) 'Integrated services: challenges in linking schools, families, and communities,' in J. Murphy and K.S. Louis (eds) *Handbook of Research on Educational Administration*, second edition, San Francisco: Jossey-Bass, pp. 443–61.

Smylie, M.A., Crowson, R.L., Chou, V. and Levin, R. (1994) 'The principal and community–school connections in Chicago's radical reform,' *Educational Administration Quarterly*, 30(3): 342–64.

Stone, C.N. (1989) *Regime Politics: Governing Atlanta 1946–1988*, Lawrence: University of Kansas Press.

Torres, R.D. and Miron, L.F. (in press) 'Economic geography of Latino Los Angeles: schooling and urban transformations at century's end,' in R. Crowson (ed.) *Community Development and School Reform*, Greenwich, CT: JAI Press.

Traub, J. (2000) 'What no school can do,' *New York Times Magazine*, 16 January (Section 6): pp. 52–7.

Tucker, D.J., Baum, J.A.C. and Singh, J.V. (1992) 'The institutional ecology of human service organizations,' in Y. Hasenfeld (ed.) *Human Services as Complex Organizations*, Newbury Park, CA: Sage, pp. 47–72.

Ullman, C.F. (1998) 'Partners in reform: nonprofit organizations and the welfare state in France,' in W.W. Powell and E.S. Clemens (eds) *Private Action and the Public Good*, New Haven: Yale University Press, pp. 163–76.

US Department of Housing and Urban Development (1995) *Empowerment, a New Covenant with America's Communities: President Clinton's National Urban Policy Report*, Washington, D.C.: US Department of Housing and Urban Development, Office of Policy Development and Research.

Wall Street Journal (2000) 'Health clinics in schools are taking on a bigger role in many states,' 9 November: 1.

Weeres, J.G. and Kerchner, C.T. (1996) 'This time it's serious: post industrialism and the coming institutional change in education,' in R.L. Crowson, W.L. Boyd and H.B. Mawhinney (eds) *The Politics of Education and the New Institutionalism: Reinventing the American School*, London: Falmer Press, pp. 135–52.

Wehlage, G.G., Rutter, R.A., Smith, G.A., Lesko, N. and Fernandez, R.R. (1989) *Reducing the Risk: Schools as Communities of Support*, London: Falmer Press.

White, J. and Hansen-Turton, T. (1997) 'Service coordination across government agencies,' in M.C. Wang and M.C. Reynolds (eds) *Development and Learning of Children and Youth in Urban America*, Philadelphia: Temple University Center for Research in Human Development and Education, pp. 105–20.

White, J. and Wehlage, G. (1995) 'Community collaboration: if it is such a good idea, why is it so hard to do?' *Educational Evaluation and Policy Analysis*, 17(1): 23–38.

5 Full-service schooling

From 'at-risk' student to full-status citizen in Australia?

Robert Semmens

> The concept of citizenship and social integration which underlies the notion of 'social exclusion' in this French tradition is difficult to grasp for people working within a liberal individualist tradition.
>
> (Gore 1995: 2)

Introduction

This chapter critically analyses the concept of full-service schooling in Australia, in relation to expected programme outcomes. Who is 'at risk' of what and how might full-service schooling make any difference in the short term and in the longer term?

The subject of 'at-risk' young people has attracted a lot of attention from various human service professions in recent years, as well as from governments and the general public. Definitions of 'at risk' may vary from notions of 'at risk of failure at school', to 'at risk of exclusion from school', to 'at risk of delinquent behaviour', to membership of a minority group, and to a generalised disaffection arising from high youth unemployment rates (Hixson and Tinzman 1990). Because this chapter is about full-service schooling it will focus mainly on students 'at risk' of exclusion from school, whether by their own choice or by official sanction.

In the state of Victoria, the proportion of young people staying on to complete Year 12 at school fell from 81.1 per cent in 1992 to 76.2 per cent in 1999 (ABS 1999). These figures reflect a national trend, although there are regional differences, with some rural areas and some impoverished urban areas considerably worse than the average. Almost half the students in the final year of school stay on reluctantly (Teese 2000) and there is strong concern in a recent report on post compulsory education pathways in Victoria (Kirby 2000) that such levels of student disaffection may be contributing evidence of an erosion of social capital (defined as 'community values'), the rebuilding of which is claimed to be essential for global competitiveness as well as social cohesion. The concept of full-service schooling therefore has some immediate attractiveness as one way of assisting students to access health, welfare and other community services. There are other young people who exclude themselves from school or who are officially excluded, and yet others who may never have been included. These groups are beyond the reach of 'full-service' schooling, although the hope is that full-service schools will reduce the numbers of young people who are disconnected from school. At this stage it is unknown whether full-service schooling can ever include all young people in any proposal for improving access to services and, if so, whether inclusion would improve their chances of access to full adult citizenship status.

Positioning full-service schooling policy

In Australia, there is a wide range of health and welfare services to youth provided by agencies across a number of government departments and non-government agencies. Service-system integration is therefore seen as desirable from management and resourcing perspectives as well as from the perspective of evaluating the quality and appropriateness of services to students 'at risk of exclusion from school'.

There have been some attempts over recent years to facilitate service system access for 'at-risk' young people through the school, variously called full-service schooling, integrated service delivery or co-ordinated services. The rationale for school-focused youth services arose from the observation (Dryfoos 1994) that many children live in vulnerable families and neighbourhoods where the incidence of poverty, unemployment, teen pregnancy, substance abuse and violence is widespread. It is a very practical response to 'at-risk' students because schools are usually located in accessible places, and services can be delivered either at the school or through the school acting as the referral agency for services provided in the community (Stokes and Tyler 1997). The claimed strength of full-service schooling is the quality of partnerships that can be developed between various community agencies and between those agencies and the school. The collaborative effort is seen as a way to improve school performance of students whose educational progress has been impeded by problems originating outside the school.

The development of full-service schooling seems consistent with the British government's concern about the viability of single solutions to complex problems. The concept of inter-agency working in Britain aims to strengthen local networks, collective self-help, and include the target community as active participants in the design and shape of local policies, including education (Oppenheim 1998). As such, it may be more comprehensive than full-service schooling in that the locus of responsibility appears to be community-based more than school-based.

The limited scope of full-service schooling is also implied in the current Victorian government report on post-compulsory schooling (Kirby 2000). The Kirby Report recommends that there be a 'whole of government' response to youth, with schools taking some, but not all, responsibility for increasing the proportion of youth making a successful transition to independent adulthood. The report recommends that all local stakeholders be encouraged to participate in problem definition and solution.

However, there is another trend emerging elsewhere which suggests that inter-agency working may also be limited in its capacity to achieve social goals, especially a goal of independent adult citizenship. Recent health research (Syme 1998) claims that there is increasing evidence that single-factor causal explanations for morbidity do not account for all the data and may not lead to improved outcomes for many groups in society. So, at the individual level, reducing cholesterol levels, quitting smoking and lowering blood pressure, or large scale anti-poverty programmes at the community level, are only partial solutions. Syme presents evidence for an upstream factor in health and well-being, 'control of our destiny', which has to do with a sense of mastery over one's environment, independent of social class, poverty, unemployment and other social indicators, although disadvantaged people more commonly lack a sense of control over their affairs. A similar conclusion is made by Moodie after many years of working with Indigenous people in northern Australia. Moodie states:

> What I learned I guess is that you realise that why people get sick is more than a germ. It's really the social and economic determinants of health – it's whether someone has got a job, it's their educational levels and really, it's the amount of control over their own destiny.
>
> (cited in Gray 1999)

While full-service schooling appears more modest in its aims than either a 'whole of government' response or the 'control of own destiny' data, it is not essentially inconsistent with these more comprehensive approaches to 'at-risk' students. Full-service schooling aims to provide an efficient and effective vehicle for co-ordinated service access and delivery, and also to enhance the autonomy of young people, involving them as far as possible in responsible decision-making about their situation, increasing their participation in the life of the school and wider community (Dryfoos 1994). The 'whole of government' and 'control of own destiny' concepts appear more comprehensive in that they attempt to account for the underlying causes of societal fragmentation and youth alienation. Such accounting may include the possibility that schools are part of the problem of youth alienation (Knight 1997), and broaden the focus from 'at-risk' students to include institutional processes as well. However, there is wide variation in full-service programmes (Semmens and Stokes 1997; Dryfoos 1994), and one cannot generalise too far about full-service programmes because some do attempt to change institutional processes as well as individual students.

Common elements of full-service programmes include: a commitment to better learning outcomes for all students; strengthening links between home, school and community; democratic school governance that includes parents, students and teachers; community participation and ownership of the programme; co-ordination between providers and agencies; involvement of local government, local employers, local health and welfare services, etc.; involvement of various community groups such as service clubs, retired people, unemployed people; in-service for teachers, parents and community workers; training of parent and student advocates; and inclusion of other social justice initiatives such as legal advice and delinquency prevention (Australian Centre for Equity Through Education 1996).

In Australia, some full-service programmes are designed and funded by the Commonwealth government and some by state governments. The Commonwealth government programmes appear to have a narrow focus on whatever is necessary to facilitate school retention and successful transition to further training and/or work in local or regional communities. This may extend to improved access to health and welfare services, if that will help to achieve the retention goal according to the collaborative wisdom of existing youth agencies, business organisations and government agencies in each programme area (*Full Service National Evaluation Discussion Paper 1*, June 2000).

Some Australian state governments have a stronger emphasis on the individual 'at-risk' student than that afforded by the Commonwealth government's focus on school to post-school statistics. These individual 'at-risk' programmes have more of a social development focus and aim to improve student engagement with schooling. Such programmes may include student involvement in decision-making about their needs, interaction with community agencies, and the involvement of professional services in the school. There are some differences in preference in relation to whether these programmes should be school-based or community-based. Some, such as the Port Phillip Project (Semmens and Stokes 1997) want professional and community services co-ordinated and located at the school, whereas others prefer the school to strengthen ties with community agencies; these maintain their autonomy and the confidentiality of client files, which may include information on client members of the family other than the student. It is argued that school access to such file data would breach client confidentiality (Stokes and Tyler 1997). The other argument for community-based co-ordination of services is that students and their families may continue to use the community agencies after the student leaves school, so the making of links to community agencies during school years will facilitate their post-school transition to independent citizen status.

The 'where to base' full-service schooling issue is tied up with sensitivities around professional and agency boundaries which need to be negotiated at the time of establishment of each full-service programme. Underlying the issue of programme location is that of theoretical model for programme development and outcomes. The issue of differential full-service models leading to different strategies and outcomes has rarely been debated in Australia, yet debate is necessary to clarify programme rationale, direction and evaluation, as well as provide theoretical grounding for connections between notions of full-service schooling and concepts such as 'whole of government response' and 'control of own destiny'. A major proportion of this chapter is therefore devoted to clarification of the relative power of current models for full-service schooling, especially their capacity to deliver particular types of services to 'at-risk' students, and also their capacity to deliver 'at-risk' students to an independent citizenship outcome.

Towards a model of full-service schooling for full citizenship

In Australia, many 'full-service' schooling programmes employ Catalano and Hawkins' (1996) social development model (Tyler and Stokes 2000). Catalano and Hawkins' draw on theories of delinquency causation, principally Hirschi's (1969) social control theory and later refinements of it such as Elliott *et al.*'s (1985) integrated theory of social bond. Catalano and Hawkins provide evidence for the differential influence of socialisation units at different phases of social development – preschool, elementary school, middle school and high school. It is postulated that these phases are separated by major transitions in the environments in which children are socialised and shifts in the balance of influence among socialising units of family, schools, peers and community according to the age of the child. For example, family is most influential with younger children, whereas peers have strong influence in the middle-school years. Transitions, with their accompanying new bonding processes, offer an opportunity to decrease antisocial behaviour traits which may have been emerging in the preceding phase. Alternatively, these traits may increase due to weak pro-social development in an earlier phase and/or inadequate intervention strategies during the transition period.

According to Catalano and Hawkins (1996), antisocial behaviour has three sources: low levels of pro-social bonding resulting in few internal constraints against antisocial behaviour; situations in which the risk of detection by valued pro-social others is low; and when a child is bonded to immediate socialising units of family, school, community or peers who hold antisocial beliefs or values.

Development of attachments and commitments to the pro-social world depends on the extent to which pro-social involvements and interactions are positively reinforced by significant others. By contrast, those who experience few rewards for pro-social interaction and involvement have high levels of early risk factors, such as poor grades at school, low social status and lack of access to pro-social leadership roles.

The influence of prior bonding and behaviour on future behaviour suggests the importance of intervening early in the development of antisocial behaviour, and targeting the primary socialising units operative at that phase of schooling. Regardless of stage, the socialising processes are seen to be the same: perceived opportunities to participate in activities within the social unit; amount of interaction with others; extent of positive reinforcement of involvement and interaction; and emotional, cognitive and behavioural skills for involvement and interaction which enhance reinforcements and perceptions of reinforcement.

Catalano and Hawkins (1996) hypothesise that intervention which focuses on the social contexts of family, school and community will strengthen 'protective factors' and weaken 'risk factors', thus increasing the 'resilience' capacity of the child in resisting pressures towards antisocial behaviour. Further, strengthening one protective factor will strengthen the effect of another protective factor and reduce the potency of risk factors. So, for example, strong family bonds will reduce the potency of bonds to drug-taking peers, as indicated in Table 5.1.

Table 5.1   The social development model

	Risk factors	Protective factors
Individual	Low self-esteem Low motivation Low academic performance Disruptive behaviour	Early identification
Family	Fragmented Disturbed parent/child relationships High mobility Low income	Training in effective parenting Integrated services Parent/school partnerships
Peers	Negative relationships Antisocial behaviour	Student participation programmes
School	Repressive discipline Large class size Unstimulating curriculum Passive learning/teaching Competitive exam-based assessment	Early focus on literacy competence Interactive, co-operative learning/teaching High expectations School-wide welfare programme
Community	Extreme poverty Neighbourhood disorganisation Antisocial norms	Integrated service provision Involvement of supportive individuals/agencies

Catalano and Hawkins' emphasis on social context 'protective factors' differentiates their model from other more clinically oriented approaches that stress measurement of 'risk factors'. These often translate into labelling the bearers of those characteristics as 'at-risk' students who are then placed in special individualised programmes outside the mainstream curriculum, and possibly in special schools (Semmens *et al.* 1998). The model for such clinically oriented programmes is outlined in Figure 5.1.

An individual development programme is defined as one which relies more on someone in authority to arrange for a problem to be diagnosed and treated, and for the client's functioning to be at least observably improved in the diagnosed deficit or risk area. A possible weakness in this approach is that, while there may be improvement in the 'risk' area, the context for the improved functioning is not necessarily addressed and there may be some regression over time, as seemed to occur, for example, with the Head Start programme (1972). In such cases there is the additional burden of a negative socially ascribed label, such as 'slow learner', 'misfit', 'disturbed' or 'school failure'. This can be isolating rather than inclusive in the life of the school and wider community. Because of the popularity of the individual development model for most of the twentieth century (Lewis 1989), particularly in the growth of the special education sector,

Identification and labelling of the individual 'deficits' (risk factors) through clinical assessment of special needs – education, disability, health, personality, behaviour.

Prescription of remedial, compensatory or other individually tailored programme by specialist teachers, social workers, psychologists and/or medical professionals in mainstream schools or segregated settings.

↓

Re-assessment of performance in diagnosed deficit areas at stated intervals and reporting of level of improved functioning.

Figure 5.1   The individual development model

Catalano and Hawkins' model is a welcome advance with its emphasis on strengthening of protective or pro-social bonding factors, although its confidence in the protective value of conventional social institutions may be misplaced in postmodern society, as discussed later in this chapter.

Further, there is still a danger of labelling students 'at risk' in schools where student health and welfare are seen as separate from school curriculum, school management and community context. It may be that Catalano and Hawkins do not go far enough. Given the dangers of risk factors becoming labels attached to vulnerable individuals, why emphasise risk factors at all? Why not concentrate on 'protective factors'? Such a focus would seek to bring the community into the school, possibly adopting a community development model for programme delivery, as has occurred with some full-service schooling projects (Semmens and Stokes 1997; Stokes and Tyler 1997).

A community development model starts with a general concern about student alienation from school and conventional society, and moves to encourage young people to gradually take more and more responsibility for identifying personal care and connection needs, with a view to developing greater understanding of how various aspects of the social system work, particularly the service system, and eventual perception of self as a contributor to that system, or even an active change agent of the system. This educative goal of community development works in much the same way as in the teaching of literacy, with a view to children increasing their competence in reading and writing to the point where they can choose to contribute to the culture through critical analysis, and possibly ultimately creating their own publishable prose, poetry or plays.

A community development model accepts that, in crisis situations, someone with specialist expertise must step in and take clinical responsibility for the client in the short term. However, a community development model does insist that this intervention be connected with the rest of the client's life. Connection or re-connection may be achieved through integration of service delivery to

Table 5.2 The community development model

Problem definition	At risk of exclusion from school
Structure and processes for community development solution	Inclusive curriculum Supportive classroom climate Student involvement in decisions about themselves Student access to co-ordinated self-help services Student participation in school governance Student-initiated activities in school and community Negotiated involvement of community agencies – e.g. employment, recreation, accommodation, etc. Networking with, between and across community agencies
Expected outcomes	Increased attendance, participation and retention rates Connection of community to, and membership of, an increasing range of agencies Engagement with interested members of the community

mainstream community schools, that is 'full-service', but it is the process for establishment of those services and the strategies for connection that make the community development model more preventive in orientation than the individual development model and the social development model. Unlike the other two main models for full-service schooling, the community development model involves students in definition of the problem, ownership of the processes for solution, and integration of the intervention programme with the mainstream curriculum of the school.

Table 5.2 presents the steps in a community development model in relation to the problem of 'at-risk' students.

The community development model invites educationists to see the school–community interaction as the basis for strengthening participation of all students, including those who may be seen as 'at risk' of exclusion, in the life of the community. It is this vision of the student as an active member of the school and wider community that drives the strategy for student involvement in decision-making about support services, and other issues of schooling, from the earliest possible age. Its disadvantage is the apparent time-lag between identification of the need to do something about the numbers of students 'at risk' and the stage when the sense of belonging in school and community has grown strong enough to make a difference to the size of the problem. The period of social action and evolution of expected outcomes may be too long for some students who are 'at risk' today. Individual development and social development models may therefore be perceived by school managers as offering more immediate and observable change within the confines of the school context.

Yet there is a weakness in all three models for full-service schooling – individual development, social development and community development. In none of the models is there any analysis of the structural sources of the growing numbers of students 'at risk', nor any explicit commitment to a particular type of society, except that connection to social institutions is seen as more (community development) or less (individual development) important for the reduction of the size of the problem. There is an assumption that social institutions are in good order and that strengthening connections for 'at-risk' students will enhance their chances to complete school and make a safe ('resilient') transition to adult citizenship. Other evidence suggests that this assumption is flawed.

Knight (1997) draws attention to the problematic situation of young people making the transition from school to destinations beyond the school. He refers to the problem of high youth unemployment rates and also cites evidence from several other perspectives – the school as a market-place, school drop-out data, the interface between schooling and youth culture, and changes in definition and management of student behaviour problems – which suggest that the school itself contributes to the disengagement of many young people from conventional social institutions, including government. Knight claims that the increasing drop-out rate from secondary schooling is partly due to the exclusionary pressures of competitive selection and partly due to fear of being a 'loser' in the highly competitive final years of school, leaving many students with few options in the high youth unemployment climate. Just as serious is his claim that there has been a 'welfarist' rather than an educational response to the problem of disruptive student behaviour. Once, the 'at-risk' student was sent out of the classroom and dealt with by the school principal, possibly in a physical way with the strap. Now the 'at-risk' student tends to be sent out of the school altogether or handed over to another profession for diagnosis and treatment. Knight concludes that 'slouching towards centralised management theories and pharmacological solutions' has resulted in increased problem behaviour. Students feel controlled and powerless, forcing them to take risks in dealing with their problems. It is not just a matter of working out ways to keep students at school or to include them in decisions about themselves, as important as these things are. Any model of full-service is therefore insufficient.

A 'whole of government' response may also be inadequate in the long term if the school curriculum is not perceived by students to increase their understanding of economic context. Knight (1999) asks: 'Inclusion for what?' None of the current models for full-service schooling sets out to teach students how to engage with their future role as citizens in a democratic society, except by osmosis. Dewey (1916) wrote a long time ago that democracy is taught through a socially interactive curriculum. Pearl and Knight (1999) reiterate that claim when they write that a comprehensive educational response is required if young people are to make a successful transition to adult citizenship status:

As the school narrows the opportunity for students to learn democratically responsible behaviour, where it lacks these resources, then students can be expected to drift towards other affiliations ... Schools have surrendered much of their power through concentrating on discipline and management to the exclusion of a general school ethos.

(Pearl and Knight 1999: 89)

A comprehensive educational response

If the school is the major social institution outside the family for bringing young people to adult citizenship, as claimed by Catalano and Hawkins and others, then a major part of the socialisation role will take place in classrooms through formal teaching of curriculum and through informal relationships with teachers and fellow students, which together constitute the social climate of the school.

In *The Democratic Classroom* (1999), Pearl and Knight take democratic education theory into modern classrooms, relating theory to the problem of youth disengagement from school and society, giving teachers and students a framework for construction of democracy in the classroom. Pearl and Knight challenge Dewey's (1916) laboratory approach to teaching democracy. They want to bring society into the school so that students can participate in solving problems related to their own future. The classroom becomes the site for initiating change through equal encouragement of all students. Pearl and Knight claim that society keeps evolving and changing anyway, so why should students not be involved in setting the agenda for the society which they are going to inherit?

Pearl and Knight begin with the claim that democratic education is as much concerned with the growth of individuals as it is with the advance of society. For them, the purpose of education is for students to be responsible problem-solvers, and for that reason the school should be problem-centred rather than child-centred or prescribed-curriculum-centred. As an example, Pearl and Knight (1999: 93) claim that students would understand the relevance of studying history if it were taught as themes of unresolved human conflict, such as war, poverty and finite natural resources. Such an approach would encourage students to participate thoughtfully and critically in the affairs of their own society, whereas the current emphasis on history as knowledge requires a leap of faith from knowledge of the past to citizen action for the common good in the future. Indeed, the current emphasis on gaining the competitive edge on one's peers at school, in order to secure a place at university and/or the job market, tends to ignore the common good altogether and redefines education as a private commodity – which is anti-democratic. For them, democratic schooling for citizenship would meet the following basic requirements:

1   Knowledge should be universally provided to enable all students to solve generally recognised social and personal problems.
2   Students should participate in decisions that affect their lives.

3   Clearly specified rights should be made universally available.
4   Equal encouragement should be given for success in all of society's legal endeavours.

(Pearl and Knight 1999: 2)

The place to begin to develop understanding about democracy is the classroom:

> No central mandate can determine how teachers relate to students nor can central authority dictate how ideas will be communicated. The nature of relationships in a classroom constitutes the heart of education and that is where reform can and should begin.

(Pearl and Knight 1999: 76)

The teacher–student relationship is dynamic and directed at the common good:

> Democratic education is used to solve problems that are real, not imaginary, important not trivial, difficult not easy … There is no abstract solution to poverty, justice, violence, crime, the preservation of the environment, and so on … For students to emerge as democratic citizens they must be able to calculate the positive and negative impact of any solution on the various individuals and groups that are affected, and on something much more difficult to define – the common good.

(Pearl and Knight 1999: 118)

Pearl and Knight present a vision of a democratic society and the role of the public school in giving students not only the credentials to live in that society, but also a sense of being a stakeholder in that society. They want debate about the structure and curriculum of schooling to include student perspectives, along with as many other perspectives as possible.

The Pearl and Knight model strengthens the community development model outlined earlier in this chapter, in that it is provided with a basis in education theory and a plan for action that begins in classrooms. It provides a cognitive curriculum foundation for the social networking emphasis of the community development model. It also re-orients the social development model because the 'social' is integrated with the intellectual, vocational, cultural and political. In another way, *The Democratic Classroom* exceeds the minimum requirement of the social development model that there be connection to at least one social institution, in that students have an active role in making the institution of schooling 'in good order' for its entire membership. In the terms of the social development model, participation in classroom and school governance is a 'protective' factor which increases student 'resilience' to adverse situations in their lives and reduces 'at-risk' factors in number and intensity.

The Pearl and Knight model also challenges, but does not discard, the individual development model for intervention in the lives of 'at-risk' students. There is still a role for experts, although the context for their involvement is different. No student is denied individual treatment, but the democratic model poses the same questions for the involvement of experts in the life of the school as it does for anyone else in the school community. The questions are: What is perceived as a problem and by whom? How is the problem defined? What is the extent of the problem? What is the interface between private and public aspects of the problem? Who is to be involved in solution of the problem, and how? How will the individual and the school community be strengthened by the proposed solution?

The initiative for expert intervention would come from the school community rather than from the central administration of the school system or from a government anxious to provide funds that might help to curb school drop-out rates. Students would gather data from as many sources as possible, including government. They may redefine the problem and invent a different solution. However, if the full-service option proceeded there would be student involvement in decision-making about the type of services and manner of delivery. Implementation of full-service schooling would be part of student demonstration of full citizenship in the wider community, now, and in the future as adults. Reports from Lewis (1991, 1994) and Holdsworth (1999) indicate that quite young students can engage in this sort of venture; according to Lewis, it is more likely to occur in primary schools at present, as secondary teachers seem more reticent to involve students in decision-making. Additionally, from their evaluation of full-service schools, Stokes and Tyler (1997) report that students may have a clearer awareness of the range and relative merits of community support agencies than their teachers.

The Pearl and Knight model requires a more fundamental re-thinking of schooling and curriculum than the authors of full-service schooling intended. But it does provide an educational response to the concerns which gave rise to the development of full-service programmes while reviving a vision for a democratic society and the role of schooling and students in achieving that vision. It makes links between society, individual needs, school processes, curriculum content and schooling outcomes, as summarised in Table 5.3.

Implementation of the Pearl and Knight model would not be imposed upon schools, although school communities would need to be fully informed about it in order to debate and make their decision. It challenges not only those currently responsible for curriculum development and school management, but also invites community debate about what sort of society we want to be.

When whole schools and school districts come to be organised for full-service to reduce the growing numbers of students 'at risk', it is time to look for alternative models for explaining and solving the problem. Beck claims that it is not 'merely' students who are 'at risk' in the globalised market economy, but Western democracy, for

> only when people have a decent place to live and a secure job can they function as citizens who embrace democracy and make it come alive ... Market fundamentalism ... is a form of democratic illiteracy.
>
> (Beck 1998: 58)

Table 5.3   The Pearl and Knight democratic model

Theory	Democratic education theory
Problem definition	How to educate students in the democratic society
Change strategy	Informing students of their civic rights and negotiating associated responsibilities Including all students in all decisions about themselves – informing, explaining, debating consulting – using logic and evidence Respecting minority view and understanding how power can be used responsibly in the interests of all members of the community Equal provision of that knowledge necessary to solve the most important personal and social problems Encouragement to equal success
Delivery system	Problem-solving curriculum in public schools, with wider community involvement in problem-solving
Expected outcomes	Sense of competence, belonging and usefulness in all students, reflected in: co-operative solving of real and important intellectual, vocational, cultural and personal problems; increased attendance, participation and retention rates; reduced violence; and, youth taking formative roles in school and the whole range of community agencies and evolving social institutions, including economic, legal and political.

It appears that none of the models for full-service schooling currently employed in Australia is sufficiently comprehensive to provide long-term direction for overcoming the marginalisation of youth generally, not just those 'at risk' of school failure. Pearl and Knight (1999) make an attempt to provide a comprehensive educational model for youth in the revival of a democratic society. They assume that teachers will gain the much stronger understanding of democratic processes that Carrington (1999) claims they currently lack, and that this understanding will be reflected in the ways that schools are managed despite the current anti-democratic nature of schools (Pearl and Knight 1999: 97). One wonders about the implications for teacher training, and how well they would be received by universities and other providers of teacher training and professional development.

There is another possible limitation to the implementation of the Pearl and Knight model and that is whether their model needs to be entirely school-based, given the existence of some young people who either do not attend school at all or who are excluded at a young age. For example, according to a review by the Victorian Department of Human Services (Department of Human Services

1997), 228 young people under its supervision at that time were identified as 'high-risk' adolescents, representing 18 per cent of the adolescent child protection population. These young people presented with serious personal or community risk and were particularly difficult to manage. They were most likely to be between 11 and 17 years of age and placed in residential care, generally as a single child, not as part of a sibling group. More than half of this group (56 per cent) had serious drug abuse problems but without access to drug and alcohol services. Twenty-seven per cent were on joint juvenile justice/protection orders, 25 per cent had suicide ideation or diagnosed mental illness, and one third of these young people had no active mental health services involvement. Non-participation in schooling was typical, although some welfare agencies provided 'day programmes' containing some education and socialisation elements for those willing to attend on a day-to-day basis.

The life situation of these young people is truly bleak, compounded by multiple, even traumatic, experiences, often resulting in damage to their capacity to trust self and others. Perhaps it is too much to expect that any model will be comprehensive enough to include pathways to full citizenship for all young people, but that is no reason to assume that excluded students are not 'at risk'. It appears at present that non-student youth cannot increase their full citizenship chances from full-service schooling. Hopefully, they are not also beyond the bounds of a 'whole of government response' as well. The Pearl and Knight model suggests a stronger emphasis on prevention – a 'control of own destiny' approach through engaging all young people in a collaborative problem-solving curriculum from the earliest years of schooling, thereby offering greater hope for achieving full citizenship in a democratic society in the long term.

Conclusion

Full-service schooling, according to whichever model is employed, may reduce the numbers of students 'at risk' of exclusion from school. In the short term, the individual development model may reduce the impact of risk factors on student performance, but the longer-term effects of negative labelling may detract from its potency to bring such students to equal citizen status. It is suggested that the longer-term interests of 'at-risk' students may be better served by the community development model because of its emphasis on prevention and strengthening ties to community agencies. Whether any model of full-service schooling can actually increase the number of young people brought safely to adult citizenship in a democratic society clearly requires longitudinal research.

Such research is necessary because the size of the youth disaffection problem is now very large (McIntyre 1994). Support for the development of a far more comprehensive model than any of the existing full-service models comes from 'control of own destiny' data (Syme 1998). Pearl and Knight (1999) propose such a model, claiming that the opportunity for involvement of all young people in collaborative investigation and solution of real and important problems for their present and future well-being will lead to a stronger sense of belonging in the society which they will inherit.

As the quote from Gore (1995) at the beginning of this chapter suggests, full-service schooling may not sufficiently challenge our liberal individualist tradition. Some re-thinking of our notion of citizenship and the relative emphasis on liberty, equality and fraternity may be necessary before 'at-risk' students, let alone 'high-risk' youth, are convinced that full-status citizenship in a democratic society is a right and a reality for them.

References

Australian Bureau of Statistics (1999) 'Transition from education to work, Australia', Cat 6227.0, unpublished data for Victoria, cited in P. Kirby (Chair) (2000) *Ministerial Review of Post Compulsory Education and Training Pathways in Victoria: Interim Report*, Victoria: Department of Education, Employment and Training.

Australian Centre for Equity Through Education (1996) *Equity Network*, 2(2):1.

Beck, U. (1998) *Democracy Without Enemies*, Oxford: Polity Press/Blackwell.

Carrington, S. (1999) 'Inclusion needs a different school culture', in R. Slee (ed.) *International Journal of Inclusive Education*, 3(3): 257–68.

Catalano, R.F. and Hawkins, J.D. (1996) 'The social development model: a theory of anti-social behaviour', in R. Catalano (ed.) *Delinquency and Crime: Current Theories*, New York: Cambridge.

Colton, M. and Hellinckx, W. (1994) 'Residential foster care in the European Community: current trends in policy and practice', *British Journal of Social Work*, 24: 559–76.

Coulter, J. (1998) *High Risk Youth*, Washington: Department of Human Services.

Department of Human Services (1997) *Overview of High Risk Adolescents in Placement and Support Services*, Melbourne: Placement and Care Branch, DHS.

Dewey, J. (1916) *Democracy and Education*, New York: Free Press.

Dryfoos, J. (1994) *Full-Service Schools: A Revolution in Health and Social Services for Children, Youth and Families*, San Francisco: Jossey-Bass.

Dusseldorp, J. (Chair) (1999) *Australia's Young Adults: The Deepening Divide*, Sydney: Dusseldorp Skills Forum.

Dwyer, P. and Wyn, J. (1998) 'Post-compulsory education policy in Australia and its impact on participant pathways and outcomes in the 1990s', *Journal of Education Policy*, 13(3): 258–300.

Elliott, D., Huizinga, D. and Ageton, S. (1985) *Explaining Delinquency and Drug Use*, Beverly Hills: Sage.

Gore, C. (1995) 'Introduction: markets, citizenship and social exclusion', in G. Rodgers, C. Gore and J.B. Figueredo (eds) *Social Exclusion: Rhetoric, Reality, Responses*, Geneva: ILO.

Gray, D. (1999) 'Doctors prescribe end to racism', *The Age*, 14 August.

Hirschi, T. (1969) *Causes of Delinquency*, Berkeley: University of California Press.

Hixson, J. and Tinzman, M. (1990) *Who are the At-Risk Students of the Nineties?* North Central Regional Educational Laboratory (NCREL), Oakbrook, info@ncrel.org

Holdsworth, R. (ed.) (1979–) *Connect*, journal of student participatory projects, University of Melbourne: Youth Research Centre.

Holdsworth, R. (1999) 'Taking young people seriously means giving them serious things to do', paper presented at Taking Children Seriously National Workshop, University of Western Sydney, Macarthur, 12–13 July.

Jones, A. and Smyth, P. (1999) 'Social exclusion: a new framework for social policy analysis', *Just Policy*, 17 (December): 11–20.

Kilpatrick, W.H. (1936) *Re-Making the Curriculum*, New York: Newsom.

Kirby, P. (Chair) (2000) *Ministerial Review of Post Compulsory Education and Training Pathways in Victoria: Interim Report*, Victoria: Department of Education, Employment and Training.

Knight, T. (1997) 'Schools, delinquency and youth culture', in A. Borowski and I. O'Connor (eds) *Juvenile Crime, Justice and Corrections*, Australia: Longman.

——(1999) 'Inclusive education and educational theory: inclusive for what?' paper presented at the Annual Conference of the British Educational Research Association, University of Sussex, 2–5 September.

Lerman, R. (1996) 'Helping disconnected youth by improving linkages between high schools and careers', paper presented at the American Enterprise Institute Forum on America's Disconnected Youth: Toward a Preventative Strategy, Washington, DC: The Urban Institute Press.

Lewis, J. (1989) 'Removing the grit', unpublished PhD thesis, LaTrobe University, Melbourne.

Lewis, R. (1991) *The Discipline Dilemma*, Hawthorn, Victoria: Australian Council for Educational Research.

——(1994) *Codes of Conduct in Schools of the Future*, Victoria: Directorate of Education.

McIntyre, P. (Chair) (1994) *Whereas the People: Civics and Citizenship Education Report*, Canberra: Australian Government Publishing Service.

Marmot, M. (1998) 'Mastering the control factor, part two', in N. Swann, *The Health Report*, Radio National, 16 November.

OECD (2000) Background paper for International Symposium on the Contribution of Human and Social Capital to Sustained Economic Growth and Well-Being in Canada, pp. 2–3, cited in P. Kirby (Chair) *Ministerial Review of Post Compulsory Education and Training Pathways in Victoria: Interim Report*, Victoria: Department of Education, Employment and Training.

Oppenheim, C. (ed.) (1998) *An Inclusive Society: Strategies for Tackling Poverty*, London: Institute for Public Policy Research.

Pateman, C. (1970) *Participation and Democratic Theory*, Cambridge: Cambridge University Press.

Pearl, A. and Knight, T. (1999) *The Democratic Classroom: Theory to Inform Practice*, New Jersey: Hampton Press.

Power, S. and Gewirtz, S. (1999) 'Reading Education Action Zones', paper presented to the British Educational Research Association Annual Conference, University of Sussex, 2–5 September.

Rayner, M. and Montague, M. (1999) *Resilient Children and Young People: A Discussion Paper Based on a Review of the International Research Literature*, Geelong: Deakin Human Services Australia, Deakin University.

Semmens, R. and Stokes, H. (1997) 'Full-service schooling for full citizenship', *Melbourne Journal of Educational Studies*, 38(2): 115–30.

Semmens, R., Stokes, H. and Downey, L. (1998) *Establishing an Integrated Service Model in the Port Phillip Cluster: An Evaluation. Working Paper 17*, University of Melbourne: Youth Research Centre.

Stokes, H. and Tyler, D. (1997) *Re-Thinking Interagency Collaboration and Young People*, University of Melbourne: Youth Research Centre.

Syme, L. (1998) 'Mastering the control factor, part one', in N. Swann, *The Health Report*, Radio National, 9 November.

Teese, R. (2000) *Academic Success and Social Power: Examinations and Inequality*, Melbourne: Melbourne University Press.

Tyler, D. and Stokes, H. (2000) *Evaluation of Civics and Citizenship Projects*, in progress, University of Melbourne: Youth Research Centre.

6   New Scotland, New Labour, New Community Schools

New authoritarianism?[1]

Stephen Baron

Introduction

In November 1998, as the Scotland Act 1998 (re)establishing a Scottish Parliament was receiving Royal Assent, the late Donald Dewar announced that 'Scotland leads the way with radical plan for New Community Schools ... one of the most innovative and modern initiatives ever carried out in British education' (Scottish Office 1998a: 1). It is the argument of this chapter that this coincidence was not accidental and that disaggregating the condensation of political themes in the New Community Schools initiative gives access to the heart of the 'New Labour' project of 'joined-up government', to the emergent Scottish polity and to key issues in the relationship between state and civil society.

In order to conduct this argument the chapter will first consider, in 'New Scotland', the centrality of 'community' and 'school' to the Scottish political tradition and their place in the agenda of the newly established Parliament. In 'New Labour', the modernising Third Way project of Blair will be considered alongside the *motif* of 'joined-up government'. In 'New Community Schools' the nature of these institutions will be explored through an analysis: of the importation of the American 'Full Service School'; of the requirements of the *New Community Schools Prospectus*; of the operational definition of good New Community Schools in the training materials and evaluation specifications produced by the Scottish Executive; and in the widely publicised account of one New Community School by a local official. In 'New authoritarianism?' conclusions are drawn about whether the New Community Schools initiative represents an empowerment of disempowered populations or the extension and fine tuning of the state's disciplinary machinery in relation to Scottish civil society.

New Scotland

The opening of the Scottish Parliament on 1 July 1999 (after a recess of 292 years) was significantly due to the work over the previous decade of the Scottish Constitutional Convention. This self-constituted body sought to draw representatives from all parts of the Scottish bodies politic and civil and to establish a consensual 'practical scheme for bringing the Parliament into existence' (Scottish

Constitutional Convention 1995: 5) A cross-party group, the Campaign for a Scottish Assembly, published a 'Claim of Right' in 1988 (Edwards 1989) and the Constitutional Convention was formally inaugurated in March 1989. It presented a blueprint for a Scottish Parliament to 'the people of Scotland' in 1995. The Convention took as given the settled will of the Scottish people for a Parliament:

> The first and greatest reason for creating a Scottish Parliament is that the people of Scotland want and deserve democracy. Their will is powerful and clear. It has been expressed calmly and consistently over a period of decades, and has strengthened rather than diminished with the passing time.
> (Scottish Constitutional Convention 1995: 6)

This 'period of decades' could arguably be stretched to one of centuries, but the impetus for a Scottish Parliament became all but irresistible in the years between the first referendum on the matter in 1979 and the second one in 1997. In Paterson's view, the desires for a Scottish Parliament 'remained minority political tendencies until the 1980s, with probably majority sympathy but no really enthusiastic support in general population' (Paterson 2000a: 49). In the first referendum, 52 per cent of those voting were in favour of devolution but, at 33 per cent of the total electorate, this failed to pass the absolute threshold of 40 per cent of the electorate set by the Callaghan Labour government. In 1997, 60 per cent of the electorate voted, with a majority of 74 per cent in favour of the (re)establishment of a Scottish Parliament. All the MPs returned to the Westminster Parliament in the 1997 general election represented parties which, in one form or another, were committed to the (re)establishment of a Scottish Parliament, there now being no Scottish Conservative MPs.

Explanations of this shift focus on the experience of Thatcherism: the Conservative Party was in a minority among Scottish MPs, its share of the Scottish vote roughly halving from 1979 to a 1997 figure of 17 per cent, creating a sense of misrepresentation and alienation from a government centred in every sense in the south-east of England; the centralising logic of Thatcherism served to increase the colonial sense of centre and periphery; the economic restructuring which liquidated 'heavy' industries had a disproportionate effect on the Scottish central belt; the burgeoning wealth created by North Sea oil visibly flowed elsewhere.

Most fundamentally, the radical individualism of Thatcherism ran counter to the deep sense of the mutual obligation which many commentators attribute to Scottish culture with its diverse, religious and secular, collectivist roots (see Fairley and Paterson 2000: 39–41 for a discussion of the doctrines of Traditional Liberalism, Social Liberalism and Group Rights in Scotland). Mrs Thatcher's 1988 jingoistic and anti-social 'Sermon on the Mound' drew a stinging rebuke from James Whyte, the Moderator of the General Assembly of the Church of Scotland; the emphasis on 'inclusion' and 'the preferential option for the poor' in social Catholicism were maintained and strengthened in the 1980s, resulting in the critique of the unfettered capitalism celebrated by Thatcherism in the 1991 Papal Encyclical *Centesimus Annus* ('After Socialism?' Group 1998). It is the Scottish sense of a moral imperative to mutual obligations and to the cultures and networks which maintain them, equated for present purposes with 'community', which is the subject of an eloquent essay by Paterson (2000a).

Paterson traces this sense of mutual moral obligations to what has been called the 'Common Sense School' of Scottish Enlightenment social philosophy trying to come to terms with the final removal of the formal institutions of state from Scotland in 1707 and the disruption of industrialisation later in the century. How could an apparently acephalous and urbanising society avoid falling into a destructive spiral of self-interest? The answers given variously by Hutcheson (instinctive benevolence), Hume (instrumental reciprocity) and – ironically, given Thatcherism's very partial mining of his work – Adam Smith ('mutual assistance is "reciprocally afforded from love" (Smith 1759)') all focus on 'common sense ... the bonds of trust and obligation that subsist among citizens' (Paterson 2000a: 41–2).

These were not idle philosophical theses but generated a distinctive civil society which was, and is, simultaneously supportive and suspicious of the state: 'anti-statist and yet public, private and yet moral, depoliticized ... and yet civic' (Paterson 2000a: 43). In centralising and increasing state power, in locating morality firmly in the private sphere and in attacking the institutions of civic society, Thatcherism was trebly offensive to the Scottish 'common sense'.

The extent to which the new Scottish Parliament articulates with such 'common sense' is thus a central issue in the new polity which can be explored through the analysis of 'community' policies.

Education – in this case, schooling – is a central component of this 'common sense', having mythical status for Scottish nationhood. For Gray *et al.*, 'to be Scottish therefore is to have and to share in what has come to be called "the democratic intellect"' (1983: 40), the right of all Scots to have access to education, to form common understandings through that education, to be assessed on merit alone but to be valued irrespective of intellectual achievement. This self-image is traced back to John Knox and the Reformation with his call in the first *Book of Discipline* of 1560 for a system of schools: elementary schools for all in upland parishes; grammar schools in towns; high schools in important towns, all feeding into universities, for which bursaries were to be provided for 'the clever poor' (Scotland 1969: vol. 1, 44–8). The figure of the 'lad o' pairts' (*sic*) haunts Scottish education: the impoverished son of the soil who, through the parish school, rises to attend one of the ancient Scottish universities and to join one of the great professions, perhaps returning to his roots as the 'dominie' (schoolteacher).

For Paterson (2000a) the Scottish education and legal systems were the institutional vestiges of nationhood on to which Scots could hold after the Union of 1707. Such professions 'became the embodiment of Scottish national identity, the holding of the nation in trust despite the absence of a national Parliament' (Paterson 2000a: 48); the professions conversely gave their allegiance primarily to civil society, the profession and the particular locality rather than to the state.

The 'dominie' was the embodiment of such professionalism most accessible to ordinary Scots. It was a crisis in this aspect of Scottish identity which provided one of the four main arguments for a remoralising of Scottish politics through the (re)establishment of a Scottish Parliament for Paterson. The demand for 'democratic accountability' of the Scottish education system was not only a demand for the central Education Department to be overseen by politicians directly elected by Scottish people but, more importantly, for education professionals to re-form their links with the communities which they served, rather than pay even more attention to school inspectors and the demands of a central bureaucracy.

It was such reasoning, at least in part, which led the Constitutional Convention to collaborate with the major teacher organisation and a newspaper to organise a conference, *Education and a Scottish Parliament* (Educational Institute of Scotland 1996), to begin to define the policy agenda. It was the only area of policy for the Scottish Parliament to be subject to such pre-devolution consultation and planning.

Three fundamental principles for the future emerged from this process:

- *Education can benefit both individuals and society* by creating 'a vibrant society of equal citizens'.
- *Education can be both utilitarian and for its own sake* by ensuring that 'the main outcome of education between generations is to enrich society's cultural capital'.
- *Education should be governed accountably* which 'forces all the partners in the system to pay attention to and understand each other'.

(Educational Institute of Scotland 1996: 4–6)

Three impediments to the realisation of these principles were foreseen:

- *The principle of subsidiarity* might not be extended beyond the Scottish Parliament in Edinburgh, thus taking existing power away from local authorities and preventing devolution to schools and communities.
- *The celebration of diversity* and the maintenance of collective interests often pull in different directions and the traditional solution for Scottish government has been to use central regulation, rather than a devolution of power, to resolve the tension.
- *The celebration of community* which lies behind the demand for a Scottish Parliament often ignores the tensions between communities and the oppressive effects of some communities on their members.

(Educational Institute of Scotland 1996: 7–9)

The extent to which the new Scottish Parliament reduces central control and enables professionals to reconnect with local communities is thus a central issue in the new polity which can be explored through the analysis of educational policies.

Paterson, in considering the move from nineteenth-century to twentieth- to twenty-first-century Scottish politics, poses a series of questions:

> But what if a public sphere does not entail a state? What if strengthened social capital may actually still be in tension with the state? What if, even, a public sphere at the beginning of the twenty-first century may increasingly require not to have a state?
>
> (Paterson 2000a: 47)

He thus foresees Scotland over the next two decades as being a testing ground between the two versions of 'public', the civic and the state, with the civic acting as a regulator of the state. The converse question, which Paterson does not pose, is: 'What if the state increasingly seeks to colonise and control the civic?'

As we have suggested above, 'community' and 'education' are individually crucial to the Scottish political experience and to the new Scottish Parliament. In combination, as 'community schools', they present a privileged moment to explore the emerging nature of the Scottish polity and its relationship with civil society. Before addressing the New Community Schools initiative we must first establish the force of the adjective 'New'.

New Labour

One of the most symbolic acts of Blair on being elected as leader of the Labour Party in July 1994 was to attach the adjective 'New' to the party and, thereafter, to ever increasing areas of social policy. The signified 'modernisation project', any opponents to which were 'forces of conservatism', was to encompass 'both ideas and organisation' in order for the Labour Party to claim the centre ground of British politics (Blair, quoted in Jones 1996: 135). Continuity with the past was claimed through showing 'how enduring socialist values can be applied in the new circumstances of the 1990s' (Brown 1994: 113), while modernisation was claimed through a move away from a focus on the state machinery as the privileged mechanism for realising social justice: indeed, the state was 'a vested interest in itself, every bit as capable of oppressing individuals as wealth and capital' (Blair 1991: 33). Community and education were pivotal concepts in this realignment.

In the modernisation project, 'community' took over from 'common ownership' as the foundation on which social justice could be established. The utility of the warm vagueness of this concept has often been noted (Baron 1988), but in New Labour it was given a newly imprecise meaning. The traditional reference points for 'community' – shared territory, local culture and stable personal identity – were seen as 'out of date and … probably gone for ever' (Brown 1994: 118). In place, 'community' was defined as 'the idea that people see themselves as mutually dependent' (Brown 1994: 119). For Blair, two major 'ethical' principles were derived from this: individuals owe a duty to one another and the broader society; and the collective power of all should be used for the individual good of each (Blair 1994). For Brown, two conclusions followed from such communitarianism:

> First, in recognition of our inter-dependence people must accept their responsibilities as individual and as citizens, and community action should never be a substitute for the assumption of personal responsibility. And secondly ... ensuring that individual rights are protected from any encroachment from the state ... examining very clearly how the community can organize its affairs in a decentralised way, more sensitively and flexibly.
>
> (Brown 1994: 119)

Given these 'Third Way' starting points (hovering, in Wheen's view, in some 'vacant space between the Fourth Dimension and the Second Coming' (cited in Hall 1998: 10), it was no surprise that the slogan with which the successful 1997 New Labour general election campaign was spearheaded was 'Education. Education. Education'. In part, this was a resurrection of the Labour Party revisionism of the 1950s under Crosland, which forged the link between social justice and economic efficiency through meritocracy: a just society which allowed every child to rise to the limits of their potential would be an economically efficient one through optimising labour market allocation of roles (CCCS 1981). In part, the new revisionism represented a decisive (post-Thatcherite) break with that of the 1950s and its 1960s. This latter had focused on the institutional structure of state education (principally the comprehensive school and the expansion of the universities) leaving day-to-day control of the process of education to the professional autonomy of teachers. The revisionism of New Labour was relatively indifferent to institutional structures, focusing instead, as in most areas of social policy, on 'what works'. This enabled New Labour to live happily with, and indeed advance, most of the Thatcherite restructuring of education. The quasi-market and selective differentiation within the state sector have been encouraged alongside an ever closer disciplining of the teaching profession; the private sector has been encouraged to flourish and offer 'leadership' to the state sector. Above all, the ends of education have been assumed to be specifiable as a simple set of 'standards' by which all (school, teachers, pupils and, increasingly, communities) will be judged.

The attributed 'needs' of the British economy in the context of globalisation are taken as the given, leaving as the only remaining issues how best to 'meet' such needs. In this, *gestalt* education shares many features with other areas of social policy. Jacques sums up Blair's first eighteen months thus: 'Having embraced modernity, he sees government as about professional management and problem-solving, rather in the manner of a modern corporate executive ... wonkery without the Big Picture runs the risk of not seeing the wood for the trees' (Jacques 1998: 2–3). The analogy with the corporation was apt and Jacques's critique telling, for, in government, one of New Labour's claimed 'Big Ideas' was to have a policy on policy: to revisit the wonkery of 'corporate management' in the guise of Modernising Government through 'ensuring that policy is more *joined-up and strategic*' (Stationery Office 1999: 6, emphasis in original) (although since 1999 this policy had made the rapid symbolic progression from the writing of the infant school to, as 'wired-up policy', the neural networking of the university laboratory; Cabinet Office 2000). How far this emphasis on joined-up government is in fact new is doubted by Paterson (2000b).

The 2000 Performance and Innovation Review of the modernisation of government programme in Whitehall (Cabinet Office 2000) sought to garner best practice from abroad and, significantly, from the devolved Scottish Executive. The creation of cross-cutting ministerial portfolios (e.g. a Minister for Communities) with parallel Committees in the Scottish Parliament was seen as 'championing' cross-cutting issues. Similarly, giving primacy in the policy-making process to eleven cross-sectoral issues (e.g. promoting social inclusion), instead of unstructured lists of scores of departmental priorities, was seen as a potential model for use south of the border.

Concurrent with the Whitehall review of the modernisation of government programme, there was a Scottish review of joined-up government (Scottish Executive 2000). This suggested that cross-cutting policies were 'increasingly being used to tackle key social and economic issues' and that 'since 1997 the Government has founded its programme of reform on tackling not only the consequences of social and economic problems, but the root causes of the problems themselves' (Scottish Executive 2000: 3). As Tett *et al.* suggest, this entails an attempt to integrate programmes both between all agencies and at all levels from policy formulation to neighbourhood action.

What is striking in this review is the assumption, consistent with more than three decades of policy of Britain and the USA, that policy co-ordination has a particular, if not unique, affinity with areas of, or populations with, 'social problems' (Baron, forthcoming). This assumption is borne out in the substance of the review, which proceeded by analysing four policy initiatives as implemented in three local authorities in Scotland (Glasgow, Highland, Stirling). The four policy initiatives were Modernising Community Care (1998); Tackling Drugs in Scotland (1999); the New Deal for 18- to 24-year-olds; New Community Schools.

As Donald Dewar claimed when launching the New Community Schools website (http://scotland.gov.uk/education/newcommunityschools/default.htm), 'New Community Schools are at the leading edge of the policies of the Scottish Executive.' It is to these which we now turn.

New Community Schools

We can now approach the New Community Schools initiative with a critical set of questions: from the discussion of the place of 'community' in the Scottish polity, we may ask whether the New Community Schools enable the institutions of civil society to act as a regulator on the actions of the state; from the discussion of the professions as carriers of Scottish identity, we may ask whether the New Community Schools represent a renewed accountability of the professions to the communities which they serve; from the discussion of subsidiarity, we may ask if the New Community Schools initiative demonstrates devolution of power beyond Holyrood (and Victoria Quay);[2] from the discussion of New Community Schools as the claimed pioneer policy of joined-up government in Britain, we may ask if the New Community Schools are indeed new and if they 'involve and meet the needs of all different groups in society' (Stationery Office 1999).

New Community Schools were not an indigenous model but an importation of the 'Full Service School' from an initiative in District 6 of New York City Public Schools in 1989. This is consonant with a long-established trend in British social policy, extended under New Labour, to seek models, and legitimacy, from the USA rather than from other states or from the adaptation of indigenous models. An old voluntary organisation, the Children's Aid Society of New York, had conducted a needs assessment of the District two years earlier and had found 'a neighborhood struggling with the city's most overcrowded school, a large population of poor, first-generation immigrant families, many young people at risk of dropping out of school, and a dangerous scarcity of health and social service providers' (Children's Aid Society 1997: 5).

In co-operation with the city's school authority, the Society spent three years converting a school (IS 218) in Washington Heights into

> a focal point in the community to which children and their parents could turn for education as well as a vast range of other supportive services. Medical, dental, mental health, recreation, youth programs, family life education and summer camping services would all emanate from this one institution, while the clear focus of every activity remained on academics and learning. And the institution would be open six or seven days a week, 15 hours a day, year round. What we proposed was not simply to use schools in the after-school hours, but to work alongside with the parents, teachers and community to ensure that children are given every chance to succeed.
>
> (Children's Aid Society 1997: 5)

Since the inception of IS 218 the model has been fully adopted in more than 600 schools in fifteen states in the USA, and a Technical Assistance Center has been established to support such developments through visits, consultancy and publication, notably Dryfoos (1994).

The idea of the Full Service School had been briefly picked up by New Labour a year before the election in a lecture by Margaret Maden at Greenwich, where she linked the themes of urban alienation (the Blade Runner problem) and of inter-agency communication and co-location (the solution). This was explicitly linked to Blair's communitarianism. The full-service school was picked up in Scotland by the Quality in Education Centre, University of Strathclyde, which organised an exploratory seminar in February 1998 addressed by HM Senior Chief Inspector of Schools Osler. His speech was notable for its spending more time arguing that HMI activities from 1988 onwards, together with current government policies, already encompassed the features of Full Service Schools than in actually analysing and developing them. In part, this can be seen as a restatement of the ideals of comprehensive schooling; in part, this can be seen as building a genealogy for a forthcoming policy initiative; in part, it celebrates Salvation through Inspection.

As a result of this seminar, a 'Pack' of source material on Full Service Schools circulated among the 'leadership class' in Scottish education (and possibly beyond). This 'Pack' consisted of: a five-page *Program Summary* from the Children's Aid Society (1996a); a two-year-old newsletter from the Society (1996b); a five-page paper in *Educational Leadership* by Dryfoos (1996), covering much of the same ground as the *Program Summary*; a feature article on IS 218 from the *New York Times* (1993); an undated manuscript by Mortimore and Whitty of the London Institute of Education, asking 'Can school improvement overcome the effects of disadvantage?'; and a set of OHP slides (source unknown) on a 'Multi-agency approach to lifelong learning'. Anne Marie McDonald, a teacher in the pilot New Community School in Clydebank (personal communication), was keen to find out more about the thinking behind the NCS. On trying to borrow a copy of Dryfoos (1994), which was liberally referenced in the Scottish New Community Schools discourse, she discovered that there was no copy available for loan in the United Kingdom and she had to import a copy from the USA.

Nine months after the Quality in Education seminar, on this apparently flimsy evidential base, Donald Dewar announced 'one of the most innovative and modern initiatives ever carried out in British education' (Scottish Office 1998a: 1) – as we have suggested above, one of the flagships of New Labour's 'joined-up government'.

The *New Community Schools Prospectus* (Scottish Office 1998b) called for proposals from local authorities for First Phase of a pilot programme, to start by April 1999. Five, later seven, 'development project' New Community Schools had already been identified for immediate starts in 1998. Two Phases subsequent to that of April 1999 were envisaged, with eventual annual funding of £12 million to establish at least two New Community Schools in each of the thirty-two local authorities by 2001. The *Prospectus* defined the 'Essential Characteristics' of New Community Schools as:

(a) a focus on all the needs of all pupils at the school;
(b) engagement with families;
(c) engagement with communities;
(d) integrated provision of school education, informal as well as formal education, social work and health education and promotion services;
(e) integrated management;
(f) arrangements for the delivery of these services according to a set of integrated objectives and measurable outcomes;
(g) commitment and leadership;
(h) multi-disciplinary training and staff development.

(Scottish Office 1998b: 8–9)

In addition to these eight necessary criteria (and formal status as a 'health promoting school') there was a further list of fifteen criteria, of which New Community Schools were likely to have 'most if not all'; these covered areas such as a flexible curriculum, extended family services and childcare, engagement with informal and lifelong learning and with higher education (Scottish Office 1998b: 10–11) An 'essential structure' for the New Community Schools were to be Personal Learning Plans by which each pupil would be assessed and 'a programme of development agreed with, *and to be supported by* parents, including targets for attainment' (Scottish Office 1998b: 11, emphasis added). The New Community Schools were to be pilots of Personal Learning Plans, which would be extended to all schools in Scotland.

Preference in selection of First Phase bids was offered to those focusing on clusters of primary schools in deprived areas which sought to forge links with the pre-5 and secondary sectors. The funding offered (£200k p.a. per New Community School) was not to cover the costs of existing service delivery by education, social work and health authorities, but the costs of integrated management, multi-disciplinary training and parental and community consultation.

With forty-five New Community Schools projects currently having run for a maximum of two years, involving over 200 schools, each being in the early stages of being evaluated locally and nationally, the dynamics of the policy on the ground are only now beginning to be surveyed (see, for example, Nixon 2001). What is possible, and revealing, is to deconstruct the implicit and explicit self-definitions of the New Community Schools policy through the staff training material produced, the required framework for the national evaluation and the self-definition recently offered by Braidfield High, one of the first 'development' project New Community Schools, on the New Community Schools website.

The Scottish Executive commissioned the University of Strathclyde to produce training materials for the New Community Schools. These consisted of ten Units, each lasting for approximately half a day, which were placed on the New Community Schools website (http://scotland.gov.uk/education/new communityschools). Seven outcomes from the training were anticipated, six of which are exclusively concerned with inter-professional relations; the seventh is concerned with how multi-disciplinary working can identify and support vulnerable children. The structure of the Units reflects these expected outcomes, with eight of the ten Units concerned with professional roles and processes with a target audience of professionals. Parents and the community are invited into the other two Units: *Inclusion/Exclusion* (which considers how professionals include and exclude and the processes by which young people and the community are excluded); and *Community Profiling* (which considers how data might be gathered on a standard range of indicators of deprivation and how 'local leadership' might be identified). Significantly, one Activity in this Unit, 'Identifying community glue', equates 'community' with the professionals of the area, focusing exclusively on the management processes of New Community Schools.

The tender document *New Community Schools: Framework for National Evaluation* provided detailed insight into the operational definition of New Community

Schools as it 'is intended to range comprehensively across aspects of New Community Schools' (Scottish Executive 1999: 2). Three 'strands' were defined: Strand 1 was concerned with evaluating the 'Essential Characteristics' above; Strand 2 was concerned with 'Monitoring Outcomes'. Strand 3 'the largest, most ambitious and most important' (Scottish Executive 1999: 20) was concerned with a summative evaluation of all the New Community Schools sites in terms of six research questions.

In Strand 1, thirty-two domains for the collection of data were identified, with pupils, parents and the community being sources of data in only seven of these. The remaining twenty-five domains were overwhelmingly concerned with issues such as 'the role, status and effectiveness of' a range of management and inter-professional relations. Where data were sought from pupils, parents and the community, they were focused on 'perceptions' of the New Community Schools and the provision of services and on the mechanisms for 'consultation' with the community. 'Empowerment' of the community did appear in one place as 'requests from pupils and their parents for improvement to the New Community Schools and/or its activities' (Scottish Executive 1999: 6).

In Strand 2, the document defines the measurable outcomes to be used to assess the achievement of the 'integrated objectives' of Essential Characteristic (f) (above). This Strand sought to monitor the outcomes of New Community Schools over time for successive cohorts of pupils and for target groups of vulnerable children ('looked after' children; the bottom quintile in terms of achievement; pupils with special educational needs). For each of the groups, four pages of detailed performance indicators were defined in terms of attainment test outcomes, free school meals, pupil self-esteem, pupil absences, staff absences, exclusions from school, inclusion of children with special educational needs, health education, health services, pupil lifestyles, community involvement, children known to social work and/or on the child protection register.

Strand 3 outlined the six domains and the data definitive of an 'effective' New Community School: the establishment of integrated inter-professional mechanisms; raised pupil attainments in public tests and examinations; raised educational expectations of participation in further and higher education and lifelong learning; reduced social problems such as crime, exclusions from school and low self-esteem; reduced social work involvement; improved pupil health.

The training materials and tender document were both operational definitions of New Community Schools from national agencies. The presentation to a New Community Schools Development Seminar in 1999 by Ian McMurdo (Director of Education, West Dumbartonshire) on Braidfield High presented a certain local definition (McMurdo 1999). A genealogy for the New Community Schools initiative in Clydebank was established in the existing practices in West Dumbartonshire Council, in the involvement of partner agencies and in a commitment to treat New Community Schools as 'a prototype of future service delivery across the Council' (McMurdo 1999: 2). The identification of Braidfield High as a site for the 1998 'development project' phase was attributed to its being in an area of multiple deprivation already subject to special area-based social policies, to its existing facilities and to the enthusiasm of the head teacher and staff. Most space was devoted to budgetary and management issues, with the steering committee of nine senior managers from local agencies plus one parent member of the school board being seen 'as crucial to effective delivery'. Apart from this sole parent representative, the community only appeared in McMurdo's vision of a New Community School as being multiply deprived and as part of a School/Parental/Business/Community Partnership; parents only appeared in McMurdo's vision as in need of support from 'joined-up working' in order to attain social inclusion, lifelong learning and active citizenship; pupils only appeared in McMurdo's vision as in need of support, of higher attainments, of healthier lifestyles and of social work alternatives to exclusion from school.

New authoritarianism?

We may start drawing conclusions about New Community Schools on a note of bewilderment about the origins and development of a policy which, as we have seen above, was launched as highly significant not only for education but for the whole 'social inclusion' agenda in Scotland, and which subsequently has been held up as a model of 'joined-up government' for the United Kingdom. Any 'rational' ideal model of research and policy development and implementation would suggest that a policy of such significance would be preceded by a period of systematic exploration of research evidence, and option appraisal and policy development. Instead, it appears that it was introduced within a year of first consideration in Scotland on the basis of 'The Pack' of dated secondary American material notable more for its enthusiasm for Full Service Schools than its analytic perspective. The attempt by HM Senior Chief Inspector Osler to establish a genealogy for the policy in the work of HMI since 1988 has an air of desperation about it. If such a 'rational' explanation of the policy is not tenable, then how can it be explained?

In part, the particular nature of the political cycle in Britain forces policy development away from the 'rational' ideal. With an unpredictable electoral cycle, essentially unfunded political parties and a civil service tied exclusively to the government of the day, the long-term development of policy becomes almost impossible. Although some interest in Full Service Schools had been expressed by New Labour in 1996, there were not the mechanisms to develop this into an operable policy. The political imperative for the New Labour government to be seen to be acting radically on issues of education and social inclusion in the new Scottish Parliament dictated that a headline initiative had to be launched in short order (but with a long heritage).

Such an organisational explanation of the strange birth of New Community Schools does not, however, help us understand why such an initiative was taken in the particular form at the particular time with the particular state logic implicit within it. It was suggested at the beginning of this chapter that New Community Schools represented a condensation of several different themes in

Scottish society. Having surveyed the first phases of the New Community Schools, we can now specify the main *motifs* of this condensation and their implications for the Scottish polity and civil society.

In part, the New Community Schools initiative can be explained by the central place of 'community' and 'education' in the Scottish political tradition at a point in time when a Scottish Parliament has been recently re-established. In part, it can be explained by the concern to restructure the organs of state into more 'corporate' modes which emerged thirty years ago but which have received a major new inflection as part of the New Labour project of modernisation through 'joined-up policy'. Similarly, the New Community Schools initiative has a long genealogy, from the Plowden Educational Priority Area experiments of the late 1960s, of attempting to address areas of social crisis through community schools. With these narratives already well established, their combination into New Community Schools was a matter requiring little additional ideological work. Addressing the questions raised at the beginning of the 'New Community Schools' section above gives access to the political logic of this condensation.

Are New Community Schools new?

The route from Henry Morris's Cambridgeshire Village Colleges via the inner-city primary schools of the Educational Priority Area experiments, the new build multi-facility centres of Wester Hailes or Cheetham Hill, to the New Community School clusters in each Scottish local authority is a tortuous one (Baron 1989; Martin 1996). One distinctive feature of that route is the gradual transition from Morris's vision of the Village College, as the facilitator of education organic to the local community, to community schools as the closer co-ordination of the agencies of the state. The findings of Tett *et al.* in this volume suggest that currently community education throughout Scotland is heavily defined in terms of inter-agency collaboration and very little in terms of the participation of local people in decision-making about the education available to themselves (as adults or as children). Similarly, the work of Lloyd *et al.* in this volume documents the development of mechanisms for preventing school exclusion which are almost entirely administrative and do not involve any challenge to the existing micro-practices of schools leading to exclusions.

The almost exclusive focus in the New Community Schools initiative on the closer integration of the agencies of the state does not, therefore, represent a departure from the current Scottish repertoire, but rather a further administrative mechanism for its realisation. In their 'vision' of community education, Tett *et al.* propose three strategic purposes for community education: parents as partners; community development; democratic renewal. The extent to which the New Community Schools initiative displays these purposes can be assessed through addressing the other questions posed at the beginning of the 'New Community Schools' section above.

Do New Community Schools, as pioneers of 'joined-up government' 'involve and meet the needs of all different groups in society' (Stationery Office 1999)?

The *New Community Schools Prospectus* has a sustained implicit and explicit emphasis on 'areas of deprivation', an assumption elaborated and operationalised in the training materials and evaluation criteria and realised in the selection of schools for conversion. It would thus appear that New Community Schools are not 'for all groups' but are targeted at areas of social crisis. The 'needs' there to be met are not those defined by the people of the locality but are those defined by the various professional groups involved (principally officials in the Scottish Executive). Further than this, practical definitions of 'need' by local people (for example, the need to escape the boredom of school by leaving at the earliest opportunity) are taken as pathological, the cultures to be changed by the professionals. Despite Halsey's 1972 conclusion from the Educational Priority Areas experiment that education cannot offer solutions to economic problems, the New Community Schools (and wide areas of social policy) are predicated on the assumption that raising individual levels of educational attainment will address the structural inequalities of British society. In this context, the understanding of the American Full Service School has been at a surface level only, the co-location and co-ordination of human services. Where the Full Service School meets the demand for the social welfare services necessary for survival (especially health services) which would not otherwise be available to the poor of New York, the New Community School focuses on the intermeshing and propagation of services which are readily available but largely unused, if not rejected, in Scotland. This leads on to a second question about New Community Schools raised earlier.

Do the New Community Schools represent a renewed accountability of the professions to the communities which they serve?

The focus of the New Community Schools as projected in the *Prospectus* and the training materials, and as reported by McMurdo (1999), is firmly on the restructuring of professional boundaries to allow easier transaction across these boundaries. In this, the New Community Schools represent a increasing professionalisation of the issues of deprivation. There is little evidence in the New Community Schools discourse of lay people increasing their power through making professionals accountable to the local community. Apart from some formal representation of management groups, 'the community' is to be consulted on terms which the professionals determine. Community 'empowerment' is defined as people making suggestions about changes in the New Community School. In training, 'the community' is only invited in to learn how it is to be profiled (as a passive object of study) and how it is socially excluded. If the New Community Schools do not represent a renewed accountability of professionals to their local communities, do they show evidence of the other tendency which Paterson suggested, an increased allegiance to the central state?

Does the New Community Schools initiative demonstrate devolution of power beyond Holyrood (and Victoria Quay)?

In the critiques of New Labour by Jacques, Hall and others (1998), a main theme is how little New Labour has moved from the Thatcherite neo-liberal economic agenda. What is not developed there is a critique of New Labour in terms of its continuation of the Thatcherite project of re-forming the state into a more authoritarian and centralised mode, a task which New Labour has set about with considerable enthusiasm. Such authoritarianism, based in New Labour's assumption that it itself is the expression of the British 'moral community', manifests itself across the range of social policies (especially in the Home Office and in Social Security). In terms of the New Community Schools, it manifests itself in the classic Thatcherite device of simultaneous centralisation and decentralisation. While the formulation of New Community Schools proposals for time-limited funding and the day-to-day operations are locally determined, the Scottish Executive, through the definition of essential and desirable characteristics of New Community Schools and, most particularly, through the fine-grained specification of success criteria in terms of the increased effectiveness of mechanisms of formal and informal social control, has established new forms of governance over a significant proportion of Scotland's welfare professionals and thus, it hopes, over the major localities of social crisis.

By way of conclusion we may now turn to the question which, we suggested above, Paterson did not ask in his discussion of the future relationship between Scottish civil society and the state: *What if the state increasingly seeks to colonise and control the civic?* In the New Community Schools initiative there is no evidence of civil society being able to regulate the action of the state. Conversely, there is an unambiguous tendency for the organs of state both to centralise power and to seek to penetrate certain sectors of civil society in order to disrupt the existing cultural mechanisms. In their analysis of the home–school discourse of the past twenty years, Vincent and Tomlinson (1997) see a 'swarming of disciplinary mechanisms' into the child's home: the New Community Schools would seem to represent not only a swarming of disciplinary mechanisms but also their increasing ordering and co-ordination.

For those hoping for 'democratic renewal' through the new Scottish Parliament this is a depressing conclusion, a conclusion which may be tempered by identification of two 'resources of hope'. First, the recent Scottish Qualifications Agency crisis suggests that the 'state' is not as monolithic as the analysis above implies (Paterson 2000c). In the face of what appears to be mismanagement on an astonishing scale by one of the central organs of the educational establishment, the grounds for an alliance between parts of the state and civil society, notably radical Members of the Scottish Parliament and local councillors, classroom teachers and parents, have been formed. Whether such an alliance can fully coalesce and challenge the definitions of the purpose, content and process of schooling currently imposed by the leadership class of Scottish education remains to be seen.

The other 'resource of hope' is that documented by Nixon (2001) in one of the New Community Schools areas. Here, he suggests that the New Community School should carry the potential for establishing the conditions specified by Apple and Beane for renewing the 'old idea of … democracy' (Nixon 2001: 6–7). He identifies professionals working in one New Community School as developing a more democratic repertoire in their relationship with local people in terms of three very ordinary activities:

- the Community Liaison Group, through which different futures for the locality are envisaged and during the process of which the meaning of being a 'professional' is challenged and re-formed;
- the Breakfast and After-School Club, which creates a 'border country' between private and public in which children are encouraged to develop their sense of responsibility for themselves and for others;
- the Personal Learning Plan, through which pupils develop 'the very Scottish culture of self-improvement and reliance, of corporate responsibility and accountability, of regard for one's own well-being and for the well-being of others'.

(Nixon 2001: 13)

At 'street level', it would seem that the 'common sense' of Scottish civil society with which we started this chapter is far from moribund.

Notes

1   I am greatly indebted to the editors, Jon Nixon, Lindsay Paterson and Melanie Walker for comments on a draft of this chapter, and to Martyn Roebuck for casting an Inspectorial eye over the text. Anne Marie McDonald of Braidfield High School, Clydebank, sourced a considerable amount of original material on Full Service Schools and traced the circulation of 'The Pack' within the Scottish policy community.
2   Respectively the site of the new Scottish Parliament building and the main offices of the civil servants of the Scottish Executive.

References

'After Socialism?' Group, Centre for Theology and Public Issues (1998) *Beyond Fear: Vision, Hope and Generosity*, Edinburgh: St Andrew Press.

Baron, S. (1988) 'Community and the limits of social democracy', in A.G. Green and S.J. Ball (eds) *Progress and Inequality in Comprehensive Education*, London: Routledge.

——(1989) 'Community education: from the Cam to the Rea', in L. Barton and S. Walker (eds) *Politics and the Process of Schooling*, Buckingham: Open University Press.

——(forthcoming) *Community and Control: Surveillance, Containment and the State*, Hounslow: Pearson Education.

Blair, T. (1991) 'Forging a new agenda', *Marxism Today*, October: 32–4.

——(1994) *Socialism*, Fabian Pamphlet 565, London: The Fabian Society.

Brown, G. (1994) 'The politics of potential: a new agenda for Labour', in D. Miliband (ed.) *Reinventing the Left*, Cambridge: Polity.

Cabinet Office (2000) *Wiring It Up: Whitehall's Management of Cross-Cutting Policies and Services*, http//www.cabinet-office.gov.uk/innovation/2000/wiring/coiwire.pdf: accessed 14.24 on 21 December 2000.

CCCS (Centre for Contemporary Cultural Studies) (1981) *Unpopular Education: Schooling and Social Democracy in England Since 1944*, London: Hutchinson.

Children's Aid Society (1996a) *Community School: Program Summary*, New York: Children's Aid Society.

——(1996b) *Newsletter*, New York: Children's Aid Society.

——(1997) *Building a Community School*, revised edition, New York: Children's Aid Society.

Dryfoos, J.G. (1994) *Full Service Schools: A Revolution in Health and Social Services*, San Francisco: Jossey-Bass.

——(1996) 'Full Service Schools', *Educational Leadership*, April: 18–23.

Educational Institute of Scotland (1996) *Education and a Scottish Parliament*, Edinburgh: Educational Institute of Scotland.

Edwards, O.D. (1989) *A Claim of Right for Scotland*, Edinburgh: Polygon.

Fairley, J. and Paterson, L. (2000) 'Scottish education and social justice', *Education and Social Justice*, 2(3): 39–50.

Gray, J., McPherson, A.F. and Raffe, D. (1983) *Reconstructions of Secondary Education*, London: Routledge and Kegan Paul.

Hall, S. (1998) 'The Great Moving Nowhere Show', *Marxism Today*, November/December: 9–14.

Halsey, A.H. (1972) *Educational Priority: EPA Problems and Policies*, London: HMSO.

Jacques, M. (1998) 'Good to be back', *Marxism Today*, November/December: 2–3.

Jones, T. (1996) *Re-Making the Labour Party*, London: Routledge.

McMurdo, I. (1999) 'Braidfield High School, West Dumbartonshire', presentation to New Community Schools Development Seminar, http://www.scotland.gov.uk/education/newcommunityschools/dev5.htm, accessed 14.35 on 7 December 2000.

Martin, I. (1996) 'Community education: the dialectics of development', in R. Fieldhouse (ed.) *A History of Modern British Adult Education*, Leicester: National Institute of Adult Education.

Mortimore, P. and Whitty, G. (no date) 'Can school improvement overcome the effects of disadvantage?' London: Institute of Education, University of London.

New York Times (1993) 'Public school offers a social service model', 8 December, A1 and B8.

Nixon, J. (2001) 'Learning as democratic action', manuscript, University of Sheffield.

Paterson, L. (2000a) 'Civil society and democratic renewal', in S. Baron, J. Field and T. Schuller (eds) *Social Capital: Critical Perspectives*, Oxford: Oxford University Press.

——(2000b) 'Scottish democracy and Scottish Utopias: the first year of the Scottish Parliament', *Scottish Affairs*, 33, Autumn: 45–61.

——(2000c) *Crisis in the Classroom*, Edinburgh: Mainstream.

Scotland, J. (1969) *The History of Scottish Education*, vol. 1, London: University of London Press.

Scottish Constitutional Convention (1995) *Scotland's Parliament. Scotland's Right*, Edinburgh: Scottish Constitutional Convention.

Scottish Executive (1999) *New Community Schools: Framework for National Evaluation*, Edinburgh: Scottish Executive.

——(2000) *Making a Difference: Effective Implementation of Cross-Cutting Policy*, Edinburgh: Scottish Executive.

Scottish Office (1998a) 'Scotland leads the way with radical plan for New Community Schools', news release 2254/98, Edinburgh: The Scottish Office.

——(1998b) *New Community Schools Prospectus*, Edinburgh: The Scottish Office.

Stationery Office (1999) *Modernising Government*, Cm 4310, London: Her Majesty's Stationery Office.

Vincent, C. and Tomlinson, S. (1997) 'Home–school relationships: "the swarming of disciplinary mechanisms"?', *British Educational Research Journal*, 23(3): 361–77.

7 Schools, community education and collaborative practice in Scotland

Lyn Tett, Pamela Munn, Helen Kay, Ian Martin, Jane Martin and Stewart Ranson

Introduction

Schools are envisaged as playing a key role in the current UK government's policy to promote social inclusion among children and young people in particular and in tackling social exclusion in general. The Social Inclusion Strategy for Scotland stresses that: 'the Government is investing heavily in programmes to promote inclusion among school-age children, including New Community Schools, Early Intervention Schemes, Alternatives to Exclusion from School and Family Literacy' (Scottish Office 1999a: 7). Furthermore, it is recognised that schools on their own cannot solve the problems associated with social exclusion. The long-term objective is to develop ways of working which integrate programmes not just within government, but at all levels of action right down to local neighbourhoods and communities (Scottish Office 1999b: 1). Thus schools are expected to work with other agencies both to prevent social exclusion taking place and to help rein-tegrate those who have been socially excluded into mainstream society.

It is not the purpose of this chapter either to analyse the government's conceptualisation of social exclusion or to comment on its policy for tackling it, save to point out that this agenda has two broad aspects: individual and community. Thus, for example, there is an emphasis on the achievement of individual children and young people, via the importance placed on literacy and numeracy and on raising attainment levels in general. There is also a desire to tackle the problems of excluded communities using health and housing initiatives and, in the school sector, a desire in England and Wales to see a timetabled slot for citizenship education. Rather, our starting point is that in the current policy context schools are expected to work with other agencies such as social work services, health services, housing agencies, community education services and local community groups to help tackle social exclusion and promote social inclusion. We already know a great deal about the problems and pitfalls of schools' work with other agencies (see Armstrong and Galloway 1994; Dyson and Robson 1999; Lloyd 1999; Kendrick 1995). These include territorial battles over budgets, different professional ideologies and structural barriers in terms of line management and reporting as well as the rather different legislative frameworks that impact on professionals. The Children Acts of 1989 and 1995 in England and

Scotland respectively, for instance, explicitly adopt a children's rights philosophy which is markedly absent in education legislation in both countries.

Little is known, however, about the nature and extent of links between schools and local agencies, including local communities. This chapter reports the findings of the first major research study in Scotland to map these links and to explore examples of effective practice in collaboration between schools and other agencies. The research was undertaken in two stages to provide breadth and depth to the findings. The first stage provided a statistical overview and a map of local community education initiatives. There was a particular emphasis on the changing local authority contexts since local government had been reorganised from a two-tier to a single-tier structure at the time of the research. The second stage of the project selected and studied in depth the links formed between ten case-study schools and their local communities.

In the first stage, three national postal surveys were undertaken in 1997 to provide an all-round perspective on schools' relationships with local community education providers, who comprise local authority and voluntary sector organisations working with young people and adults in a range of informal educational contexts. The first survey, completed by head teachers or their deputies, collected information about school links with these providers. The second survey asked the Principal Community Education Officers in the thirty-two local councils to define the key purposes of work in their areas. The third survey sought information from Chief Executive Officers on the local policy context, with particular reference to organisational structure and the extent of decentralised decision-making in the thirty-two council areas. Here we report on the findings of these surveys and the subsequent in-depth analysis of ten case-study schools.

Using these data we will, first, focus on the details of collaboration as described by the schools in order to identify the extent of the base on which the integrated service delivery envisaged by government policy would need to build. Such policy is predicated on the assumption that learning needs in the community are many-sided, and meeting them partly depends on professionals with different skills working together. We will then go on to examine key dimensions of collaborative practice revealed by a more detailed analysis of the case studies, with a view to highlighting rather different models of collaboration which, in turn, promote rather different notions of social inclusion. It should be noted that while the focus is on one particular researched activity there were usually many other collaborative activities taking place in the case-study location. Indeed, the activity could be at the centre of a complex web of relationships between the school and a variety of community education organisations.

The extent and nature of school–community links

The initial survey of all Scottish schools elicited information on three key elements of school–community links: provision, collaboration and participation. First, three aspects of community education *provision* were explored from the schools' perspective. These were: the provision of facilities (including community rooms and libraries); the provision of adult learning opportunities (including parent education and guidance for adults in the community); and the provision of opportunities for young people (including youth groups and after-school clubs). Second, information was collected on school *collaboration* with community education providers: which providers did schools work with most often to develop, manage, deliver, fund and evaluate four core activities, that is, the formal curriculum, the hidden curriculum, extra-curricular activities and support for individual pupils? The third aspect explored was *participation* in decision-making. Information was collected on representative groups who were involved in schools, including school boards, parent–teacher associations and pupil councils, and whether and to what extent they were involved in school development planning (SDP). Each of the three aspects contained items which were successively more demanding. For example, under 'provision', the letting of rooms was viewed as less demanding than the provision of adult education opportunities or the provision of after-school clubs. Furthermore, each of the aspects was seen as successively more demanding of collaborative activity. Thus it was less demanding to provide opportunities than to share decision-making about school matters.

The results of our analysis of the 1,687 returned questionnaires from primary and secondary schools (64 per cent of the sample) are detailed below in terms of the categories outlined above (see Blair *et al.* 1998 for further details).

Provision

While most schools reported that they let accommodation to community groups, the offering of other, more challenging opportunities to the local community was rarer. Schools were clearly more likely to offer provision that put little strain on – or indeed, enhanced – limited resources. Most schools' provision appeared designed to enhance as far as possible – or, at least, not to disturb – their core business of educating children.

Collaboration

Respondents reported very little collaborative practice: that which was reported tended to centre on the formal curriculum and take place with other schools. While collaboration tended to involve the joint creation and delivery of activities, joint funding and management arrangements were far less common. Collaboration with community groups, local authority community education services and voluntary agencies together constituted only 20 per cent of collaborative occurrences.

Participation in decision-making

School governance and management were more representative than participatory. Professional control of schools was evidenced by the predominance of professional educators in school groups and school development planning. Likewise, community groups and customer groups were less common in schools, leading us to speculate that most schools defined their communities primarily in terms of their student constituency rather than their locales.

Schools and collaborative practice

While most schools did not have strong links with their communities we wanted to study further those that did. In order to do this we identified schools that had strong school–community links in the three areas of provision, collaboration and participation in decision-making outlined above. From these, ten case studies of different community education locations were selected which represented a range of: local authority types; schools' demographic characteristics; community partners; and activities. Four different categories of collaborative activity were studied: school–home–community links; health education; work with troubled children and young people; adult education. These activities were known to be providing challenging opportunities for partnership and collaboration in many schools, as they frequently required particular kinds of expertise that most teachers do not have. Moreover, these activities were areas of policy interest when the research was undertaken (see Tett *et al.* 1998 for further details).

The schools selected as case studies had taken part in at least one of these collaborative activities. Representatives of the partners and participants in the collaborative activity, including the head teacher and teachers, parents and pupils, local authority managers, community and voluntary workers, were inter-viewed in each of the ten localities. A topic list was used as guidance for the interviews; the questions asked focused on a description of the identified activity including the history of its development, its current operation and issues relating to collaboration and participation between the school and other community and voluntary organisations. Other issues covered were the description of the school and its community, the community education system and the policy context. All these interviews were transcribed and analysed. Documentary material relating to the identified activity as well as to the school was collected and used to inform the interview data.

The study found that in general there were three principal factors that contributed to effective collaboration:

- *added value from collaboration*: effective collaboration was sustained where all partners were able to achieve 'more' with 'less'. This was exemplified in the adult education activities, where resources of space, facilities and staff expertise had been used to provide more opportunities for both adults and pupils;
- *extended range of provision due to collaboration*: only through collaboration in the health education programmes and the home/school/community projects were providers able to offer sufficient breadth in the scale and scope of interventions;

- *complementarity in provision*: the most demanding form of collaboration was required to deal with situations involving complex social issues such as social exclusion, defined by the European Community (1993: 10) as: 'the multiple and changing factors resulting in people being excluded from the normal exchanges, practices and rights of modern society'. In particular, work with troubled young people required multi-organisational approaches.

It was hypothesised that organisations would need to share – or at least not have conflicting – values, purposes, tasks and conditions for collaboration to be effective and for satisfactory partnerships to be developed. This was confirmed by the research which showed how ostensibly the same collaborative activity might, in different settings:

- be underpinned by rather different values;
- have different purposes;
- define tasks differentially in order to realise these purposes;
- deliver community education under a variety of conditions.

Table 7.1 summarises these key differences by comparing the same collaborative activity in different case-study schools, in terms of values, purposes, tasks and conditions of the partners involved. Thus partners working together may have conflicting values and purposes: they may see the task differently and they may be operating under different conditions.

The study highlighted some of the resultant tensions between potential partners:

- In adult education activities there were tensions between those committed primarily to supporting the academic achievement of pupils and those whose aim additionally was to increase the involvement of the wider community.
- In the projects designed to promote home/school/community links there were conflicting perspectives of parent involvement. For some, there was an expectation that parents would learn to extend an interest in the development of their own children's education by learning how to work as unpaid classroom helpers. For others, the emphasis was placed on the recognition of the parent's own educational needs and the development of appropriate learning experiences for the parent as an individual.
- Another constraint to effective collaboration was the competing professional cultures and traditions which limited the type of collaboration considered feasible; this was evident in the health education projects, where different approaches to sexual health education led to conflicts between youth workers and school teachers.
- A final constraint was lack of time and money. This was especially evident in the voluntary sector, where dependence on short-term external funding,

Table 7.1 Summary of key differences in the activities

	Adult education	Health education	Home/school/community links	Troubled young people
Values	Proactively promoting equality of opportunity *vs* Reactively responding to community	Achieving measurable educational outcomes *vs* Collaboration to achieve academic and social goals	Meeting needs of parents as well as children *vs* Parents' role to be involved in education of children	Social and academic education for all *vs* Academic education for majority undisturbed by disaffected young people
Purposes	Providing education for pupils *vs* Providing for whole community	Promoting sense of community *vs* Providing information	Promoting parents' own education *vs* Supporting children's education	Involving young people in decision-making *vs* Minimising effect of problematic behaviour
Tasks	Providing responsive education *vs* School-focused education	Active collaboration *vs* Providing services	Community education best able to involve parents *vs* Head teacher best able to involve parents	Developing all pupils socially and academically *vs* Sub-contracting out of difficult pupils
Conditions	Provision of programme *vs* Participation in decision-making	Promoting academic standards *vs* Promoting safe and friendly environment for all	Utilising skills of identified community worker *vs* No additional staff resources available to school	Collaborative sharing of expertise *vs* Complementarity of expertise

subject to competitive bidding, was a key constraint in planning and sustaining collaborative work with troubled young people.

Despite the difficulties described above, respondents identified a number of benefits from collaborative action:

- the opportunity to develop a broader curriculum;
- making school facilities available to the wider community;
- access to a wider range of skills and expertise;
- the co-ordination of a range of different services which contribute to educational work in communities;
- the growth in adult confidence which develops from the wider conception of their role as educators;
- the development of employment as a way out of poverty through a range of programmes;
- an understanding that the school is part of the community and the recognition of the complementarity of the contribution that each can make to the other.

The local authority context

The management structure in local authorities has had an effect in each area on the strategic planning for community education as provided through the community education service and through community and voluntary groups. Severe budget cuts, on top of local government reorganisation in 1995, have led local authorities to experiment with new management structures, but only some of these have been successful in developing and implementing new policies for the delivery of community education, in the view of our interview sample.

The role of the Community Education Service varied across and within local authorities. In some areas there was an emphasis on the *strategic development* of work in terms of commissioning, monitoring and evaluating the services provided by community and voluntary groups. In other areas, Community Education Service workers were *involved directly* in the provision of community education.

There was a diversity of perceptions among local authority managers of the purpose of community education, some aiming for universal provision, others targeting resources on particular areas and initiatives. There was also a diversity of arrangements for the delivery of community education.

The general reduction in funding had led to a review of priorities in the Community Education Service and new ways of working had been introduced. Several authorities had focused on the development of home–school–community links as a priority. Some schools in these areas were being encouraged and supported by the authority to develop parental education through projects run by the Community Education Service which promoted parental involvement in their children's education and in community organisations.

With the development of inter-departmental co-operation, several case-study authorities were developing links between the Community Education Service and Departments of Economic Development to provide vocational training for adults and young people that would support regeneration and provide continuing education. In addition, new approaches were being developed in youth work to give young people more 'voice' in the affairs of institutions and the community.

The relationship between councillors and their communities was also changing. Local authorities were searching for new ways to consult and involve their local communities: councillors in some areas were more involved in meeting local representatives and seeing for themselves the outcomes of local projects. The Community Education Service was perceived as having a strategic role to play in supporting community participation in emergent forums which, in some local authorities, were taking on a central role in local democratic renewal.

Overall, strategic thinking by local authorities on the relationship between schools and community education was at an early stage of development. Consequently, many collaborative activities between schools and community education were being developed in practice-based environments without the support of a council policy.

Frameworks for understanding the variety of practice

The analysis of the data relating to collaborative practice in schools and the pattern of provision in local authorities led to the conclusion that differing conceptions of the purposes of community education, and the structures required to fulfil these purposes, turn on two fundamental dimensions of practice:

- institutional boundaries;
- pedagogic purpose.

Underpinning these dimensions were different ideas about the role of local authorities in encouraging participation in local decision-making. In addition, the rather different, even rival, professional socialisation and traditions of teachers on the one hand and community education workers on the other illuminated the analysis. First, however, a brief description of the two dimensions of practice is provided at the two levels of analysis, the school and the local authority.

Institutional boundaries at the school level

Each profession defines itself in terms of specialist skills and knowledge. Such specialisation helps to distinguish one profession from another. It also separates the professional from the lay member of the public. In understanding different approaches to collaborative practice, it is important to acknowledge the existence of *professional boundaries* and to examine whether such distinctions of professional knowledge and skills are sharply defined or blurred.

Pedagogic purpose and practice at the school level

The orientation of the community educator may be particularistic, focusing upon the personal and educational development of the individual, whether pupil, young person or adult. Alternatively it may be holistic, with a focus on the development of the community as a whole and a vision of learning as having a dual purpose in the development of both the individual and the community.

Institutional boundaries at the local authority level

Services may be organised in such a way that boundaries are certain to arise between different parts of the community education system, as between schools and the Community Education Service. Or there may be no strategic plan to bring rival departments together.

Pedagogic purpose and practice at the local authority level

In this area there is a continuum of purpose and practice. It ranges from an orientation towards community development that aims to encourage effective and responsible citizenship to an individualistic orientation, concerned with universal provision of education rather than being responsive to both the articulated and the unvoiced requirements of the community.

The relationship between these two dimensions results in a matrix of four quadrants in which the different purposes of community education can be characterised as follows:

- Quadrant A: individualistic perspective/high institutional boundaries (*student development*)

  The purpose of community education is designed to support the work of schools and focuses upon addressing the problems that frustrate the progress in the learning of students. Institutions define roles and rules in ways that can create a boundary between the school and other professionals, and between the school and community education professionals and the community.

- Quadrant B: holistic perspective/high institutional boundaries (*citizen development*)

  In this category the community education system recognises the challenges of social and economic regeneration: it is involved in education and training to enable members of the community not only to gain employment but also to improve the quality of individual lives. Yet professional and institutional traditions can still frustrate collaborative working.

- Quadrant C: holistic perspective/low institutional boundaries (*whole community development*)

  In this perspective, the local authority, the institutions and agencies recognise the importance of community development as well as lifelong learning. They form collaborative partnerships to ensure effective provision of education to enable members of the community to participate as citizens in the practice of local democracy.

- Quadrant D: individualistic perspective/low institutional boundaries (*individual development*)

  Community education seeks to support the learning needs of all individuals in the community: pupils; young people outside school; their parents; and the lifelong learning needs of adults in the community. To support these needs, institutions strive to become responsive to the expressed needs of the community and to establish collaborative patterns of working with other organisations and agencies. The quadrants are illustrated by Figure 7.1.

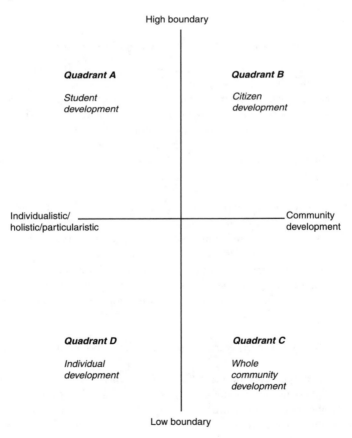

Figure 7.1   Pedagogic purpose and practice

Although some case studies provide examples of one model shaping the practice of the system as a whole for that area, other case studies show that different models can coexist in the same authority. The local authority may adopt a particular model in the development of its strategic policy, while at the same time individual schools within that local authority area can adopt a very different model in the direct provision of education. The data suggest that the distribution of interests and power in a locality will define which model predominates.

In examining the data, it was found that working partnerships always involved the agency of the people who were working together and the structures that made such interactions possible. Using the framework developed above, the key factors in particular models of partnership in community education are described and summarised in the following section.

High boundaries are the result of:

- the organisation and management process that leads to two partners having separate spheres of operation;
- declining resources that make it necessary for the partners to concentrate on what is considered their core business;
- situations where professional roles are in conflict;
- divergent views on the role of the participants in the activity, or the providers of the service, or both;
- different groups being given priority by the partners in the collaboration: for example, only the parents of pupils attending the school or only people living in poverty.

Low boundaries are the result of:

- management organisation and processes that place value on joint decision-making by the various partners;
- a commitment by institutions to collaborative working which includes the wider community;
- institutional responsiveness to the articulated views of the community;
- a shared view of the roles of either participants in the activity, or the providers of the service, or both;
- an appreciation of the strengths to be gained from the complementary roles of professional workers.

An individualistic approach is the result of:

- an emphasis on the individual growth of participants;
- no means for the community to raise problems of concern to them;
- not involving people in decision-making;
- not utilising or valuing the skills of the community;
- universalistic provision focused on individuals;

- predetermining policy and practice objectives;
- a focus on income-generating work that is responsive to the demands of the most articulate.

A community development approach is the result of:

- having mechanisms for, and a commitment to, responding effectively to the issues and problems identified by the community;
- the community having control over, or a least influence on, decision-making, and having the structures in place that allow such decisions to be implemented;
- having methods for developing the 'voice' of socially excluded groups and communities;
- a commitment to community participation in decision-making that leads to responsive, demand-led provision.

Overall, then, the analysis suggests that it is possible for partnerships to exist in a wide range of circumstances and situations. Where boundaries are low and a community development approach is taken, collaborative partnerships are more likely to encourage the development of democratic participation in local communities, a key goal of the policy to combat social exclusion. Such partnerships have at their core a commitment to lifelong learning and to promoting community capacity and empowerment.

A new role for schools?

Our research has also raised questions about the proper role of schools within a community education system. As Watt (1989: 185) points out: 'Community education transcends schools, but a community education process that bypasses schools is inconceivable.' However, the position of the school has often been ambiguous within a system that, as we have suggested, requires shared values and purposes between collaborative partners. Our case studies are typical of the wide range of networks within which schools work. As we have indicated, the conditions within which schools operate affect the types of collaborative activity in which they engage. The local socio-economic and political context will influence how a school can engage with parents and others to develop education for the community. But at a time when increasingly autonomous schools are being urged to work in 'partnership', there is a need to reflect on what type of school will best develop such partnerships. Building partnerships, as our frameworks have indicated, results in collaborative activity which supports both the values and purposes of the school and the values and purposes of the community. Such activity necessarily sits on the boundary between the school and community and is as much about schools' development as about community development. The successful school will be involved in community building and regeneration as a value and a purpose. This is what Sergiovanni (1994: 8–9) terms the '*gemeinschaft*' school – the school that values kinship, neighbourliness and collegiality above rational, contractual relationships (*gesellschaft*). Merz and Furman (1997), using the same theory, conclude that schools have become too '*gesellschaft*' which is undermining a sense of community. Schools which value community building and regard it as a prime institutional purpose will, we suggest, be more successful in shaping collaborative partnerships. This requires the community to be involved in shaping education and creating a learning community. While our case study schools provided examples of an interest in, and commitment to, a vision of learning communities and indeed demonstrated this in aspects of their practice, there are institutional barriers preventing '*gemeinschaft*' being at the heart of schooling – the purposes of teaching and learning.

One barrier is pedagogical, since many schools would claim to encourage lifelong learning, either directly through teaching approaches that promote enjoyment and a sense of achievement thereby enhancing motivation to learn in their pupils, and/or by encouraging adult participation. Yet the scope for a negotiated curriculum is heavily circumscribed in Scotland by the demands of the 5–14 curriculum, Standard Grade syllabuses and so on, and this is unlikely to change. Furthermore, the introduction of performance targets in terms of pupil attainment leads to teacher attention being focused on those aspects of the curriculum for which they are publicly accountable. This observation is not intended as a criticism of the curriculum in Scottish schools or to diminish the importance of key skills such as numeracy or literacy. Rather, it is to remind ourselves that the 'core business' of schools as currently constructed by education policy-makers is not identical to the key purposes of community education. This is explicitly recognised by teachers and community education workers themselves, as the following extract from one of our interviews makes clear.

INTERVIEWER: Is the community education service in the driving seat in initiating developments in relation to urban regeneration?

RESPONDENT (COMMUNITY EDUCATION MANAGER): We deliberately encourage the formation of education manager groups to look specifically at these kinds of areas but we're very often in the driving seat of getting these things started. A school is always first and foremost a school; all these other things could be seen as diversions. The Chair of Education said she was in the forefront of encouraging development of community schools as a resource, yet the school's priority must be to ensure that testing is going on and that the performance is going up all the time in relation to pupils.

Schools also have a very limited capacity currently to promote learning to participate in a democratic community. 'Citizenship education' and the like have as yet no place in the formal curriculum in Scotland. At most there is a very limited opportunity to pursue ideas about democracy and participation through provision for personal and social development. However, this provision in its own right has a small slot on the timetable in most schools and encompasses many other aspects of personhood beyond notions of active citizenship. The informal curriculum may provide experience of organising and managing clubs and societies. The hidden curriculum of schools typically sends messages about the hierarchical and status-driven nature of school organisation with little or no opportunity for pupil involvement in decision-making. There are a few notable exceptions, of course, where pupil councils or their equivalent play a real part in decisions about school life.

Certainly many schools work with parents as partners, both to improve children's learning and to enhance parents' own education. Yet even the most successful and dynamic schools in this regard would not claim to reach all parents and it was evident from our mapping study that the vast majority did not see themselves as actively involved in either community development or democratic renewal. This is not intended as a criticism of schools. Rather, it is to recognise the limited role they can play given current government priorities for schools and the severely constrained budgets under which they operate. Thus if we are to enact a vision of learning communities, schools as currently constituted can only be a small part in a much more complex system which will involve further and higher education institutions as well as the Community Education Service and voluntary organisations (Ranson 1994).

Each partner in collaboration brings their own tradition to community education that sets limits about what they can contribute to the whole. Head teachers as well as community education workers and managers acknowledge these limits in the contribution of each partner.

> We're teachers and we certainly have a community worker in the school, but the one thing you've got to be aware of is that the community worker in a community school isn't just there for the youth work. Originally I saw the youth project as requiring a skill level that we didn't have and if I could release a teacher then I would get both staff development and the staffing for the group required. One of my worries is that people think that you can just do it and I don't think you can. It's quite difficult and you have to have a skilled person, at least in the early stages, till you acquire these skills yourself.
>
> (Head teacher)

Discussion – towards a vision of community education

In the global age of information technology, learning will be at the centre for individuals, institutions and communities, as all will need to acquire new skills and capabilities to equip them for a world of continuing change, risk and uncertainty. The research findings suggest that community education is particularly well placed to address the needs of the learning age: that is, of developing the capabilities of individuals, of reaching out to build networks of collaborative learning and support, and of enabling community development and democratic renewal. The essence of learning in such a learning society is for citizens to recover their sense of agency, to learn to take more control over their lives and to work co-operatively with others to renew their communities (see SCEC 1995).

Discussions with teachers, local authority managers, community educators and voluntary organisations about who community education is for reveal a variety of purposes. Some are concerned that community education is seen as having primarily a social welfare function and being targeted only at the poor, when it should be accessible to all. Others argue that, in an ideal world, community education would be for everyone. However, the constraints of available resources and local authority and government priorities mean that community education will need to focus services on supporting disadvantaged communities, empowering local people to gain the confidence and skills to participate in local decision-making within their community. This broad community-based programme often includes working in partnership with economic regeneration teams to improve job opportunities, and gives a new role in facilitating the work of decentralised committees and forums.

The findings from the case studies suggest that this need to clarify a sense of direction is leading to an emphasis on three strategic purposes:

- *Parents as partners*: professionals across the community education system are increasingly recognising the significance of parents, as complementary educators enhancing their children's learning, as partners in the management and governance of schools, and as learners, all these activities contributing to the development of the community.
- *Community development*: this involves being responsive to community needs in the widest sense, supporting local involvement in democratic processes by working with and through local organisations. Community development is about supporting and encouraging people to become actively involved in the regeneration of their area.
- *Democratic renewal*: at the heart of this conception is the perceived potential of community education to contribute to the process of democratic renewal now under way in Scotland. Some local authorities recognise the potential; community education is an under-utilised service as far as democratic participation skills are concerned. Others have proceeded further, perceiving in an active local democracy an opportunity to build a learning partnership with the community for social and economic regeneration.

Informing the debate about meaning and purpose is an emergent reconceptualisation of community education. Teachers and community education workers can express a set of purposes, which captures the potential of community education to contribute to the issues that lie at the heart of social and economic regeneration. This implies a commitment to:

- inclusiveness;
- recognising social as well as academic goals;
- raising expectations through educational achievement;

- valuing complementary professional skills;
- involving local people in decision-making;
- democratic participation and active citizenship.

The community education system grows out of diverse institutions, agencies and services, each contributing its distinctive specialist knowledge and skills. It is possible for a school to be immersed in all the layers of purpose for community education and community regeneration. Yet this research suggests that institutions and services believe there are core functions that shape all their work. Schools, for example, face statutory constraints that, in the last resort, limit what they can contribute to the community education system as a whole. However, if they are to contribute their distinctive quality they need to work collaboratively in partnership with others. As Rigsby *et al.* (1995: 7) argue, 'A fruitful way to think about schools is to see them as structures that are intricately and irrevocably interwoven into others, all of which serve political, economic, cultural, religious and social aims.'

This study of the work of schools and of their collaborative activities shows that in each community there is a great diversity of learning needs which can only be addressed through a variety of professional skills. Plural interests and needs require the complementarity of specialisms. However, although joint professional development can reinforce the understanding and valuing of collaboration, the threats and pressures facing the community education system can accentuate the limits of professional boundaries.

Conclusion

The literature (e.g. Dyson and Robson 1999; Huxham, 1996; Shiver and Newburn 1996) and the case studies outlined above point to the very real possibilities of collaboration between schools and other agencies. They suggest that where professionals share a common purpose, where they are able to work jointly and where they are able to build up trust over time, then partnerships are successful. Collaboration, however, has endemic problems. These arise both from the different priorities that agencies establish and from the different definitions of 'need' that govern their work. This leads us to suggest that schools and community education have distinct but complementary roles to play in promoting active citizenship and in combating social exclusion. If such partnerships are to work towards the development of an inclusive education system that involves all children, parents and the wider community, there needs to be agreement about its meaning and purpose. Such a system requires, as Lloyd (2000: 267) suggests in the context of school exclusion, '[schools] emphasising both social and academic goals rather than narrowly academic aims, [having] ... flexible and open pupil–teacher and home–school relationships, strong interprofessional relationships, a supportive senior management and a responsive local authority'. However, despite the commitment of some teachers and schools to reach beyond the institution to serve and draw in the community, the pressure of public accountability systems on schools is likely to continue to focus attention on raising pupils' levels of attainment, easily (if not unproblematically) measured and described. Educational qualifications are a positional good, affecting entry to further and higher education and to the labour market. Increasing attainment is thus a very important aspect of the social inclusion agenda and a demanding goal for all involved.

It may be that the broader conception of education advocated by the Scottish Executive that 'the potential of all children can only be realised by addressing their needs in the round' (Scottish Office 1998: 2) will open out the opportunities for collaboration. However, in the end schools and community education have different kinds of 'core business'. Schools by themselves, as we have pointed out, have a limited capacity currently to promote learning to participate in a democratic community. This means that democratic renewal depends on a dual commitment by the new Scottish state: not only to use schooling to help prepare young people to become democratic citizens, but also to support and enhance people's capacity in civil society to be active citizens in a democracy. In other words, education needs communities as much as communities need education.

The findings from the study of collaborative partnerships on which this chapter is based and from work on developing 'inclusive' schools in the UK and the USA (see Ball 1998; Merz and Furman 1997; Rigsby *et al.* 1995; Tett *et al.* 2001) suggests that:

- A multi-agency approach to the needs of children and their parents provides added value, extends the range of provision available and provides the means of dealing with complex social situations such as those leading to social exclusion.
- Collaboration between the school, other professionals, parents and the community in multi-agency projects is difficult and requires time, effort and a sharing of perspectives if it is to be successful.
- Inter and intra professional training and discussion is essential if people are to understand the strengths to be gained from the complementary roles of the different professions.
- It is important that all agencies share and are committed to the aims of the project and that a holistic approach is taken that recognises both the internal school community and the external wider community.

Partnerships are potentially valuable if people are realistic about their possibilities and constraints. Community workers and other informal educators have a significant role to play in this, but first potentially difficult and divisive questions of purpose, values, tasks and conditions have to be tackled. On the evidence of the case studies and a critical reading of the relevant literature, policy-makers and practitioners need to be aware of the issues detailed above if they are to contribute to the move towards a more inclusive education system. The full potential of schools and community education can therefore only be realised when they are both seen as essential elements within a coherent and comprehensive *community education system.* This is understood as a way of organising education and making available opportunities for learning throughout life which is relevant and responsive to all communities of interest, aspiration and need (see Martin 1996). If democracy is to be renewed in Scotland, education, always a key signifier of cultural identity, must be at work in the lives of its diverse communities – in order, ultimately, to promote the common life in community (see Scottish Office 1999a). Such a learning society demands a commitment to the kind of dialogue that has always been part not only of the philosophy and pedagogy of community education but also of the distinctively Scottish traditions of democratic intellectualism and common sense (see MacIntyre 1981).

We speculate, however, that schools' commitment to collaborative practice will tend to focus on those arrangements which foster individual achievement. Our data suggest that the most demanding form of partnership is that plotted as Quadrant C, involving a holistic perspective and low institutional boundaries. This is the quadrant in which schools are involved with other agencies in whole community development, with learning the vehicle for encouraging democratic participation in civil society. Might this be the kind of collaboration that schools are more reluctant to develop because of the many demands on them and the ambitious nature of the goals for such collaboration? With these issues in mind, we hope the analysis presented here will help plot the various models of collaborative practice that unfold and provide a useful way of analysing the multifaceted strands of social inclusion policy.

References

Armstrong, D. and Galloway, D. (1994) 'Special educational needs and problem behaviour: making policy in the classroom', in S. Riddell and S. Brown (eds) *Special Educational Needs Policy in the 90s*, London: Routledge, pp. 25–46.

Ball, M. (1998) *School Inclusion: The School, Family and the Community*, York: Joseph Rowntree Foundation.

Blair, A., Tett, L., Martin, J., Martin, I., Munn, P. and Ranson, S. (1998) *Schools and Community Education: The Mapping Study*, Edinburgh: Moray House Institute of Education, University of Edinburgh.

Commission of the European Community (1993) *Background Report: Social Exclusion, Poverty and Other Social Problems in the European Community*, ISEC/B11/93.

Dyson, A. and Robson, E. (1999) *School Inclusion: The Evidence*, Newcastle: Department of Education, University of Newcastle.

Huxham, C. (ed.) (1996) *Creating Collaborative Advantage*, London: Sage.

Kendrick, A. (1995) 'The integration of child care services in Scotland', *Children and Youth Services Review*, 17: 5–16.

Lloyd, G. (2000) 'Gender and exclusion from school', in J. Salisbury and S. Riddell (eds) *Gender, Policy and Educational Change: Shifting Agendas in the UK and Europe*, London: Routledge, pp. 63–78.

MacIntyre, A. (1981) *After Virtue*, London: Duckworth.

Martin, I. (1996) 'Community education: the dialectics of development', in R. Fieldhouse (ed.) *A History of Modern British Adult Education*, Leicester: National Institute of Adult Continuing Education, pp. 109–41.

Merz, C. and Furman, G. (1997) *Community and Schools: Promise and Paradox*, New York: Teachers College Press.

Ranson, S. (1994) *Towards the Learning Society*, London: Cassell.

Rigsby, L.C., Reynolds, M.C. and Wang, M.C. (1995) *School-Community Connections*, San Francisco: Jossey-Bass.

SCEC (1995) *Scotland as a Learning Society: Myth, Reality and Challenge*, Edinburgh: Scottish Community Education Council.

Scottish Office (1998) *New Community Schools: The Prospectus*, Edinburgh: Scottish Office.

——(1999a) *Social Inclusion Strategy for Scotland*, Edinburgh: Scottish Office.

——(1999b) *Social Inclusion Summary*, Edinburgh: Scottish Office.

Sergiovanni, T.J. (1994) *Building Community in Schools*, San Francisco: Jossey-Bass.

Shiver, M. and Newburn, T. (1996) *Young People, Drugs and Peer Education: An Evaluation of the Youth Awareness Programme, Home Office Drugs Prevention Initiative Chapter 13*, London: HMSO.

Tett, L., Ranson, S., Martin, I., Munn, P., Kay, H. and Martin, J. (1998) *Schools and Community Education for the Learning Age*, Edinburgh: Moray House Institute of Education, University of Edinburgh.

Tett, L., Munn, P., Blair, A., Kay, H., Martin, I., Martin, J. and Ranson, S. (2001) 'Collaboration between schools and community education agencies in tackling social exclusion', *Research Papers in Education*, 16(1): 1–19.

Watt, J.S. (1989) *Parental Involvement: Developing Networks between School, Home and Community*, London: Cassell.

8 The nature of special educational needs partnerships

Enid Mordaunt

Introduction

Partnership has long been considered to be an important way of working within schools in both England and Scotland (Cave 1970; De'Ath and Pugh (eds) 1984a/b; Macbeth 1989; Wolfendale (ed.) 1989; Jowett *et al.* 1991; Munn (ed.) 1993). The extensive literature, which also encompasses Europe (SO 1998a), covers many aspects of school life. With the development of Parent Partnership Schemes or Services (PPS), it also became an established way of working in the area of special educational needs (SEN) (Blamires *et al.* 1997; Wolfendale (ed.) 1997; Wolfendale and Cook 1997). This chapter sets out to examine the nature of those SEN partnerships, offering a comparative picture of England and Scotland.

At the outset, it should be noted that although the SEN statutory procedures in the two countries are similar there are notable differences. In England, local education authorities (LEAs) issue children with statements, while in Scotland education authorities (EAs) issue records of need. In England, it is standard practice for all children attending a special school to be statemented, whereas about 25 per cent of Scottish children attending special schools do not have a record of need. The SEN procedures in England follow the Code of Practice (DfE 1994a), currently under review; this chapter makes reference to the proposed revised Code (DfEE 2000), which at the time of writing was out for consultation. There is no direct equivalent to the Code in Scotland, although there are a range of good practice documents, which are considered in this chapter. In Scotland, it is normal practice for those 'professional advisers involved in an assessment' (SOEID 1996: para 101) to attend a case conference. There is no direct equivalent in the Code.

The chapter falls into three sections, beginning with an examination of the policy-setting of SEN partnerships, including the rights of parents and children within this arena, since effective partnerships are embedded in human rights: 'Governments should take a lead in promoting parental partnership, through both statements of policy and legislation concerning parental rights' (UNESCO 1994: paras 59–62). The chapter then moves on to an exploration of the nature of SEN partnerships and concludes with a more detailed examination of such partnerships within the context of a specific research project, as current and future developments are considered.

The study

This chapter is based on data gathered during a research project entitled 'Justice in SEN assessment procedures in England and Scotland', funded by the ESRC (no. R000237768) and run jointly by the Universities of Edinburgh and Glasgow. The nature and effectiveness of procedural justice was considered from the standpoint of all the key players in the SEN procedures; however, it was when the standpoints of parents and children were particularly examined that the nature of partnerships within the SEN process emerged as a vital aspect of the procedures.

The project fell into two phases. Having established the context of the research by means of a review of the legislation and policy documents, the purpose of phase one was to gain an overall picture of SEN procedures across the two countries. This mapping exercise was achieved by means of a postal survey of English and Scottish education authorities. Detail was added by means of data drawn from seventeen key informant interviews, including civil servants, representatives of voluntary organisations, elected members, local authority officers and educational psychologists (EPs). Using criteria developed from phase one and from an examination of SEN statistics, four education authorities were then identified as case study authorities.

Phase two took the form of case studies. From the four authorities, two of which were in England and two in Scotland, sixteen case study children were identified from each authority. A range of semi-structured interviews was conducted with the key players connected to each case. These included the children, parents, EPs, head teachers, special educational needs co-ordinators (SENCOs), class teachers, medical officers and, where applicable, social workers. The case studies put flesh on the bones of the procedures as live cases were followed as they worked their way through the statutory assessment procedures. The variety of research methods employed enabled data to be cross-checked.

The policy settings of England and Scotland

SEN partnerships are set within a policy framework that began with Warnock (HMSO 1978) and continues today. The now famous words of the report: 'Parents can be effective partners only if professionals take notice of what they say and how they express their needs, and treat their contribution as intrinsically important' (*ibid.*: para 9.6) have informed policy over the subsequent decades. If Warnock established the bedrock of SEN partnerships, the paths that such policies then took have differed in Scotland and England, emerging from different historic policy contexts. The term 'partnership' is more closely examined in the following section of this chapter; for the moment, if we take it to mean that both children and parents have the right to participate in any decision-making process

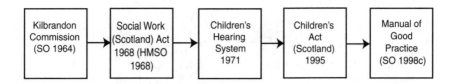

Figure 8.1   The development of partnership in Scotland

related to the child and to express an opinion about the child, then distinct traditions emerge in the two countries.

Figure 8.1 shows the development of partnership within the welfare tradition
in Scotland. The Children Act (Scotland) (HMSO 1995) has been described as 'a
first attempt to translate into Scottish legislation the principles of the UN
Convention' (Marshall 1997: 46). This welfare setting is further extended in the
Manual of Good Practice (SO 1998c: Part 1), which sets out the policy and legal
setting of SEN in Scotland, encompassing international statements: 'These legal
rights are not comprehensive but indicate the extent to which international and
domestic law now *cherish* children as individuals developing in their own right
and under the protection of the State' (*ibid.*: 14, emphasis added).

Meanwhile, in England the development of SEN partnership has taken the
route of legislation, as shown in Figure 8.2. That is not to say that SEN legislation does not exist in Scotland: of course it does (Education (Scotland) Acts
1980, 1981). The point is that, while SEN partnerships emerged in both countries from good practice, in England they have developed via the route of
legislation and regulation while in Scotland they have remained as good practice.
One of the results of such different traditions is that the basic right of appeal
has the appearance of fractured policy in Scotland, remaining complex and
forbidding to parents and children, unlike in England where SEN appeals have
one route via the SEN Tribunal, introduced by the 1993 Education Act. Within
the infrastructure of the appeals system, conciliation is an aspect of partnership
(Hall 1999) which, it would seem, is about to be strengthened (DfEE 2000;
proposed SEN and Disability Rights in Education Bill). LEAs are to be required

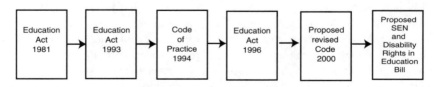

Figure 8.2   The development of partnership in England

to 'provide conciliation arrangements, which can demonstrate independence and credibility in working towards early and informal dispute resolution' (DfEE 2000: 12).

Parents as partners

The notion of parents as partners in their children's education is a well-developed concept in both countries (DfE 1994b; SO 1995), emerging not as a direct result of a particular policy but, rather, developed from the mainstream approach of working with parents as partners within schools generally. In Scotland the approach adopted has remained at the more general level (Eales and Watson 1994), although it has not been confined to the field of education (SO 1999b). Reflecting this approach, the Scottish Executive currently funds 'Enquire', a national advice service for SEN. In England, the notion has been more formally and specifically developed, notably in a special needs setting with the expansion of the PPS.[1]

Within a mainstream setting, partnership with parents was the specific focus of a Scottish discussion paper (SOEID 1998), which sought to develop and acknowledge parents' rights and responsibilities in both formal and informal relationships with their children's schools. The subsequent White Paper (SO 1999a) then indicated a number of targets, some of which were already under-way. The purpose of the targets was to strengthen further the relationship between parents, children and the school community. In particular it noted: 'The responses to *Parents as Partners* showed enthusiasm on the part of schools and authorities for involving parents in decision making on education issues and for clear and frank exchanges of information on issues of concern to parents' (*ibid.*: 41).

In England the approach has been more formal, with legislation strengthening both a partnership style of working and parental rights and choice (Education Acts 1996: Part 4; 1993: Part 3; 1981). The Code of Practice (*op. cit.*) underpinned this legislation as it considered parents as crucial to effective SEN delivery. Partnership with parents was presented as an aspect of procedural justice, since parents were presented as a vital aspect of the SEN procedures and as key players with a right to be heard (DfE 1994a: 1:2; 2:28).

The Code had a three-pronged approach, consisting of parent partnerships, the development of the roles of the SENCO and the Named Person. These three were interwoven, strengthening and supporting each other. A definite boost was afforded PPSs by the Grants for Education Support and Training (GEST) funding, enabling LEAs to identify Parent Partnership Officers. Such officers developed telephone advisory services and direct casework making home visits to offer parental support when mediation or conciliation proved necessary. The funding also advanced schemes for the identification and training of Named Persons and the routine provision of written information for parents (Wolfendale and Cook 1997). However, time-limited funding resulted in the negative effect of injecting into the schemes a level of uncertainty, as those leading the schemes held temporary appointments (*ibid.*). Subsequently, such schemes became eligible for support from the Standards Fund, which replaced GEST funding as central government continued its commitment: 'We propose to encourage an expansion in the number and scope of parent partnership schemes' (DfEE 1997a: 27).

The Code drew attention to parent partnership arrangements, since school governors were required to include in their SEN policy statement information related to 'partnership with bodies beyond the school', including 'arrangements for partnership with parents' (DfE 1994a: 2:10(3)). This was a statutory requirement (Education Act 1993: s161; see also DfE 1994c). The proposed revised Code takes a more developed view of partnership. Most importantly, there is to be a requirement that: 'All LEAs must make arrangements for parent partnership services' (DfEE 2000: 2.8), to be underpinned by the proposed consultation document on the – as yet unpublished – SEN and Disability Rights in Education Bill. Thus the service, which began life as a set of voluntary schemes and examples of good practice, has gradually acquired a sense of greater permanence.

The development of parent partnership was evident in the two case study authorities in England, where both had a funded scheme, designated officers and documentation. In one authority, where funding was due to become full-time, name changes had also taken place, so the scheme was now called a 'service' while the officer was called a 'co-ordinator'. The Parent Partnership Coordinator considered the changes in terminology better reflected the type of work she did, making it sound more permanent.

Children as partners

The place of children in SEN partnerships is at best low key. In neither country did the original Education Acts of 1980 and 1981 recognise the right of children to express a view concerning their education and for that view to be taken into account. In later guidance (DES 1989; SOEID 1996), however, children were to be encouraged as partners in the assessment and decision-making process. Not only were children invited to present their views but they were also to be enabled to participate in the assessment procedures (SOEID 1996: paras 65, 79, 81–3). The most recent Standards in Schools etc. Act (2000: s2(2)), albeit mainly focusing on mainstream issues, reinforces the approach of the Children (Scotland) Act 1995 by its approach to the involvement of children when decisions are taken about them.

In England, the 1994 Code sent out mixed messages on the nature of partnership in relation to children. The terminology within the Code relating to the right of children, separately from their parents, to participate in the assessment process, was much more problematic than that relating to their parents. On the one hand, the term used was 'involving the child', which carried less weight than the phrase used for parents, which was 'parents as partners'. On the other hand, stated as a 'principle' was that: 'children have a right to be heard. They should

Table 8.1   Defining legislation and policy documents

	Scotland		England
Date	*Document*	*Date*	*Document*
1968	Social Work (Scotland) Act		
1978	Warnock Report (HMSO 1978)		
1980	Education (Scotland) Act	1981	Education Act
1981	Education (Scotland) Act		
1989	Convention on the Rights of the Child (UN 1989)		
1994	HMI: *Effective Provision for SEN* (SOEID 1994)	1989	Children Act
		1993	Education Act
1995	Children (Scotland) Act	1994	Code of Practice (DfE 1994a)
1995	Parent's Charter updated (SO 1995)	1994	Parent's Charter updated (DfE 1994b)
1996	Circular 4/96 (SOEID 1996)	1994	*Special Educational Needs: A Guide for Parents* (DfE 1994d)
1998	*A Manual of Good Practice in Special Educational Needs* (SO 1998c)	1996	Education Act
1998	*Special Educational Needs in Scotland: A Discussion Paper* (SO 1998b)	1997	*Excellence in Schools* (White Paper) (DfEE 1997b)
		1997	*Excellence for All Children: Meeting Special Educational Needs* (Green Paper) (DfEE 1997a)
		1998	*Meeting Special Educational Needs: A Programme of Action* (DfEE 1998)
1998	Human Rights Act 1998		
1999	*Targeting Excellence* (White Paper) (SO 1999a)	2000	SEN code of Practice & SEN Thresholds (DfEE 2000)

be encouraged to participate in decision-making about provision to meet their special educational needs' (*ibid.*).

The approach of the proposed revised Code is more clearly defined, affording a separate chapter to what is now called 'pupil participation' and beginning by firmly placing such participation within a rights setting (UN 1989). While there appears to be a recognition of children as separate from their parents, there is still no legal right for a child to participate in the SEN procedures, only an expectation. Children still cannot bring their own appeals. None of the case study authorities involved children as fully as they involved their parents, with officers preferring to see such involvement as a parental responsibility: 'I mean, presumably, when the draft [statement] goes out to the parents … if it came to me I'd get my child … and go through it with them' (Senior Officer, English LEA 1).

In drawing this section of the chapter to a conclusion, it should be noted that the bureaucratic nature of the English assessment process has been criticised. However, it has equally been recognised that such an approach ensures that 'LEAs made decisions about children on a rational, informed and challengeable basis rather than on the basis of professional prejudice or whim with a consequent denial of children's and parents' rights' (Watt 1997: 6). Finally, the reader may find it useful to refer to Table 8.1, which sets out those documents that have played a key part in the development of SEN partnerships. Included in the Table is the Human Rights Act (HMSO 1998), the effect of which is still to be tested in the area of the rights of children and parents to participate in the SEN procedures.

The meaning of partnership

Having established the policy setting of SEN partnerships, consideration is now afforded to the meaning of such partnerships. So far, this chapter has recognised that partnerships exist between parents, children and other key players in the SEN procedures. There is a need for a more exact examination of the term, since it is now acknowledged to exist between all players in the process (DfEE 2000). The proposed revised Code recognises the complex and extended ways in which partnerships can operate. There is no longer the single focus on parents, as though partnership were a simple two-way transaction between parents on the one hand and all other players on the other. Figure 8.3 illustrates Model 1, called

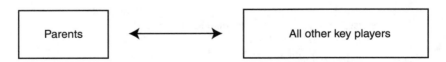

Figure 8.3   Model 1: the divide

Source: based on DfE 1994a: 2.28

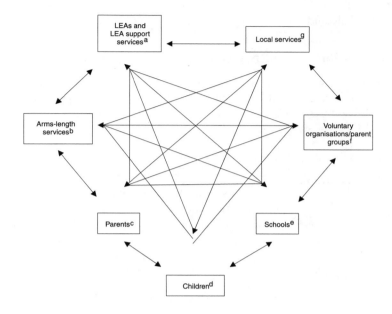

Figure 8.4   Model 2: the web

Source: based on DfEE 2000, especially chs 2, 3 and 10

Notes:
[a] LEAs and LEA support services include elected members, officers, centrally funded specialist teachers, behavioural support services, counsellors, EPs, advisers, education welfare service
[b] Arm's-length services include, e.g., parent partnership service, independent parental support, Connexions service, Connexions personal adviser, Learning and Skills Council
[c] I.e., those with parental responsibility
[d] Not limited to older children and young people
[e] Including staff and governors
[f] E.g. IPSEA, National Children's Bureau
[g] Other local services include health services, local authority social services departments, early years development and child-care partnership, child and adolescent mental health services

here 'the divide', and shows how parents appear to be pitted against other players in the procedures. Policy, at this stage of development, acts to encourage and exhort partnership to extend across the divide: 'The school-based stages should therefore utilise parents' own distinctive knowledge and skills and contribute to parents' own understanding of how best to help their child' (DfE 1994a: 2:29).

The proposed revised Code, however, indicates a range of partners. Called here 'the web', Model 2 demonstrates a more developed understanding of partnership, one which depends on the interconnected policies of all the players involved in the procedures and implies a greater sense of equality between all players (see Figure 8.4). This approach is exemplified in chapter two of the proposed revised Code, where a range of parties is explored. The concept of partnership has the opportunity to become an operational principle, since it fundamentally underpins the approach of the proposed new Code.

Characteristics of SEN partnerships

In this second section, we will consider in a more systematic manner what is meant by partnership within the setting of the SEN statutory assessment procedures. Table 8.2 displays the distinct characteristics that partnerships in general exhibit:[2]

Table 8.2   Characteristics of partnerships

Partnerships are:	
•	expressed by means of basic elements;
•	driven by self-interest;
•	concerned with trade-offs and compromises;
•	not necessarily between equal bodies;
•	between bodies who retain their own identity;
•	dependent for their survival on the unique qualities that each member brings;
•	created to bring benefits to each member;
•	expressed in terms of a 'greater good';
•	organic relationships rather than static end results;
•	ultimately tested.

In examining the nature of SEN partnerships, these characteristics will be considered more closely.

The essential *basic elements* of a partnership set out those aspects that form its defining nature, acting as a common bond drawing partners together – for example, the good of the child. As one interviewee indicated, it was particularly important for all parties to work together, because 'you're impacting on children and young people. And if you're antagonistic towards one another, and one partner doesn't understand what the other's doing, and there isn't a common goal, the kids get lost in the middle of it' (elected member, England). The basic elements of an SEN partnership were identified by interviewees as trust and understanding, it being necessary to: 'Work … together and respect … the differences, the different roles that people have got and different bits that you bring to the table, as it were' (elected member, England).

To speak of *self-interest* is generally to speak pejoratively, but self-interest can be legitimate to the parties to a partnership. When a local authority is driven by Best Value (Local Government Act 1999) or places the good of all children in their purview above the individual good of a single child, or when parents place the needs of their own child above all other concerns, each is driven by self-interest:

> Partnership with parents means working closely with them, but remembering that we are here to meet the needs of the child, not the needs of the parents, and we have to provide an equitable system for all. This sometimes implies refusing parents' requests for additional resources which would be incompatible with the principle of equity.
>
> (senior officer, England)

Mutual recognition of what drives each side can lead to the positive outcome of an empathetic realisation of each other's concerns and aspirations, so that when compromises are needed to break a stalemate they are more likely to occur since 'give and take is at the heart of it' (civil servant, England). The path to such give and take was identified by civil servants as conciliation, which has been afforded a role of greater significance in the proposed revised Code (2.9). There must be a 'pragmatic recognition on both sides that there was a need to give ground, to shift position' (civil servant, England).

Preferred outcomes may not necessarily begin by being based on the single most important aim of what is best for the child. For the parent, this may be a desire for private education at the education authority's expense, while for an officer it may be a concern to place the budget before an open examination of all available options. However, through consideration of the statutory advice, parties may *trade off* their original preferred outcomes, reaching a *compromise* in order to achieve a positive outcome for the child. There was evidence in one LEA that parents were both willing and able to see the bigger picture, modifying their expectations for the general good:

> [the LEA] look at a statement and they give the child what they think they can give them, if you see what I mean. Because, obviously they've got other children to think of who are just as desperate as Roxanne, and you know they've got to be able to give them the time that they need as well. You can be very selfish and say, 'Well, but my Roxanne needs this and my Roxanne needs that,' but you've got to think there are other children who need that first.
>
> (mother, English LEA 2)

At face value, the *inequality of the parties* to an SEN partnership appears to be problematic, because without a sense of equality the partnership would founder as the strong prevailed. However, partnership is a more complex, dynamic and robust process than that would suggest. In SEN procedures, parents and children have traditionally been seen as the weaker partners in comparison with professionals from education and health, and officers and elected members of local authorities. Indeed, in the research there was a view that such a balance of power was as it should be: 'If society believed that parents were the right people to educate children, society would not run schools. It's as simple and as straight-forward as that' (elected member, Scotland). However, a partnership with workers in the SEN field can lead parents and children to a new, stronger voice, enhancing their roles. While it was recognised that:

> Partnership ... always implies a sense of equality between the participants ... Technically that isn't necessary because you have senior partners and junior partners in business enterprises ... I would regard that as a difference in degree rather than of kind.
>
> (voluntary organisation trustee)

Parents have traditionally played such a junior role; there was among inter-viewees a general recognition that parents have more power than formerly, being less likely to 'play ... the client role' (Wolfendale 1983: 114):

> I suppose ... [parents as partners] implies that we've moved radically away from the situation that used to exist twenty years ago ... when ... the atti-tude was one of paternalism by the professionals. And we knew best. We're the experts and if you listen to us, then this is what we think should happen. And if the truth be told, sometimes parents were bullied into accepting things that maybe they didn't want to accept. I think that was wrong.
>
> (civil servant, Scotland)

In the two English case study authorities, one had a more active PPS than the other. Where the service was the more active, it was more common for case study parents to be at ease with the procedures. Parents indicated that they knew what to expect in the statement because they had been informed of the content of all reports written during the assessments: 'Yes, they've told me everything that they're doing. And I have a lady come round who's called Parents' Partner. She comes round' (mother, English LEA 2). In the authority where the service was at a lower key, parents more commonly expressed feelings of having to enforce their rights: 'I have felt involved because I've made myself involved, because I've pushed myself forward' (mother, English LEA 1) and of confusion: 'I don't really understand what's going off behind closed doors' (mother, English LEA 1).

While it was stressed that authorities 'must listen very carefully to parents, take them along ... and they must play a major role in the decision-making process' (civil servant, Scotland), one interviewee speaking from a background in social work indicated that: 'The problem with professionals is that we regard ourselves as the experts in our own procedures and expect other people to accept ... our management and government of these' (voluntary organisation trustee). This interviewee considered there to be very few professionals used to operating in a 'true partnership mode', because he felt it was difficult enough for profes-sionals to work with each other, let alone with 'the humble lay people whom they regard as their clients'.

Partnership was seen to be about moving away from the extremes because problems arise if the balance of power in the SEN partnership tips too far in any one direction. Recognising this dilemma, one civil servant indicated that some professionals felt the balance had now tipped too far, so that partnership had 'jumped to the opposite pole where parents always know best' (civil servant, Scotland). This was considered to be equally unacceptable, 'because that's not always in the best interests of the child. And it's really the child who is at the centre' (*ibid.*). Again, civil servants saw an important role for conciliation in maintaining such a balance, where the conciliator would try to bring the parents down to earth when their expectations were totally unrealistic, while at the same time attempting to lever up the LEA provision when it was not meeting requirements.

It is important for each party in the SEN partnership *to retain their identity*. Thus, parents would neither be expected to play the role of a pseudo-professional, 'second-guessing the outcome of psychological testing' (voluntary organisation trustee) nor the role of the client 'ineffective in child management, and need[ing] the "topping up" of professional expertise in order to function and do their parental duty' (Wolfendale 1983: 146). Instead, parents would be valued and, in turn value themselves for what they offered as parents. In this way, a recognition of each party's identity enables each to exercise their *unique quality*, essential if the partnership is to survive: 'Each person needs to recognise the weight of the other person's knowledge and experience and respect it ... The concept of partnership implies that ... [reports on the child] would be weighted equally' (voluntary organisation trustee).

Thus, each party to the partnership has brought something that is unique to them and is needed by the other party: 'at the end of the day, the parent is the person who knows the child best, is closest to their needs' (civil servant, England). This unique offering has within its nature an element of proactivity; there can be no passive partners. Interviewees generally considered that the unique contribution of parents was 'advice about the child's care and welfare' (elected member, Scotland) and the parental 'experience of that child throughout life' (voluntary organisation trustee). This was considered to be especially true of SEN children, where the particular needs may have developed over a period of time with the parent being aware of its various manifestations. Interviewees indicated that parents provided stability; while professionals came and went, parents knew the history and provided insight and continuity. However, several interviewees drew a distinction between the parents' care and welfare input and the professionals' educational decisions. One interviewee thought that spending taxpayers' money on training education professionals 'only to say, "Well, actually, the parents know best." Well, why do we bother? It's absurd' (elected member, Scotland).

This interviewee considered that parents had a limited role in the partnership relationship, when educational decisions were being made:

> I think that parents are the worst people to make decisions about their children on an educational basis. Most parents have a totally wrong view of their children's abilities, strengths and weaknesses, even if your child doesn't

have special needs. Most of us would like to think that we had offered to this world a genius or a child of such special character that was going to create huge changes in the world. But, of course, that doesn't happen.

(*ibid.*)

Some parents of SEN children were considered to be even less able to reason on their child's behalf than other parents, since wanting the best for their child could cloud the judgement of parents: 'Sometimes parents have the potential to make things more difficult for their kids' (elected member, England). While it was generally accepted that parents had a right to have a voice in the SEN procedures, more than one interviewee emphasised that such a stance left unresolved those situations where the parents are a pernicious influence in the child's life.

The *benefits* from SEN partnerships can be a reduction in levels of anxiety as parents are informed and, therefore, empowered to develop a voice within the procedures. While the provision of written information for parents may initially cause more work for the education authority, it can save time in the longer term. The opportunity for mediation at critical points in the assessment process may avert appeals and litigation, as greater confidence in the assessment process develops (DfEE 2000: 8.15). However, initially better-informed parents can lead to increased numbers of SENT appeals as increased parental confidence enables parents to make use of their rights: 'It's not necessarily a bad thing that people exercise a right that exists' (senior officer, English LEA 2).

Partnerships are often expressed in terms of the *greater good*, for example to reinforce human rights. Furthermore, partnerships could well lead to improved, targeted provision, which in turn could result in greater educational achievement and fulfilment of the child. Once SEN partnerships reach a critical level, they can positively affect the reputation of the education authority, with the result that parents approach assessment and provision expecting a supportive system, geared to their needs. This will result in fewer appeals and more general benefits for all parties to the partnership.

SEN partnerships are not ends in themselves, but rather a means to the end of best provision. Like other partnerships, they should be considered as *organic*, constantly developing and therefore needing constant nurturing. They are 'extremely fragile. Months and even years of trust and mutual respect can be destroyed overnight if a lack of respect and inequalities are perceived. You have to "walk the talk" ' (Crouch 1998: 9). Partnerships may be unwittingly fractured by the wider education authority, not simply by those in close contact with parents. Local authority SEN partnerships, like those in commercial organisations, depend on:

having people 'on song' with the brand ... at all times ... the brand does not depend solely on those employees who have obvious links with customers. The security man answering out-of-hours calls may have a more direct influence over customer relations than the managing director ... A sale or a reputation ... may be ... lost in a moment of employee exasperation or inattention.

(Stevens 1998: 14)

SEN partnerships, like all partnerships, will be *ultimately tested*. It is at such a point that the basic foundations of the partnership need to be strong: 'If you're working as partners you're less likely to be in a situation where there's misunderstanding and friction and accusations ... You might disagree but at least you understand why you disagree' (elected member, England). Partnerships are also tested by changes in personnel, a challenge for education authorities to transform what has been called the 'human capital' (Golzen 1998: 20) into 'structural capital'. In other words, authorities must protect the knowledge and commitment to partnerships of individuals so that such working becomes part of the cultural fabric. In that way partnerships will not evaporate when key figures leave.

The future of SEN partnerships

In this third and final section, current developments of SEN partnerships will be considered. As we saw at the start of the chapter, there are SEN partnerships that have developed informally and there are those that are underpinned with legislation. In Scotland, SEN partnerships have remained at the informal end of the spectrum, while in England they have progressively moved to the formal end; see Model 3 in Figure 8.5.

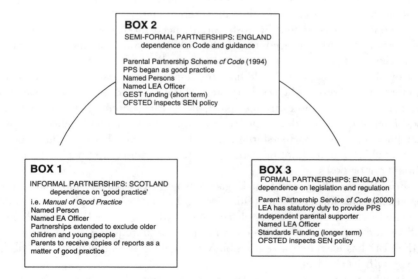

Figure 8.5　Model 3: the spectrum of partnerships

Box 1 in Figure 8.5 shows the current position in Scotland, where SEN partnerships are informal: that is, they depend on good practice rather than
guidance, regulation or legislation. The general intention of Scottish documents
(SO 1998c; SOEID 1994, 1996) was to offer a standard approach of SEN assessment procedures countrywide by offering exemplar material. However, these
documents are unlikely to have any widespread, lasting effect, since they are not
underpinned with regulation, are unenforceable and do not offer standards
against which HMI (education) could inspect. Lacking such underpinning,
aspects of good practice generally have a tendency to slip into oblivion, become
hostages to budgetary considerations or become hijacked by vested interests.
Because it is in the nature of good practice documents that they offer exhorta-
tions rather than instructions, the result has been that Named Persons are
seldom used and parents do not receive copies of statutory reports (SOEID
1996: para 96).

The current debate in Scotland indicates a wish by some key players to reject
the system of recording completely. The line of reasoning taken is that to open
records of need for some children is in direct opposition to the agenda of inclusion, as this emphasises those children as being different from their peers.
Naturally, not all the key players in the process see a record of need in that light,
since it continues to offer some children legally protected access to resources
deemed appropriate to their needs. There are dangers in a simple move away
from recording without putting in place at least some of the infrastructure seen
in England, namely nationwide school-based procedures that offer a child with
special needs the resources they need to access the curriculum. Such procedures
would also need to be tied into a system of inspection to ensure that EAs and
schools everywhere were delivering this commitment.

It could be argued that Scottish parents need more opportunities to act as
partners in the SEN procedures of their children and that the surest way of
achieving such opportunities is by a more formalised system. All parents, regardless of place of residence, should have the right to access partnerships. If there is
no formal system then the vested interest of the stronger partners may well take
over. It is pointless those stronger partners assuring parents that they have the
best interest of the child in mind, because this smacks of munificence, not partnership. Access to a partnership relationship within the SEN procedures should
be available to all and not be dependent on the localised approaches of EAs: it
should not be post-code justice.

Box 2 shows the position in England, where SEN partnerships have devel-
oped in a semi-formal setting (DfE 1994a). The Code, although not legislation
itself, was introduced by means of legislation (Education Act 1993: sects 157–8).
LEAs and schools across the country have been required to follow it and
OFSTED has exercised a responsibility to monitor the implementation of the
Code (DfE 1994a: 1.5).

Should any part of a code be violated or ignored, no criminal offence or
breach of the civil law has been committed (Evans 1998). However, should decisions be made in complete disregard of the terms of the SEN Code, then such 'a

departure from the Code of Practice can be evidence towards proving, for example, that an assessment was inadequate, or that provision is not appropriate' (*ibid.*: 27).

Within such a setting, partnership arrangements have had an uneasy status, exemplified by the point at which parents accessed their children's statutory reports. In both case study LEAs, parents received copies as indicated by the Code (4.38), but because these were semi-formal arrangements, LEAs interpreted when to issue the reports differently. In LEA 1 parents received their copies with the draft statement, although EPs gave an immediate copy to parents. Many parents in this LEA, when interviewed, expressed the wish to see the reports before they received the draft statement in order to resolve immediately any aspect of any of the reports with which they disagreed. English LEA 2, however, expected parents to receive reports before they were submitted to the LEA. Typically, interviewed parents indicated that because they had discussed the report with the writer and had received copies in advance of the proposed statement, they felt fully informed and approved of the conduct of the process.

Attention was drawn to parent partnership arrangements in the 1994 Code, since school governors were required to include in their SEN Policy Statement information related to 'partnership with bodies beyond the school' which included 'arrangements for partnership with parents' (DfE 1994a: 2.10(3)). This was a statutory requirement of the 1993 Act (s161; see also DfE 1994c). There was no parallel legal requirement placed on LEAs to establish actual PPSs. However, the pump-priming funding through GEST, over a three-year period from 1994 to 1997, offered a base-line from which to work (Wolfendale and Cook 1997: i). Because arrangements for such schemes were semi-formal, they developed from good practice in a non-standard manner (DfEE 1998: 46). This was borne out by the two case study LEAs, where the schemes were funded at different levels and where one was more proactive than the other. There was a subsequent difference in the take-up rate of Named Persons and a demonstrable difference in the level of understanding of the parents of the procedures and of their rights. PPSs may have begun as good practice, but they rapidly developed into a nationally networked scheme with a dedicated newsletter.

Box 3 shows the developing position in England as SEN partnerships become formally organised and their funding longer-term. The central government consultation exercise (DfEE 1998), based on the Green Paper (DfEE 1997a), set a timetable for action. It identified six themes to be the focus for action, one of which was 'Promoting Partnership in SEN' (DfEE 1998: 4–7). Partnership in this document had a wide focus and, leading to the approach taken in the proposed revised Code, did not confine itself to partnership between parents and other key players. The programme of action covered improving multi-agency working (*ibid.*: 5.3–6), including health, education and the careers service. It also identified the Standards Fund to support pilot projects for speech and language therapy, in which education, health, parents and voluntary organisations would work together (*ibid.*: 5.7–8). There was also a commitment to consider ending the distinction between educational and non-educational needs and provision in statements (*ibid.*: 5.9). Furthermore, the programme of action placed an emphasis on multi-agency working at transition post-16 (DfEE 1998: 5.10–12).

As central government consults on a new Code, many of the issues above are reflected in the proposed revisions. For example, the Connexions service is given a brief to support those aged 13–19 who are 'disadvantaged ... or those likely to underachieve, including those with SEN but without statements' (DfEE 2000: 9.21). It is also envisaged that schools, having consulted the Connexions Personal Adviser, would draw up a Transition Plan for individual young persons: 'There will need to be close collaboration with LEA staff and other professionals involved with the young person' (*ibid.*: 9.21). There is proposed further underpinning of partnership arrangements via legislation in the SEN and Disability Rights in Education Bill, announced in January 2000, but so far postponed from the current parliamentary session for lack of time. This Bill is expected to alter the status of the PP Service, since the proposed revised Code indicates that 'All LEAs have a statutory duty to provide parent partnership services, they do not have to deliver the services themselves' (*ibid.*: 12).

This chapter has set out to do two things. First, it has offered a conceptual framework of partnership in general terms, which forms a base-line and a context within which other chapters can be read. Specifically, it then applied the framework to what partnership means in a special needs setting in England and Scotland. Second, it has presented examples of partnership at work with data drawn from a current research project, placing the varying styles of partnership within a spectrum. The spectrum highlights how two neighbouring countries, with the same foundations for SEN procedures, have developed in distinctly different ways. Finally, the spectrum shows how the more formal arrangements offer the weaker partners – parents – a more secure status within the partnership by establishing more exactly their rights within the process.

Partnership has travelled a long route from its initial concerns to involve parents in the education of their children to the current concerns to establish collaborative working across agencies, where parents, children and young people are key players. Other chapters take up this expanded notion of partnership, exploring examples from a wide range of settings beyond SEN. The need for integrated policy, spanning aspects of government that have not traditionally worked in partnership, forms a common theme running through each chapter.

Notes

1 For fuller discussion of the emergence of parent partnerships see Wolfendale and Cook (1997: 1–3).
2 These characteristics were developed from an examination of a range of partnerships found in public services, business and industry (see Mordaunt 1999).

References
Blamires, M., Robertson, C. and Blamires, J. (1997) *Parent–Teacher Partnership: Practical Approaches to Meet Special Educational Needs*, London: David Fulton.
Cave, R. (1970) *Partnership for Change: Parents and Schools*, London: Ward Lock Educational.

Crouch, N. (1998) 'Partnerships with people', in T. Nash (ed.) *Partnerships with People: Improving Business Performance Through Your People*, London: Director Publications.

De'Ath, E. and Pugh, G. (eds) (1984a) *Working Together: Parents and Professionals as Partners*, Partnership Paper 1, London: National Children's Bureau.

——(eds) (1984b) *Parental Involvement: What Does It Mean?*, Partnership Paper 2, London: National Children's Bureau.

DES (1989) *Assessments and Statements of Special Educational Needs: Procedures within the Education, Health and Social Services*, Circular 22/89, London: DES.

DfE (1994a) *Code of Practice on the Identification and Assessment of Special Educational Needs*, London: DfE.

——(1994b) *Our Children's Education: The Updated Parent's Charter*, London: HMSO.

——(1994c) *The Organisation of Special Educational Provision*, Circular 6/94, London: DfE.

——(1994d) *Special Educational Needs: A Guide for Parents*, London: HMSO.

DfEE (1997a) *Excellence for All Children: Meeting Special Educational Needs*, Cm 3785, London: The Stationery Office.

——(1997b) *Excellence in Schools*, Cm 3681, London: The Stationery Office.

——(1998) *Meeting Special Educational Needs: A Programme of Action*, Sudbury, Suffolk: DfEE.

——(2000) *SEN Code of Practice on the Identification and Assessment of Pupils with Special Educational Needs*, London: DfEE.

Eales, J. and Watson, J. (1994) *Health Education in Scottish Schools: Meeting Special Educational Needs*, Edinburgh: Scottish Office Education Department.

Evans, W. (1998) 'The problems of interpretation and guidance: the consequences of SENCO action from a legal point of view', in J. D. Davies, P. Garner and J. Lee (eds) *Managing Special Needs in Mainstream Schools: the Role of the SENCO*, London: David Fulton.

Golzen, G. (1998) 'All in the mind', in T. Nash (ed.) *Partnerships with People: Improving Business Performance Through Your People*, London: Director Publications.

Hall, J. (1999) *Resolving Disputes between Parents, Schools and LEAs: Some Examples of Best Practice*, London: DfEE SEN Division.

HMSO (1968) *The Social Work (Scotland) Act 1968*, Edinburgh: HMSO.

——(1978) *Special Educational Needs*, Report of the Committee of Enquiry into the Education of Handicapped Children and Young People (Chairman Mrs H.M. Warnock), Cmnd 7212, London: HMSO.

Jowett, S., Baginsky, M. and MacNeil, M.M. (1991) *Building Bridges: Parental Involvement in Schools*, Windsor, Berks: NFER/Nelson.

Macbeth, A. (1989) *Involving Parents: Effective Parent–Teacher Relations*, Oxford: Heinemann Educational.

Marshall, K. (1997) *Children's Rights in the Balance: The Participation–Protection Debate*, Edinburgh: The Stationery Office.

Mordaunt, E. (1999) '"Not for wimps": the nature of partnership', paper presented at BERA Conference, September, University of Sussex.

Munn, P. (ed.) (1993) *Parents and Schools: Customers, Managers or Partners?* London: Routledge.

Scottish Office (SO) (1964) *Children and Young Persons: Scotland*, Report of the Kilbrandon Commission, Cmnd 2306, Edinburgh: HMSO.

——(1995) *The Parent's Charter in Scotland*, updated, Edinburgh: HMSO.

——(1998a) *Parents as Partners*, EPA/UK Presidency Conference, Edinburgh: The Stationery Office.

——(1998b) *Special Education Needs in Scotland: A Discussion Paper*, Edinburgh: The Stationery Office.

——(1998c) *A Manual of Good Practice in Special Educational Needs*, Edinburgh: The Stationery Office.

——(1999a) *Targeting Excellence: Modernising Scotland's Schools*, Cm 4247, Edinburgh: The Stationery Office.

——(1999b) *Responding to the Childcare Challenge*, Edinburgh: The Scottish Office.

Scottish Office Education and Industry Department (SOEID) (1994) *Effective Provision for Special Educational Needs*, a report by HM Inspectors of Schools, Edinburgh: SOEID.

——(1996) *Children and Young Persons with Special Educational Needs: Assessment and Recording*, Circ 4/96, Edinburgh: HMSO.

——(1998) *Parents as Partners: Enhancing the Role of Parents in School Education*, discussion paper, Edinburgh: The Stationery Office.

Stevens, J. (1998) 'Is your brand image people-based?' in T. Nash (ed.) *Partnerships with People: Improving Business Performance through Your People*, London: Director Publications.

UNESCO (1994) *The Salamanca Statement and Framework for Action on Special Educational Needs*, Paris: UNESCO.

United Nations (1989) *Convention on the Rights of the Child*, Brussels: United Nations.

Watt, J. (1997) *Excellence for All Children – Green Paper on Special Educational Needs*, consultation response, London: DfEE.

Wolfendale, S. (ed.) (1983) *Parental Participation in Children's Development and Education*, London: Gordon and Breach.

——(1989) *Parental Involvement: Developing Networks between School, Home and Community*, London: Cassell.

——(ed.) (1997) *Partnership with Parents in Action*, Tamworth: NASEN.

Wolfendale, S. and Cook, G. (1997) *Evaluation of Special Educational Needs Parent Partnership Schemes*, DfEE Research Report 34, London: HMSO.

9 Supporting pupils with special health needs in mainstream schools

Jane Lightfoot, Suzanne Mukherjee
and Patricia Sloper

Introduction

In this chapter we use data from research and development work we have undertaken between 1996 and 2000 to reflect on the position of pupils with special health needs within relevant policy guidance for supporting children in mainstream schools. By 'special health needs' we mean needs arising from a chronic illness or physical disability. The discussion identifies areas where policy guidance might be strengthened to provide better support for these pupils.

'Inclusion' of pupils with a variety of special needs has been an explicit policy goal since the 1981 Education Act. Statistics point to the success of this policy: Norwich (1997) reports that, by 1996, the proportion of pupils aged between 5 and 15 being educated in special schools was 1.4 per cent, the lowest ever. In relation to pupils with special *health* needs, while it has long been the practice for pupils with some chronic conditions – such as asthma, diabetes and eczema – to be educated in mainstream schools, Botting and Crawley (1995) have shown that developments in medical technology now mean that a growing number of children are surviving with long-term and sometimes complex needs, and are able to join their peers in mainstream schools.

Some of the most prevalent chronic conditions among children are: asthma (12 per cent); eczema (8–10 per cent); diabetes (1.8 per cent); epilepsy (0.26–0.46 per cent); congenital heart disease (0.2–0.7 per cent); cerebral palsy (0.2 per cent); and cancer (0.17 per cent) (Edwards and Davis 1997; House of Commons Health Committee 1997; Botting and Crawley 1995). Although the numbers of these children are small in relation to the whole school population, they do suggest that most medium to large secondary schools would include affected pupils.

A recent research review by Wallander and Varni (1998) shows that pupils with chronic health conditions are 'at risk'; that is, on average they perform less well academically and have higher rates of psychosocial problems than their peers. Studies reveal a higher absence rate as one factor behind this discrepancy, along with the impact of illness on psychosocial well-being through feelings of isolation caused both by absence and by other limitations on participating in school life (Fowler *et al.* 1985; Midence and Elander 1994; Nettles 1994).

Moreover, research by Sloper *et al.* (1994) found that poor academic progress compounded psychosocial problems for this group of children.

Many different education and health professionals potentially have a part to play in supporting pupils with special health needs, including: teachers; Local Education Authority (LEA) learning support staff; school care assistants, administrative and catering staff; school nurses and school doctors; therapists; and medical consultants. It follows that collaboration is needed among these professionals to ensure appropriate support is in place for individual pupils. However, existing research points to evidence of poor co-ordination, both within health services – between staff in hospital and community services – and between staff in health and education (Bolton 1997; Larcombe 1995). Particular problems reported by school staff include a lack of clarity as to who to contact in the NHS for advice and information about an individual child (OFSTED 1997), and wide variation in medical consultants' responses to their attempts to obtain health-related advice and information (Dyson *et al* 1998). While some consultants gave prompt information, others responded only after a considerable delay, or even not at all, on grounds of confidentiality. Such difficulties reveal the continued lack of health-related information available to school staff as reported in a number of earlier studies – Bradbury and Smith (1983), Eiser and Town (1987), Court (1994), Stevens *et al.* (1988) – the provision of which could help them understand the child's condition and to provide appropriate support to ensure that these pupils get the most from school life.

In this chapter we first give a brief overview of the two projects we have carried out which provide the empirical data informing our policy analysis. We then go on to outline three key policy guidance documents and explore the 'fit' between these and practice, as revealed by our research data. In a closing section, we discuss areas where policy guidance might be strengthened to provide better support for pupils with special health needs.

The projects: an overview

Between 1996 and 2000 we carried out two projects with a focus on the health-related needs of pupils in mainstream school who have a chronic illness or physical disability. Our shorthand titles for these projects are the 'service support' project and the 'health/ school communication' project. The purpose of this overview is to provide a context for an examination of the 'fit' between policy and practice, rather than to report the projects in detail. The methods and findings of the projects are reported more fully elsewhere (see Lightfoot *et al.* 1998 and 1999; Mukherjee *et al.* 2000a and b).

The 'service support' project

The first project was a research study funded by the NHS Executive National Research and Development Programme and carried out between October 1996 and September 1998. The research sought to identify the support needs of pupils with special health needs, as expressed by pupils themselves, by their parents and by teachers. We were particularly keen to investigate pupils' views, since this was a gap in existing research despite increasing emphasis – for example in the United Nations *Convention on the Rights of the Child* (1989); and the Children Act, 1989 – on the rights of children to have decisions made in their best interests and to have their views heard.

Given the lack of previous research on support needs, our research was exploratory and we adopted a qualitative approach. We collected data in respect of pupils attending schools in three LEAs and obtaining clinical care from three NHS Trusts. A total of thirty-three pupils in mainstream secondary schools and aged between 11 and 16 took part. Between them, a wide range of health conditions was represented: for example, severe asthma, cerebral palsy, diabetes, juvenile arthritis, spina bifida, cystic fibrosis, cancer, muscular dystrophy and ME (myalgic encephalomyelitis). Fourteen of the pupils had a Statement of Special Educational Needs (SEN) on account of their illness or disability. Parents from 58 families took part, 33 of whom were parents of these young respondents. The remaining 25 parents had children with special health needs attending primary schools. Thirty-five teachers took part in the study.

Summary of findings

That young people attached importance to school was evident in their accounts of efforts they made to attend and to take part in the various facets of school life. Although these young people were actively managing their health condition at school in a variety of ways, there were areas where they encountered difficulties and valued support from others: minimising the impact of absence; minimising exclusion from aspects of school life; easing peer relationships; and having someone to talk to for emotional support. Parents and teachers reported similar issues and also identified medical care as an area of difficulty: for example, unclear responsibilities for medical care and equipment provision in school.

Overall, having 'a teacher who understands' emerged from the young people's data as crucial for appropriate support: that is, teachers who know about their health condition, understand its impact on school life and can make any special arrangements needed in school. In turn, teachers reported a wide range of information needs for which they needed advice from a medical expert, for example: general information about the condition and how it affects the individual child; the pattern of treatment and prognosis; and the impact of the condition on school life, such as likely absence, pain, tiredness and side-effects of medication, and the level and types of appropriate physical activity. This information was needed to make special arrangements for individual pupils, such as: permission to leave the classroom on request; extending home-work deadlines; organising an appropriate alternative to PE sessions; and planning school trips.

However, both pupils and teachers reported wide variation in the extent to which their needs for support were being met. Although examples of good practice were reported, pupils who did not have access to good support experienced a number of difficulties, including: not being believed by some teachers that they were experiencing symptoms; and being unnecessarily excluded from some activities and/or inappropriately forced to take part in others, such as PE. Support appeared idiosyncratic, according to the ethos of individual schools, the personal interest of individual teachers and medical consultants, and the level of knowledge of individual school health staff.

Overall, the research revealed a number of weaknesses in meeting pupils' support needs systematically. Within schools, responsibilities for this group of pupils were unclear, both in terms of who should have lead responsibility for co-ordinating support (including raising awareness among colleagues) and for medical care. Systems for communicating information between school staff were also reported as weak. While teachers were able to articulate their health-related information needs, they reported these as largely unmet, owing to weak arrangements for communication between health staff and teachers. It followed that many struggled to be the 'understanding teacher' which pupils identified as so crucial for good support.

These findings, along with evidence of the growing number of pupils in mainstream schools with special health needs, suggest that attention is needed to ways in which this group of pupils can secure support more systematically to enable them to make the most of school life. Staff in one of the three research sites subsequently expressed an interest in working with the research team in a development project, using the research evidence as the basis for improving local inter-agency communication.

The 'health/school communication' project

The aim of this second project was to develop an improved communication system between local health and school staff in respect of pupils in mainstream schools who have a chronic illness or physical disability. The research team secured funding to support the staff from the NHS Executive Northern and Yorkshire Regional Research and Development Programme, and the project was carried out between January 1999 and June 2000. Prior to the development work, we carried out a research phase in which we interviewed twenty local health staff about their experiences of communication with teachers. These data were needed to add health staff's perspectives on communication to the existing evidence from pupils, parents and teachers obtained in the earlier study. After the research evidence had been presented to local health and education staff, thirteen volunteers formed a working group. Three members of the working group were from the LEA, three from schools, and seven from the NHS Trust. The researchers recruited five local parents and four pupils to advise and comment on the working group's plans. With the research team in a facilitating role, the staff working group devised a model for improved communication and, by the time our funding came to an end, had prepared for its implementation.

Summary of findings from health staff

The data from health staff both confirmed evidence about health/school communication from other sources and also shed light on difficulties experienced by health staff. Information and advice which health staff passed to teachers, and how they went about doing this, varied widely. The flow of information was most consistent where pupils had a Statement of SEN, since there was an established system for passing on and reviewing information about the child's needs. Health staff valued efforts made by teachers who passed on health-related information to colleagues in school and eased arrangements for visiting health staff, although not all teachers were thought supportive in health matters.

A strong concern for health staff in sharing information with teachers was confidentiality, since they saw codes of confidentiality in the NHS as stricter than in schools. Other communication difficulties were practical: the lack of time for health and school staff to contact one another, and uncertainty about who in schools held responsibility for liaison in respect of this group of pupils. Health staff also reported wide variation in practice among health colleagues in passing information to each other. The chosen practice of consultant paediatricians emerged as crucial, since they were the source of much information. While school doctors saw themselves as a key link with schools, a lack of clarity among consultants as to the school doctor role resulted in the limited transfer of information to school doctors for onward communication to school staff.

The new model for health/school communication

The working group decided that they needed to introduce a system which clarified *who* was responsible for passing on information about this group of pupils and *what* information they were routinely expected to pass on, and to produce a *standard* set of documents for collecting information. The intention was to develop a model which would be as simple as possible and which would not place a heavy additional burden on staff, in particular teachers. What was developed, while research-based, necessarily builds upon the local context, including existing resources available. As such, it was designed to fit the local circumstances, rather than for generalisability. The model has five linked components:

- a named teacher in every mainstream school;
- a named health professional for every mainstream school;
- a standard health register in every school;
- a standard individual health care plan for pupils with an illness or disability;
- a 'Smart card' for pupils with an illness or disability.

The named teacher has designated responsibility for pupils with special health needs, including liaison with LEA and NHS staff. Each school decides who should take on this role. The named health professional is a school doctor. In each school, the named teacher and named health professional are responsible for setting up a health register of all pupils with a medical condition and/or health-related support needs, and for reviewing this at least annually. The named health professional has responsibility for writing, updating and reviewing health care plans for individual pupils, in conjunction with parents and the named teacher.

Overall the model is designed to improve communication between staff about a pupil's health-related needs at school. By contrast, the 'Smart card' (laminated and of credit-card size) is held by pupils. Written on the card is any information that they might want to pass quickly and discreetly to teachers. It was proposed by pupils and is intended to overcome difficulties they experience when teachers refuse to believe their health-related requests.

The model has been written up in the form of joint LEA/NHS Trust guidelines for local staff, and was 'launched' at a local head teachers' conference in March 2000. A copy of the guidelines was sent to all schools and relevant health staff. School doctors have received relevant training. The model went 'live' in the autumn term of 2000, with an audit scheduled for spring term 2001.

The 'fit' between policy and practice

In this section we identify key relevant areas of national policy guidance and use the research data to examine their interpretation in practice. Pupils with a chronic illness or physical disability straddle the policy boundary between education and health: there is no single policy document which identifies their needs and gives guidance on support. However, this group of pupils does feature in policy guidance in both education *and* health. At the time our research was carried out three guidance documents were particularly relevant, and we consider each of these in turn:

- the *Code of Practice on the Identification and Assessment of Special Educational Needs*, issued following the Education Act 1993 by the (then) Department for Education and the Welsh Office (1994);
- guidance on *Supporting Pupils with Medical Needs*, published jointly by the Department for Education and Employment and the Department of Health (1996);
- the Department of Health's (1996) good practice guide on *Child Health in the Community*.

Code of practice on the identification and assessment of special educational needs

Policy

The 1993 Education Act (section 156) identified a child as having 'special educational needs' if he or she 'has a learning difficulty which calls for special educational provision'; that is, provision additional to or different from provision generally available in the local area. The Code was issued under the Act to give practical guidance – primarily to schools and to LEAs – on managing their response to the 20 per cent of pupils who the Code estimates will, at some time, have SEN. The Code argues that there is a continuum of severity of SEN and that the needs of the vast majority of pupils can be met through the resources of their school, with outside help if necessary. Under the Code, pupils with SEN are allocated to one of five stages of severity on a school's SEN Register. Early stages are managed by the school with outside specialist experience being brought in from Stage 3 upwards. Nationally, only around 3 per cent of pupils have needs complex or severe enough to place them at Stage 5, where a formal Statement of SEN allocates additional resources to support the child at school following a statutory assessment by the LEA and other relevant agencies, including the NHS where appropriate. In each school a designated teacher – the Special Educational Needs Co-ordinator (SENCO) – is responsible for day-to-day operation of the school's SEN policy, including maintenance of the Register, and for liaison with colleagues, parents and other agencies.

Where do pupils with a chronic illness or physical disability fit into the Code? Despite its undoubted focus on special needs arising from *learning* difficulties, the legal definition of SEN in the 1993 Act (Section 156) does include children with a disability 'which prevents or hinders them from making use of educational facilities' (now Section 312 in the 1996 Education Act). In addition, the Code draws attention to the *potential* impact which a child's medical condition may have for his or her education: 'Some medical conditions may, if appropriate action is not taken, have a significant impact on the child's academic attainment and/or may give rise to emotional and behavioural difficulties' (para 3.89).

In anticipating the consequences for education of 'medical needs', the Code urges collaboration between those who have expert knowledge about the child:

> Children with identified medical needs will not necessarily have an associated learning difficulty, but the consequences of their illness or disability ... may lead to future difficulties if there is not close co-operation between the school, the relevant child health services, and parents.
>
> (para 2.49)

Although legislation imposes duties on agencies to help each other in respect of pupils with SEN, the provisions are weak. Under Section 166 of the 1993 Education Act (now Section 322 in the 1996 Act), health authorities must comply with an LEA request in connection with pupils with SEN, subject to 'the reasonableness of the request in the light of available resources' and unless they consider that the help is 'not necessary'. Nevertheless, each health authority must have a 'designated medical officer' to lead the local NHS contribution to assessment of pupils with SEN.

Practice

In our research, teachers reported that the focus of the Code on *learning* difficulties meant that its application to pupils with a chronic illness or physical disability was unclear. Pupils in the study who had a Statement of SEN had constant and clear-cut needs for additional resources: for example, a need for personal assistance with medical procedures, toileting or with mobility. Other pupils had needs considered by teachers as much more difficult to relate to the Code's guidance in terms of whether – and, if so, where – to place them on the staged SEN Register. For example, some pupils' needs for support were intermittent (in a medical crisis) or were essentially preventative in terms of their impact on education (such as repeated absence risking falling behind with the curriculum). Teachers were concerned about equity in support among this group of pupils, since scope for wide interpretation of the Code meant that pupils with similar needs could be recorded on the Register – and so be supported – very differently, both between and within schools.

Two particularly important aspects emerged as to how the Code is interpreted for this group of pupils; first, whether the child has a Statement and, second, whether the child's needs are included on any stage of the Register. Apart from the general function of the Statement to identify and secure additional resources for school-based support, for pupils with an illness or physical disability having a Statement was also important in providing a formal mechanism for communication between teachers and health staff. Teachers said that only for pupils with a Statement was there a *system* through which they would know the identity of the child's key health professional(s). In addition, only for these pupils was there an expectation that everyone working with the child would meet annually to review the child's progress and discuss how best to support the child. For children without a Statement, teachers felt that education and health operated as 'two very separate worlds' and that trying to find the appropriate NHS contact could be like 'stabbing in the dark'.

The research found that registering pupils on stages of the Code below formal Statementing both provided a mechanism for raising awareness among school staff about a pupil's special needs and identified a person – the SENCO – with lead responsibility for co-ordinating support. Evidence from the teachers in our study (nearly all of whom were SENCOs) suggests that interpretation of the Code for pupils with special health needs varies widely. Crucially, SENCOs argued that a strict interpretation of the Code would mean focusing on pupils with learning difficulties. It followed that, if pupils with health conditions *per se* were not on the SEN Register, then they were technically outside the remit of the SENCO.

In practice, schools' interpretation of the Code fell into one of three categories. In the first category, schools did register pupils with special needs of any kind, so using the Register as a device to raise awareness among school staff of pupils who have health conditions and of any special arrangements made for them. In the second category of schools, the SENCO took an *ad hoc* decision whether to place a child with a health condition on the SEN Register, according to their judgement as to how important it was that colleagues be alerted to the pupil's health needs. In the third category of schools, the Code was interpreted more narrowly as applying only to pupils with learning difficulties. In these schools, either another system – such as a medical register – was used to inform staff about pupils' health needs or, as some teachers reported, no system was in place. For teachers with experience of using medical registers, keeping them up to date could be problematic, as was getting the balance right between confidentiality and making sure that all staff involved with the individual pupil had the relevant information. Secondary schools appeared to have more difficulties than primary schools, owing to the larger number of staff involved with each pupil.

Regardless of whether a pupil was on the SEN Register, and so formally within the remit of the SENCO, in practice SENCOs reported taking responsibility for this group of pupils 'by default', since colleagues turned to them for advice about pupils with special needs of any kind. While SENCOs regarded themselves as ordinary class teachers with a co-ordinating role, they thought colleagues saw them as having expert medical knowledge. Such an assumption was unrealistic for SENCOs, who had insufficient non-contact time and training to meet these expectations. Confusion was also apparent among the health staff we interviewed in the 'communications' project as to whether they should be liaising with SENCOs about pupils with special health needs. Some pupils did not like the assumption that the SENCO had lead responsibility for meeting their support needs in school. Four of the young people in our study mentioned that they did not like being expected to turn to the SENCO for emotional support, since they thought SENCOs prioritised pupils with learning difficulties and so took their health-related worries less seriously.

In the local model developed in the 'communications' project, the working group took account of these ambiguities about the SENCO role by being careful when proposing a 'named teacher' for each school that this would not automatically be a role allocated to the SENCO. Instead, each school should decide who would be the most appropriate person.

Supporting pupils with medical needs

Policy

The growing number of pupils in mainstream schools with medical needs has exposed a 'grey area' as to the responsibilities of school staff at the boundary between education and medical care. In 1996, the DfEE and DoH issued joint guidance aimed at clarifying the situation through setting out the legal position and providing a guide to good practice. The guidance was intended to assist schools in drawing up policies on managing medication and to put in place systems to support pupils with medical needs in school.

The guidance defines children with 'medical needs' as those with 'medical conditions which, if not properly managed, could limit their access to education' (DfEE/DoH 1996: para 7). The guidance cites the Health and Safety at Work

Act 1974 as relevant law, which makes it clear that it is the employer – generally the school's governing body or the LEA – who is responsible for health and safety policy, which should include procedures for supporting pupils with medical needs. However, the guidance also makes it clear that it is parents who are responsible for their child's medication: there is no legal duty which requires individual members of school staff to administer medication; this is a voluntary role and the head will normally be responsible for deciding whether the school can assist (para 11).

Drawing up clear protocols in the form of an 'individual health care plan' is recommended to identify and clarify the level of medical support needed at school (para 75). The good practice guide includes a pro-forma plan which focuses on daily care requirements, what to do in an emergency and follow-up care. In addition to the child, parents and school staff and NHS professionals (school health staff, GP or other health professional) may need to contribute to the plan, which should be reviewed annually (paras 75 and 77).

Practice

In practice, our evidence suggests two types of difficulty with the guidance: first, it appears to have been poorly disseminated; and second, it is insufficiently precise in clarifying responsibility for the provision of medical care in school, despite this being its original purpose.

The good practice guide was issued to LEAs, but was available to schools only on request. Knowledge about the guidance, including the concept of an individual health care plan, was poor among the teachers in our study. Ironically, in their discussions teachers said that there was a need for clear protocols for individual pupils covering medication and what to do in an emergency, which is precisely what the pro-forma individual health care plan in the guidance was designed to provide.

A 1997 Health Select Committee investigation into the clinical needs of children at school concluded that the guidance had failed in its aim to clarify responsibilities for this group of pupils. Our findings endorse this view. While parents are held responsible for their child's medication in the guidance, parents in our study reported school policies to be unclear about the respective obligations of parents and school staff. Parents who were asked to come into school to deal with medication queried this in principle and wanted someone in school to take on this responsibility. For their part, while some teachers in the study did take on a voluntary medical role, others were concerned at the possibility of litigation should something 'go wrong'. Some teachers reported pressure from LEAs not to offer such support on these grounds, although this would be contrary to the spirit of the guidance which encourages LEAs to cover the legal liability of teacher volunteers.

In the 'communications' project, staff drew on the pro-forma individual health care plan in the national guidance to develop their local plan. They started by widening the scope of the plan from the emphasis on 'medical needs' in the national guidance to a broader need for health and school staff to share health-related information. In this way, the plan was explicitly linked with the commitment to introduce other related mechanisms locally, such as school health registers and 'Smart' cards. In designing their local pro-forma, the working group took account of criticisms of the existing guidance by: spelling out staff responsibilities; striving to achieve a consistent approach across schools; and making clear that teachers who had received training for specific 'medical' procedures would be legally indemnified by the LEA. Named contacts in the NHS Trust and the LEA were also identified to provide advice in interpreting the local guidelines.

Child Health in the Community: A Guide to Good Practice

Policy

In 1996, the DoH issued this good practice guide in respect of all child health services, including the school health service (SHS) which has a range of functions in respect of the health of school-aged children. One objective of the SHS is 'minimising the consequences of illness and disability in children for their education' (DoH 1996: para 8.1). Inclusion of more pupils with disabilities in mainstream schools is cited (para 8.5) as one of the factors which has led to a shift in recent years from the traditional universal 'medical inspection' model of the service to a more selective focus. Within this more selective focus, the SHS is expected to provide information and advice to schools about individual pupils, and to make a contribution to the assessment and support of pupils with SEN and medical problems in school (para 8.6).

Practice

In practice, our evidence reveals some reservations about the value of the SHS as the key health service contact for schools, along with communication difficulties between school and NHS staff more generally. In our study, teachers all saw the SHS – and in particular the school doctor – as their key point of contact with the NHS in respect of pupils with a chronic illness or physical disability. However, teachers also reported wide variation in the level of support they received, a finding consistent with other research on the practice of school health professionals (for example, Lightfoot and Bines 1997).

Even where individual school doctors were helpful, in general teachers were not keen to route requests for medical information and advice through them, for two reasons. First, the school doctor was seen by teachers as having a particular focus on the learning implications of illness and disability, and not as an expert on medical conditions *per se*. Second, routing requests for information through the school doctor inevitably resulted in a delay in receiving the information, as confirmed by school doctors themselves in the 'communications' project, who spoke about variation in practice among consultant paediatricians in passing information to school doctors. For both these reasons, teachers said that they would prefer to have direct contact with a child's lead health professional, typically a consultant.

SHS staff were reported by parents and young people as largely irrelevant in the pattern of pupils' care, with their medical needs catered for by specialists away from the school setting. A few parents and young people even raised concerns about the extent to which their school doctor's knowledge about specific conditions was up to date. Although the school nurse is a more frequent visitor to individual schools than the school doctor, young people in our study saw her role as focusing on universal health checks for all pupils, and so of little relevance to their own special needs.

Turning to communication difficulties between health and education staff, although teachers reported a wide range of needs for specific health-related information and advice to help support individual pupils, these needs remained largely unmet, owing to the lack of a mechanism for systematic communication between teachers and health staff caring for individual pupils. All types of respondent in our study – young people, parents and teachers – wanted health staff to be more proactive in taking responsibility for collating and passing information *routinely* to schools. All the young people wanted school staff to have health information so as to understand their support needs at school. Both parents and teachers thought that, while health staff possibly assumed that parents were passing on information to schools, some parents may be unwilling and/or unable from time to time to do so. It followed that health staff needed actively to seek consent from parents and pupils to pass on information needed by school staff.

Research data from health staff in the 'communications' project revealed communication difficulties experienced by health staff, both *between* health and school staff and *among* health staff themselves. In developing the local model for improved health/school communication, the working group chose not to opt for closer contact between the child's lead health professional and school staff, but rather sought to strengthen the role of the school doctor as an intermediary for this group of pupils.

Discussion

It is clear that education policy for 'inclusion', together with medical advances, mean that a growing number of pupils in mainstream schools are likely to require attention to their special health needs to get the most from school life. Our research indicates that pupils with a chronic illness or physical disability and their teachers have a range of health-related support needs, but that provision of support is variable. For schools to operate as a setting for a wide range of health-related support, systems and lead responsibilities are required to identify the needs of these children and to put appropriate support in place. For support to work, pupils' views are needed, along with close co-operation in practice between health and school staff.

Despite these requirements being implicit in policy, analysis of relevant guidance alongside the research evidence suggests that children with a chronic illness or physical disability are a somewhat hidden group. At policy level, the fact that relevant guidance is spread among a number of documents in itself obscures clear definition of these pupils as a group with particular support needs. Straddling the remit of two government departments – education and health – may also serve to weaken their identity as a group, although the DfEE and DoH have pledged to collaborate more closely (DfEE 1998).

Policy guidance could be strengthened in respect of this group of pupils in two key ways. First, the health-related support needs of pupils and their teachers could be made more explicit. Second, guidance could encourage and foster better communications between education and health staff.

Since we embarked on our research, policy attention has again been paid to pupils with SEN. Following publication of the Green Paper *Excellence for All* (DfEE 1997) and the resulting *Programme of Action* (DfEE 1998), a revised Code of Practice on SEN has been drafted (DfEE 2000a). Revisions are aimed at a focus on preventative work and promoting effective school-based support, both of which would be relevant for pupils with special health needs. Involving pupils in decision-making is also given greater emphasis. Designated medical officers are to be asked to consider how the new powers in the Health Act 1999 – allowing pooling of budgets and integration of commissioning or providing functions between the NHS and Local Authorities – can best support services for children with SEN. Such consideration could benefit pupils with special health needs: for example, funding for specialist equipment and aids currently falls between the remit of the two agencies.

In addition, there are signs that disabled children may be emerging as a distinct group among pupils with SEN. Although the draft revised Code of Practice makes clear that education legislation does not distinguish between SEN and disability, attention is drawn to the breadth of definition of disability in the Disability Discrimination Act 1995, which could include a significant proportion of children with SEN. Recently, attention has been paid to education as a gap in existing disability discrimination legislation, with the new Special Educational Needs and Disability Act (2001) designed to fill this gap. Under the Act there is a new duty on education providers to plan strategically and make progress in increasing disabled pupils' accessibility to schools' premises and to the curriculum. The practicalities of doing so are being supported by an allocation of £220million to mainstream schools between 2001 and 2004 to 'improve access for disabled pupils' (DfEE 2000). It seems likely, then, that in future closer attention will be paid to the support needs of disabled pupils in school. While this is a welcome step, we would also hope that the needs of other pupils with chronic illness do not remain hidden.

In the absence of clear national guidance, one way forward is to take a more 'bottom-up' approach through making improvements to local practice. In this chapter we have outlined how health and education staff in one area have attempted to do this. At the time of writing, it is too early to assess the impact of their new local model, both on communication between staff and, crucially, on the appropriateness of support for pupils with special health needs. Fundamentally, whatever benefits may accrue locally to individual pupils from this work, it still seems likely that a national policy 'push' is likely to be needed to secure support on a more systematic basis for this hitherto hidden, but growing, group of pupils.

Acknowledgements

With regard to the 'service support' project, we would like to thank the young people, parents and teachers who took part. This project was funded by the NHS Executive National Research and Development Programme Mother and Child Health Initiative (Grant ref. MCH: 139). With regard to the 'health/school communication' project, we would like to thank the staff involved, in particular the health staff we interviewed and the members of the working group. Our thanks are also due to the parent and pupil advisers. The work of the research team for this project was funded by the NHS Northern and Yorkshire Regional Research and Development Programme under the theme 'Improving the quality of health and social care by better communication' (Project ref. RCRC42C). The views expressed in this paper are those of the authors, and not necessarily those of the NHS Executive or the NHS Executive Northern and Yorkshire.

References

Bolton, A. (1997) *Losing the Thread: Pupils' and Parents' Voices about Education for Sick Children*, London: National Association for the Education of Sick Children.

Botting, B. and Crawley, R. (1995) 'Trends and patterns in mortality and morbidity', in B. Botting (ed.) *The Health of Our Children: Decennial Supplement*, Office of Population Census and Surveys Series DS no. 11, London: HMSO.

Bradbury, A.J. and Smith, C.S. (1983) 'An assessment of the diabetic knowledge of school teachers', *Archives of Disease in Childhood*, 58: 692–6.

Court, S. (1994) 'The health–education boundary: a study of primary school teachers' understanding of childhood illness and its potential to disrupt the educational process', unpublished MSc thesis, University of Newcastle upon Tyne.

Department for Education/Welsh Office (1994) *Code of Practice on the Identification and Assessment of Special Educational Needs*, London: DfE.

Department for Education and Employment (1997) *Excellence for All Children: Meeting Special Educational Needs*, London: The Stationery Office.

——(1998) *Excellence for All: Meeting Special Educational Needs – A Programme of Action*, London, The Stationery Office.

——(2000a) Draft Revised SEN Code of Practice, online, available: www.dfee.gov.uk/sen/standard.htm

——(2000b) £220 million to improve access for disabled children in schools and £172 million for students in other settings (DfEE news 482/00, 6 November), online, available: www.dfee.gov.uk/news/

Department for Education and Employment/Department of Health (1996) *Supporting Pupils with Medical Needs in School*, Circular 14/96, London: DfEE.

Department of Health (1996) *Child Health in the Community: A Guide to Good Practice*, London: NHS Executive.

Dyson, A., Lin, M. and Millward, A. (1998) *Effective Communication between Schools, LEAs and Health and Social Services in the Field of Special Educational Needs*, Newcastle upon Tyne: Special Needs Research Centre, Department of Education, University of Newcastle upon Tyne.

Edwards, M. and Davis, H. (1997) *Counselling Children with Chronic Medical Conditions*, Leicester: BPS Books.

Eiser, C. and Town, C. (1987) 'Teachers' concerns about chronically sick children: implications for paediatricians', *Developmental Medicine and Child Neurology*, 29: 56–63.

Fowler, M.G., Johnson, M.P. and Atkinson, S.S. (1985) 'School achievement and absence in children with chronic health conditions', *Journal of Pediatrics*, 106: 683–7.

House of Commons Health Committee (1997) *Health Services for Children and Young People in the Community: Home and School*, third report, London: The Stationery Office.

Larcombe, I. (1995) *Reintegration into School after Hospital Treatment*, Aldershot: Avebury.

Lightfoot, J. and Bines, W. (1997) *Keeping Children Healthy: The Role of School Nursing*, York: Social Policy Research Unit, University of York.

Lightfoot, J., Wright, S. and Sloper, P. (1998) *Service Support for Children with a Chronic Illness or Physical Disability Attending Mainstream School*, Final Report NHS 1576 10.98, York: Social Policy Research Unit, University of York.

——(1999) 'Supporting pupils in mainstream school with an illness or disability: young people's views', *Child: Care, Health and Development*, 25(4): 267–83.

Midence, K. and Elander, J. (1994) *Sickle Cell Disease: A Psychological Approach*, Oxford: Radcliffe Medical Press.

Mukherjee, S., Lightfoot, J. and Sloper, P. (2000a) 'The inclusion of pupils with a chronic health condition in mainstream school: what does it mean for teachers?' *Educational Research*, 42(1): 59–72.

——(2000b) *Improving Communication between Health and Education for Children with Chronic Illness or Physical Disability*, Final Report NHS 1740 7.00, York: Social Policy Research Unit, University of York.

Nettles, A.L. (1994) 'Scholastic performance of children with sickle cell disease', in K.B. Nash (ed.) *Psychological Aspects of Sickle Cell Disease: Past, Present and Future Directions of Research*, New York: The Howarth Press.

Norwich, B. (1997) *A Trend towards Inclusion: Statistics on Special School Placements and Pupils with Statements in Ordinary Schools, England 1992–96*, Bristol: Centre for Studies on Inclusive Education.

Office for Standards in Education (1997) *The SEN Code of Practice: Two Years On*, London: OFSTED.

Sloper, P., Larcombe, I.J. and Charlton, A. (1994) 'Psychosocial adjustment of five-year survivors of childhood cancer', *Journal of Cancer Education*, 9: 163–9.

Stevens, M.C.G., Kaye, J.I., Kenwood, C.F. and Mann, J.R. (1988) 'Facts for teachers of children with cancer', *Archives of Disease in Childhood*, 63: 456–8.

United Nations (1989) *Convention on the Rights of the Child*, London: HMSO.

Wallander, J.L. and Varni, J.W. (1998) 'Effects of pediatric chronic physical disorders on child and family adjustment', *Journal of Child Psychology and Psychiatry*, 39: 29–46.

10 Housing and schooling

A case study in joined-up problems

Jill Clark, Alan Dyson and Alan Millward

Introduction

The establishment by the incoming government in 1997 of a Social Exclusion Unit (SXU) indicates the extent of concern currently about those groups within society which are systematically 'excluded' from the benefits and opportunities to which most members of society have access. The SXU has been particularly keen to stress that social exclusion in this sense is a 'joined-up problem' and that, in the Prime Minister's words, 'joined-up problems demand joined-up solutions' (Blair 1997). This constitutes a welcome recognition that deep-rooted social problems tend to have a multiplicity of causes and that single-strand remedies are unlikely to be successful. In particular, this has meant that it has become possible to see issues in apparently disparate areas of social and economic policy as forming part of a complex nest of problems which cannot be dealt with in isolation.

Housing and education: a 'joined-up' problem?

Despite this, connections between housing and education remain, in both research and policy terms, relatively under-explored. As the Chartered Institute for Housing comment, 'The connection between housing and education may not be the most obvious. This is reflected in the lack of comprehensive research investigating how the two interact.' They add that, 'Much of the work on the housing–education link has concentrated on homeless children's development' rather than on wider issues (CIH, 1995: 9). Certainly, there is a growing under-standing of some of the grosser impacts of problems associated with housing on schools. Homelessness, as CIH point out, is one such problem, and so too are the problems of schools on some of the country's most troubled estates (Power and Tunstall 1995; Social Exclusion Unit 1998). It is not difficult to understand how 'sink estates' tend to be reflected in 'sink schools', nor how each drags the other into a cycle of decline. However, most children are not homeless, and most of those who live in social housing do not live on 'sink' estates. Yet we know little or nothing about the less dramatic aspects of housing–schooling interactions.

Given this lack of understanding, it is scarcely surprising that there is little policy co-ordination, whether at national, local or area level, between housing and education. It is probably true to say that, at local level, education departments tend to see health and social services as natural partners, while at national level DfEE likewise works more closely with the Department of Health than with the Department of Environment, Transport and the Regions. At area level, there are marginally more developments, with both social landlords and schools involving themselves in wider community issues through what are becoming known as 'Housing Plus' (Housing Corporation 1997; Pearl 1997) and 'Schools Plus' (Social Exclusion Unit 1998) respectively. However, the early evidence suggests that although both schools and landlords may be working in the same communities addressing related aspects of the same 'joined-up problems', it is relatively rare for them to see each other as major partners or to consider in any detail the implications of their policies and actions for each other (Evans 1998).

This chapter, therefore, seeks to fill in at least a few of the gaps in our understanding of these issues.

The investigation

We report here a case study of a primary school – 'Granville Primary' – serving an area of predominantly social housing.[1] Granville Primary is unusual in that it has a particularly close relationship with the dominant social landlord in the local community – a housing association with a long-standing reputation for attempting to create sustainable communities rather than merely providing 'bricks and mortar'. At the time of our study, the landlord supported the school in three ways: financially, by nominating representatives to serve on its governing body, and indirectly through funding initiatives within the community (such as a new nursery) which had educational implications. To this extent, the management of housing on the estate and of the estate's school were more closely bound up with one another than might commonly be the case elsewhere.

The study originated in a series of concerns raised by the staff of Granville Primary School about what they saw as an increasing level of difficulties presented by children in the school, and the relationship between this increase and changes in the landlord's lettings policy in recent years. The first phase of the study focused on exploring these concerns through interviews with relevant stakeholders – school staff and governors, housing association officers, community representatives and professionals in other agencies. The school provided quantitative data on its pupil population (reading test and national assessment scores, exclusion rates, placements in LEA Units, details of the Special Needs Register, changes in pupil roll, etc.) and other agencies were also invited to supply data about the local community (e.g. crime statistics, tenants' survey, GP case-load).

A workshop was held for school staff and other stakeholders at the end of phase one of the research, and the school drew up an action plan. This led directly to the second phase of the investigation, which was chiefly concerned with monitoring and supporting this plan. In addition, an attempt was made to trace linkages between the landlord's lettings policy and the difficulties experienced by the school. This involved matching (in anonymised form) performance data on pupils with housing data related to their families. Moreover, throughout the investigation, parallel data were collected (albeit less intensively) in two comparator areas in order to differentiate idiosyncratic features of the Granville situation from any that might be more generic.

The policy context

Developments in education and in housing policy in England during the 1980s and 1990s parallel each other in important ways. The story of the education reforms in this period has been rehearsed many times and is by now well known in the education community (see, for instance, Ball 1993; Ball *et al.* 1996; Bowe *et al.* 1992; Chitty 1989; Gewirtz *et al.* 1995; Gold *et al.* 1993). The story of housing reforms is perhaps less familiar. In essence, the break-up of local authority monopoly and the introduction of market forces which took place in education were replicated in the housing field. On the one hand, the introduction of the 'right to buy' for council housing tenants meant that many of the more desirable council properties were sold off to some of the (relatively) better-resourced council tenants. On the other hand, councils lost their dominant role as providers of social housing in a more diversified sector and became, instead, 'enablers' of other providers – notably housing associations. In return for their enhanced role, housing associations were required to accept tenants nominated by the local authority on the grounds of their housing need. They had also increasingly to call upon private finance rather than public funds to support their work, which, in turn, required them to set higher rents. Paradoxically, this had the effect of making social housing affordable more easily to people on housing benefit (who do not have to meet these higher rents out of their own income) than for those who are somewhat better off and are therefore not eligible for benefit. (For a fuller, critical overview of these developments, see Malpass 1996.)

The consequence of these policy shifts has been an increasing polarisation within areas of social housing (Burrows 1997). As the (relatively) better-resourced residents gravitated towards owner-occupation, so those residents with fewest resources and the greatest needs gravitated to the remaining areas of social housing in which they could afford to continue to rent their homes, frequently with the support of housing benefit. This has, of course, meant that areas of social housing have experienced varying degrees of turbulence since the late 1980s. In some areas this turbulence has been dramatic, with high levels of unemployment, an increasing proportion of young people, a significant and increasing number of single-parent households, a tendency for schools on these estates to perform well below the national average and a wide range of associated social problems (Power and Tunstall 1995).

Recent Social Exclusion Unit reports on neighbourhood renewal (Social

Exclusion Unit 1998, 2000) point to a pattern of multiple disadvantage on the 'worst estates' in the country, emphasising the extent to which the difficulties confronting these estates constitute 'joined-up problems' and highlighting the implications for schools in such areas. However, they fail to point out two aspects of the housing–schooling interaction that are of particular concern to us here. First, it seems probable that the turbulence caused by housing policy changes has been compounded in its effect on schools by the turbulence caused by education policy changes. Although doubts have been raised about the nature and extent of polarisation in schools (Gorard 2000), case study evidence such as that presented here strongly suggests that, if the population of social housing estates has become residualised, then the population of local schools is likely to become doubly so as more aware and better-resourced parents exercise their right to choose schools in less problematic areas else-where. Second, it is entirely likely that these destabilising effects are not restricted to the 'worst estates'. Even estates which are not in a spiral of decline are likely to have experienced shifts in population, and even schools which are not 'failing' are likely to be dealing with more problematic pupil populations. Granville Estate and its primary school constitute, we suggest, an example of this phenomenon.

The changing estate and school: perceptions

Granville Estate, comprising just under a thousand properties, is a suburb of a medium-sized English city. It is unusual among social housing estates in having been built in the early years of this century as something of a 'model' commu-nity where good-quality houses, each with their own garden, are surrounded by trees and open spaces, where the countryside is nearby and where a range of community facilities – shops, church and community centre – meet the material, spiritual and social needs of residents. As such, it always attracted a cross-section of what one long-stay resident described to us as 'the respectable working class', and sustained a thriving social life underpinned, we were told, by a shared set of communal values and behaviours.

In recent years, the estate has begun to change. As a result of the policy changes outlined above, the landlord was required to accept local authority nominations and to let on the basis of housing need. Inevitably, therefore, many of the 'new' families coming into the estate were experiencing a range of social and economic stresses. At the same time, refurbishment programmes and new build meant that these families tended to be concentrated in particular parts of the estate, while older residents were decanted into purpose-built sheltered accommodation on the periphery or out of the estate entirely.

At about the same time, the primary school serving the estate began to notice a change in its pupil population. Granville Primary is a medium-sized school (over 350 pupils were on roll at the start of our fieldwork) which was originally conceived as an integral part of the comprehensive facilities provided for the residents of the estate. It is for this reason that the landlord has been so closely involved in the governance and funding of the school and that both teachers and residents have seen it as making a distinctive contribution to the quality of life on the estate. As one former pupil told us,

> we were a very special school that people came to see. There were television programmes made on us. We were a model open-air school. We have a videotape over at the school of a programme made in the early fifties where they showed the PE lessons and things. It was very much a school to be a model for others, big windows, south-facing, beautiful gardens, pond.

However, staff now working in the school were increasingly concerned about a series of changes for the worse which recent years had brought with them. These fell into three main areas:

* *Pupils' entry skills*: as one teacher put it to us, pupils in the school currently, 'lack a sort of background awareness and knowledge'. This meant that the school now had to teach them things, particularly in terms of language and social skills, that had always been seen as essentially the responsibility of the family.
* *Pupil attainment*: not surprisingly, staff felt that this lack of prior attainment was reflected in pupils' attainments while they were in the school. The decline in attainment, they felt, was evident right across the curriculum, was particularly marked in basic skills, especially literacy, and was reflected in the school's poor performance in its LEA 'league tables'.
* *Pupil behaviour and social skills*: teachers felt that the behaviour of children had declined alongside the decline in academic standards. Increasingly, they reported, the school has had to deal with an aggressive and disruptive minority of children, who tended to involve a wider group of children in their misbehaviour and who consumed disproportionate amounts of teacher time and attention.

The explanation offered by most teachers for these problems was in terms of the changing population of the estate. This, they felt, threatened the norms and standards that the school demanded and that had once characterised the community as a whole. One teacher explained:

> I think in a way there's no longer the social mix that we used to have. When I first came here it was a genuine estate and you had all the different professions, people who worked at the factory. You had a general social mix. I think there was more of a family life too. [Young] children had both parents at home. I think the parents, some of the parents that I know individually, are struggling to keep their children on the straight and narrow, and they're insisting on their standards but they're finding it very hard because they're surrounded by problem families. And I suppose – I mean I don't know this,

but I suppose – it's very difficult sometimes to stand up and say your bit if you're surrounded by problems who might take it out on you.

In particular, teachers tended to identify the failure of parents – especially lone parents – to develop the learning and behaviour skills of their children as the major causal factor in the school's decline:

> I think it's a lack of experience, a lack of skills amongst parents ... they are coming with a lack of concentration skills; a lot of them watch television, I think; a lot of them watch videos; a lot of them play on computer games; a lot of them don't know about books, don't sit, as far as I can work out, they don't sit and look at a book. They don't play, a lot of my little ones ... Really, I think a lot of these parents need help ... I think we do have a lot of single-parent families which do struggle. I mean, they try their best, but it is a struggle.

Under these circumstances, the school, which had historically been an integral part of the community, was now swimming against the tide of change within that community, seeking to uphold norms and values to which some families no longer subscribed. Put simply, the children it was educating were no longer the children of what we earlier saw called the 'respectable working class'.

The problems facing the staff of the school were compounded by three additional pressures. First, the landlord's lettings policies meant that, as the numbers of school-aged children on the estate increased, so the school had witnessed a dramatic increase in its pupil roll. In the year when most of our fieldwork was undertaken, for instance, the roll had climbed from just over 290 to well over 360 – an increase of some 25 per cent. The light and airy classrooms which were once the pride of the school had suddenly become cramped and inflexible spaces in which children constantly brushed up against one another and where the tolerance of both pupils and teachers was rapidly exhausted.

Second, teachers were aware that they were becoming increasingly accountable in public for pupils' attainments. There was a sense of bitter injustice among the staff we interviewed that the public reporting of attainments took no account of the social background from which the school's intake was drawn. As one teacher put it:

> It makes you very despondent when you know how much effort you put in to try and redress things and it's not measured very much. I mean, I have a child in my class now who was a non-reader in September, and he has made great strides but I think he'll still be 'W' [the bottom of the National Curriculum assessment grades] and that's nothing really. It isn't measured, the progress he's made. And I find that very sad. I find it very sad for the child; I find it sad for myself.

This sense of injustice reached something of a climax at the time of our fieldwork, as the school faced an OFSTED inspection. Even though it emerged from

164 *Jill Clark* et al.

the inspection with some credit, the tension prior to the event and the exhaustion after it were tangible.

Third, as the attainments of pupils apparently declined and as the behaviour of some pupils became more problematic, so parents on the estate were beginning to exercise the right which education legislation now gave them to choose schools elsewhere. As the teacher explained:

> It is a matter of great concern that we might, we could, we may well have done – lost children from the school whose parents do not want them to mix or be with those children that do not behave in the way that they feel they should. And that will skew the school population more and more … into a group which becomes more difficult. It'll be, it could be, a sink school if you're not careful.

The changing estate and school: evidence

When we set the perceptions of school staff, residents and other stakeholders against the 'hard' evidence of change that we were able to identify, our findings were somewhat ambiguous. Certainly, there was evidence that the population of the estate had changed in recent years and that it now contained more families who were experiencing poverty and other forms of stress. However, there was no evidence that the difficulties in Granville were any greater than in a number of other areas in the same city. Indeed, they were a good deal less acute than in many of the most problematic estates in the country (Social Exclusion Unit 1998) and Granville was far from embarking on any terminal decline.

Similarly, there was good evidence that the population of the school had changed and that it contained more children with low attainments and more who presented behavioural difficulties than had historically been the case. However, there was no evidence of an overall, year-on-year decline. Instead, there were 'pockets' of 'problematic' children in particular year groups, causing very real difficulties to their teachers but certainly not presenting the school with a hopeless situation.

It would, however, be too simplistic to dismiss the concerns either of residents or of the school staff as unfounded. The key to us seemed to be not the *absolute* level of difficulty (in terms of poverty, low attainment and so on) so much as the degree of *change* in that level. The longer-stay members of the school staff in particular were imbued with the sense that this had been 'a very special school' with particularly positive relationships between teachers and pupils and with particularly strong support from its community. They had developed practices and procedures based on these expectations, but as these expectations increasingly fell out of line with reality, it was difficult for them to be readjusted, or for the staff to develop new ways of working.

There were a number of areas where this was evident. One was in relationships with parents. Granville Primary was by no means insensitive to the need to involve parents in supporting their children's learning. The staff, therefore, set up a range of parental involvement activities of the sort which work in many schools and had worked here in the past. Unfortunately, these activities did not generate the response which the staff expected. One teacher, for instance, told us what had become of her parent–child reading scheme:

> [Another teacher] and myself run these 'Pals' groups, which is extra reading … and I think we sent out eighteen letters and I think we got nine replies – that's half – and then to the actual meeting only four turned up. And I've just looked at their books this morning and of those four, there's only two doing it properly.

Although we never found teachers being anything less than understanding of the difficulties which many parents faced, such experiences simply reinforced the view that the children's – and therefore the school's – problems were largely due to the inadequacies of those parents. As the head put it, 'There's a clash of values here between the school and a good number of our – a good portion of our catchment.' The consequence of this attribution was, inevitably, that the problems within the school were seen as having causes in the community which it was quite beyond the capacity of the school to address. There was, therefore, simply a sense of helplessness in the face of what were seen to be overwhelming difficulties. As one teacher told us in reporting her unsuccessful attempts to model appropriate behaviour to her pupils: 'for some it's water off a duck's back. They'll do it while you're there. They're only doing it because you're there, basically. If you turn your back on them, they'll resort to their own behaviour.'

This mention of behaviour difficulties points to a second area where the same phenomenon was evident. In response to these difficulties, the head had changed his approach to children, abandoning, to some extent, the positive approach which had previously worked so well in school. As he told us:

> I'm now having to address children in a way I wouldn't have done ten years ago … we have had to adopt different stances to deal with these children which are, to some extent, alien to us. We don't want to have to behave in that way.

The school had adopted a more punitive approach, including the use of detentions. However, this was not altogether effective. As one teacher told us:

> the children in the detention room, generally speaking it's the same children over and over again because these are the children with behaviour problems. It's not what we want to do but it's the only way that we can really cope.

As a result, the constant battles over behaviour were draining on the staff and reduced their educational input to children. The head explained:

> It's exhausted them on occasions, and it's diverted them away from what they should be doing. It's affected the learning of other children and it's

affected the way they would teach those children. I think that's one of the most radical changes I've noticed in the school.

A similar situation was evident in respect of literacy teaching. In response to the perceived – and indeed, actual – decline in pupils' attainments, the school had employed a part-time special educational needs co-ordinator (SENCO), who effectively operated as a remedial reading teacher. However, this strategy was no more effective than the behaviour strategy – and for very similar reasons. As one teacher explained:

> We've got more special needs children. I think there's over a hundred in the school and we have to provide for these. So these children get less of our SENCO's time because she only works three days and this is a financial problem so she cannot give them extra time. Also the outside support team have had their hours cut. So children who would have been getting extra help from outside of school … that has been cut right down, so basically I think two of our children get it in the whole school now.

Looking from outside the school, it was not too difficult to see why these strategies were not working. Faced with a changing population of both pupils and parents, the school had failed to develop approaches that were sufficiently different from those that it had used in the past. It had put a little more effort into its parental involvement schemes, had begun 'tightening up' (in the head's words) its approach to behaviour management and had employed a teacher to do some remedial teaching. However, it had not thought through from first principles how it might respond to the changed situation. It had not, for instance, addressed the curriculum and teaching practices in ordinary classrooms, or sought to become a community school, or developed inter-agency strategies for addressing pupils' difficulties. Not surprisingly, therefore, its efforts were taking a great deal out of the staff, but producing very little change among the pupils and their families.

Saying this, however, begs the question about how, precisely, the school could have gone about such a fundamental reorientation of its approach. Despite the extent to which they were struggling with the current situation, the head and his staff were described to us in glowing terms by some informed observers. One commented that 'there are some outstanding teachers, teachers that I look at and think, "I wish I could have taught a class like that." ' Another paid similar testimony to the head: 'He's an excellent, devoted headmaster and he has a tremendously hard job there. He does, he really does.'

If such comments were only partly true, it is evident that the head and staff of the school were at least 'good enough'. If, therefore, they were not able to generate solutions to their problems, there are real doubts as to how far many schools – certainly, many small primary schools – would be capable, from within their own material and intellectual resources, of reconstructing themselves and addressing the 'joined-up problems' which Granville Primary was facing.

Moreover, at the same time as the need for a 'joined-up solution' was manifesting itself, the school was under increasing pressure to focus more intently on its 'core business' of teaching and learning. The OFSTED inspection at the start of our involvement with the school drained the staff and led the head to put on hold any community-oriented developments for some time. Towards the end of our fieldwork, the school experienced the annual publication of its position in the league table of pupil attainments. It was firmly rooted at the bottom, and we left the head disheartened and disillusioned.

Certainly, in the case of Granville Primary it was difficult to see where support was to be found to help it work more proactively with its community. As we have seen, Granville Estate was no 'worse' than other estates in its city. The consequence was that the other agencies active on the estate – including the LEA and its services – tended not to see Granville as a particularly problematic area. Although they provided adequate levels of service, they were therefore not inclined either to invest disproportionately in the estate or to engage in ambitious inter-agency approaches and regeneration schemes. There were, for instance, no plans for Education Action Zones or Health Action Zones, and no ways to access moneys for New Deal for Communities or Excellence in Cities initiatives.

The only agency that saw Granville as particularly problematic, in fact, was the housing association which was its landlord, and hence it invested heavily in both the school and the community. However, in matters to do with the school, the landlord was guided by the head teacher and therefore tended to support the school's traditional approach (it was, for instance, the landlord which, effectively, paid for the remedial teacher). Moreover, there were some indications – to put it no more strongly – that the more proactive the landlord became in the community, the more other agencies retreated into their minimum statutory obligations.

Granville Primary, therefore, may not have been a failing school, and its estate was not apparently entering on a spiral of decline. Nonetheless, here we had a school which was facing a set of problems not of its own making – a change in its pupil population, a decline in attainments and behavioural norms, a reduction of the support which it could automatically expect from its parent body – and which were significantly destabilising its established practices. These problems were certainly 'joined-up', if only because they emanated from housing as well as education policies. However, there was no evidence of a joined-up solution emerging that would offer either the school or its pupils effective support.

Some implications for inter-agency working

What, then, can we learn from the Granville situation about the key themes of this book – in particular about the problems and possibilities of inter-agency working and about its relation to social inclusion/exclusion?

The first lesson is that we have to conceptualise 'inter-agency working' some-what more broadly than is usually the case. It is, the Granville situation suggests, no longer adequate to think of joint working simply in terms of collaboration among the individually oriented 'caring' agencies such as education, social services and health. Other aspects of public policy impact on schools, on children within those schools and on the families in which those children grow up. In this case, our focus has been on housing. However, there is good reason to believe that other aspects of policy – transport, economic development, employment, policing and so on – have equally powerful impacts. 'Joining up' policy, therefore, does not simply mean linking the services that deal with families at risk or in crisis; it means developing a co-ordinated approach which eliminates risks at source. Indeed, it is no accident, as Moss *et al.* suggest (1999), that countries which place greatest emphasis on collaboration to meet personal, family and community crisis may be precisely those which do least to develop good universal provision.

The second lesson relates to this. Just as joint working tends to be focused on the most vulnerable individuals and groups, so it also tends to be focused on the most 'needy' areas. Certainly, many of the current government's initiatives – Education Action Zones, Surestart, Excellence in Cities, Health Action Zones and so on – are focused in this way.

Not surprisingly, areas such as the Granville Estate, where problems are not – or not yet – acute, tend to be overlooked in such initiatives as attention, energy and resources are targeted on areas, particularly the inner cities, where problems are more dramatic. The danger is, of course, that, as areas such as Granville are left to their own devices, the 'good-enough' gradually becomes the 'not-quite-good-enough' and the problem becomes a crisis. By this time intervention may well be too late.

The final lesson relates to the deep ambiguity which is endemic in government policies regarding education and social exclusion. This ambiguity can be detected in the dilemmas which Granville Primary faces. On the one hand, it is expected to focus on children's attainments, is resourced with this in mind and is judged almost solely according to its success in this respect. On the other hand, it is unlikely to raise attainments in the long term without undertaking some fundamental work in its community which would take it away from its 'core business' of teaching. This same ambiguity is also evident in the comments of Rob Smith, in introducing the DfEE's recent *Schools Plus* report:

> Our overall aim was to develop a coherent and comprehensive approach to supporting the learning of every child in deprived communities. This would require teaching to be focused, stimulating and productive, as well as schools being fully utilised as agents for broader change in communities. The result *should* be a strengthening, rather than any erosion, of schools' pupil-focused efforts.
>
> (DfEE 1999: 4, our emphasis)

Whether what *should* be is what actually *is* remains to be seen. The implications for schools serving disadvantaged communities, however, are clear: they have to focus on academic excellence in the same way as all other schools, and *at the same time* they have to undertake an extended community role. Whether such schools have the capacity – in terms of the resources, the expertise and the energy – to carry out such a dual role is, to say the least, a moot point. Whether, moreover, the drive for 'standards' in which they are required to engage is compatible with this wider role is equally problematic. The message from the centre, however, is as unambiguous as it is unrelenting: they must simply work harder than other schools to achieve all that is expected of them (OFSTED 2000).

Somewhere beneath the dilemmas which schools such as Granville Primary face lurk the ambiguities of the government's social inclusion agenda. Social inclusion, like motherhood and apple pie, is an ideal from which it is difficult to dissent. However, it is equally difficult not to wonder whether some of the structural features of the society within which disadvantaged citizens are being so vigorously *in*cluded are not precisely the ones which are generating their *ex*clusion. The attainment-focused, reputation-sensitive, beleaguered schools which the standards agenda and the education market, at their worst, create might themselves unwittingly be responsible for alienating disadvantaged children and families from the education process that is their pathway to 'inclusion'. One final piece of 'joining up' that is needed, therefore, is the development at government level of a 'joined-up' vision of what an inclusive society might look like, and of the role that schools might play in such a society. It remains to be seen whether this government or any likely successor is capable of such a task.

Notes

1   This study was sponsored by the Joseph Rowntree Foundation and is reported at greater length in J. Clark, A. Dyson and A. Millward (1999) *Housing and Schooling: A Case-Study in Joined-Up Problems* (York: YPS).

References

Ball, S.J. (1993) 'The market as a class strategy in the UK and US', *British Journal of Sociology of Education*, 14(1): 3–19.

Ball, S.J., Bowe, R. and Gewirtz, S. (1996) 'Circuits of schooling: a sociological exploration of parental choice of school in social class contexts', *Sociological Review*, 43: 52–78.

Blair, T. (1997) Speech given by the Prime Minister on Monday 8 December 1997, at the Stockwell Park School, Lambeth, regarding the launch of the government's new Social Exclusion Unit.

Bowe, R. and Ball, S.J., with Gold, A. (1992) *Reforming Education and Changing Schools*, London: Routledge.

Burrows, R. (1997) *Contemporary Patterns of Residential Mobility in Relation to Social Housing in England*, York: Centre for Housing Policy University of York.

Chartered Institute of Housing (1995) *A Point to Prove: Why Housing Matters*, Coventry: CIH.

Chitty, C. (1989) *Towards a New Education System: The Victory of the New Right?* London: Falmer Press.

Clark, J., Dyson, A. and Millward, A. (1999) *Housing and Schooling: A Case-Study in Joined-Up Problems*, York: YPS.

DfEE (1999) *Schools Plus: Building Learning Communities. Improving the educational chances of children and young people from disadvantaged areas: a report from the Schools Plus Policy Action Team 11*, London: DfEE.

Evans, R. (1998) *Housing Plus and Urban Regeneration: What Works, How, Why and Where?*, Liverpool: European Institute of Urban Affairs, Liverpool John Moores University in association with the Housing Corporation.

Gewirtz, S., Ball, S.J. and Bowe, R. (1995) *Markets, Choice and Equity in Education*, Buckingham, Open University Press.

Gold, A., Bowe, R. and Ball, S. (1993) 'Special educational needs in new context: micropolitics, money and "education for all"', in R. Slee (ed.) *Is There a Desk with My Name on It? The Politics of Integration*, London: Falmer Press, pp. 51–64.

Gorard, S. (2000) 'Questioning the crisis account: a review of the evidence for increasing polarisation in schools', *Educational Research*, 42(3): 309–21.

Housing Corporation (1997) *A Housing Plus Approach to Achieving Sustainable Communities*, London: Housing Corporation.

Malpass, P. (1996) 'The unravelling of housing policy in Britain', *Housing Studies*, 11(3): 459–70.

Moss, P., Petrie, P. and Poland, G. (1999) *Rethinking School: Some International Perspectives*, Leicester: Youth Work Press for the Joseph Rowntree Foundation.

OFSTED (2000) *Improving City Schools*, London: OFSTED.

Pearl, M. (1997) *Social Housing Management: A Critical Appraisal of Housing Practice*, London: Macmillan.

Power, A. and Tunstall, R. (1995) *Swimming Against the Tide: Progress or Polarisation on Twenty Unpopular Estates*, York: Joseph Rowntree Foundation.

Social Exclusion Unit (1998) *Bringing Britain Together: A National Strategy for Neighbourhood Renewal*, London: The Stationery Office.

——(2000) *National Strategy for Neighbourhood Renewal: A Framework for Consultation*, London: The Stationery Office.

11 'Some woman came round'

Inter-agency work in preventing school exclusion

Gwynedd Lloyd, Andrew Kendrick and Joan Stead

Introduction

This chapter will give an account of the current policy context and practice in relation to the issue of exclusion from school in Scotland and then discuss some emerging themes from a current research project, funded by the Joseph Rowntree Foundation,[1] which is looking at inter-agency practice effective in preventing exclusion from school. It will refer to the accounts of service-users – young people who have been excluded or are at risk of exclusion, and their parents – and explore their understandings of the different professionals involved in their lives. It will then briefly discuss some initial conclusions derived from interviews with the professionals and from observations of inter-agency professional meetings. Finally it will discuss the implications for policy and for successful inter-agency practice.

The policy context for inter-agency working

Inter-agency work is not always easy, and a number of issues have been identified: the barriers caused by different professional cultures and working practices (Cullen *et al.* 1996; Leathard 1994); the protection of budgets and resources by the different agencies (Kendrick 1995; Lloyd and Munn 1999; Wilson and Pirrie 2000); varying commitment to inter-agency work in different schools and social work areas (Kendrick 1995). The principle of inter-agency working has been central to many recent developments in working with young people, both those specifically at risk of exclusion from school and those caught up in wider processes of social exclusion. However, joint working between social work, education and other agencies has a much longer history in Scotland. Indeed, the Kilbrandon Report (Scottish Office 1964) proposed that children and young people in difficulty should be dealt with in 'social education departments' managing both education and social services in an integrated way (Schaffer 1992; Kendrick 1995). While 'social education departments' were never established, collaborative responses have been formalised in 'youth strategies' in Scotland since the early 1980s (Pickles 1992; Kendrick 1995).

Youth strategies, as developed in a number of local authorities, varied in their scope. Some youth strategies incorporated a broad, community development approach, bringing together agencies working with young people and community representatives to develop a range of opportunities and activities for young people in their area. For other youth strategies, the starting point was in keeping children out of residential education and developing a range of community-based resources to support children whose needs were not being met in mainstream education. Multi-disciplinary, school-based meetings were developed in most authorities which bring together representatives from school guidance, learning support, school health, educational psychology, the social work department, the community education department and often neighbourhood-based voluntary sector projects, to develop school-wide strategies and to consider cases of young people experiencing difficulties in school and at risk of school exclusion.

The Children (Scotland) Act 1995 specifies a statutory duty for local authorities to produce and publish Children's Services Plans in consultation with health agencies, voluntary organisations, representatives of the Children's Hearing System, and housing agencies. The legislation emphasised the 'corporate responsibility' of the local authority. The Scottish Office (now the Scottish Executive) set out five strategic aims for Children's Services Plans:

- to ensure the welfare of children;
- to clarify strategic objectives in relation to services;
- to promote integrated provision of services and effective use of available resources;
- to ensure a consistent approach to planning by local authorities;
- to establish a high standard of co-ordination, co-operation and collaboration between service departments within local authorities, between different local authorities and with other agencies and organisations which have a contribution to make to effective provision of local services.

(Scottish Office 1997)

Barriers to joined-up working

The Labour government has increasingly stressed the importance of 'joined-up' working or partnership working. As part of the government's Social Inclusion Strategy, the 'Making It Happen Strategy Action Team' was set up to make recommendations about ways of overcoming professional, organisational and cultural barriers to promoting social inclusion. In its report it identifies three types of barriers to effective joint working:

- *Structural and functional barriers*: fragmentation of public services because of the range of organisations involved in their delivery; agencies structured around the services to be delivered rather than the areas or groups served.

- *Process barriers*: inflexibilities caused by the financial procedures of agencies; the processes of some central government funding which encourages short-termism and forced partnerships.
- *Cultural barriers*: professions and organisations can have their own way of doing things which may involve ill-informed views of the other organisations and professions with which they deal (Scottish Executive 1999).

The Making It Happen Strategy Action Team also make a number of recommendations focusing on:

- training for partnership working;
- leadership on commitment to partnership working;
- review of resource allocation issues which prevent partnership working;
- setting targets for partnership working;
- fostering a learning culture through dissemination of good practice across agencies and organisations;
- streamlining of partnerships.

(Scottish Executive 1999)

Central to the development in the government's social inclusion strategy – indeed, described as being 'at the leading edge' of the strategy – is a pilot project for New Community Schools drawing on the Full Service School concept from the USA (see Chapter 4, this volume). As part of the New Community Schools initiative, the Scottish Executive commissioned a literature review entitled *Multidisciplinary Team-working: Beyond the Barriers? A Review of the Issues*. It concluded that, at the moment, 'there is very little evidence regarding the efficacy of multi-disciplinary team working in educational settings' (Wilson and Pirrie 2000a: 4; Wilson and Pirrie 2000b). So the issue of multi-agency working has been on the agenda for a long time in Scotland but clearly has been given additional impetus through a range of current politically driven policy initiatives. One policy initiative, key at both national and local council level, focuses around a drive to reduce the numbers of children excluded from school.

Exclusion from school in Scotland

There are several key differences in the legislation and guidance on exclusion in England and Scotland (Munn *et al.* 2000). In England there is a stipulated length of fixed term exclusions and a restriction of parental rights to choose a school if their child has been excluded more than once. In Scotland the length of an exclusion is a matter for the education authority to decide. The law in Scotland does not use the terms 'temporary' and 'permanent' exclusion but, according to the national Guidance, either 'temporary exclusion' or 'exclusion/removed from the register' of the individual school (Scottish Office 1998a).

Comparisons of number or rate of exclusion between Scotland and England are difficult as there are different ways of describing exclusion and of collecting data. Recent Scottish Executive statistics, derived from a fairly new approach to data gathering following the Guidance on Exclusion, allow for more comparison, but again there are issues about the accuracy of these figures due to the difficulties experienced by councils in collecting accurate data from schools (Scottish Office 1998a; Scottish Executive 2000a). Parsons compares Scottish and English numbers, based on figures recorded by education authorities, which suggest that the rate of 'exclusion/removed from the register' in Scotland in 1997/1998 was a tenth of that recorded as 'permanent exclusion' in England (Parsons 2000). These figures have limited validity as the Scottish figures are inconsistent in their application of the categories (Parsons 2000). One council, for example, recorded as 'removal from the register' pupils who had been excluded from school and then subsequently enrolled in another, whereas one of the largest councils counted such a move as temporary exclusion as pupils remained educated by the council. This has led to suggestions that children are not permanently excluded from school in Scotland. Sadly, this is only the case in the sense that the formal label is not that of permanent exclusion – there are still excluded children with no full-time educational placement.

In Scotland there are no Pupil Referral Units specifically for excluded pupils, although there is a range of units and schools, ranging from units designed to support pupils part-time in mainstream or to reintegrate them, to day and residential schools for children and young people with 'social, emotional and behavioural difficulties'. As in other parts of Britain, the rate of reintegration of pupils into mainstream, once they have been out for some time, is low (Lloyd and Padfield 1996; Farrell and Tsakalidou 1999). Recent figures from the Scottish Executive show disproportionate rates of exclusion for children with Records of Need (like a Statement of Special Educational Needs in England), 'looked after' children and children entitled to free school meals.

The law on special educational needs in Scotland, discussed in this volume by Tisdall, requires that special educational provision be made for those who have greater difficulties in learning than their peers. In a rather tautological model, a child or young person has 'a "learning difficulty" if additional arrangements need to be made to enable them properly to access the curriculum' (SOEID 1996: para 9.2). Difficulties in learning are defined widely and described as being caused by a variety of factors, including a child's behaviour or social and emotional development. Thus the perceived presence of social, emotional and behavioural difficulties (SEBD) can be a reason for a child or young person being considered to have special educational needs. Where such special educational needs are seen to be pronounced, specific or complex and to require continuing review, the education authority is required to open a Record of Needs. Considerable variation in levels of Recording are found within and between education authorities (Closs 1997). This variation is most marked in relation to social, emotional and behavioural difficulties, where some pupils may have Records whereas others, even many of those in full-time special educational provision, may not.

A confusing policy context

The Guidance on the 1995 Children (Scotland) Act could apply to 'children with special needs', 'children with emotional, behavioural and mental health problems' and those whose 'educational development is suffering' (Tisdall, this volume). This means that children who are excluded or at risk of exclusion from school may be considered in terms of education law and procedures *and/or* in terms of the social welfare law and procedures of the Children (Scotland) Act 1995, including those relating to the Children's Hearing System. The rights of children and families in each are different. This is confusing, not only for children and families but also for professionals. The Children (Scotland) Act 1995 gives children and young people the right to have their views considered – this right is not specified in the educational law and procedures for the assessment of special educational needs. In Children's Hearings children and families will be present and must understand the basis on which decisions are made (Kendrick 2000). The position of children and families in relation to school-based multidisciplinary meetings varies considerably, as discussed further below.

The 'right' to schooling and the presumption of inclusion

The Standards in Scotland's Schools etc. Act 2000 introduces for the first time in any British education law a 'presumption of mainstream education' (see also comments in this volume by Tisdall). The Guidance for Education Authorities on the presumption of mainstream states that 'The intention behind the new duty is to establish the right of all children and young persons to be educated along with their peers in mainstream school unless there are good reasons for not doing so.' However, it also argues that: 'The new duty ... acknowledges that the needs of some children may be best met through special provision' (Scottish Executive 2000b: 2). There are two main reasons why this might be the case: first, if there are particular reasons why an individual child might need some small-scale or highly specialised setting, and second, very relevant to the issue of exclusion, if the inclusion of one child 'may be incompatible with an education authority's duty towards all of the children in its care. Children regularly displaying severely challenging behaviour, for example, can have negative effects on the education of children around them' (Scottish Executive 2000a: 4).

Importantly, also in the context of thinking about exclusion, the new Act gives all children of school age the *right* to be provided with school education. Previously parents had a duty and education authorities had a duty to provide an adequate and efficient education, but children had no specified rights to receive schooling. However, the possibility of disciplinary exclusion is still clearly specified in the Act, although it does impose new duties on education authorities to make special arrangements to ensure that pupils who do not attend school because they are excluded, as well as those who are caring for relatives or are too ill to attend school, receive an adequate education. A Circular will be issued to authorities offering guidance in the interpretation of the aspects of the Act relating to exclusion and to their duty to make appropriate educational provision, although such provision may be part-time and take place outwith school.

Scottish Executive initiatives around exclusion

The government in Scotland has specifically addressed the issue of school exclusion and problem behaviour in school in three policy and funding initiatives: Promoting Positive Discipline, the Ethos Network and the Alternatives to Exclusion initiative (Munn *et al.* 2000). The latter has the explicit aim of reducing the need for and incidence of exclusion from school. Again central to this initiative is effective multidisciplinary and inter-agency co-operation and the guidance on this sets out good practice as including:

- mechanisms for ensuring that, at an early stage, schools and other agencies inform each other about pupils in difficulty and discuss those difficulties;
- mechanisms for co-ordinating a full range of appropriate assessments involving teachers and professionals from other agencies, and integrating these to provide a picture of the whole child;
- mechanisms for jointly planning, undertaking and reviewing programmes of intervention to address underlying difficulties identified;
- joint mechanisms for the placement and review of pupils in special provision; and
- mechanisms to ensure appropriate collaboration between education, social work and, where appropriate, other agencies, with regard to pupils in residential provision or children who are being 'looked after' by the local authority in children's homes or other contexts.

(Scottish Office 1998b: 19)

Researching inter-agency practice in preventing exclusion

The aspects of good practice specified above in preventing exclusion are the focus of the research described here. From the preceding discussion it will be apparent that the Scottish Executive has a demonstrable commitment to reducing disciplinary exclusion from school which, as in England, is viewed as part of a wider problem of social exclusion. Equally, however, recent education legislation and guidance still allows for both exclusion and special out-of-school placement of pupils whose behaviour is viewed as unacceptable, both in terms of the welfare of the individual pupil and in terms of the welfare of the wider school community.

Most education authorities, while wishing to retain the ability to exclude, have policies – and in some cases quite long-established procedures – designed to reduce exclusion and to promote more effective inter-agency working to support children and young people in their family and in their local school. Inter-agency 'joined-up' working, as argued throughout this book, is very much on the agenda, but its effectiveness in educational contexts is under-researched.

Our research project, funded by the Joseph Rowntree Foundation, had four main aims:

- to outline the context in which inter-agency initiatives have developed in three Scottish councils with regard to the prevention of disciplinary exclusion from secondary schools;
- to investigate the effectiveness of inter-agency initiatives in relation to the prevention of school exclusion in the three Scottish councils;
- to explore stakeholders' perceptions of inter-agency initiatives;
- to identify factors which facilitate or inhibit the development and/or effectiveness of such provision.

The research process involved collaboration with three councils which were involved from the beginning in discussing the research design, locating statistical data and in identifying schools to take part. A sample of thirty young people was selected, who had been excluded in the past or who had been at risk of exclusion, but who were now being supported through multi-agency initiatives in the six study schools (five young people, boys and girls, in each school). Interviews took place with most of the young people and their families (mainly their mothers) and involved professionals. Interviewees were asked to talk about their perceptions of the aims of the multi-agency initiatives; involvement in the process of decision-making and planning; inter-agency relationships; perceived success of the initiatives in relation to the individual young people and more generally. In addition, interviews were held with key informants in the different agencies to identify general issues concerning the development, success and sustainability of the multi-agency initiatives.

In order to provide a more detailed context for interview data in relation to the thirty young people identified, agency case records were scrutinised to collect information on educational progress and involvement with other agencies. Meetings of school-based multidisciplinary teams were observed directly to further understand and contextualise personal and professional interactions with each school. Following the methodology set out by Parsons and Castle (1999), estimated costs relating to involvement of the thirty sample young people in multi-agency initiatives were derived from interviews, case record analysis, and requests for calculation of hourly costs from agencies.

The project was still in progress at the time of writing, and we therefore can only point to emerging themes and make tentative claims. Young people were selected for participation in the research on the grounds that the school felt that their cases showed effective inter-agency working and their schools had equally been suggested by their council on the grounds that they were working successfully to prevent exclusion. This allowed us to focus on what constitutes good practice in this work. Interviews have also, however, pointed to a number of more problematic aspects of collaborative working to avoid exclusion.

Progress so far has allowed us to identify some key issues/questions. These include:

- what counts as inter-agency work
- the key position of inter-agency meetings
- level/nature of participation of young people and parents in decision-making meetings
- roles and responsibilities of professionals, and
- the perceptions of these by service-users
- the qualities of an effective 'helper'
- issues to do with the complexity of the legislative and policy context
- the broad general question as to what counts as effective: formal outcomes in relation to individual perceptions.

What counts as inter-agency work

In all three councils there was an explicit commitment to joint policy-making across council services, particularly education and social work. This was documented in policy papers and structured in meetings, especially around resource allocation. In Council C there had been a recent restructuring to merge the education and social work departments at council management level; however, the distinctiveness of their services had not yet altered. This council was also developing a quasi-market model for delivering its services to schools in preventing, and developing alternatives to, exclusion.

Schools in all three councils had a multi-agency decision-making forum. These meetings varied in their style and composition but were a key feature of strategies to support young people in trouble in and out of school and to avoid exclusion – of course, they might also sometimes agree to exclusion. When different professionals in our study were asked about inter-agency working, many focused initially or exclusively on the inter-agency meetings rather than, for example, direct jointly planned work with young people, although such work does take place. Indeed, what our interviewees understood by terms such as 'inter-agency', 'inter-professional' or 'multi-agency' was not always clear.

Inter-agency meetings and the level/nature of participation of young people and parents in decision-making meetings

The meetings were a key focus for thinking about young people in trouble in school. They had some common features but also key differences across the three councils. In Glenmore Council multi-disciplinary teams were called

School Liaison Groups. Their management, and the channel for most referrals, was the responsibility of school senior management. A key role within this was '[t]o ensure that parents or carers are informed of a referral to the SLG and are actively and positively involved in the subsequent programmes' (Council policy paper). There were three levels of decision-making. Level 1 was 'in school' and consisted of a regular meeting of school staff. Level II was for consideration of referrals to support services outwith school, for example to the council's pupil support centre which offered part-time attendance and outreach support. Professionals presented might include guidance staff, Learning Support, the designated link from the area social work department, a representative from the council-wide support centre, someone from the local youth project, educational psychologist, nurse. Level III was referral for residential placement outwith the authority, and used only for very small numbers. Joint planning with the social work department was through the 'link worker' who attended Level II – informal discussions regarding social work involvement can take place at SLG. Parents might be invited to a meeting but often seemed not to attend. Pupils were not invited. Smaller sub-groups would meet with pupils and parents.

In Wallace City Council there was also a staged intervention structure. New guidelines for the school-based Pupil Support Groups were launched as part of the council's joined-up 'working together' policy in June 2000. Key partnerships were identified as: education, social work, health services, police, voluntary sector, parents and young people. The Pupil Support Groups (PSGs) should assess, co-ordinate assessment, recommend appropriate strategies and identify appropriate resources. Apart from representatives from key agencies as above, a 'working together' dedicated project representative should also attend PSGs plus other case-related staff as appropriate. (Dedicated project staff were based in teams which support several schools in different parts of the city.) Parents should always be informed of PSG and should be included in a meeting to discuss proposed support plans. Information on individual pupils might be passed on within participating agencies only with parental/guardian permission. The head teacher should review the work of the PSG, and PSGs should consider matters of school policy relating to pupil inclusion.

In Douglasshire Council, inter-agency meetings also formed part of a tiered structure. SAT (School Assessment Team) Level 1 involved the initial assessment undertaken by the school once a problem had been identified. It would not involve any visiting professionals. These meetings therefore fell outwith the research parameters. SAT Level 2 focused on 'within school' resources which could include those professionals whose input fell within the range of what the school would normally access as a result of practice agreements and contracts (for example, school psychologist, case social workers, visiting therapists). Each secondary school held a SAT Level 2 meeting every month. These SATs acted as a mechanism for controlling referrals to CATs. CAT (Community Assessment Team) was a forum that managed access to all resources outwith school. There was a requirement that certain people attend a CAT meeting (for example, chair, parent/guardian, pupil, teacher, case psychologist, case social worker and any other person as specified on the referral). A CAT would only take place in exceptional circumstances if any of these individuals were not present.

So one key difference was that in Douglasshire Council young people and parents were always expected to attend the meetings (and all of those involved in our research had attended), whereas in the other two councils, although there was a good deal of professional contact with parents, it was more common for them to meet with a subgroup of professionals prior to and/or following a meeting of the formal larger group. There was a recognition by parents from Douglasshire that 'having all these people' round a table indicated that things were being taken seriously. One mother, who was now positive about the help she had received through attending the meetings, describes how many parents must feel to begin with:

> At the first ever meeting I went to I was so nervous I had to take my mum with me because I was so nervous, because I thought they were going to end up taking him away.
>
> (mother, School 1)

Another parent said she had been to so many meetings she had become used to them, but

> To start with it's quite intimidating. You're sitting there and Charlie used to cry all the way through them and I used to sit and cry with him [laughs].
>
> (mother, School 2)

Pupils' views were mixed, although there was a general feeling that the meetings were important and that they should attend, with only one young person saying that he 'didn't care'. One young woman, for example, was able to recall the names of all those present at her meetings and was confident and positive about participation.

In the other two councils, where there was less direct participation by parents and young people, the meetings were able to take a more strategic role, sometimes discussing broader aspects of provision to support pupils rather than being entirely case-based as in Douglasshire Council. One observed meeting in Wallace City Council was attended by the assistant head teacher, two guidance staff, the Educational Welfare Officer (attendance officer), educational psychologists, school doctor, Learning Support teacher. The aim of the meeting was to discuss the new school intake for next session, in the light of particular pupils being identified as having special needs or where there may be cause for concern. One hour was allocated for this meeting, at which many pupils were discussed. Other agencies which were mentioned as already being used by the pupils, or those that should be considered by School 3, were CRUSE (for a pupil recently bereaved), psychological services, physiotherapy, speech therapy and English as an Additional Language support.

This more strategic use of the meeting may sometimes make for more effective understanding between professionals, as it allows for the discussion of professional skills and responsibilities, but this is clearly set against the lack of direct participation by young people and families in meetings where decisions may be made about them.

'Some woman came round': does professional role matter?

The title of this chapter reflects a theme emerging from interviews with parents and young people, that perhaps they may not know or even care about the differences in role and status of the professionals in their lives. What was important was that a professional intervention was seen as helpful and not intrusive. A young woman attending a secondary school and a youth strategy support centre, each part-time, after exclusions from two previous schools for – in her words – 'giving cheek to teachers', felt that she had found a good balance of support, but was not always clear about the professional status of those who had been working with her.

> I asked her if she had a social worker and she said, 'Well, there was this woman once who helped.'
>
> (field notes, School 4)

It may be about getting the right help at the right time. Often a cause of frustration for parents, pupils and professionals was the time it took to provide support. Some parents felt that there was a tendency to feel optimistic about issues being resolved in early meetings, but some disillusionment about delays or failure to produce some outcomes:

> I go to them all [with emphasis] every one. I've been at hundreds. It drives you nuts – it's just the same thing, you sort it, it goes on and on.
>
> (mother, School 2)

Another issue often raised was about the nature of the relationship between young people, parents and professionals. The mother quoted below distinguished strongly between those professionals who treated her in an equitable way and those who talked down to her. This comment is about her daughter's social worker:

> I don't consider myself one of the privileged classes. He speaks very properly and real [imitation of 'posh' accent] and you'd think he's come in here and go 'oh, oh' but he doesn't. Although he talks properly he's, he's very – he talks to me on my level. I don't like people that talk to me like they are talking down to me.
>
> (mother, School 3)

In one interview, jointly held with a young man and his mother, she talked about the support offered by the assistant head responsible for behaviour support in School 1:

Mother: Mr N., he doesn't talk down to you, he talks to you.
Interviewer: Sure.
Young man: He doesnae tell me what to do, he asks you to do it.

This young man had been given some additional support from a local authority youth social work agency. He was very positive about this relationship, about the fact that the worker was male and that he saw him as credible in the community. He didn't see him as a social worker (Triseliotis *et al.* 1995):

> T.C., my dad used to talk to him at the football all the time … He's a voluntary helper I seen.
>
> (young man, School 1)

A young man who felt that the support he was given was effective said that:

> My mum and my social workers are good friends and if I'm not in [school] and my mum doesn't phone to say I'm not in, she'll know I'm truanting.
>
> (young man, School 2)

Parents interviewed all expressed care and concern for their son or daughter, and although some were critical of the school for its treatment of their child, often they were understanding of how the actions of their child might have made things difficult in school. Some parents disliked the way they were spoken to by some school staff – one mother said that she felt as if she was being punished along with her child. One parent of a boy frequently excluded from a previous secondary school, when asked about how she felt about all the different professionals who had been involved, said that she would do whatever it took to get her son back on track, and she had never felt uncomfortable or that people talked down to her.

> They don't come at you badly – they explain things.
>
> (mother, school 4)

Changing professional roles

Some of the professionals most valued by parents and young people were the semi-specialist 'children in trouble' workers, sometimes described as group workers or youth social workers, perhaps working in council-run support units or in neighbourhood-based voluntary sector projects. Such staff involved in group work with young people may, for example, have varied original professional qualifications: teaching, social work, community education/youth work and/or outdoor education. This development perhaps reflects the other side of the changing role of some professionals involved in this kind of work: for example, the well-documented move of area team social workers away from casework towards becoming case managers (Malin 2000). This has also to some extent been true of educational psychologists in Scotland, who have moved towards a model which emphasises consultancy (Liddle 2000). An often mentioned difficulty in inter-agency working, described earlier as a cultural barrier, involves lack of knowledge on the part of different professionals of the roles and responsibilities of each other. This difficulty was mentioned by some professionals here and may also reflect the changing roles, structural changes within councils and the rapidly developing policy context.

The complexity of the legislative and policy context

We argued earlier that the policy context for the work involved in preventing or establishing alternatives to exclusion is confusing. This work involves professionals trying to collaborate in relation to legislation and policy which is not joined up at national level. It is clear from interviews in this project with young people, families and professionals that most do not have a comprehensive picture of the rights and responsibilities of families and of professionals as specified in the rather different laws and procedures. At council level, the changing policies and associated procedures on exclusion, pupil support and inter-agency working, as well as those associated with the social work departments and the Children's Hearing System, are difficult enough for the professionals involved in these complex systems to understand, but even more so for those on the periphery, like class and subject teachers. (Some school staff suggested that sometimes their subject teaching colleagues represent the greatest challenge in terms of inter-professional understanding and the development of shared purpose.)

In their study of inter-agency collaborative working in areas of high social need, Easen *et al.* argued that collaboration could be seen as located across two dimensions (2000). These were boundedness and context, the first 'indicating the extent to which the attempt at collaboration had clearly specified outcomes, timescales and procedures' and the second the 'extent to which collaboration focussed on individual clients or on wider community contexts'. The most bounded form of collaboration was found to be in child protection procedures, where the context was clearly about an individual child and the procedures clearly specified. This may be a useful model for analysis of the collaborative work in this study and will be developed further in the final research report (Stead *et al.* 2001). The formal inter-agency meetings themselves may have been mentioned most frequently by professionals as examples of inter-agency work, as they were the most bounded with formal guidelines for procedure specified by the councils. The boundedness of the shared decision-making guidelines/procedures for the meetings about young people is much greater sometimes than the specificity of the possible professional support/intervention which was planned to follow, where professionals may be less aware of the roles and processes in other agencies.

It may be assumed that the principal dislocation in understanding occurs between professionals who are practically involved but not aware of policy and those policy workers who are not aware of practical implications. Our study suggests that the picture is more complicated than this. Practitioners often had incomplete pictures of policy context, but nonetheless their practice was influenced both by the level of their understanding of policy and by their opinion of current policy initiatives. The perception of the current policy on inclusion was very mixed, with some school guidance teachers, for example, expressing hostility:

> Other people have to suffer these kids. The balance is already wrong.
>
> (guidance teacher, School 1)

There is a question as to whether the complex and confusing policy context affects delivery of a service in practice. It may be argued that some professionals appear to be offering appropriate support to families, and it may not matter to those families which agency they represent or whether they understand the policy context of their work.

'They must be doing well – I'm still here' (young man, School 2)

We cannot address, in this chapter and at this stage in our research, the broad general question as to what counts as effective. We have spoken to a number of young people and parents who believe that they have received effective support, and that this support has been relevant to preventing disciplinary exclusion. They have not always been clear about the professional status of helpful people, but have valued those who were there at the right time and who were fair, non-judgemental and treated them as equals. This raises questions about whether the skills and attitudes valued by parents are or should be cross-professional – should these be a feature of all professional interventions?

It may, of course, be that it is easier for some professionals to appear to be fair and non-judgemental. One assistant head, for example, was valued by parents for his support for their children. In this school the head teacher was seen as 'hard' and unsympathetic, as the person who excluded, whereas the assistant was seen as helping to prevent exclusion. This division of roles possibly suited the school and may to some extent have been deliberate, rather than necessarily reflecting personal differences between the individuals concerned. Workers who have no statutory responsibility for formal intervention are also sometimes considered to be more able to give less apparently judgemental support. A further issue worthy of exploration involves the extent to which this kind of work may be more professionally marginal for some professionals. School staff may define their professional role in more narrowly 'teaching' terms; their professional training may have not included any focus on 'helping' skills, like listening or empathy, found in training for others such as social workers or youth workers.

What counts as success?

Different kinds of outcome may be perceived as successful or not by the various participants. The notion of exclusion may be understood differently, and therefore also the definition of success. In this context, success was usually defined as the absence or reduction of the incidence of temporary disciplinary exclusion. However, a number of the young people in the study, identified by their school as successful examples of inter-agency practice, were no longer attending school. So, for example, a young man now attending a special school full-time, another attending a voluntary sector work-based scheme full-time, a young women spending half her day in an off-site support unit – these are all considered successful. The absence of exclusion is not therefore defined as inclusion in a mainstream education setting. Equally there is the possibility that young people seen as successful examples may include some of those whom school staff may prefer to be included, such as one young woman with major problems in the community yet not really presenting a significant behaviour difficulty for the school. She and some others were described as 'nice' or 'able' pupils, which may echo other research findings suggesting that sometimes schools may construct pupils as 'worthy or unworthy' of support (Munn et al. 2000).

Sometimes success has been defined as an outcome of inter-agency decision-making, when perhaps the school may have been able to do more before seeking a referral to the meeting. For example, the mother of the pupil who is now in full-time special school felt he responded well to one-to-one support but had not been offered the support of a learning support assistant in mainstream. Another mother of a pupil now permanently placed elsewhere felt that her son might have benefited from a place in the school where he could go when he found himself getting into difficulties in class. There was a clear tension expressed occasionally between staff in some schools, who felt that there was not enough support provided by other agencies, and professionals from those agencies, who suggested that the school could do more within its own resources before asking for help from outside.

At the start of this chapter we identified some of the difficulties of inter-agency working. This research has also found structural and functional barriers in the fragmentation of public services, because of the range of organisations involved in their delivery. Restructuring in the councils is addressing this, but at the same time may contribute to a sense of confusing and constant change. The development of the idea of a quasi market for pupil support services may add to such confusion. Some process barriers can be seen to result from some central government funding which might foster short-termism and forced partnerships. The Alternatives to Exclusion funding mentioned earlier, for example, is three-year time-limited, and concerns are being expressed about the continuance of some funded work. Differences in professional culture, in training in the professional skills for working with challenging young people, and in the centrality of these to the professional self-concept of different groups, are also evident.

Conclusion

The research is still in progress. However, it is already clear that the complexity of the interpersonal processes and of the policy and legislative context, both nationally and locally, means that there may be a series of fragmented and overlapping notions of effectiveness, which cohere in particular ways in relation to the interests and opinions of different participants. Alternatives to exclusion do not always keep young people included in mainstream school. Professional practice from the range of agencies involved in this research is both valued and criticised by practitioners and young people and parents, yet what is seen as good practice by the young people and parents seems to be simple in its focus. Key here was the notion of the right help, at the right time and in the right place. The right help was fair and non-judgemental, and treated young people and parents as equals.

It may be, however, that the complexity of policies and procedures and the lack of clarity about professional roles may make it difficult for the position of young people and parents always to be kept central, in order to protect their rights and to ensure that the potentially damaging consequences of school exclusion can be avoided.

Notes

1   A complete account of the research and full analysis of the data is available in our final research report (Stead *et al.* 2001).

References

Closs, A. (1997) 'Special educational provision', in M.M. Clark. and P. Munn (eds) *Education in Scotland, Policy and Practice from Pre-School to Secondary*, London: Routledge.

Cullen, M., Johnstone, M., Lloyd, G. and Munn, P. (1996) *Exclusion from School and Alternatives*, three reports to the Scottish Office, Edinburgh: Moray House Institute of Education.

Eason, P., Atkins, M. and Dyson, P. (2000) 'Inter-professional collaborative practice', *Children and Society*, 14: 355–67.

Farrell, K. and Tsakalidou, K. (1999) 'Recent trends in the re-integration of pupils with emotional and behavioural difficulties in the United Kingdom', research report, University of Manchester.

Kendrick, A. (1995) 'Supporting families through inter-agency work: youth strategies', in M. Hill, R. Kirk and D. Part (eds) *Supporting Families*, Edinburgh: HMSO.

——(2000) 'The views of the child: Article 12 and the development of children's rights in Scotland', presentation, 13th International Congress on Child Abuse and Neglect; Implementing the United Nations Convention on the Rights of the Child: Myth or Reality. International Society for the Prevention of Child Abuse and Neglect, Durban, 3–6 September.

Kendrick, A., Simpson, M. and Mapstone, E. (1996) *Getting It Together: Changing Services for Children and Young People in Difficulty*, York: Joseph Rowntree Foundation.

Leathard, A. (ed.) (1994) *Going Inter-Professional. Working Together for Health and Welfare*, London: Routledge.

Liddle, I. (2000) 'Recording the needs of children with SEN. The future role of educational psychologists', paper presented at ESRC seminar Disability and the Restructuring of Welfare. Edinburgh.

Lloyd, G. and Padfield, P. (1996) 'Re-integration into mainstream. Gi'e us peace', *British Journal of Special Education*, 23(4): 180–6.

Lloyd, L. and Munn, P. (1999) 'Educational services for children with emotional or behavioural difficulties', in M. Hill (ed.) *Effective Ways of Working with Children and Their Families*, London: Jessica Kingsley.

Malin, N. (ed.) (2000) *Professionalism, Boundaries and the Workplace*, London: Routledge.

Munn, P., Lloyd, G. and Cullen, M. (2000) *Alternatives to Exclusion from School*, London: Paul Chapman.

Parsons, C. (1999) *Education, Exclusion and Citizenship*, London: Routledge.

——(2000) 'The Third Way to educational and social exclusion', in G. Walraven, C. Parsons, D. Van Veen and C. Day (eds) *Combating Social Exclusion through Education*, Leuven-Appeldoorn: Garant.

Parsons, C. and Castle, F. (1999) 'The economics of exclusion', in C. Parsons (ed.) *Education, Exclusion and Citizenship*, London: Routledge.

Pickles, T. (1992) 'Youth strategies in Scotland', in G. Lloyd (ed.) *Chosen with Care? Responses to Disturbing and Disruptive Behaviour*, Edinburgh: Moray House Publications.

Schaffer, M. (1992) 'Children's Hearings and school problems', in G. Lloyd (ed.) *Chosen with Care? Responses to Disturbing and Disruptive Behaviour*, Edinburgh: Moray House Publications.

Scottish Executive (1998) New Community Schools Prospectus, accessed November 2000: www.scotland.gov.uk/library/documents-w3/ncsp-00.htm

——(1999) Making It Happen: Report of the Strategy Action Team, accessed November 2000: http:www.scotland.gov.uk/inclusion/docs/maih-oo.htm

——(2000a) *Exclusions from Schools, 1998/99*, press release, Edinburgh: Scottish Executive.

——(2000b) *Draft Guidance on Presumption of Inclusion in Standards in Scottish Schools, etc., 2000*, Edinburgh: Scottish Executive.

Scottish Office (1964) *The Kilbrandon Report*, HMSO Edinburgh.

——(1997) *Scotland's Children: The Children (Scotland) Act 1995 Regulations and Guidance*, Edinburgh: Scottish Office.

——(1998a) *Guidance on Issues Concerning Exclusion from School*, Circular 2/98, Edinburgh: Scottish Executive.

——(1998b) *Alternatives to Exclusion Grant Scheme, Specification for Bids*, Edinburgh: Scottish Executive.

Scottish Office Education and Industry Department (SOEID) (1996) *Children and Young Persons with Special Educational Needs: Assessment and Recording*, Circular 4/96, Edinburgh: Scottish Office.

Stead, J., Lloyd, G. and Kendrick, A. (2001) *Still Hanging on in There. A Study of Inter-Agency Work to Prevent School Exclusion in Three Councils. Research Report*, York: Joseph Rowntree Foundation.

Triseliotis, J., Borland, M., Hill, M. and Lambert, L. (1995) *Teenagers and the social work services*, London: HMSO.

Wilson, V. and Pirrie, A. (2000a) *Multidisciplinary Teamworking Indicators of Good Practice*, Edinburgh: Scottish Council for Research in Education.

——(2000b) *Multidisciplinary Teamworking: Beyond the Barriers? A Review of the Issues*, Edinburgh: Scottish Executive.

12 Social inclusion or exclusion?

Recent policy trends in Scottish children's services for disabled children

E. Kay M. Tisdall

Introduction

Both conceptually and practically, 'joined-up' or 'inter-agency' working is central to the social inclusion policy agenda (O'Connor and Lewis 1999; Room 1995; Scottish Executive Social Inclusion Network (SIN) 1998). Reacting to criticisms of past urban regeneration programmes, government documents insist that social inclusion policies and programmes are based on devolved decision-making, supporting local people to take responsibility for their own communities (SIN 1998: para 3.10). In Scotland, as well as in England and Wales, children and young people have been identified as a key group who are at risk of social exclusion.

The disability and special needs literatures are replete with research findings and writings describing how the present educational and inter-agency process for disabled children, along with the gaps between services, lead to their social exclusion (e.g. Armstrong and Davies 1995; Dobson and Middleton 1998; Oliver 1996; Watson *et al.* 2000). How well are recent policy trends improving the social inclusion of disabled children?

While all children are affected by changes in welfare services, children with disabilities and their families may be particularly affected by policy changes in both universal (e.g. education and health) and selective (e.g. social security, housing and social work) welfare services. This chapter proposes to concentrate on two service areas – social work and education – that have been subject to considerable change in Scotland within recent years. 'Child care' services for children have been radically reformed by the combination of new unitary local authorities and the implementation of the Children (Scotland) Act 1995. While legislated for under the previous government, the Act has similar ideas to those presently promoted by the New Labour government: the Act promotes 'joined-up thinking' through a 'corporate' approach to children's services, a 'mainstreaming' of services for disabled children, and 'partnership with parents'. Scottish education policy has been the subject of extensive consultation and policy decisions since New Labour was elected in May 1997. Moving away from a discourse of the 'market' and 'parental choice', New Labour has put forward policies on raising standards and setting targets and on early intervention, and has adopted the rhetoric of 'partnership with parents'. This is exemplified by the Standards in Scotland's Schools etc. Act 2000 and subsequent policy documents.

This chapter will discuss policy changes and directions within these two areas of social work and education. In particular, it will consider (from the perspective of their potential impact on disabled children): in what ways the different changes and directions are compatible or contradictory; in what ways they take account of the rights of disabled children, as established by the United Nations; and how well they meet the government's proposed fight against 'social exclusion'.

Introduction to recent changes

The Children (Scotland) Act 1995 is the first comprehensive revision of Scottish child care law since the Social Work (Scotland) Act 1968. For children with disabilities, the 1995 Act is revolutionary because it includes them within 'mainstream' child care legislation. The preceding White Paper *Scotland's Children* (Social Work Services Group (SWSG) 1993) dedicated a chapter to children with disabilities and began it with a commitment to re-orienting services:

> Social work provision for children with disabilities has progressed over the past 20 years but often in a piecemeal way. While services have developed they have continued to concentrate largely on the disability rather than on the child, and children's needs are in some cases accommodated within services designed essentially for adult care, even though children with disabilities have more in common with other children because of their childhood than they do with adults with corresponding disabilities.
>
> (SWSG 1993: 20)

In the 1995 Act, this problem was addressed by including children affected by disabilities within new local authority duties for 'children in need'. Local authorities must safeguard and promote the welfare of 'children in need' in their areas, preferably by promoting children's upbringing within their families, by providing a 'range and level of services appropriate to the children's needs' (Section 22).

The Act and accompanying guidance (SWSG 1997) emphasise the need for preventive services, partnership with parents and children's rights both to be protected and to be consulted. Increased and improved inter-agency co-operation is another consistent theme, underlined by the 'corporate' definition of local authority within the Act and the requirement on local authorities to prepare and publish children's services plans. The Act's initial remit precluded a complete inclusion of health services within it but sections were inserted as the Bill went through Parliament, seeking to encourage closer co-operation for children's services.

In practice, inter-agency co-operation has been either hampered or helped by local government reorganisation, which occurred in April 1996. The two tiers of

Scottish local government (Districts and Regions) were amalgamated into thirty-two all-purpose unitary authorities, ending the separation between, for example, housing and recreation services on the one hand and social work and education on the other (see Craig *et al.* 2000 for discussion of impact of local government reorganisation on children's services).

The revised guidance on assessing 'special educational needs' (SEN) (Scottish Office Education and Industry Department (SOEID) 1996) recognises, to some extent, education's corporate duties under the 1995 Act. For example, education's responsibility for 'children in need' is referred to and the educational needs of 'looked after' children discussed. Certain principles introduced in the 1995 Act, such as partnership with parents and listening to children's views, are similarly threaded throughout the SOEID guidance. While re-orienting the system, the guidance itself is only a re-interpretation within the limits of the Education (Scotland) Act 1980 as amended.[1] The 1980 Act remains the foundational legislation, with its category of 'special educational needs' and system of assessment and recording SEN. (For further description of Scottish SEN system, see Closs 1997 and SOEID 1996.)

In 1998, the Scottish Office issued a thin (twenty-four pages in large print) if glossy discussion paper, *Special Educational Needs in Scotland*. It deliberately did not seek to address all aspects of SEN provision, but 'a number of areas of particular concern which have been the subject of recent representation to the Minister and the Department' (SOEID 1998a: 3). Under the new Scottish Executive and Scottish Parliament, the government approach has been less sanguine. The Executive established the Riddell Committee, to address educational issues for children with 'severe low incidence disabilities'. Its recommendations (1999), however, have wider ramifications: for example, inter-agency liaison should be improved; further support is required to include young disabled people within schools; good practice should be disseminated on how the views of disabled children and young people can be heard. The Beattie Report (1999) considered young disabled people's post-school education and training, and made numerous recommendations for agencies working together. The Education, Culture and Sport Committee of the Parliament, struck by the range of concerns expressed as the Standards in Scotland's Schools etc. Bill was introduced, began an Inquiry into Special Needs Education (2000).

While the need to overhaul the SEN system has only recently been recognised by the government, the opposite would be true for Scottish education more generally. Once New Labour came into government, the Scottish Office/Executive has made a new announcement virtually every week, with a dizzying array of new funds and interventions. Certain themes emerge:

1   *An emphasis on early intervention and inter-agency co-operation, particularly to prevent educational failure*: e.g. the Sure Start Programme, a National Child Care Strategy, a pre-school place for every 4-year-old, funds through the Early Intervention Programme to raise standards of literacy and numeracy in primary school, baseline assessment, and New Community Schools.

2   *An emphasis on 'partnership with parents'*: along with the SEN discussion paper, a discussion paper titled *Parents as Partners* was issued in January 1998 (SOEID 1998c). New community schools will also, according to the government, involve parents in their children's schooling (Scottish Office 1998a). Local authorities will have to state how they will involve parents in their children's schooling, within their annual report on improvement objectives.

3   *An emphasis on standards and targets*: the government has committed itself to raising educational standards; as part of this commitment, it issued provisional targets to each school in regards to attendance and qualifications (Scottish Office 1998b). The Standards in Scotland's Schools etc. Act 2000 has introduced a cascade of targets, from national priorities set by the Scottish Executive, to local authority improvement objectives, to schools creating school development plans.

4   Education has always been core to the war on 'social exclusion' and the Social Inclusion Unit within the Scottish Office has identified non-attendance and school exclusions as key priorities (Scottish Office 1998c). Money has been made available for initiatives to prevent such educational exclusion, along with up-dated guidance on school exclusions (SOEID 1998b) informed by the first substantial Scottish research on that topic (Munn *et al.* 1997).

Compatibility or contradiction?

Local authorities have thus been reeling from a combination of change over the past five years, from local government reform in 1996, to new children's legislation implemented in 1997 and an ever-changing educational agenda. The New Labour government has encouraged 'joined-up thinking', to break down unhelpful divides between professionals and services, to see the connections between different problems and thus greater potential to develop more effective solutions. To what extent has such 'joined-up thinking' been applied to the interface between social work and education services?

Gaps are evident in assessment, definitions and legal duties. New assessments were introduced by the 1995 Act for children affected by disabilities and their carers. These new assessments now sit alongside numerous other assessments that children with disabilities may experience. Guidance from both the SWSG (1997) and the SOEID (1996) recommends co-ordination of such assessments, to avoid unnecessary duplication for children and their families. The legislation, however, does not make such co-ordination particularly easy – especially for older children – due to the different ages and legal requirements for assessments.

The requirements for SEN assessments are far more stringent and specific in education legislation than are the 'welfare' assessments under the 1995 Act. For example, no specific appeal structure was established in the 1995 Act, while there is within the 1980 Act. Parents, or a young person, must be sent a copy of a completed Record; no such requirement is laid out in the 1995 Act. No legal link is made within the 1995 Act between the assessment of need and actual services being delivered, unlike the Record of SEN. The SWSG guidance (1997) does make numerous suggestions in relation to assessments, for children affected by disability, and hopefully encourages good practice.

No guidance has been issued from the Scottish Office, to help children, parents or professionals sort through the definitions of 'disability' within social work and 'special educational needs' within education legislation. A child with 'special educational needs' is not necessarily a 'child in need' under the 1995 Act. The SWSG guidance (1997) does suggest that 'children with special needs', 'children with emotional, behavioural and mental health problems' and those whose 'educational development is suffering' be considered as children having needs. Local authorities, however, have considerable discretion in determining who is a 'child in need'. Research from England and Wales (Social Services Inspectorate (SSI) 1994, 1998a, 1998b) indicates that local authorities have had problems reconciling their specific duties to children with disabilities and their duties towards 'children in need' more generally. Local authorities have been confused about the fit between disabled children and 'children in need', and development of services (with notable exceptions) was often slow or simply not present.

Even though the Acts were being legislated for coterminously, the Children (Scotland) Act 1995 fails to incorporate the more up-to-date definition of disability as provided for in the Disability Discrimination Act 1995.[2] While the disability legislation itself could be accused of not adequately considering its applicability to children, it does recognise the social contribution to an individual's disability. With the DDA's extension into education, these differences may cause increased confusion.

Research from England and Wales, which have worked with both categories for over eight years now, suggests the agencies can have trouble working together because they have different conceptualisations of what is a 'child in need' (Audit Commission 1994; Department of Health 2000). As local authorities have the power to refine the definition of 'children in need' for their own areas, the definition provides considerable flexibility to meet local needs and demands. Such flexibility, though, has some disadvantages. Children in one area might be eligible for a service but not eligible in another. Given the smaller size of most local authorities in Scotland, migration between local authority areas may grow and local authorities with good services for particular needs (e.g. for children with disabilities, or young people who are homeless) may have increasing demands on their services.

Children's services plans could provide an answer to at least some of these difficulties: they could ensure agencies generate a common understanding of 'needs', across the different legislative requirements, and they could ensure that agencies collaborate in service planning and provision. The corporate definition of local authority within the 1995 Act aids such intra-local authority co-operation. Recent educational initiatives, on the other hand, could disrupt such co-operation and future planning. The Scottish Office/Executive has been forwarding New Labour's agenda through substantial funds for particular initiatives, in a deliberate attempt to alter the educational agenda through financial incentives. The initiatives and deadlines for programme bids have been tight, with the potential for disrupting decisions already made in earlier planning for children's services. The Standards in Scotland's Schools etc. Act 2000 introduces new annual planning responsibilities on both local authorities and schools – and no amendment was accepted to encourage co-ordination between these educational plans with the existing requirements for three-year children's services plans.

The evaluation of these educational initiatives, and schools more generally, will be judged mainly through the raising of educational attainment and meeting related targets. The New Labour government has sought to introduce a more sensitive means of producing 'league tables' and setting targets, by using the proportion of students eligible for free school meals, so as to recognise the 'value added' by schools rather than raw scores. Children's baseline assessments, in time, could also be used for more sensitive grading. But, however sensitive, such attainment measures and related targets create certain incentives for schools that could potentially exclude those most 'in need'. Schools' financial interests – and perhaps very survival – will be served by raising those students who are just below meeting such targets to just above. Schools will not benefit from addressing the needs of children at either end of educational attainment. Some disabled children may well not be attractive to schools: they cost too much financially and in kind, with their actual progress unrecognised by the targets schools must meet. As responsibility is increasingly devolved to schools, and smaller local authorities have less access to specialist support to offer schools and students, those students most disadvantaged may become even more so as compared to their peers. The Scottish Executive is well aware of these criticisms, as it consulted on its National Priorities paper (Scottish Executive Education Department 2000); it will take innovative and thorough thinking, however, to ensure that its 'mainstream' targets do not exclude children and that it has sensitive targets to foster the potential of disabled children.

Rights of disabled children

Along with a potential conflict between the individual and collective needs of children, the 1980 and 1995 Acts set out different expectations of what needs will be met and the rights of children more generally. The 1995 Act is predicated on the principle of children's best interests, as described above, along with the right of children to have their views heard. The Act was specifically introduced with the government's intention to fulfil its obligations under the UN Convention on the Rights of the Child, which requires a child's best interests to be a primary consideration in all actions concerning children (UN 1989: Article 3) and a child's views to be given due weight in all matters affecting the child (Article 12).

The 1980 Act, on the other hand, contained none of these principles for education. But the Standards in Scotland's Schools etc. Act 2000 now includes, after substantial outside pressure on the Scottish Executive, new rights for children:

Section 1: It shall be the right of every child of school age to be provided with school education.

Section 2: It shall be the duty of the authority to ensure that the education ... is directed to the development of the personality, talents and mental and physical activities of the child or young person to their fullest potential.

In carrying out this duty, the authority shall have due regard, as far as is reasonably practicable, to the views of the child or young person in decisions that significantly affect the child or young person.

Section 5 requires consultation with children and young people on an education authority's annual statements of improvement objectives.

Section 6 requires the school development plans to state how head teachers plan to consult pupils and seek to involve the pupils, on decisions about 'the everyday running of the school'.

The Act is thus revolutionary in the UK for giving the child a right to education. Section 2 is nearly a direct quote of Article 29 (1) (a) of the UN Convention. Children's views now need to be considered, in line with Article 12 of the UN Convention. The emphasis on 'every' child underlines the inclusive intention – that is, disabled children also have these rights.

The UN Convention, along with a general non-discrimination article specifically mentioning disability (Article 2), also has a specific article for 'handicapped' children. Article 23 (1) states that a disabled child should 'enjoy a full and decent life, in conditions which ensure dignity, promote self-reliance, and facilitate the child's active participation in the community'. An even stronger commitment to inclusive education was signed by the UK government in 1994, commonly called the Salamanca Statement, arguing that regular schools with an inclusive orientation are:

> the most effective means of combating discriminatory attitudes, creating welcoming communities, building an inclusive society and achieving education for all; moreover, they provide an effective education to the majority of children and improve the efficiency and ultimately the cost-effectiveness of the entire education system.
>
> (CSIE 1994)

While legally untested, the wording of Section 23 (1) in the Children (Scotland) Act 1995 could be used to promote inclusive services (although the wording clearly takes a deficit model of disability). 'Children in need' services must be designed to:

- minimise the effect of his/her disability on a disabled child;
- minimise the effect of the disability of another family member on any child adversely affected;
- give those children 'the opportunity to lead lives which are as normal as possible'.

Interactions with other legislation may provide further support to these measures. The Disability Discrimination Act (DDA) 1995 requires public services to be accessible to all disabled people. Taken together with Section 23 (1), would this mean that local authority services should be accessible for disabled children, from swimming pools to day-care?

The proposed extension of the DDA to education (DfEE *et al.* 2000) could provide another impetus towards inclusion. The consultation paper outlined the proposal to:

> make it unlawful for education providers to discriminate against a disabled child by:
>
> a treating a child less favourably on the grounds of the disability than a non-disabled child, without justification, in the arrangements made for the provision of education;
> b failing to take reasonable steps to change any policies, practices or procedures which place a disabled children at a substantial disadvantage compared to a non-disabled child; and
> c failing to take reasonable steps to provide education using a reasonable alternative method where a physical feature places a disabled child at a substantial disadvantage compared to a non-disabled child.
>
> (DfEE *et al.* 2000: Annex A1, para 2)

The problematic qualifiers of 'reasonable' remain, and Scottish children's organisations have reacted unfavourably to the failure to require physical adjustments (as is proposed for post-16 education). England and Wales have been promised a new duty on education providers 'to plan systematically to increase the accessibility of schools for disabled children', which has not yet been promised nor the details (yet) developed for Scottish legislation. One argument for the exclusion of physical adjustments is the opportunity for parents to choose alternative schools for children, whereas there may be only one college offering a particular course. This, however, misses the realities for children living in rural and remote areas (a particular issue for much of Scotland) – they may have only one choice of a local school.

With the Standards in Scotland's Schools etc. Act, Scottish educational law has now caught up with other UK education legislation in having some promotion of integration/inclusion. The Scottish Executive introduced an amendment into the Bill as it went through Parliament, to create a presumption for mainstream schooling. This amendment was subject to considerable controversy, with many confused by the legal wording (so the media ran stories that the parents' right to choose a mainstream school was actually *worsened* by the amendment) and others critical of the 'get-out' clauses in subsection 12A (2) and the deficit-based wording. Interestingly, it allows for children's views to be considered within the choice of schools, which again was inserted after consultation with outside agencies.

The new section represents the current 'balance' the Scottish Executive and Parliament are promoting for school inclusion. As stated in the 1998 consultation paper:

> For the majority of children with special educational needs the fullest inte-
> gration into mainstream education, with appropriate support, will be in
> their best interests. The needs of others will be best met partly or wholly in a
> specialist setting.
>
> (SOEID 1998a: 4)

There is a strongly voiced and felt concern of certain parents' groups that special schools must be an option – inclusion has not necessarily worked for their chil-
dren and/or they feel that special schools are the best option for their children. In short, the Scottish Office/Executive is ruling out a fully inclusive education policy for disabled children but wishes to move towards inclusion.

Key reports, such as the Beattie Report (1999), take a strong stand promoting inclusion of disabled people but do not identify physical proximity as a necessary component. Yet the physical separation of disabled children from their peers has been a fundamental aspect of both social and educational exclusion, according to disability advocates (e.g. Hall 1997). Research on schools demonstrates how children's peer groups tend to be built around school (e.g. Hill and Tisdall 1997). The recent interest in children, space and geography would suggest that where children are is important to their lives, experiences and futures (e.g. James *et al.* 1998). This increasingly common idea that where children are does not affect their inclusion bears further scrutiny. There are many examples of children who were integrated into mainstream schooling but were not 'included' (e.g. see Watson *et al.* 2000). Physical proximity is clearly not enough to ensure inclusion. But until children spend less of their waking hours in education, in the physical space of schools, *where* children are surely does matter for their social inclusion.

Conclusion: social inclusion?

As mentioned above, education has been identified as a key problem – and solu-
tion – for the social inclusion agenda of the New Labour government. Lowering non-attendance, be it through truancy or school exclusions, is a priority, along with raising educational attainment.

Yet the position of disabled children – who as a group have poorer attainment than their peers (Hirst and Baldwin 1994) and who may be disproportionately excluded from school (Booth 1996) – has been virtually ignored within discus-
sions of social inclusion. The information is already there, for those involved in the social inclusion/exclusion decision-making, to see how the concept of social exclusion could apply to disabled young people. This absence looked set to change, with young disabled people a priority group on the excluded young people's social inclusion action team. The team's report, however, left out this group entirely. No Social Justice targets are set for disabled children and their

families. The benefits of the 'social exclusion' discourse is its potential (at least theoretically) to incorporate process as well as risk factors and outcomes (Room 1995). These benefits are not yet being systematically applied to services and policies for disabled children; disabled children are not yet fully included on the social inclusion agenda.

Disabled children have become more central to Scottish local authority services. Their inclusion within the Children (Scotland) Act 1995 appears to have galvanised many local authorities and become a focus in children's services planning. Many plans name joint assessment and better-integrated services as priorities for action. The UN Convention on the Rights of the Child and other international statements highlight the rights of disabled children; the right of children to have their views considered is now regularly cited in social work documents and is now starting to emerge in educational policy. Commitments have been made to a more democratic participation in the Scottish Parliament (Consultative Steering Group 1998), with increasing attention to how young people can be meaningfully involved. These methods could ensure that disabled children's views are heard, as well as their parents. Both child care and education legislation now have some requirements (albeit qualified) to listen to children's views.

The recent policy changes, however, have not always demonstrated the 'joined up thinking' recommended by the present government. No attempt has been made to rationalise the different definitions of need that determine service eligibility nor the potential tensions between legislative duties contained within various Acts. While the SWSG has been responsible in the Scottish Office for issuing guidance on the 1995 Act, the SOEID and now the Scottish Executive Education Department has been announcing initiatives and policy directions with a seeming lack of consideration as to how they would affect long-term local authority planning and may conflict with the Act's priorities. While the 1995 Act may seek to ensure the needs/rights of disabled children are considered across services, the radical changes in general education policy do not appear to have been evaluated for their potential impact – for good or bad – on disabled children. The Scottish Executive now appears willing but not yet able to 'mainstream' disabled children in their 'mainstream' educational policies. Whether mainstreamed or not, both child care and educational legislation operate largely on an individual basis, concentrating on assessing individual children. Neither takes on fully the 'social model of disability' (see Oliver 1990, 1996), with a requirement to remove barriers or fundamentally change society and its institutions.

The new Scottish Parliament now has control over virtually all welfare services that affect children: from health, to social work, to education. The Scottish Parliament has considerably more time for legislation than was ever available for Scottish legislation in Westminster and, almost inevitably, it wishes to 'make its mark' and be considerably interventionist with its legislative powers. Local authorities are currently trying to provide (education and social work) services under requirements primarily designed for larger authorities, with larger economies of scale. While the decentralisation of local government reform allows for more community accountability and flexibility to local needs, it also can cause inequity across local authorities in service provision. The Scottish Parliament and local authorities may well find themselves in tension, with the Scottish Parliament potentially wishing to centralise or to issue national standards, to ensure equitable and quality services.

If the political will was created, policies could be changed so as to address the gaps and tensions between legislation and to enact more fully international commitments to the rights of disabled children. While equal opportunities/anti-discrimination legislation is a reserved power of Westminster, the Scottish Parliament does have a remit to promote equal opportunities. The incorporation of the European Convention on Human Rights into UK law will invariably lead to more judicial testing in the courts. While the ECHR is frequently criticised for not being a child-friendly document (e.g. see Kilkelly 1999), it has been used to promote indirectly certain rights for children (such as the banning of the physical punishment of children in state schooling). Article 14 of the ECHR prohibits discrimination, under any of the ECHR's other articles. Age is already recognised as a potential ground for discrimination and, tacitly, disability (see Kilkelly 1999 for discussion).[3] The European Court of Human Rights recognises the roles of other international conventions and is ever more frequently making reference to the UNCRC. Such cross-referencing should also now occur in Scotland, as required by the Scotland Act 1998.

Special educational needs legislation and policy is almost definitely going to change over the next few years, with the government preparing for a large-scale consultation in due course. Policies for disabled children could look radically different in Scotland in just a few years – if they rise in political and policy priority, and their rights are considered systematically and consistently in policy changes and initiatives.

Notes

1   The Education (Scotland) Act 1981 contains the core legislation for 'special educational needs'. It amended the Education (Scotland) Act 1980, so technically the basic legislation is the Education (Scotland) Act 1980 as amended. For this chapter, the combination of these two acts will be referred to as the 1980 Act for simplicity.
2   'Subject to the provisions of Schedule 1, a person has a disability ... if he has a physical or mental impairment which has a substantial and long-term adverse effect on his ability to carry out normal day-to-day activities' (Section 1 (1)).
3   Notably, however, parents have not been able to gain a mainstream school place for their disabled children when a proper assessment has been carried out of the children and proper account taken of parents' views on their children's needs. See Kilkelly 1999.

References

Armstrong, D. and Davies, P. (1995) 'The transition from school to adulthood: aspiration and careers advice for young adults with learning and adjustment difficulties', *British Journal of Special Education*, 22(2): 70–5.

Audit Commission (1994) *Seen But Not Heard*, London: HMSO.

Beattie Report (1999) *Implementing Inclusiveness Realising Potential*, Edinburgh: Scottish Executive.

Booth, T. (1996) 'Stories of exclusion: natural and unnatural selection', in E. Blyth and J. Milner (eds) *Exclusion from School*, London: Routledge.

Closs, A. (1997) 'Special education provision', in M.M. Clark and P. Munn, P. (eds) *Education in Scotland: Policy and Practice from Pre-School to Secondary*, London: Routledge.

Consultative Steering Group on the Scottish Parliament (1998) *Your Views on How the Scottish Parliament Should Work*, Consultation Paper 2.4.98, Edinburgh: Scottish Office Constitution Group.

Craig, G., Hill, M., Manthorpe, J., Tisdall, K., Monaghan, B. and Wheelaghan, S. (2000) 'Picking up the pieces: local government reorganisation and voluntary sector children's services', *Children and Society*, 14(2): 85–97.

CSIE (1994) *Inclusive education – the UNESCO Salamanca Statement (1994)*, http://inclusion.uwe.ac.uk/csie/slmca.htm

Department for Education and Employment (DfEE), Scottish Executive, Scotland Office, The National Assembly for Wales (2000) *SEN and Disability Rights in Education Bill*, London: DfEE.

Department of Health (2000) *Consultation: New Guidance on Children's Services Planning*, London: Department of Health.

Dobson, B. and Middleton, S. (1998) *Paying to Care: The Cost of Childhood Disability*, York: York Publishing Services.

Hall, J. (1997) *Social Devaluation and Special Education: The Right to Full Inclusion and an Honest Statement*, London: Jessica Kingsley.

Hill, M. and Tisdall, K. (1997) *Children and Society*, London: Longman.

Hirst, M. and Baldwin, S. (1994) *Unequal Opportunities: Growing Up Disabled*, Social Policy Research Unit. London: HMSO.

James, A., Jenks, C. and Prout, A. (1998) *Theorizing Childhood*, Cambridge: Polity Press.

Kilkelly, U. (1999) *The Child and the European Convention on Human Rights*, Dartmouth: Ashgate.

Munn, P., Cullen, M.A., Johnstone, M. and Lloyd, G. (1997) *Exclusions and In-School Alternatives*, Interchange 47, Edinburgh: The Scottish Office.

O'Connor, W. and Lewis, J. (1999) *Experiences of Social Exclusion in Scotland*, Research Findings 73, Edinburgh: Central Research Unit, Scottish Executive.

Oliver, M. (1990) *The Politics of Disablement*, London, Macmillan.

——(1996) *Understanding Disability: From Theory to Practice*, Basingstoke: Macmillan.

Riddell Report (1999) *Report into the Education of Children with Severe Low Incidence Disabilities*, Edinburgh: Scottish Executive.

Room, G. (1995) 'Poverty and social exclusion: the new European agenda for policy and research', in G. Room (ed.) *Beyond the Threshold: the Measurement and Analysis of Social Exclusion*, Bristol: Policy Press.

Scottish Executive Education Department (2000) *Improving Our Schools. Consultation on National Priorities for Schools Education in Scotland*, Edinburgh: Scottish Executive.

Scottish Executive Social Inclusion Network (1998) *Social Inclusion: The Strategic Framework*, http:www.scotland.gov.uk/inclusion/

Scottish Office (1998a) *Scotland leads the way with radical plan for New Community Schools*, press release, 4 November, http://www.scotland.gov.uk/frame2n.htm

——(1998b) *Targets to raise standards in Scottish schools*, press release, 4 March, http://www.scotland.gov.uk/frame2n.htm

——(1998c) *Social Exclusion in Scotland: A Consultation Paper*, Edinburgh: The Stationery Office, or http://www.scotland.gov.uk/frame2n.htm

Scottish Office Education and Industry Department (1996) *Children and Young Persons with Special Educational Needs: Assessment and Recording*, Circular 4/96, Edinburgh: SOEID.

——(1998a) *Special Educational Needs in Scotland*, discussion paper, Edinburgh: SOEID.

——(1998b) *Guidance on Issues Concerning Exclusion from School*, Circular 2/98, Edinburgh: SOEID.

——(1998c) *Parents as Partners: Enhancing the Role of Parents in School Education*, discussion paper, Edinburgh: SOEID.

Social Services Inspectorate (SSI) (1994) *Services to Disabled Children and Their Families. Report of the National Inspection of Services to Disabled Children and their Families, January 1994*, London: HMSO.

——(1998a) *Removing Barriers for Disabled Children: Inspection of Services to Disabled Children and Their Families*, Wetherby: Department of Health.

——(1998b) *Disabled Children: Directions for their Future Care*, Wetherby: Department of Health.

Social Work Services Group (SWSG) (1993) *Scotland's Children: Proposals for Child Care Policy and Law*, Cm 2286, Edinburgh: HMSO.

——(1997) *Scotland's Children. The Children (Scotland) Act 1995 Regulations and Guidance, Volume 1: Support and Protection for Children and their Families*, Edinburgh: The Stationery Office.

United Nations (1989) *Convention on the Rights of the Child*, London: HMSO.

Watson, N., Barnes, C., Corker, M., Cunningham-Burley, S., Davis, J., Priestley, M. and Shakespeare, T. (2000) *Lives of Disabled Children*, http://www.hull.ac.uk/children5to16programme/

13 Inter-agency strategies in early childhood education to counter social exclusion

Findings from six European countries[1]

Emer Smyth

Introduction

This chapter discusses the provision of early childhood education for children from disadvantaged backgrounds in six European countries: Belgium (Flanders), Ireland, the Netherlands, Portugal, Scotland and Spain. 'Early childhood education' is used in a broad sense to include all educational measures targeted at children under the compulsory school age. In practice, however, it is often difficult to disentangle educational measures from broader childcare provision. Such provision addresses a diverse set of objectives, including promoting the educational and social development of young children and facilitating the access of parents to employment or training, either as ends in themselves or as a means of countering social exclusion. While some services (particularly pre-school provision in mainstream primary schools) are clearly 'educational' in focus, other provision, such as play-groups, often incorporates an emphasis on educational development in a broader sense. Provision in the six European countries entails a combination of these 'welfare' and 'education' functions. The extent to which these two perspectives facilitate inter-agency co-operation will be discussed in the remainder of this chapter.

The first section outlines the level and nature of early childhood educational provision in the six countries and the extent to which it targets children from disadvantaged backgrounds, however defined. The second section presents some examples of projects which have been designed to target these young children, focusing on programmes which involve inter-agency strategies. A broad definition of 'inter-agency' is adopted, encompassing all of the groups involved in young children's education; this perspective takes account of parental involvement as well as the role of statutory and voluntary organisations. Conclusions are presented in the third section of the chapter.

Early childhood education in Europe

European countries, including the six countries examined here, differ significantly in the level and nature of early childhood education for young children in general and for disadvantaged children in particular. Figure 13.1 shows rates of

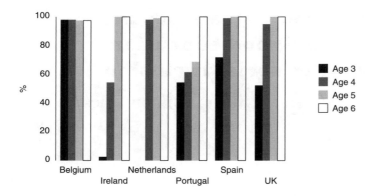

Figure 13.1   Educational participation among young children in the study countries, 1998
Source: OECD 1998

participation in education among children aged 3 to 6 in the study countries. Almost all young children in Belgium take part in early childhood education, even though school attendance is not compulsory until the age of 6. Participation rates are negligible for 3-year-old children in the Netherlands and Ireland, but increase sharply for older children due to the high proportion of children who attend 'infant' classes in primary schools before the compulsory school entry age. In both Spain and the UK,[2] there is a dramatic increase in participation between the ages of 3 and 4. In contrast, educational participation is relatively low among Portuguese children under the age of 6.

No systematic information is available on the participation of young children from disadvantaged backgrounds in early childhood education. It is clear, however, that their situation will be affected by overall levels of participation in the country as a whole. Given the very high levels of participation among children in Belgium, almost all children from disadvantaged backgrounds will experience three years of education prior to entering the compulsory schooling system. However, this may mean that existing inequalities in educational outcomes between less and more advantaged children are maintained unless specific measures are designed to improve the position of socially excluded children. In the other countries, the lower level of participation among very young children is likely to mean that levels are especially low among children from disadvantaged backgrounds. As a consequence, lower participation among poor children is likely to reinforce their initial disadvantage.

In addition to differing in the level of provision, European countries also differ in the nature of early childhood educational provision. In most countries, there is a sharp distinction in provision on the basis of age, with services for children under 3 under the auspices of welfare authorities and services for older children administered by education authorities. This distinction is likely to lead to a fragmentation of services for young children and to impede the development of a more integrated and holistic approach to meeting their needs (Randall 2000). The 'welfare'/'education' dichotomy is even more starkly evident in provision for children from disadvantaged backgrounds.

In Belgium, 'welfare' provision is targeted at children under the age of 3 while 'educational' provision is targeted at those aged 2½ to 6 years of age. In Flanders, services for children under 3 are regulated and subsidised by Kind en Gezin, an organisation which has a wide remit in terms of child care, preventative health care and social work support. Some of this provision is specifically targeted at children living in poverty (see below). The majority of 3 to 5-year-olds in Belgium attend nursery schools, which are usually part of primary schools. Nursery schools are regulated by the Department of Education with a separate inspection system from childcare services. While the approach adopted is child-centred, research has indicated that provision at this stage is mainly oriented to preparation for primary school (Delhaxhe 1989). In spite of the potential of the Kind en Gezin model for integrated service delivery, the Flemish system has been criticised for the persistence of structural differences between the childcare and education sectors and it has been argued that there is a need for greater co-ordination between the systems (OECD 2000b).

In Ireland, there is limited provision of early childhood services (Hayes *et al.* 1997) and, as in many other countries, there is an artificial divide between 'welfare' and 'education' functions. Publicly funded provision for very young children targets those 'at risk' while other provision includes play-groups and private pre-schools. The majority of 4 and 5-year-olds attend 'infant' classes in primary schools. A significant issue is the lack of co-ordination and standardisation of early childhood education services, with as many as ten government departments involved in such services (Department of Education and Science 1999). This issue led to the drafting of a White Paper on Early Childhood Education. The paper emphasises the importance of integrating service provision, particularly for disadvantaged children, and recommends the establishment of a unitary Early Childhood Education Agency to this effect. These recommendations currently await legislative implementation. Specific measures in Ireland designed for children from disadvantaged backgrounds, including the Rutland Street Project, the Early Start Programme and centres for pre-school Traveller children, will be discussed in the following section.

In the Netherlands, the main form of provision for children under 4 is play-groups, with the majority of children commencing primary schooling at the age of 4 (on a voluntary basis) (Moss 1990). There appears to be no specific pre-school provision for children from disadvantaged backgrounds with the exception of some broader community-based projects (see below).

In Portugal, there is also an age-based distinction between welfare and education services for young children. The Ministry of Labour has responsibility for services for children under 3 years of age as well as for family support services. Kindergartens under these auspices operate a 'social welfare model' with access depending on family background characteristics and 'need'. The Ministry of Education has responsibility for services for 3 to 6-year-olds and coverage of pre-school provision has expanded rapidly since 1997, although the level and nature of provision varies by geographical location. There are few specific projects for disadvantaged children with the exception of the Amadora Project (see below) (Bairrão *et al.* 1989; Moss 1990). It has been argued that the multiplicity of providers in Portugal, along with the complex division of functions between them, has led to a compartmentalisation of responsibilities and has impeded the development of a holistic view of child and family needs (OECD 2000a).

In Spain, provision is divided into two levels: the first cycle which covers children under 2 years of age and the second cycle which covers children aged 3 to 5 (Palacios 1989). Unlike the situation for Belgium and Portugal, all responsibility for children under 6 years of age lies with the Ministry of Education. However, the type of provision may vary by age with 'custodial' services (including day-care centres and work-based care centres) for very young children and pre-primary school for 4 to 5-year-olds. There is no clearly defined policy for pre-school children from disadvantaged backgrounds, although some measures (such as multi-disciplinary teams in schools) are designed to provide additional services to this group in the context of mainstream provision.

In the UK (including Scotland), a distinction persists between care-focused and education-focused settings, although new programmes introduced under the Labour government have focused on the development of 'joined-up' provision (see below). The Department for Education and Employment now has overall responsibility for early childhood education. The education of children between the ages of 2 and 5 is provided for under the Education Act 1996. State-funded child care for children under 3 years of age is targeted at those in need. Since 1996, local authorities in Scotland have been obliged to provide services for 'children in need'. For other groups, there is a shortage of low-cost day nurseries in Scotland (Powney *et al.* 1995). Pre-school provision for children over 3 tends to be educational in focus, with 4-year-olds spending two-thirds of their time in activities directly relevant to the primary school curriculum, regardless of the type of centre they attend (Powney *et al.* 1995). In 1997 the Scottish Office produced a curriculum framework for children in their pre-school year. This framework covers the following key areas: emotional, personal and social development; communication and language; knowledge and understanding of the world; expressive and aesthetic development; physical development and movement. Pre-school education is subject to external inspection on the basis of nationally specified 'output standards'.

In the UK as a whole, there is some evidence that children from socially deprived backgrounds are less likely to receive pre-school education, and that where they do so, the quality of care they receive is likely to be lower (Eurydice 1994). However, the 1996 Task Force in Scotland recommended a comprehensive intervention strategy with particular emphasis on overcoming the 'disadvantages and inequalities of social and domestic background' (SOEID, 1997). The measures which target pre-school children from disadvantaged backgrounds in Scotland are discussed in the following section.

In summary, Belgium, Ireland, the Netherlands, Portugal, Scotland and Spain differ in the level and type of provision for early childhood education. However, a number of common issues are apparent. First, in many systems there is a distinction between provision focused on 'welfare' and that focused on 'education', a distinction which is likely to impede the development of successful inter-agency strategies for young children. Thus, 'education'-based services may often fail to take account of the broader welfare needs of the child while educational activities may not be integrated into services for very young children, although this represents a crucial stage in their development. Second, children from disadvantaged backgrounds tend to be the focus of 'supplementary' programmes rather than having their needs addressed within mainstream provision. The nature of provision for children from disadvantaged backgrounds is discussed in greater detail in the following section.

Intervention programmes for disadvantaged children

Four kinds of programmes targeted on disadvantaged children can be identified in the six countries studied. These include:

1   structured education programmes;
2   flexible delivery of pre-school services to certain groups;
3   home-based intervention programmes which focus primarily on the child;
4   interventions aimed at both children and parents (and sometimes, the wider community).

These types of programme differ in their potential to involve inter-agency strategies. Structured education programmes are more likely to be school- or centre-based and can often have very low levels of inter-agency co-operation. Some programmes involve parents in their activities but parents may often have a 'supplementary' role, providing back-up and support for the programme rather than having a key role in decision-making within the school or centre. Structured education programmes may also involve other education stakeholders, although such involvement is not extensive. Home-based and 'flexible' services tend to have higher levels of direct parent involvement, although again services are likely to be directed by a group of professionals. At the other end of the continuum, 'two-generation' or community-based interventions will tend to involve a wider range of agencies, almost by definition. These interventions are based on the premise that young children's educational needs cannot be separated from their broader social, economic and welfare needs. As a result, they seek to involve a broad array of statutory, voluntary and community-based agencies in service design and delivery. This approach is probably the most difficult to implement, involving the integration of hitherto fragmented agencies, but would appear to have the most potential to address the needs of young children. The remainder of this section outlines some examples of good practice in early childhood education aimed at disadvantaged children, focusing on the extent to which such measures reflect a 'joined-up' approach.

Structured education programmes for pre-school children

The development of early childhood education programmes in Europe has been strongly influenced by projects targeted on disadvantaged children initiated in the United States from the 1960s onwards. Such programmes have been found to have positive effects on children's cognitive and intellectual development, at least in the short term, with longer-term influences on school achievement and retention (see, for example, Barnett 1995; Reynolds *et al.* 1997; Weikart 1996). Interventions were found to be particularly successful when pre-school and primary school services were integrated (Zigler 1995) and where child-focused activities were linked to parent-focused activities (Gomby *et al.* 1995).

The Rutland Street Project, initiated in Dublin in 1969, was influenced by the experience of such interventions in the United States. The aim of the project was to develop strategies to prevent school failure in disadvantaged areas, particularly through preparing young children for integration into primary school. The project targeted 3 and 4-year-old children through a two-year structured programme. The project recognised that the educational needs of disadvantaged children could not be solely addressed through school-based activities and that a broader approach would be required. For this reason, it actively sought to involve parents in the activities of the project, establishing a Mothers' Club, an Advice Centre, and regular parent–teacher meetings. Social workers linked to the school project also carried out casework with some of the families (Holland 1979; Kellaghan 1977).

An evaluation of the Rutland Street Project indicated an improvement in intelligence scores and pre-school readiness among children by the end of the two-year programme. However, there was some falling-off of intelligence scores among participants in their first three years in primary school. In addition, a survey of mothers indicated positive attitudes towards, and satisfaction with, the pre-school, along with greater involvement in the education of their children (Kellaghan 1977). Positive benefits of programme participation were evident among young people at the age of 16. In particular, they received greater encouragement from their parents to stay on in school and were more likely to take state examinations than their peers (Kellaghan and Greaney 1993).

The Early Start Programme, initiated in Ireland in 1994, drew on the approach and curriculum developed through the Rutland Street Project. The aim of the programme is to enhance the overall development of the child, to ensure a smooth transition to full participation in the formal education system, and to offset the effects of socio-economic disadvantage. It is targeted at 3 and 4-year-old children living in disadvantaged areas and currently caters for more than 1,500 pupils in forty schools. Each class is run by a primary school teacher and a qualified childcare worker. Parental involvement is a particular feature of the programme and occurs on three levels: the day-to-day running of the centre;

taking part with their children in the centre's activities; and participation in an advisory group in the centre.

An initial evaluation of the Early Start Programme found no significant improvement in children's cognitive, language and motor behaviour following programme participation. However, children were found to have improved school-readiness on entry to primary school (Educational Research Centre 1998). In addition, some concern has been expressed over its displacement of existing community-based childcare services (often run by local groups of parents themselves) (NESF 1997).

Structured educational programmes in Scotland have tended to focus on the development of literacy skills among young children in the early stages of primary education. Such programmes have targeted schools serving economically disadvantaged areas. The Pilton Early Intervention Project was set up in Edinburgh and involved additional teaching in the early years, the provision of nursery nurses for the infant classes, and home-link teachers to promote parental involvement in children's learning. Home–school link teachers were given the task of supporting parents in their role as educators of their own children. This involved holding workshops for parents on early literacy in both pre-school and early primary years, the development of resources to enable parents to stimulate literacy and the provision of opportunities for children and parents to work together. Evaluation indicated clear improvements in children's literacy levels over the first three years of the project. However, there was some variation between classes which was likely to relate to individual school and teacher effectiveness (SOEID 1997; Lothian Regional Council 1995, 1996, 1997). A similar project was initiated in Wester Hailes schools with nursery nurses or classroom assistants provided in early years classes. These nurses/assistants are actively involved in literacy development, and progress has been reported for participating classes (SOEID 1997).

In 1997, these early intervention programmes were extended to a national basis, initially for a period of three years (subsequently extended to five years). The aim of the national Early Intervention Programme is to raise standards of reading, writing and numeracy in the first two years of primary school. Additional funding provided by government and local authority grants provides extra support in schools through the employment of learning support teachers, educational psychologists, classroom assistants and home–school link personnel. Local authorities are not specifically required to target schools in disadvantaged areas, but it seems that it is now established that the Early Intervention Programme funding should be allocated to schools on the basis of their socio-economic status. The numbers of children receiving free school meals and in receipt of clothing grants have been used as indicators for the selection of schools to participate in the programme. However, there is some autonomy on the part of local authorities in deciding the nature of funding allocation. The programme is currently being evaluated; initial research indicates some positive perceptions on the part of teachers to children who have participated in the programme (Fraser and Pirrie 1999).

A similar approach of targeting provision on disadvantaged areas is evident in the Belgian (Flemish) context. The Extended Care (Zorgverbreding) programme, initiated in 1993, is a preventive programme aimed at children at risk of school failure. Resources are targeted on schools with a certain percentage of children from families living in poverty. A parallel programme (educational priority policy) provides similar resources for schools with a high percentage of children from immigrant backgrounds. Additional resources allow for extra teaching hours and for the facilitation of parental involvement in the school. The programme covers the last two years of pre-school and the first two years of primary education. Schools are required to design an action plan which optimises: skills development; monitoring of pupils; teaching techniques; co-operation within the school; and co-operation with parents. Evaluation of the programme indicates that the number of teacher hours spent on extended care has a significant positive effect on pupil progress. Other research has indicated that the programme has resulted in greater confidence among teachers in detecting and remedying developmental problems. However, the extent of the direct involvement of parents in school life remains unclear (OECD 2000b).

A number of the structured educational programmes considered have shown positive benefits for the young children involved. In general, it has been recognised that the broader needs and circumstances of the young children should be considered in service delivery, and all of the projects have made some efforts to involve parents in their activities. However, the extent to which parents have 'ownership' over such projects remains unclear; in many cases, they assume a back-up or supportive rather than central role. Furthermore, a number of critics have argued that such programmes can serve to direct critical attention away from wider socio-economic issues and the nature of the educational system itself to focus attention on parents and children (Bernstein 1974; Connell 1994).

Flexible delivery

A number of countries have developed special provision to reach young children who do not usually have access to, or participate in, early childhood education services. The groups targeted are mainly Traveller children or those living in isolated rural areas.

In the Irish context, there are fifty-four pre-school facilities for Traveller children, catering for approximately 660 children. The state provides 98 per cent of the tuition costs for up to three hours a day for the school year. Transport costs are almost fully funded by the state, with additional support provided for the purchase of equipment. The health authorities contribute towards the cost of care assistants and the provision of meals. These pre-schools represent a co-operative effort between a range of agencies, with funding provided by the Department of Education and Science and health centres while centres are managed and run by a range of voluntary organisations. It has been argued that these pre-schools can have a positive role in preparing children for integration into primary school. However, the lack of guidelines for practice and curriculum along with the absence of systematic in-service training and support for staff has been criticised (Task Force on the Travelling Community 1995).

In Spain, there are two such programmes: La Casa de los Niños and travelling pre-schools. La Casa de los Niños is targeted at children under 4 (and their parents) living in remote rural areas; more recently the service has been extended to working-class urban areas. The objectives of the programme are for children to socialise and engage in activities with other children, and for parents to exchange information and experiences in collaboration with educators from whom they receive guidance and support. Centres are staffed by a teacher and an educator, and run by a director in each area.

Travelling pre-schools (Preescolar na Casa) are educational services provided in sparsely populated rural areas. The programme is an educational intervention with children under 6 and their parents, with the assistance of systematic and regular guidance by professionals. The programme supports parents in carrying out educational activities with their children. Periodically, meetings with children from other families are organised for play or to carry out group projects. The programme has been seen to have positive effects on children's integration into compulsory schooling. However, issues such as the difficulty in involving parents (particularly fathers) and scepticism on the part of 'mainstream' teachers have been raised.

Travelling pre-schools were also introduced into Portugal in 1993. Their objective is to promote development among pre-school children who live in remote areas with no nursery facilities. The network of nursery school teachers reaches 170 children in seventy-five localities.

It is interesting to note that it is usually 'supplementary' programmes, often directed at particular groups (such as Traveller children) that have incorporated greater flexibility into their service delivery. In general, this has not been matched by increased flexibility within mainstream educational provision. These services have tended to involve parents, but levels of involvement vary markedly, as does the involvement of other statutory and voluntary agencies.

Home-based intervention programmes

Home-based intervention programmes aim to support parents as educators of their children. Due to their heavy demands in terms of resources and personnel, they tend to be less commonly implemented than the other types of programmes.

In Scotland, the Lothian Region Home Visiting Scheme involved trained teachers visiting the homes of 2 and 3-year-olds for one hour per week to encourage mothers in the educational development of their children. However, some caution has been expressed about the potential impact of this scheme on damaging mothers' self-confidence in their own child-rearing practices by failing to recognise and take account of the home culture (SOEID 1997).

In the Netherlands, a home intervention project using structured activities designed to prepare the child for school was implemented. Local mothers were involved in training other parents. However, evaluation indicated mixed results in terms of the impact on children. There were positive effects for the development of language skills among Moroccan children, but no effects on other dimensions of child development (Eurydice 1994).

A home-based intervention project was implemented on a pilot basis for disadvantaged pre-school children in a provincial town in Ireland (the Kilkenny Project). The objective of this programme was to increase the quantity and quality of mother–child interaction in order to facilitate the development of school-related concepts and skills among pre-school children. The curriculum was centred around perceptual–cognitive activities, imitative play, manipulative activities and language, and involved home lessons of one hour spread over a two-year period. An evaluation of this programme indicated no marked advantage accruing to participants in terms of performance in ability tests (Archer and Kellaghan 1975)

These measures overlap somewhat with the 'two-generation' measures discussed in the following section. However, home-based intervention programmes can be seen as focusing more closely on promoting the educational development of the child (by working with the parent) while community-based interventions may also have specific goals for parents, including the promotion of access to training and employment.

'Two-generation' and community-based interventions

A number of examples of community-based interventions were evident in the countries considered. These projects usually took as their starting-point the need to adopt a holistic approach to the needs of young children, placing their educational needs within a broader social and economic context.

In the Belgian context, projects set up by Kind en Gezin tend to adopt an integrated approach to the delivery of services to children and their parents. Kind en Gezin runs and subsidises day-care centres, and operates preventive health-care centres in disadvantaged areas. A funded day-care centre, De Wurpskes in Leuven, involves a co-operative effort among a number of voluntary organisations in a disadvantaged district in order to provide educational support to parents and activities for children.

The Koffiepot, Centre for Work, Knowledge, Living and Well-being, is a community project in a working-class district of The Hague (in the Netherlands) with a relatively high proportion of immigrants. Its aim is to involve statutory and community stakeholders in involving mothers in their children's education as well as helping to develop job opportunities for local mothers (Schwab 1994).

In Spain, maternity/infant centres provide integrated services for parents and children. Some target mothers during the child's first year of life, trying to provide information and training, and allowing for an exchange of experiences with other mothers and a space of their own. Other services target both parents of children under 3. They have a role in the provision of social, educational and health information and services. In addition, the Proyecto Granada targets parents and children (including those from the Gypsy community) in training, cultural and educational activities. Initial results suggest that this project has assisted the integration of children into mainstream schools (Eurydice 1994).

Other locally based projects in Spain provide services jointly to parents and children. Capitulaciones 92 in Granada provides support to families with children under 3 through training, group meetings, play and learning activities. This initiative has been found to have positive developmental outcomes for children. Parents are better trained to stimulate their children's physical, intellectual, emotional and social development. In addition, parental awareness of local services for their children has improved. Elsewhere, Proyecto Avanzada has taken an integrated approach to service provision for families, involving the early detection of children and mothers at risk, and support for mothers on an individual or group basis. The existence of multi-disciplinary teams (of psychologists, social workers, etc.) in mainstream schools in Spain can also be seen as leading to a 'joined-up' approach.

The Amadora Project in Portugal is a project in which educational, health and social welfare agencies integrate their efforts to respond to the socio-educational needs of at-risk children and to promote family and community involvement in dealing with social problems. The project has been undertaken in two of the most deprived areas in the district of Lisbon (Bairrão *et al.* 1989). Similar initiatives, using integrated approaches to the needs of children at risk and the promotion of family and community involvement, have been integrated into general programmes targeted at those experiencing socio-economic disadvantage (e.g. under the Integra Programme).

The current Labour government in Britain has strongly emphasised the need for 'joined-up' policy in relation to young children and their families. A range of new programmes aiming at the delivery of more integrated services have been introduced, including Sure Start, Early Years Development and Childcare Partnerships, Education Action Zones and Early Excellence Centres. However, not all of these programmes have been introduced in Scotland. Sure Start Scotland was launched in 1998. The aim of the programme is the promotion of the physical, intellectual and social development of children under 4, especially those experiencing socio-economic disadvantage. It builds on existing services to provide a range of supports, including outreach, family support, child care and health care, for children and parents. Contact with parents commences with a visit by outreach workers within three months of a child being born. The programme is explicitly cross-departmental in nature, aiming to deliver integrated services to children and their parents. In July 2000 an additional £315 million in funding was announced for the programme. The programme will be subject to on-going evaluation but it is too early to assess its success in meeting its objectives.

Community-based interventions appear to have considerable potential for developing successful inter-agency co-operation in service delivery. However, many of these services are still at a relatively early stage of development. A number of potential limitations should also be considered. First, such interventions are highly resource-intensive and their success requires an on-going commitment to the provision of such resources. Second, it can be difficult to evaluate the 'success' of such interventions since they aim to address a diverse set of goals, including the educational development of young children, the support needs of parents, and so on. Third, these interventions may be supplementary to existing services which may remain fragmented.

Conclusions

This chapter has indicated the diversity of provision for early childhood education for disadvantaged children in six European countries: Belgium, Ireland, the Netherlands, Portugal, Scotland and Spain. In many of the countries, services for young children remain fragmented, thus inhibiting the development of a more holistic approach to meeting their needs and those of their parents. Structured education programmes appear to provide some positive results in terms of young children's development. Some of these programmes strongly emphasise parental involvement and a number draw on supports and resources from other agencies. However, such programmes tend to be heavily school-centred in design and delivery, they vary in the extent to which they actively promote parental involvement, and they are often unable to address the broad range of factors which lead to social exclusion among young children and their families. Home-intervention programmes are resource-intensive and run the risk of locating the 'problem' within individual families rather than the wider socio-economic context. Programmes which feature flexible delivery, as evidenced by the Spanish experience, have also been found to provide an efficient way of reaching marginalised groups. In overall terms, community-based services would appear to have the greatest potential to address the diverse needs of young children and their families. However, many such integrated service programmes (such as Sure Start in Scotland) are at a very early stage of development and it can be very difficult to evaluate the success of such measures given the extremely diffuse nature of their goals. The examples of good practice considered in the six countries concerned do, however, indicate the importance of adopting a more holistic and integrated approach to the needs to young children living in disadvantaged circumstances.

Notes

1 This chapter draws on research funded under the Socrates Programme (see Nicaise 2000). In particular, the contribution of Breda McCabe is gratefully acknowledged.
2 Separate figures are not available for children in Scotland.

References

Archer, P. and Kellaghan, T. (1975) 'A home intervention project for pre-school disadvantaged children', *Irish Journal of Education* 9: 28–43.

Bairrão, J., Barbosa, M., Borges, I., Cruz, O. and Mecedo-Pinto, I. (1989) 'Care and education for children under age 6 in Portugal', in P.P. Olmsted and D.P. Weikart (eds) *How Nations Serve Young Children*, Michigan: High/Scope Press.

Barnett, W.S. (1995) 'Long-term effects of early childhood programs on cognitive and school outcomes', *The Future of Children* 5(3): 25–50.

Bernstein, B.B. (1974) 'A critique of the concept of "compensatory education"', in D. Wedderburn (ed.) *Poverty, Inequality and Class Structure*, Cambridge: Cambridge University Press.

Connell, R.W. (1994) 'Poverty and education', *Harvard Educational Review* 64(2): 125–49.

Delhaxhe, A. (1989) 'Early childhood care and education in Belgium', in P.P. Olmsted and D.P. Weikart (eds) *How Nations Serve Young Children*, Michigan: High/Scope Press.

Department of Education and Science (1999) *Ready to Learn: White Paper on Early Childhood Education*, Dublin: Stationery Office.

Educational Research Centre (1998) *Early Start Preschool Programme: Final Evaluation Report*, Dublin: ERC.

Eurydice (1994) *Pre-School and Primary Education in the EC*, Brussels: European Commission.

Fraser, H. and Pirrie, A. (1999) 'Improving standards of literacy and numeracy in the early years of primary school: preliminary findings from the national evaluation of the Early Intervention Programme in Scotland', paper presented to the European Conference on Educational Research, Lahti.

Gomby, D.S., Larner, M.B., Stevenson, C.S., Lewit, E.M. and Behrman, R.E. (1995) 'Long-term outcomes of early childhood programs: analysis and recommendations', *The Future of Children* 5(3): 6–24.

Hayes, N., O'Flaherty, J. and Kernan, M. (1997) *A Window on Early Education in Ireland*, Dublin: DIT.

Holland, S. (1979) *Rutland Street*, Oxford: Pergamon Press.

Kellaghan, T. (1977) *The Evaluation of an Intervention Programme for Disadvantaged Children*, Slough: NFER.

Kellaghan, T. and Greaney, B.J. (1993) *The Educational Development of Students following Participation in a Preschool Programme in a Disadvantaged Area*, Dublin: Educational Research Centre.

Lothian Regional Council (1995, 1996, 1997) *Deprivation, Early Intervention and the Prevention of Reading Difficulties*, Lothian: Lothian Regional Council, Department of Education.

Moss, P. (1990) *Childcare in the European Communities 1985–1990*, Women of Europe Supplements, European Commission.

NESF (1997) *Early School Leavers and Youth Unemployment*, Dublin: National Economic and Social Forum.

Nicaise, I. (ed.) (2000) *The Right to Learn: Educational Strategies for Socially Excluded Youth in Europe*, Bristol: Policy Press.

OECD (1998) *Education at a Glance*, Paris: OECD.

——(2000a) *OECD Country Note: Early Childhood Education and Care Policy in Portugal*, Paris: OECD.

——(2000b) *OECD Country Note: Early Childhood Education and Care Policy in the Flemish Community of Belgium*, Paris: OECD.

Palacios, J. (1989) 'Child care and early education in Spain', in P.P. Olmsted and D.P. Weikart (eds) *How Nations Serve Young Children*, Michigan: High/Scope Press.

Powney, J., Glissov, P., Hall, S. and Harlen, W. (1995) *We Are Getting Them Ready for Life: Provision for Pre-Fives in Scotland*, Scotland: Scottish Council for Research in Education.

Randall, V. (2000) 'Childcare policy in the European states: limits to convergence', *Journal of European Public Policy* 7(3): 346–68.

Reynolds, A.J., Mann, E., Miedel, W. and Smokowski, P. (1997) 'The state of early childhood intervention: effectiveness, myths and realities, new directions', *Focus* 19(1): 5–11.

Schwab, A. (1994) *The Koffiepot: Centre for Work, Knowledge, Living and Well-Being in Laakwartier-Noord*, The Hague.

SOEID (1997) *Early Intervention: Key Issues*, Edinburgh: Scottish Office Education and Industry Department.

Task Force on the Travelling Community (1995) *Report of the Task Force on the Travelling Community*, Dublin: Stationery Office.

Weikart, D. (1996) 'High-quality preschool programs found to improve adult status', *Childhood* 3(1): 117–20.

Zigler, E.F. (1995) 'Meeting the needs of children in poverty', *American Journal of Orthopsychiatry* 1: 6–9.

14 Involving parents in their children's education in Japan and Scotland

Contrasts in policy and practice

Hiroyuki Kasama and Lyn Tett

Introduction

Parents' involvement in their children's education can position them as customers, managers or partners, and these constructions have a strong effect on how their rights and responsibilities are regarded (see Munn 1993). Policy statements by the governments of the UK use an implicit deficit model, where parents, especially those from the working-class and minority ethnic communities, are assumed to be unwilling educators of their children, who needed to be harnessed to the educational aims of the school (see Crozier 1998). In Japan there is also a strong emphasis on parental involvement, but there is no assumption that this will be difficult to achieve. Rather, the problem is seen as stopping parents from becoming over-anxious about their children's achievement (see Lynn 1988). Making comparisons between two countries that have different cultures is one way of illuminating practices that can be taken for granted as 'normal'. In this chapter we do this by comparing schools' expectations of parents and parents' expectations of schools in Japan and in Scotland, and the contrasts in policy and practice that underpin these differences. The two authors have taken different responsibilities. Hiroyuki Kasama has provided the perspective from Japan, and also the case studies, and Lyn Tett has provided information about the Scottish system and the comparison between the two countries. The differing perspectives reflect the differing cultural perspectives of the two cultures.

In both countries the importance of the relationship between schools, community and parents has been emphasised by governments. 'The school deep-rooted in the community' is a phrase that has been used in Japan as one of the ideal features of education. Creating good relationships between schools and parents is an important school policy, and many people think that the school should have a central role in the community. In Scotland, collaborative relationships between parents, school and community are also strongly emphasised. Parents are expected to play an increasingly important role in their children's education and there is a particular focus on the ways in which this can be encouraged in order to help raise children's attainment (see McMillan and Leslie 1998; SOED 1996). In a situation where the structure of society and the role of education is changing, involving parents as partners in their children's education is becoming an important issue in both Scotland and Japan.

In this chapter we will examine first Japanese cultural and ideological expectations about education and schools. Second, two case studies of primary schools, one in Japan and the other in Scotland, will show the differing ways in which parents are involved in these contrasting schools. Then the views of a small group of Japanese parents whose children attend Scottish schools will be reported, so that their views of the different strengths and weaknesses of the two systems can be considered. Finally we will examine the policy differences in the two systems and how these are translated into practice.

Parents and education in Japan

There is a strong expectation that Japanese parents will help their children to study. This has been true for a long time. A survey carried out by the Prime Minister's Office in the 1960s showed one-third of boys' parents wanted to give their children higher education at any cost. Most other parents also answered that even if the burden were heavy they would try as much as possible (Kobayashi 1976: 109–10). Nowadays, this tendency is becoming even more common. Behind this situation lay a great change in the industrial structure of the country. Thrush and Smith (1980: 54, 62) state:

> The growth in heavy industry and service areas has placed pressures on the educational system to produce more potential white-collar workers. Increasing national income has made expansion in higher education possible ... Parents, wanting to provide a 'sure future for their children', engage in 'boundary jumping' to ensure their children are enrolled in the 'right' school.

In order to ensure their children's future, parents endeavour to encourage their children from their early years and struggle with meeting the cost of supplementary education. For example, there is a special private supplementary school called *Juku*. It is common to see children attending *Juku* between two and five days a week and studying two to three hours a day. According to a Ministry of Education survey in 1998, 36.9 per cent of primary school children and 71.8 per cent of public junior high school students were attending *Juku*. There is even a kind of *Juku* for 2 or 3-year-olds. Employing a tutor or enrolling on a correspondence course is also common, with correspondence courses even for kindergarten children. In Japan, these kinds of learning support systems are becoming a big industry, and parents choose one or more for their children. Lynn (1988: 74) argues:

> Japanese parents are well aware of the importance for their children of obtaining the educational credentials of graduation from a high status senior high school and university, and they transmit their concern for

educational achievement to their children during the course of their upbringing.

Japanese society is fairly homogenous. According to a Ministry survey in 1999, around 80 per cent of people said that they felt they belonged to the 'middle class'. It is not easy to discern poverty in Japan, and neither the Japanese themselves nor visiting foreigners are aware of it (Yoshida 1995). Of course, there is the matter of family poverty and problems relating to children's schooling. Research indicates that the retention rate of children in high school from families on welfare benefits is 75 per cent and from single-parent families around 85 per cent (Okano and Tsuchiya 1999), compared with a national average of around 95 per cent across Japan.

Why are Japanese parents so committed to their children's education? Sometimes mothers are much keener than fathers. What is the motivation to urge children to study? Kobayashi (1976: 111) pointed out that 'in Japanese society, education has long been considered an effective way of climbing up the social ladder'. According to him, the system was already established in the Edo period (1600–1868), in the Shogun feudal age. Today there is a phrase '*Gakureki Shakai* (academic pedigree)' (Thrush and Smith 1980: 62) which means that educational background will strongly influence the course of people's lives and careers. Particularly, the system of new college graduates gaining lifetime employment was so common that academic background became much more important than one's professional career. A good school background makes it easy to have a connection with the big well-established companies. There is therefore a strong motivation for parents to support their children's learning (Gakken 1997).

However, some other factors must be considered. First, there is an atmosphere that diligence is valued, as Dore and Sako (1989: 21) describe it, arising from 'older Confucian traditions – the belief that self-development, self-cultivation are desirable in themselves and a condition for citizen self-respect'. People almost have an obsession about working hard, and there is a tendency to look at a person who fails in studying as a failure in life. Academic failure can easily become a severe stigma for children, and something parents are afraid of. Second, a kind of 'opportunism' must be pointed out. Everybody goes to high school and university, so people think that their children must go to a higher school. Ironically, this has caused some problems, such rising numbers of dropouts from high school and the university becoming a 'play park', where students don't study hard. Third, it is argued that women, after leaving work to marry and have children, can't find any identity except in their role as mothers. So parents, particularly mothers, are trying to fulfil themselves through their children: children's good academic results are seen as a result of good child-rearing, thus they become good mothers. Fourth, good private universities have their feeder schools, and when children enter this system early they are absolved from taking school entrance examinations. Paradoxically, parents are eager to encourage their children to study at a very young age precisely because they want to protect them from the 'entrance examination war'. Fifth, of course parents want their children to have knowledge as human beings, but compared with other reasons this seems less important to many people. Finally, there is another issue regarding the curriculum, which has been getting too condensed and difficult, particularly in the early years of primary school. Many children cannot keep up with learning in school and are now dropping out. Most parents are afraid of this and seek to find ways of supporting their children.

This is the general picture of the reasons parents become involved in their children's education. In order to show the types of activity that they engage in, we now turn to a more detailed examination of the collaborations that take place in Japan, using a case study.

School, teachers and parents in collaborative activity in Japan

Japanese school administration

The Ministry of Education is the core of the Japanese education system. It has significant influence in establishing the standards of Japanese education such as the national curriculum (called the Course of Study), textbook authorisation, class sizes, salaries and so on. The Ministry of Education oversees local boards of education, and municipal boards of education are under the control of the local agency. Schools are administered under the supervision of municipal boards of education. The boards usually regulate the following items (Ministry of Education 1994):

1   provision and maintenance of facilities and equipment;
2   employment of personnel, assignment of school duties, leave of absence and official travel of personnel;
3   classroom organisation and administration;
4   educational activities such as instructional planing and special curricular activities;
5   school attendance;
6   common use of instructional materials, notice and approval of instructional materials;
7   school terms and holidays;
8   school lunch.

The boards also have a function to appoint and dismiss teachers and personnel, and arrange teachers' rotation among schools. The term served by a teacher and deputy head teacher in any school is usually around three years. There are no representatives from parents or the community who have any responsibility for school governance.

Involving parents in Japan: case study of K Primary School in Hokkaido

This case study is set in Hokkaido, a northern island of Japan which was developed by settlers from mainland Japan and where schools were established as the first public facility for the support of settlers. So in some rural areas in Hokkaido some people still become members of school PTAs in the area where they live, even if they don't have any children at the school (Tamai 1996: 81–4). K Primary School is a public primary school. In 1999 there were 264 children from 200 families. Each grade has two classes except Primary 1 and 3. Each class has about twenty-five children due to the low birth rate. All the mothers were born in Japan and less than five percent of the fathers are unemployed. Very few of the mothers whose children are in the first two years of school have full time jobs. Overall just a few of the children are getting some financial support due to their economic and social circumstances.

There are three kinds of collaborative activity with parents and the school. First the school takes an initiative, second the parents, and third there are co-ordinated activities like a PTA. Also, the first activity can be separated into two aspects, the formal school policy and each classroom teacher's informal endeavour.

Involving parents – initiatives by the school

Formal school policy

The day for class visits   There are special days two or three times a term when parents (mostly mothers) visit and see a class being taught. Teachers show off their teaching skills and parents observe, but normally parents' concern is their children's behaviour during the class, so this is a kind of performance to show the children's development. After the lesson, children are dismissed and a teacher–parents meeting is held. At that time teachers introduce their teaching policy and classroom management, discuss children's development and make any requests to parents; it then becomes a time of questions and answers and chatting. Most mothers come to school on that day. Even if they have jobs they take time off, and it is very useful time to communicate with each other.

A home visit   A teacher visits all the homes of the children at the beginning of the first term. It takes several days; each visit lasts about half an hour. The teacher asks about the child's everyday life in the home and has a discussion with the mother. It is also a good time to get to know each other and for teachers to learn about the child's family background.

Individual profile card   At the beginning of the first term parents submit a profile card of their child, filled out not only with the address and emergency contact telephone number but also with notes on the child's character, some health records, their expectations of school, requests for teaching, points for concern, and so on.

Liaison notebook   In the first grade there is a special notebook which parents can use to contact the teacher. If something happens, such as the child becoming ill, a relative dying, or signs of bullying, and parents want to say something to the teacher or school, they use this notebook to contact the school.

Curriculum information letter   Every week a newsletter is published in each grade which introduces the following week's study plan, events and things which are going to be needed in classes such as art and handicraft. Using this letter, parents check the child's school bag every day and prepare ahead.

A report card   At the end of term – so three times a year – children get a report card. All subjects are divided into sub-contents and each content is reported. There is a part where the teacher gives his/her views, and when they return the card parents also write their reply.

School events   There are many school events which parents attend, to cheer on their child or for their own interest, such as an athletics meeting, marathon race, literary arts exhibition or drama festival.

Classroom teacher's informal work

Classroom newsletter   In addition to the curriculum information letter, some teachers make their own classroom newsletters. It shows what happens in the classroom, and may include photographs, children's descriptions, drawings, teacher's comments, etc.

Diary exchange   Most Japanese teachers do this but it is not compulsory. Every day children write a diary and bring it to the teacher; then it is returned to the children with some comments. Sometimes parents also write something about the children so it becomes a letter notebook, too. It is not easy work, but it makes a great relationship between teachers and families and is very useful for practising writing.

Homework   Teachers assign a homework sheet to children according to the curriculum. These sheets may be produced by educational material companies or by the teachers themselves. In the case of the latter, sheets can be tailored easily to the children's needs and abilities.

Making relationships – initiatives by parents

Parents' meeting with the teacher   A meeting is held at least once a year; several times a year is more common. This meeting is held in the community centre or in a restaurant, outside the school. The first meeting is particularly important, because at that time the membership and role of the PTA are decided. Other meetings are just for communication and fun, or may sometimes be held after big school events. Usually, this meeting is just attended by mothers.

Family recreation with the teacher   At least once a year, there is a half or whole day of family recreation. Hiking, outdoor games, sports, barbecue and so on are planned by mothers, and fathers, brothers and sisters also attend. It is one of the biggest events in the programme of classroom activities.

PTA activities

The PTA activities are also vital and are quite structured. Every class chooses four people for the school committee. There are three committees and their roles are as follows:

* *Planning committee*: planning and organising the PTA festival and several lectures for parents. There are also general tasks of co-ordinating information between classroom and school.
* *School life committee*: environmental safety checks around the school and maintenance of the PTA's flower garden; planning, carrying out or organising sports events in which parents also participate, and volleyball tournament matches.
* *Information committee*: editing and publishing the PTA school newspaper three times a year.

Every committee has a meeting at least once a month in school, and there is a meeting of committee representatives with members of the school executive several times a year. Policy is decided in this meeting, and then each committee starts to carry out its work. Committee representatives also attend a city-wide committee of PTA organisations once or twice a year.

Within each class, after the committee members have been chosen, several roles for school events and classroom events are assigned to the rest of the members – organising the school fête, cleaning the school after athletic meetings, planning parents' round-table conferences and family recreation days. This involves as many members as possible, thus making as little work as possible for each one. There is also a parents' circle learning computing, supported from the PTA budget, together with lectures and cultural study classes.

The above is an outline of ways of involving parents in school in Japan. Although some of the details are very particular to this school, most of the general practices referred to in the school are formal policy and can be seen in any school in Japan. But compared to the interest in their own children, in recent times fewer parents have wanted to be members of the PTA committee or attend the lectures. This is because they are busy – in particular, the number of working mothers is increasing – and they don't want to have too much responsibility. However, although it may take several parents' meetings, a committee is always formed.

School, teachers and parents in collaborative activity in Scotland

Scottish school administration

At the heart of the Scottish system is the concept of the fairly autonomous school operating within a strong national framework. There is a separate legislation system that sets out the nature of provision in Scotland and the agencies responsible for its delivery (Bryce and Humes 1999). Central government determines how much money is allocated to local councils but not how that money is spent. Councils have a range of responsibilities and powers that are supportive of their main duty of ensuring the provision of adequate and effective school education, but these statutory responsibilities are stated in very general terms (Bloomer 1999: 157). Devolved school management means that budgets are devolved to individual schools in relation to pupil numbers, property maintenance and staffing. While the curriculum is designed centrally, there remains scope for decision-making at the level of the school and the individual teacher. National guidelines, contained in the Memorandum setting out the programme for 5 to 14-year-olds, recognise that different children develop at different speeds (Kirk and Glaister 1994). The curriculum remains relatively fluid and flexible, and its interpretation depends heavily on the professional judgement of teachers, either individually or collectively (Darling 1999: 34). Thus, in Scotland, the education system is much more decentralised than in Japan.

Involving parents in Scotland: case study of D Primary School in Edinburgh

D Primary School is situated in a densely populated area in the middle of Edinburgh. There are 200 children from 108 families. Unlike the Japanese case study, many of the fathers are unemployed, there are a number of single parents and many parents are poor. Sixty per cent of the children are eligible for free school meals, and 20 per cent have English as their second or third language. Each grade has one class. There is a nursery school situated in two of the classrooms. This is an area of quite high unemployment, and many families who are in work have very low wages. For the minority ethnic groups, mainly from Pakistan and Bangladesh, people (mainly fathers) work long hours in 'take-aways' and restaurants. Most of the mothers have jobs working for a few hours in the small shops locally while their children are in school.

Involving parents – initiatives by the school

Formal school policy

The day for class visits While schools are required to make formal communication with parents by offering parents' consultation times, they are not specifically set out in terms of time required. In this school parents are formally invited to visit the school twice a year but can drop in informally at other times.

A home visit This is not a formal requirement, but there is a part-time 'home–school liaison' member of staff who would visit any families that the school felt were experiencing particular difficulties.

Individual profile card In Scotland these are called enrolment forms, and they are a statutory requirement.

School information letter Every month a newsletter is published that describes the school's activities. It includes some information about the curriculum, and also activities for parents.

A report card As in Japan, at the end of term (so three times a year) children get a report card. All subjects are covered and there are comments from the teacher.

School events As in Japan, there are many school functions which parents go to see. These include fund-raising events as well as events for the children, and have been an effective way of involving parents in the school.

Home-based 'activity packs' Number sacks, story sacks, reading books, including some in minority languages such as Urdu, are all available for parents to borrow from the school to enable them to work with their children at home. The materials are accompanied by straightforward suggestions about how they can be used. The minority ethnic worker and the home–school liaison worker offer extra support to any parent who needs it.

Education programme for parents Every week during term-time, a programme is arranged for parents that includes keep fit, visits to the local library, museums and art galleries, and basic education. This last is organised in collaboration with the Community Education Service and takes place in the designated parents' room.

Classroom teacher's informal work

Classroom news poster/letter Once a month, each class produces a record of what has happened in terms of events. It is mainly about the children's activities and achievements. It is displayed in poster form with pictures in the parents' room and as print in a one-page summary that is taken home by every child.

Homework   Teachers will assign a homework sheet to children. In Primary 1 this happens no more than once a week. If the children are having difficulties then their parents will be approached by the classroom teacher to see if they need any extra support.

Making relationships – initiatives by parents

Maintaining the parents' room   Parents maintain the displays on the walls. These include photographs of the children and staff on outings, and displays of national costumes and flags from India, Pakistan, Bangladesh, China and Saudi Arabia, representing the countries of origin of the families in the school.

End-of-term social   The minority ethnic group has an end-of-term party in the parents' room that all the staff attend during the morning break. Everyone is on first-name terms and friendly and open with each other.

Advising the school about non-Christian religious festivals   Parents inform the school about other religious festivals such as Eid, and children, staff and parents celebrate them during the school day.

Volunteer helpers   There is a range of activities, from helping to organise the classroom, to being helpers on outings, to acting as a collector of children, which all involve parents. Each year a parent is nominated as the organiser of the volunteers.

School board and PTA activities

Both school board and PTA activities are important ways of involving parents in the life of the school. The powers of the school board include an involvement in the selection of senior staff and a general oversight of school spending, but they have no locus in the curriculum or day-to-day management. Four parents sit on the school board, and they see their role mainly as supporting the head teacher in his efforts to improve their school's facilities. Of these four, two are also members of the PTA and have taken the roles of chair and secretary. There has not been an election for these posts for the last five years, as there has been only one nominee for each. The PTA sees its main function as fund-raising and has a termly event such as a sale of work or a coffee morning that the majority of parents will participate in. The elaborate structure set up in Japan does not apply to Scottish schools. Paradoxically, although, through the school board, parents have powers established by statute, such is the tradition of support for the school staff that parents have fewer formal responsibilities than those in Japan (see Munn 1993).

In order to further review the differences in approaches to involving parents between Japan and Scotland, we now turn to an examination of a small group of Japanese parents who have experienced Scottish education.

Japanese parents' opinions about Scottish education

There is a Saturday School in Edinburgh where around ninety children who attend Scottish primary schools study Japanese. Almost all of them will go back to Japan in a few years. A questionnaire was used to ask twenty-eight Japanese parents for their impressions of Scottish education, their child's study conditions and their involvement in Scottish schools.

Most of the parents appreciated the 'open door' policy of Scottish schools and agreed that visiting the school was easy and they felt welcome in the school. They found both classroom teachers and head teachers very friendly and approachable. One mother said, 'In Japan it was common that my opinion was not accepted by the school, but in Scotland teachers listen to my opinion and requests and then I can see that some things have changed.' Several mothers agreed with her opinion and talked about their experiences. One had involved a child's diet, another a child's isolation in his class, and the last one was about a child's trouble among friends. A mother wrote:

> When my child had a small problem with others I met the classroom teacher and talked about that. The teacher looked after my child carefully and encouraged him to be friends with others. (My child couldn't speak English well.) In Japan, teachers may just say something but in Scotland that teacher always let my child be close to her and encouraged him by taking his hands.

Another mother wrote: 'In Scotland, teachers teach children so individually that they know each child's character very well and then they can deal with the child's needs.' Many parents put a high valuation on this kind of emphasis on individuality and learning according to each child's pace. It may be related to class sizes and the existence of the assistant teacher system. In Japan, class size is up to forty children per teacher, and the team teaching system is not common yet.

However, only 20 per cent of parents were satisfied that they had enough information about their children's learning in the Scottish school. A lot of parents did not think the amount of homework was appropriate, either. Several parents wanted their children to have their own textbooks, and one wrote that

> I think it is not good that children don't have their own textbooks, and are not allowed to bring them home. If a child could bring textbooks home, it would be helpful for the child to study at home and for me to support his learning.

In Japan, every child has their own textbooks (they are free) and they bring them between home and school every day. Parents also receive a report card three times a year, at the end of each term, and many exam papers. Through these materials, Japanese parents can easily find out what their child is studying and what the learning attainment is, so they can support their child.

Although many Japanese parents were satisfied with communication with teachers in Scotland, they wanted to have more opportunities to meet teachers and get information about their child's learning. Some wanted to have regular meetings with the classroom teacher, and others wanted to have a set day for class visitation. A mother wrote, 'teachers always tell us not to hesitate to come and ask them anything, but my English is so poor that I can't go to school easily. I hope that there will be more regular meeting times.' This opinion seems very Japanese: Japanese parents weren't used to behaving spontaneously, so it was easier for them to go to school if the meeting time was fixed. Parents also wanted more information. One parent wrote,

> I would like to know a year's curriculum. I think it is not enough that an academic report is provided just once a year. I don't know what my child is learning, particularly about ethics, religion and social studies. It is hard to know my child's attainment from school information.

Another parent suggested, 'I feel that printed materials are less than in Japan, e.g. school newsletters. When my child was in P1, a teacher announced by word of mouth that children must bring something to school and my child didn't understand.'

There is a clear contrast between satisfaction with general communication and dissatisfaction with information about a child's study in the relationship between teacher and parents. Parents want to know precise and concrete information about their child's learning in school. However, information about how parents should support their children is also important. A Japanese mother said, 'Even if I know the answer to the question, I don't know how to teach it to my child.' The school must grasp each child's needs and give this information to the parents with a definite 'prescription', which shows what and how parents should do.

Concerning school events which parents attend, most parents say that they are well organised and give them a lot of opportunities to meet other parents and to get to know different cultures, unless they are too shy to participate. A mother also accepted the importance of the diversity in Scottish schools, saying 'My child used to have a prejudice about handicapped people but it seems to be disappearing. He has close contact with physically handicapped children in school and sees them frequently in town.' On the whole, it appeared that if Japanese parents didn't have to think about how their children must adapt to the Japanese 'entrance examination hell', they would be satisfied with Scottish schools and education. This is because they think that their children are respected for their individual character in school and that children have some choice over what they want to do.

Furthering parental involvement

What do these three case studies tell us about the different ways in which parents are positioned and position themselves in the two countries? Clearly, the ways in which schools work with parents have an important influence on the ethos of the school and the education that happens both within the school walls and, more informally, in the home. Parents are an important group that schools must work with if they are to achieve their goals, but how teachers construct the relationship with parents is crucial. It can range from a democratic partnership, at one end of the spectrum, where the importance of the different focus of the educational work of parents is acknowledged and mutually constructed sets of expectations about what each group can expect of the other are developed. At the other end of the range, the relationship can be conceived of as a one-way linear process where teachers inform or instruct parents about how they can support the work of the school. This in turn has wide implications for the way in which the role of parents in helping their children to learn and in their children's socio-emotional development is conceived. It also has an effect on social justice if some groups of parents and their children are treated differentially because of, for example, their socio-economic status.

There is a clear policy difference between the two countries as to why the importance of the relationship between school and parents is emphasised. The difference reflects each country's problems and the purposes of the educational reforms that have been introduced. In Scotland, the emphasis is on supporting parents to help their children learn in order to raise attainment (Caddell *et al.* 2000). The link between parental participation in children's early learning and children's achievement and aspirations has been demonstrated in a number of studies (Fraser 1996; McMillan and Leslie 1998; SOED 1996). HM Inspectors of Schools (1999) have also argued that 'parents are important partners in the drive to improve standards of literacy and numeracy'. The underlying policy premise here, however, is that teachers must teach parents how to be educators in a one-way linear process of informing them about what they must do.

In contrast, in Japan the importance of the relationship between parents, community and school is very much concerned with children's character-building but not with their academic achievement, which is the responsibility of the teacher. Of course, these cannot be separated clearly in the development of the whole child, but early learning such as the acquisition of literacy and numeracy is seen as a less important issue in Japan. Particularly, given the increase in educational problems such as bullying, refusal to attend school, school violence, suicide and so on, collaboration between school, family and community is regarded as an extremely important matter for children's social development. 'Education of the heart', morality and citizenship are more emphasised, and a school is not considered to be doing its job unless it is making strong links with parents and the community (Advisory Organ of the Prime Minister, Youth Affairs Administration 1999). The change from the six-day to the five-day school week is another factor. In 1993, Japan introduced a five-day school week every second and fourth week, and this will be every week from 2002. With this decrease in the school week, family and community have much more responsibility for child care.

On the other hand, it is normally expected not only that the school will build children's scholastic ability but also that each family will take care of their children individually in ensuring that their children learn. Many opportunities and materials for learning – such as *Juku*, or cram school, private supplementary schooling, tutor or correspondence courses that support children's learning – surround children and parents. A wide range of workbooks and reference books related to subjects and levels are also available at bookshops. All parents are expected to take for granted their high level of responsibility for supporting their children's learning. This assumption and the absence of investigations into the effects of socio-economic influences on children's development has meant that parental involvement in raising children's academic attainment is viewed as unproblematic.

In contrast, the clear class differential in parental involvement in both Scotland and the rest of the UK (see Crozier 1998; Cuckle 1996; Tett and Crowther 1998; Tizard *et al.* 1988; Vincent and Warren 1998) has been the subject of considerable research and discussion. The importance of class and culture in parents' interactions with teachers is shown in these studies to be influenced by parents' socio-economic status and confidence about their competence as educators of their children. Evidence shows that working-class parents strongly support their children's education by showing an interest, giving encouragement and so on, but not by relating strongly to the school. This tends to be because they are aware of the cultural differences, particularly in relation to the teachers, that make it difficult for them to influence school practices. This means that participating in the activities that the school feels are appropriate to 'good' parents is seen as rather pointless (see Reay 1998; Tett 2001). Since both school staff and educational policy-makers focus on participation in school-based activities as the key measure of parental participation, such parents are regarded as not participating in their children's education (see Tett *et al.* 2000). Such 'non-participation' can then be translated by teachers into assumptions of a parental deficit, arising from differences in values between the home and the school, that enable them to blame parents for children's under-achievement.

In Japan there is the same focus on school-based activities but, because the school administration is so centralised and systematised, the school often follows a set pattern. For example, many Japanese schools hold a teacher's welcome and farewell party, sponsored by the PTA, in an expensive hotel. The mothers, as classroom representatives, not only pay a lot themselves for this but must also encourage the attendance of other parents who do not want to go to such a party. This example is not a small matter to be laughed away, but a symbol of the kind of formalism that can be seen throughout Japan. The implication of this is that even though this tradition is unpopular with many parents it is difficult to change, especially where there is a conservative head teacher or PTA representative. The bigger the school, the stronger the tendency to work in a 'top-down' way, to convey the wishes of the head teacher to those under him or her. Another contributory factor to the conservatism in Japanese schools is the situation of head teachers and deputy head teachers. The length of service of these administrative posts is only three or four years in every school. Such a term is definitely too short to make changes or to introduce new school policy. It is perhaps understandable that the school does not want to take the risk of changing anything, but then parents' dissatisfaction increases.

Another contrast between Japan and Scotland is the availability of space and facilities open to parents. The spaces available in many schools in Scotland are not there in Japan. When the PTA members have a meeting, they can use a room, with permission, but there are no 'drop-in' spaces in the schools in Japan. The school is the place for children's study from start to finish, but not the place where parents can spend time talking with other parents and relaxing. One reason for this difference in Scotland is the role that community educators play in collaborating with schools in providing classes and supporting facilities for parents. If parents are seen as people with an important contribution to make to the life of the school and the community, then they are viewed differently by the school and see themselves more positively (see Tett 2001).

Learning in the community, inviting people to the school from the community and attending or organising events with the community are also very important factors in making an effective link between school and community. In Scotland, many primary schools include learning about their local community as an important topic in the curriculum. Although there is a similar curriculum in primary schools in Japan, it tends to be made light of by both teachers and parents, because this kind of knowledge is not asked for in the entrance examinations. Some schools have a very interesting programme in which, with the help of local people, children are given the experience of making some special product typical of the community as well as studying in the classroom. Inviting people who have special knowledge or skills to the class is also adopted, but again this is seen as not very important because it does not contribute to the set curriculum. In general, co-operation between school and community is becoming weaker in Japan, but some schools in Hokkaido still have a strong relationship and hold school events and community events. Where this is the case, local people appreciate the work of teachers and consider that these events help children identify with the community (Tamai 1996: 149–50).

Through this research on involving Scottish and Japanese parents, it has become clear that the role of information is important. Communication between teachers and parents, with the information that parents desire, increases parents' trust in teachers. Parents come to understand their role, and sometimes those who have not been involved in their children's schools begin to change (Vincent and Warren 1998). In our Scottish case study school, parents felt that they were clearly informed about activities going on in the school. They found speaking to the class teacher the most effective means of finding things out; parents' evenings were also highly valued. Many parents indicated that teachers were always willing to offer help and advice. However, when it came to specific information about their own child and their progress in the school, the response was more mixed. The evidence seems to indicate, therefore, that the school was doing well at communicating with parents, but was not necessarily communicating the things parents want to know most about. This point was also highlighted by the Japanese parents whose children were at school in Scotland, and shows the difficulty of engaging with parents on their own terms.

In Japan it has been emphasised that schools should give information about their educational purpose, the school policy and any problems the school has, not only to parents but also to everyone in the school district. The school must recognise that if it needs the co-operation of parents and the community, it will first have to leave its narrow-minded world. A report of the Ministry of Youth Affairs said that schools should have public meetings to inform parents and the community and regularly provide parents with information about the curriculum, its contents, the goals of learning and the general ways of effective support. Clearly, information about their individual child's work is also a very important matter for parents. In Japan this is an important priority, whereas in Scotland schools provide much less detail and do not necessarily feel that parents need this information.

Conclusion

We can see that, while there are differences between Scotland and Japan, the importance of parental involvement is largely uncontested, although the justification for such involvement is different. Concern about the link between socio-economic background and children's learning was the starting point in Scotland, whereas in Japan it arose from a concern with children's character-building. In Japan, teachers reach out to the home through home visits, whereas in Scotland parents are mainly expected to come into the school. However, in neither country are parents seen as educational agents with their own agendas for their children beyond that relating to academic attainment. In Japan, every school has specified at least a minimum standard of collaboration between school and parents, but sometimes schools lack flexibility and cannot deal with individual children's problems or parents' requests. On the other hand, in the Scottish schools individuality is much more respected and the parents are able to have responses from the school that take account of their child's individual characteristics. This is partly a reflection of the greater flexibility of the curriculum in Scotland, whose interpretation depends on the professional judgement of teachers, whereas in Japan it is specified in considerable detail and is not open to local variation.

McNamara *et al.* (2000) use the metaphor of 'mobilisation' to describe the involvement of parents in their children's education. They argue that the current policy context in the UK means that parents need to be mobilised to education policy-makers' aggregate notions of school improvement, rather than parents' own agendas regarding their individual child's progress and happiness. In both Scotland and Japan, teachers are expected to involve parents in the life of the school but have little training, time or experience in doing so. As Bastiani (1989:

183) points out, parent–school partnership takes place very much on the *profes-sional's* terms, is conceptualised through professional ideology and articulated through professional language, all of which create barriers for parents. Under these circumstances, many parents experience such 'partnership' in terms of 'inequality, social distance and powerlessness'. If the school is to become more open to the voices of parents and the community, and parents are really to become educational partners, there needs to be a range of opportunities that would enable teachers to listen to and act on parents' opinions and requests.

What is clear, as Hannon (1998: 141) points out, is that

> to involve parents is not to give away teachers' professional expertise. [Rather it is] to take on the challenge and stimulation of working with adults and young children in the conviction that anything that teachers believe they can accomplish alone, they can do better in collaboration with parents.

What is missing from the policy and practice context in both countries is the will and the resources to enable teachers and parents to work together to create mutually constructed, feasible sets of expectations that would make partnership a reality. While this is the case, then the motivations and self-positionings of parents will be ignored and the social injustice of blaming parents for the educa-tional failure of their children will continue. As long as the responsibility for monitoring children's schooling rests on individual parents – usually mothers (David *et al.* 1993) – and is not shared with school officials, teachers and social services of all sorts, then working-class and poor children's school success will be compromised. A public discourse that lays the responsibility on the family, espe-cially mothers, for academic success or failure justifies a public educational system that intensifies inequalities, if only by concealing the economic conditions that underlie the creation of inequality.

References

Advisory Organ of the Prime Minister, Youth Affairs Administration (1999) *15th Youth Affairs Council Report*, Tokyo: Youth Affairs Administration.

Bastiani, J. (1989) 'Professional ideology versus lay experience', in G. Allen, J. Bastiani, I. Martin and K. Richards (eds) *Community Education. An Agenda for Educational Reform*, Milton Keynes: Open University Press.

——(1993) 'Parents as partners: genuine progress or empty rhetoric?' in P. Munn (ed.) *Parents and Schools. Customers, Managers or Partners?*, London: Routledge.

Bloomer, K. (1999) 'The local governance of education: an operational perspective' in T.G.K. Bryce and W.M. Humes (eds) *Scottish Education*, Edinburgh: Edinburgh Univer-sity Press.

Bryce, T.G.K. and Humes, W.M. (eds) (1999) *Scottish Education*, Edinburgh: Edinburgh University Press.

Caddell, D., Crowther, J., O'Hara, P. and Tett, L. (2000) *Executive Summary: Valuing Parents as Partners*, Edinburgh: City of Edinburgh Council.

Crozier, G. (1998) 'Parents and schools: partnership or surveillance?' *Journal of Education Policy*, 13(1): 125–36.

Cuckle, P. (1996) 'Children learning to read – exploring home and community relationships', *British Educational Research Journal*, 22: 17–32.

Darling, J. (1999) 'Scottish primary education: philosophy and practice' in T.G.K. Bryce and W.M. Humes (eds) *Scottish Education*, Edinburgh: Edinburgh University Press.

David, M., Edwards, R., Hughes, M. and Ribbens, J. (eds) (1993) *Mothers and Education: Inside Out?* London: Macmillan.

Dore, R. and Sako, M. (1989) *How the Japanese Learn to Work*, London: Routledge.

Fraser, H. (1996) *Early Intervention in Reading: Evaluation Report 1995/6*, Edinburgh: Moray House Institute of Education.

Gakken (ed.) (1997) *Japan As It Is*, Tokyo: Gakken Company.

Hannon, P. (1998) 'How can we foster children's early literacy development through parent involvement?' in S.B. Neuman and K. Roskas (eds) *Children Achieving: Best Practices in Early Literacy*, Delaware, USA: International Reading Association.

HM Inspectors of Schools (1999) *Early Intervention: 1997–1998*, Edinburgh: HMSO.

Kirk, G. and Glaister, R. (1994) *5–14: Scotland's National Curriculum*, Edinburgh: Scottish Academic Press.

Kobayashi, T. (1976) *Society, Schools, and Progress in Japan*, Oxford: Pergamon Press.

Lynn, R. (1988) *Educational Achievement in Japan*, Basingstoke: Macmillan.

McMillan, G. and Leslie, M. (1998) *The Early Intervention Handbook*, Edinburgh: City of Edinburgh Council.

McNamara, O., Hustler, D., Stronach, I., Rodrigo, M., Beresford, B. and Botcherby, S. (2000) 'Room to manoeuvre: mobilising the "active partner" in home–school relations', *British Educational Research Journal*, 26(4): 473–90.

Martin, J., Tett, L. and Kay, H. (1999) 'Developing collaborative partnerships: limits and possibilities for schools, parents and community education', *International Studies in Sociology of Education*, 9(1): 59–75.

Ministry of Education (1994) *Education in Japan: A Graphic Presentation*, Tokyo: Ministry of Education Press.

Munn, P. (1993) *Parents and Schools: Customers, Managers or Partners*, London: Routledge.

Okano, K. and Tsuchiya, M. (1999) *Education in Contemporary Japan*, Cambridge: Cambridge University Press.

Reay, D. (1998) *Class Work. Mothers' Involvement in Their Children's Primary Schooling*, London: UCL Press.

SOED (1996) *Partners in Learning*, Edinburgh: SOED.

Tamai, Y. (1996) *Hokkaido no Gakko to Chi-iki Shakai*, Tokyo: Toyokan Syuppan.

Tett, L. (2001) 'Parents as problems or parents as people? Parental involvement programmes, schools and adult educators', *International Journal of Lifelong Education* 20(2): 188–98.

Tett, L. and Crowther, J. (1998) 'Families at a disadvantage: class, culture and literacies', *British Educational Research Journal*, 24(4): 449–60.

Tett, L., Caddell, D., Crowther, J. and O'Hara, P. (2000) 'Parents and schools: partnerships in early years' education', paper presented at the BERA Annual Conference, September.

Thrush, C.J. and Smith, R.P. (1980) *Japan's Economic Growth and Educational Change 1950–1970*, Nebraska: EBHA Press.

Tizard, B., Blatchford, P., Burke, J., Farquhar, C. and Plewis, I. (1988) *Young Children at School in the Inner City*, London: Erlbaum.

Vincent, C. and Warren, S. (1998) 'Becoming a better parent? Motherhood, education and transition', *British Journal of Sociology of Education*, 19(2): 177–93.
Yoshida, K. (1995) *Nihon no Hinkon*, Tokyo: Kenso Shobo.

15 Exploring the tailored approaches of the New Deal for 18–24 year olds

Jane Salisbury

Introduction

Over the last decade, many countries have witnessed a shift away from unconditional entitlement to social assistance towards greater emphasis on obligations and conditions tied to the receipt of financial aid. Increasingly as part of this process recipients must work or train in order to be eligible for benefits. The shared aim of what are increasingly described as 'Welfare to Work' schemes is to increase economic activity rates, through the creation of 'active' benefit systems for all people of working age which improve employability, reinforce work incentives and reduce costs and welfare dependency. Several 'Workfare' programmes are in place across Europe where, despite a range of labour market circumstances, unemployment experienced by population subgroups is a major concern across European nations (Trickey and Loedmel 2000). EU Member States are committed to providing a 'New Start' for all those under 25 who have been unemployed for six months (Laarson 1998; Finn 2000). Young people in the UK are currently the subject of an ambitious programme of welfare reform. Though unemployment figures for the 18–24 age group have been falling recently, over 100,000 young people remain in the official unemployment figure of 5.1 per cent (Drury and Dennison 1999). In response to continued high levels of unemployment among the disadvantaged and fears of social disintegration, the Labour government introduced a raft of time-limited, welfare to work schemes under the positive label 'New Deal'. This chapter explores the 'joined-up thinking' and attempts at 'joined-up working' that policy architects recommend for the successful operationalisation of the New Deal for 18–24 year olds. In particular, it examines the difficulties arising around the full-time education and training option.

New Deal

In the UK the launch of the New Deal programme in April 1998 followed a range of earlier initiatives – YOP, YT, ET, Training for Work, etc. (Avis *et al.* 1996; Yeomans 1998) to support young people who, in the conventional sense, 'don't make it in the British education system' (Hodgson and Spours 1997).

Although the entire programme consists of four strands, for 18–24 year olds, for over-25s, for single parents and for people with disabilities, the focus of this chapter is on the New Deal for 18–24 year olds. The New Deal programme offers young unemployed people the choice between a subsidised job, work in the voluntary sector, work with the environment task force or full-time education and training. All options include a training and/or education element, most of which will be provided by further education colleges.

New Deal for 18–24 year olds is part of what the Labour government see as a comprehensive and 'joined-up' approach which might be more successful in reducing the alienation of young people from society. Given the reality of fractured youth transitions (MacDonald 1998) and differential access to education, training and the labour market noted by the DfEE (1998), the Select Committee (1998) and the Prince's Trust (1997), the development of programmes to involve disadvantaged young people has been welcomed. Early promotional and operational literature for the New Deal emphasised the individual focus of the New Deal programme and the tailoring of 'one-off' customised training schemes. Individual clients are supported by a personal advisor based at the Employment Service who works with them for the duration of their programme. Via their New Deal Personal Advisor (NDPA), access to a range of formal and voluntary agencies is possible. The NDPA's task is to work in a client-centred way to assist individuals to reduce barriers to employability. This work begins in what has been optimistically termed 'The Gateway'. It describes a period of four months which starts when an individual has been claiming Jobseeker's Allowance (JSA) for six months. The Gateway is the first stage of the New Deal for Young People (NDYP) in which clients develop plans jointly with their NDPAs to find a job, to enhance their employability or to prepare for the four New Deal options. 'Clients receive support and advice from NDPA that is tailored to the individual's needs and circumstances. NDPAs provide structured support and advice and training with regard to job search, basic skills and personal problems that relate to employability' (Hasluck 2000: 25).

In working in a 'joined-up way' with statutory and voluntary agencies to help the client sort out health, housing, relationship, family problems and skills deficits which may be impacting on their ability to obtain work or undertake training, it is expected that a client's employability will be enhanced. Documents describe this joined-up mode of working as something of a panacea; not only is it more efficient and reduces the specialist and fragmented provision that existed before New Deal's launch in January 1998 (often cited as a key problem for jobless young people and those at risk of social exclusion), but it also drives down costs.

The policy thrusts deriving from imperatives of both economic and social improvement agendas have an interconnectedness which affects the lives of many young people across a range of social contexts. New Labour appear to have understood the need for multi-dimensional and multi-agency approaches to the problems of disaffection, non-participation and social exclusion. The New Deal initiatives, creation of the Social Exclusion Unit (SEU), in particular its work on disadvantaged neighbourhoods, and the setting up of Regional Development

Agencies, all exemplify this approach (Hayton 1999). While the impact of the individual and combined effects of such policies remains to be evaluated, New Labour's belief that the state has an active role to play in creating opportunities for individuals to become part of a more inclusive society is clear.

Recent official evaluations of New Deal commissioned by the DfEE (for example, Hales and Collins 1999; Legard *et al.* 1998; Walsh *et al.* 1999; Hasluck 2000) have drawn attention to a number of caveats and operational difficulties, the majority of which are also highlighted here via data from an in-depth qualitative research project.

Introducing the research study

The focus of this research project is upon the 'implementation gaps', in particular the workings of Employment Service personnel and college staff who strive to interpret and work within the relevant policy guidance for the NDYP. The chapter draws upon a single qualitative case study in South Wales and describes the interaction and articulation of the 'main players' who facilitate New Deal education and training options.[1] Though samples were small – three New Deal Personal Advisers and one senior quality manager from the Employment Services were interviewed, along with four link tutors/co-ordinators from further education (FE) colleges and two Careers Officers – the qualitative data generated revealed some of the realities, barriers and frustrations of inter-agency work. Some implications for policy and practice are identified for this large-scale initiative to 'break the log jam of unemployment, poverty and social exclusion' (DfEE/Employment Service 1997).

The subsequent sections of the chapter use 'informant voices' to render visible commonly reported experiences of those 'frontline' Employment Service and FE college staff about their day-to-day delivery of New Deal. A later section explores the specific problems as experienced by FE colleges as they strive – and in many cases struggle – to provide appropriate flexible and individualised education and training for New Deal clients

Inter-agency 'joined-up' working and New Deal

Inter-professional and inter-agency working has long been seen as a means to a variety of ends, such as ensuring that the totality of people's needs are both recognised and met, achieving economies in resource use and bridging the gap between and within statutory and voluntary organisations. The importance of an inter-professional approach between institutions and staff implementing New Deal is emphasised in much of the official operational literature, where working as a team is stressed. The purpose of inter-professional or multi-agency working is described by Mathias *et al.* (1997: 21) as the coming together of individuals from different professions and disciplines with specialist knowledge and skills, to give and share information, determine needs, formulate plans and provide appropriate services. There is an acceptance that pooling resources and integrating advice, training and action planning will allow for a 'seamless service' for individual New Deal clients. Of course, as several commentators point out, such joined-up working also reduces costs and reflects government's economic rationalist agenda (Hodgson 1999; Stokes and Tyler 1997).

Researchers emphasise that working collaboratively is not easy; it involves crossing occupational boundaries with professionals setting aside the 'primacy' of their own disciplines and demonstrating a receptivity and willingness to listen to the views of colleagues from other occupational settings. Mackay (1995) points out that it is difficult enough to work intra-professionally in one's own organisation without the added challenge of working effectively both inter-professionally and inter-organisationally – with professionals outside. Data presented below and in later sections illustrate these difficulties well.

It became apparent early on in the data collection that the Employment Service and FE colleges, which have been directed by central government policy to work in partnership with Training and Enterprise Councils (TECs) and employers, had experienced many difficulties. Interview data have revealed some operational difficulties and indeed tensions both for 'clients' (claimants) and various staff in the FE colleges which provide the education and training options. The enactment and mediation of New Deal policy for the Full Time Education and Training Option (FTET) has, in the words of one informant: 'been fraught with problems connected to excessive bureaucracy, delayed funding and the academic year shaped by Awarding Bodies!' (link tutor, FE college).

Some positive working relationships between collaborating agencies have been developed since the launch of New Deal. In particular, NDPAs reported very favourably on their named and linked or responsible staff at local FE colleges.

> I ring [name] up at the college at least three times a day and I have to say he's always able to clarify a course query or at least call me back with the details I need. At the start we were all a bit too formal and didn't want to appear ignorant but now we've moved on to a more honest and direct way of talking.

Retrospective accounts provided by Personal Advisors of their early encounters with FE college prospectuses and liaison with designated link tutors indicated that many had felt 'totally overwhelmed' and 'really overfaced by the depth and breadth of information to be absorbed'. One Personal Advisor stressed that prior to her work as an NDPA she had been 'largely ignorant of the range of courses and qualifications now on offer at the local college'. As with other NDPAs who emphasised that they had 'really learned on the job in the first six months', there was a frank acknowledgement that the Employment Service preparatory training could 'never really prepare you sufficiently well for the PA role'. Their accounts testify to the significance of their experiential learning:

I know – just from *this* office, that all of us involved in PA work found things out literally as we met up with different problems. We were learning on a day-to-day basis through different people and cases.

Similarly,

No two clients are the same … you think they might be but … well, I've made some cock-ups but they are fine here at ES [Employment Service] as long as I'm honest. The link tutor at [name] college has also been really patient with me!

In contrast to the NDPAs, FE staff responsible for facilitating and managing the New Deal full-time education and training options were far more cautious in praising their Employment Service counterparts. In particular, many felt dissatisfied with the guidance provided to New Deal clients.

We find here that what happens in the Gateway period is often a mystery to us. There's supposed to be a lot of diagnostic work but – well, it really does depend upon the New Deal Advisor. Some of the clients are not always focussed when they arrive here.

(New Deal Link Officer)

One senior college manager felt that valuable weeks in the Gateway were wasted when clients could have been assessed more rigorously and 'more realistic matching into appropriate courses' might have resulted.

I'm *angry* sometimes when very soon, often within ten days, it becomes very clear that a New Deal student has been wrongly allocated to a course! Really, it's immoral because the NDPAs are just setting them up to *fail*!

(Link tutor/manager)

Several FE tutors agreed that the Gateway is a time when 'some basic skills teaching and screening should take place'. Such assessment, many felt, would enable a better matching of clients into appropriately levelled courses and would probably reduce later drop-outs. The Gateway period was perceived by college staff and New Deal co-ordinators as an area of activity that could be much improved.

Across the FE staff interview transcripts, however, were several sympathetic remarks reflecting their ability to empathise with the changed work roles of benefits officers who had become NDPAs. The clichéd phrase 'we've all had a steep learning curve' was used with predictable regularity:

They've [NDPAs] been at the sharp end of it all, too … My concern is you cannot turn a person into a Guidance Officer overnight!

(College manager/liaison for New Deal)

The knowledge, skills and attitudes of a professionally trained Careers Officer were reported to be lacking in Personal Advisors, though this was seen as 'understandable given that PAs have been asked to do too much too quickly ... how can they [Personal Advisors] be sufficiently expert in counselling or in careers guidance work?' Indeed, FE staff speculated upon the extent and quality of training provided for the NDPAs. Three of them explained that communication with young people presented particular issues, and that specialist training should be available to all PAs advising clients in the 'crucial' Gateway period. There are particular skills in working confidentially and productively with young clients, as several informants acknowledged.

> The difficulty of getting some of the young people to talk and express their needs and wishes is great ... this aspect of the PA's work should not be underestimated.
>
> (Link tutor)

One New Deal Personal Advisor explained her discomfiture when working with particularly needy young people.

> The clients coming into the Gateway are often – well, quite disadvantaged, some of them have major difficulties and problems with basic skills and of course they don't want to own up to things like this ... It is really hard to get them sorted out with something meaningful ... I often feel uncomfortable, unhappy after a session [interview].
>
> (NDPA)

Drury and Dennison (1999: 176) report that, at least in the UK, training across the different benefits departments varies considerably. Although officers in Job Centres, Benefit Agency offices and Housing Benefit departments often specialise in working with young people, only those dealing with hardship claims receive detailed instructions on communication. Emotionally vulnerable young people are frequently involved in hardship claims, and thus the Benefits Agency (1994) has provided advice for officers involved. An interview with a senior quality manager for New Deal described a series of training events that Personal Advisors in the Employment Service (ES) had experienced. Though proud of the training menu, the manager acknowledged that

> We at the ES are getting better at dealing with the individual client problems but obviously we have a long way to go ... Some of the young adults have such serious difficulties, almost *too upsetting* to describe.

Interview data revealed that the NDPA role differs greatly from the Employment Service (ES) roles that preceded it; those PAs interviewed were aware of this contrast. Recent formal reviews of New Deal also recognise this:

'The NDPA role ... requires important interpersonal skills and specific skills relating to advice, guidance and mentoring. Not all ES staff have the experience or innate skill to undertake the NDPA role without training and support from their organisation' (Hasluck 2000: 59–60).

Observational research strategies were not a feature of the present study, thus it remains an empirical issue how far any training, where it exists, informs the actual practice of those NDPAs whose routine work is with clients in the Gateway or four option phases of the New Deal. It was widely acknowledged among college staff that if the quality of advice and steerage about FE provision given in the Gateway was improved, better matching of clients to courses and programmes would generate more completions and fewer drop-outs, and would increase the acquisition of credentials by participants which could potentially enhance their employability. Indeed, completions and retentions of New Deal FTET clients was a major anxiety for all colleges involved and is discussed in the next section.

Pressures and problems at colleges

Retention: 'Keeping 'em in, getting them through'

LINK TUTOR FOR NEW DEAL: Not a week goes by here [at college] without a meeting, a memo or such like about the three Rs.

JS: Sorry? Do you mean the old "reading, riting and rithmetic" stuff?

TUTOR: No [laughter]. It's shorthand for recruitment, retention and results. Basically, it's a summary of how *all* our students are funded, not just the New Dealers – but with New Deal retention is a *very* real issue for us.

At several stages in their interviews, FE staff raised and returned to issues of retention and funding. All those interviewed for this study highlighted the challenges presented by certain demotivated FE participants and those poorly attending New Deal 'clients' who sooner or later drop out. One interviewee described how, in the early phase of the New Deal initiative, a number of the 'graduates' of the first Gateway period had

> just disappeared before their ITP [Individual Training Plan] was even typed up! They'd been and gone before we could blink, leave alone get them organised into departments and college life.
>
> (College manager, liaison for New Deal)

Another college co-ordinator explained how:

departments didn't know they [New Dealers] were here on the books until we'd lost them – and, of course, their funding!

All informants from FE colleges reported similar experiences of 'disappeared', 'lost' and 'vanished' students and were able to report on the ways in which they had since developed tighter systems in an attempt to secure funding for New Deal clients.

> We lose fewer at the beginning now because we have an intensive ten-day induction period to college, to job search, to mentoring, and all ITPs are completed within these ten days.

The excessive bureaucracy and clerical red tape required of colleges by Employment Service regulations was much criticised, with one college co-ordinator describing the 'fifty-plus dreaded proformas accompanying each New Deal recruit'. Moreover, the time-consuming administrative work and overfrequent progress reporting required by ES had, it was felt, contributed to some teaching staff's hostility to the New Deal initiatives.

> Tutors were often too slow to alert me to student absence and registers and official documentation was a mess – they [tutors] just want to get on with their teaching! To get around this, management has now devolved registers, time sheets and signing in to one colleague who is also a personal mentor for New Deal people … she walks the college at least twice a day to keep attendance and progress data up to date. So ES can be satisfied. Our tutors really appreciate *not* having to do the paperwork on New Dealers!
>
> (New Deal manager, college)

Interviewees from the four FE colleges acknowledged that overall non-completion rates for New Deal FTET students were too high. Current drop-out rates were seen as unacceptable and problematic in many cases:

> Of the hundred or so people that started, only 30 per cent of these finished. That's just not good enough, and collectively we've got to do something to improve this situation.
>
> (Co-ordinator for New Deal)

> Last September [1998], we had fifty odd that started on the full-time option here, but I'm sorry to say that only twenty completed – it's awful, isn't it?
>
> (Link tutor)

Such withdrawal and drop-out rates were described as 'horrific wastage' and condemned as a 'substantial waste of national resources' by one co-ordinator. FE staff, along with Employment Service NDPAs, felt that the students 'at risk' of non-completion comprised a number of identifiable groups within the New Deal 18–24 year old clients. They agreed that a number of the characteristics of the New Deal community accounted for a substantial proportion of withdrawals and non-completions.

> These young people have the dice really stacked against them – their chances of success are low because they're inside or up against so many problems.
>
> (Link tutor)

> So many of the people in the Gateway who don't get jobs and who *have* to progress to options have not got much going for them at all, so it's not surprising that they don't cope well.
>
> (Personal Advisor)

Poor motivation, low self-esteem, prior educational experiences, financial problems and health and family difficulties were typically identified as components of the non-completion problem by most interviewees in the study.

Earlier in-depth research by the Further Education Unit (FEU) and Further Education Development Agency (FEDA) (Martinez 1995) on causes of student withdrawal lends considerable empirical support to current evidence. Davies (1999), describing college information systems and procedures for identifying the causes of student withdrawal, points out that it is very difficult for a college to identify in advance students who are at risk of non-completion, and, further, to cater for such students if they could be identified.

In contrast to mainstream FE students funded via FEFCE (or FEFCW in Wales), who are largely a blended heterogeneous learner population, students on the New Deal FTET option are a clearly labelled, defined and well-documented group. As a client group they require detailed, separate administrative paperwork and are embedded in a more punitive funding formulae. By official definition, the 18–24 year olds are a needy group at risk of becoming socially marginalised, and those who are unable to secure employment during the sixteen-week Gateway often fail because of severe basic skills deficits. Moreover, many clients on the full-time education and training option represent the extreme end of non-achievement (Slater 2000). It is acknowledged that such learners may view education as irrelevant, may have previously been rejected or failed by the system that is inviting them back in, and may have low self-esteem, motivations and aspirations (Kennedy 1997; Social Exclusion Unit 1999).

Most FE staff interviewed took considerable care not to make over-simplistic causal links between 'drop-out' and the New Deal further education and training option. Their accounts revealed the complex factors at play which shaped the learners' identities, their participation levels and completions. Table 15.1 provides a summary of reasons identified as contributing to poor completion.

Table 15.1 College staff's perceptions of factors shaping New Deal client drop-outs from full-time education and training

Perceptions of perceived ease of FTET options (on behalf of client and PA)	Some clients believed the FTET route and going to college would be a soft option.
Low basic educational levels	Many clients found that their lack of basic skills could not sustain them through a course.
Prior history of non/poor attendance in compulsory education	The routines of regular and timely attendance were not a norm carried over from school days and many clients found it difficult meeting this expectation.
Time of year client joins the already started course programme	Clients' ITPs often meant that they joined an existing class where group dynamics had already formed and much course coverage done. This reinforced their often low self-esteem.
Course contents and programme planning	Many clients felt that they were wrongly located in programmes which they felt were not relevant to their perceived needs and the result of poor advice from PAs and inflexible but cost-effective infilling policies of the college.
New Deal as a stigmatised status	College monitoring and tracking of clients made them feel stigmatised and different. They had less vacation than peers funded via Funding Council formulae and felt unequal and more 'controlled'.
Staff relations and attitudes	Teaching staff were often irritated and unhelpful when New Deal clients arrived to join an already existing (up-and-running) course. ND clients felt their late arrival had made them 'miss too much' and this made them a nuisance for teachers and peers.
Clients' massive personal problems	A range of overwhelmingly difficult circumstances connected to health, rehabilitation, relationship, poverty and lifestyle impacted negatively on clients in their New Deal student roles.

Problems arising from poor attendance and motivation were seen by college staff as an outcome of the time pressures and targets of the New Deal. In conceptualising and operationalising the full-time education and training option, it was argued that planners had allowed inadequate time. Getting many young people to feel confident about coming on to a course and then developing authentic relationships with significant others in educational or work settings unfamiliar to them had been underestimated in terms of time needed. Some NDPAs and college staff had begun to appreciate this early on, and to feed back their experiences to regional quality managers.

The worryingly low retention rates and patterns of absenteeism were seen by New Deal co-ordinators and link tutors as deserving of detailed investigation:

> The sector needs to know 'what works' and whether one particular college's approach or effective strategies are transferable to others.

Clearly, student course completions are a matter of key importance for funding to be secured. Furthermore, such qualifications contribute to a college's measurable outputs towards NACETT's (1998) most recent and revised set of targets (NTETs), to be achieved by 2002. Last and most crucially, acquisition of skills and qualifications, however modest, is important in enhancing a New Deal client's employability.

The interviews revealed that there were wide variations in retention performance both within and between institutions. One NDPA reflected on the 'amazing work of the Building and Construction section in keeping some very difficult lads motivated and involved'. At the college level, also, it was acknowledged that:

> Some departments are just better with these types of learner than others ... in fact, it is true to say that some teachers know how best to work with the kinds of young people we have here on New Deal.
>
> (New Deal college manager)

> We know from our experience to date that the majority of young people coming through to us from New Deal need extra support, sensitive induction and guidance and, ideally, their own college-based personal mentor on hand all the time.
>
> (Co-ordinator)

Accounts from New Deal liaison staff, both co-ordinators and managers, were unified in their descriptions of college systems being unable to cope fully with the range of issues confronting them. Despite trying to understand the various forces impacting negatively upon New Deal learners via the use of personal tutors and mentoring staff, colleges frequently referred back to the NDPAs at the Employment Service.

> Very early on in the first weeks of the New Deal, I realised – or it became obvious – that we didn't have the capability for dealing with the many issues and problems the young people were bringing to college from outside.
>
> (College co-ordinator for New Deal)

At the time of the fieldwork interviews, statistical material available on dropouts at college level was limited to general approximations of percentages

completing or leaving; analysis by age, gender or course was not being undertaken. However, New Deal liaison staff explained that there were wide variations
and inconsistencies in retention performance within their own institutions and
FE institutions nationally.

> Unfortunately our drop-out rate is very high – it's really very problematic …
> its current rate is 45 per cent, which is unacceptable, though I think colleges
> across the UK are also having difficulties and, like us here at [college name],
> wondering about the economic viability of the full-time education and
> training [FTET] option.
>
> (Link tutor)

Official statistical breakdowns of starts and completions are at present not
available for public use, though monthly returns are forwarded to the Government
Statistical Service (see Welsh Office 1999 and National Assembly for Wales 2000),
which then produces quarterly official bulletins. Behind these hard and somewhat
'cold' numerical data are the complex lives of real people: each number represents
a client of the New Deal initiative, a young person in receipt of a benefits-linked
individualised training programme 'choreographed' via the collaborative working
of professionals from the Employment Service and FE sector.

'Clients', claimants or learners

The vocabularies used to talk about New Deal participants reflected a speaker's
day-to-day involvement with them and also, to a degree, their perspectives about
the initiative. Not surprisingly, perhaps, there was a tendency for Employment
Service Advisors to use the term 'claimant' or elide 'claimant' with 'client'
during interviews. The 'clientised script', however, had permeated the vocabularies of the NDPAs, who spoke of 'identifying the young person's needs as a
client of New Deal', 'helping the client to sort out his domestic difficulties',
'working with the New Deal people, advising them as clients', and

> pointing out the client's choices, their options and their responsibilities to
> the New Deal programme and reminding them that when all's said and
> done, they are still a claimant.
>
> (New Deal Personal Advisor)

The interview extract quoted above is revealing. 'Clients' can choose an option,
but their choices are made within parameters which are set externally. If at the
end of the Gateway period the client refuses to sign up for an option, as a
'claimant' s/he will be conscripted to one of the four options by the NDPA. In
the words of Prime Minister Tony Blair, 'There will be *no* fifth option of
remaining on benefits!' (PM 1997).
    Severe benefits sanctions occur when a New Deal participant fails to
enrol, attend or participate in their individualised option programme. This

underpinning punitive sanction rather explodes the myth behind the client-centred rhetoric of the New Deal. It also contrasts with the perspective which emphasises the individual as 'learner', which the colleges might be expected to hold!

In terms of the FTET option, the individually tailored programmes created via the learner's Individual Training Plan (ITP) mean that they can join a course at any point in the year. The official documentation emphasises the individual focus of the New Deal and the tailoring of 'one-off' customised schemes, in which colleges 'must ensure that entry into provision is available throughout the year rather than at traditional times in the calendar' (Employment Service 1998: 3). It is this flexibility with the attendant requirements of that 'roll-on roll-off' individualised delivery that colleges have struggled to provide, and have in some cases resisted. Furthermore, this 'flexibility' requirement, coupled with stereotyped views of '*the* New Deal learner' has contributed to the generalised perception that 'New Deal is a nuisance'.

Political commitment to the New Deal concept varied widely within departments. Two co-ordinators reported that some lecturers and heads of department had become unhelpful and had developed hostile attitudes to participants on the FTET option as a result of their attendance patterns and persistent lateness.

> You can see colleagues groan at the idea of another New Deal student being dropped into the middle of an existing programme ... it's a lot of work for staff having to go over the stuff that's already been covered.
>
> (College co-ordinator for New Deal)

Teaching staff were reported as finding it increasingly difficult to spend additional valuable time, resources and attention on New Deal students, some of whom are their most challenging and troublesome learners.

NEW DEAL MANAGER: To be perfectly honest with you, some teaching staff here perceive New Dealers as a nuisance – as having too much extra work attached to them, they're troublesome in different ways.

JS: Can you say how – in what ways are they troublesome?

NEW DEAL MANAGER: Well, as you well know, they're not long-term unemployed for nothing. In terms of basic skills many of them are really lacking, and then some of them are what you'd call disaffected – they really don't want to know anything to do with learning! I'd be dishonest and unfair if I didn't try to explain why our staff are so reluctant to get involved.

This negative labelling of New Deal learners by FE teachers and the accompanying teacher expectations about 'these types of students' (see earlier section and Table 15.1) derive in part from the everyday work realities in contemporary further education. In contrast, however, more constructive and sympathetic views also existed.

Reflecting a more learner-centred focus, fears at the college level included a concern that as an intervention New Deal might not necessarily enhance an individual's employability at all. It was acknowledged that though the FTET option might have this potential, its current funding level and delivery, which involves 'infilling' young people into existing courses, could result in a complex and frustrating cycle of disengagement and *un*intended exclusion from learning.

> The underconfident returners, those people who haven't really ever seen themselves as learners – who dip their toe back into education under the New Deal Scheme, are taking quite a risk … in my view, what we currently provide could be quite a turn-off.
>
> (New Deal college manager)

Those individuals with fragile learner identities (Rees *et al.* 1997) rooted in prior experiences in compulsory schooling could be 'switched off' from engaging with the learning opportunities made available under the FTET option.

> Funding [for New Deal] is such that we are compelled to insert FTET [pronounced 'efftet'] young people into existing programmes … I have to confess this is *not* ideal, but cost-effective infilling is how we've coped here at [name] College. The *tailoring* you referred to is really theoretical.
>
> (College co-ordinator for New Deal)

Particular difficulties in implementing customised, learner-centred provision were attributed to the low funding and prescriptive nature of the policy. Those co-ordinating the FTET option and liaising with Personal Advisors based at the Employment Service had an impossible task. In Marsh's (2000: 2) words, they had the challenge of trying 'to fit an over-conceived flexibility and individually tailored programme of 30 hours a week over a 50 week year, into an over-rigid college framework operating over a shorter academic year combined with an inflexible curriculum delivery pattern!'

At the Employment Service and college levels, both sets of players are caught up in mediating policy, albeit in different ways and in different settings, and their localised interpretations shape young people's experiences. Analysis of interview transcripts reveals their underlying perspectives on young people who are seen as 'needy' and as needing things done to them. This deficit model of the young person is indeed narrow and is a perspective which rarely incorporates young people as active agents in the collaborative processes of joined-up working.

New Deal as a stigmatising label

There are some considerable tensions for students in being identified by teaching staff and other student peers as 'New Deal people' (see also Marsh 2000).

Someone who'd been doing reasonably well on an A-level course asked specifically *not* to be identified as a New Deal person. Now, we were happy to collude and be discreet with this lady because *theoretically* under her New Deal funding she should not have been doing an academic course. She was halfway through the A level, so we negotiated with the Advisor for her to continue. It wasn't easy and the student strongly resisted the label.

(New Deal Manager)

The college staff alluded to the stigmatising possibilities, and it was clear from their accounts that college systems for tracking New Deal clients had raised issues around identities and labelling.

It's true, they [New Deal clients] *do* want to be seen like just another student in the crowd, but as I say to them – you're *not*, you're in receipt of funding and travel allowances and you *are* different. There are clear rights and responsibilities.

(Link tutor)

The requirements for New Deal students to register and 'sign in' for New Deal studies were explained as cumbersome, not only by college managers but by students themselves who, it was reported, felt 'over-controlled' and policed.

One man – he's doing our plumbing course – well, he is a very good student and the department say he's fine – a regular attender, never misses. He refuses to sign in in the mornings and afternoons at the special 'drop in/sign in' point – so I've allowed his department to do registration forms.

(Link tutor)

The surveillance and policing of the New Deal learner required by the Employment Service was described as coming 'into sharp relief during the college vacation periods, when regular students on Funding Council provision have two weeks off and the New Dealers only a couple of days!' To accommodate this statutory and by comparison ungenerous two-week holiday allowance for participants on the FTET option, colleges have resorted to various strategies which attempt to leave the majority of their teachers' vacations untouched. Such strategies include arranging work experience placements and taster programmes with local employers and developing 'stand-alone self-supported study kits' for individuals to complete off-site during the college vacations. Because New Dealers did not share the half term and holiday breaks of their peers, they felt different, unequal and, in the words of one college link tutor, 'labelled and discriminated against, which didn't help them develop a positive learner identity!'

Inter-agency relations were initially thwarted and affected by a number of intra-organisational inhibitory factors; these included differences in administration, working modes and contrasting priorities. NDPAs working for the Employment Service strive to secure jobs for their clients during the Gateway or option periods: indeed, this is their central objective. Once a client is enrolled upon an FTET option, however, the college's objective is for that client to *complete* his/her training programme and secure the qualification outcome. Thus, somewhat conflicting tensions exist around the roles of those personnel interacting with the New Deal participant. Staff working in incorporated FE colleges must respond to local market demand and supply to niche markets in terms of local employers and potential learner groups (see, for example, Jephcote and Salisbury 1996; Lucas and Mace 1999). Moreover, colleges have to work within the policy imperatives of 'widening participation' and promoting receptivity to 'lifelong learning' (DfEE 1998; Kennedy 1997; Parry and Fry 1999; Tight 1998), and interviewees reported that many classroom teachers felt a kind of dissonance and unease about limiting the New Deal learner's access to NVQ level 2 qualifications.

> It does seem quite immoral to make someone who is doing okay on an Access to Humanities course move to a low-level vocational programme just because her Benefit Officer has moved her into the Gateway and New Deal programme.
>
> (Link tutor for New Deal)

Across the interview transcripts of college informants there was a clear congruence in the view that those few New Dealers who are capable of higher-level study should have access to it. This again reflects the 'claimant *vs* learner' tension. New Deal was seen as being too employment-focused and too orientated to the achievement of short-term job targets.

> Shouldn't the government be aiming for long-term sustained employment that longer training or education programmes might provide? New Deal can be seen as a bit of a quick fix, and I'm not clear that some of its rules and regulations will help provide a learning society!
>
> (College manager for New Deal)

FE link tutors who facilitate and manage, in various ways, the New Deal FTET option emerge as a 'seriously challenged' group; they have to forge workable and practical interpretations of a policy which somewhat undermines notions of a learning society and lifelong learning. New Deal Personal Advisors similarly are up against performance targets and cyclical job evaluation. 'Joining up' aspects of their clients' lives, working holistically to advise individual young people and direct them into 'options', demands expertise and specialist knowledge, and not just missionary zeal!

Policy implications and concluding remarks

This case study has rendered visible a hitherto *un*researched aspect of New Deal provision and organisation. It has highlighted the changes in roles, status and responsibilities for Employment Service and FE college professionals. The moving boundaries, imperatives and targets between these different 'state workers' (Finn 2000), and the necessary links between them, clearly present numerous challenges. The Labour government has linked the transition to active benefit regimes with radical changes in the bureaucracies delivering and administering them. Recent official evaluations have considered a wide range of issues and evidence relating to New Deal for Young People (NDYP). A key point emerging from monitoring and evaluation is the need to enhance the scope and quality of the NDPA advisory role (Hasluck 2000).

Clearly, the access to and quality of what is learned by New Deal students cannot occur through policy alone. The full-time education and training (FTET) experience of the young person on New Deal depends significantly upon the practices of FE colleges, teachers, employers and Employment Service Advisors. Put simply, access to meaningful training which enhances an individual's employability does not occur through the rhetoric and imperatives of policy-makers. A quality programme of tailored, individualised learning is the result of the willingness and capacity of colleges and the efforts of teaching staff to deliver skills and knowledge in ways that enable each individual to engage in processes of authentic and meaningful learning.

Despite NDPAs and college staff's use of case management approaches, there is a limit to the compromises possible to accommodate real differences in individual needs. Cost-effective infilling of clients into existing curricular provision will continue as a poor surrogate for tailored ITPs until colleges are funded more realistically. Furthermore, the flexibility desirable for meeting heterogeneous learner needs is limited in programmes which are codified and underpinned by compulsion.

Centralised and mandatory programmes, like the New Deal for Young People, which aim to be integrative and ameliorative but which are framed within a strong sanctioning policy, have created tensions between those professionals trying to work in a 'joined-up' manner. The guidance, educative and social work elements which contribute to a positive learner/trainee identity are at odds with the surveillance and policing roles involved in monitoring claimant participation. Indeed, labelling and stigmatisation are but two social processes reported by informants which reinforce poor self-esteem and may have negative impacts in the long term.

This research must be interpreted as a selection of comments from people working within the New Deal policy framework on a day-to-day basis. Its value is not as an overall assessment of the New Deal, though its findings complement and augment 'officially' commissioned evaluations. As a set of 'insiders' accounts, however, it provides some insights into the problems of implementing New Deal as well as highlighting tensions in the policy thrusts deriving from Labour's economic and social improvement agendas.

Acknowledgements

I am grateful to those FE college and Employment Service staff who shared their experiences of New Deal with me and who gave so freely of their time. I also wish to thank Cardiff University's School of Social Sciences for supporting the research project, and finally, Diana Taylor for help with transcription and word-processing drafts of this chapter.

List of abbreviations

NDPA   New Deal Personal Advisor based at the Employment Service
PA   Personal Advisor
NDYP   New Deal for Young People (18–24 year olds)
ES   Employment Service
FEFCE   Further Education Funding Council (England)
FEFCW   Further Education Funding Council (Wales)
NACETT   National Advisory Council for Education and Training Targets
FTET   Full-time Education and Training Option of the New Deal
ITP   Individual Training Plan
NTETs   National Education and Training Targets

Notes

1   Documentary analysis and semi-structured interviews with Employment Service Personal Advisers, Careers Officers and link tutors in FE colleges formed the main research methods of the case study. The study was carried out over a six-month period from January to June 1999.

References

Avis, J., Bloomer, M., Esland, G., Gleeson, D. and Hodkinson, P. (1996) *Knowledge and Nationhood; Education, Politics and Work*, London: Cassell.
Banks, M.H., Bates, I., Breakwell, G., Bynner, J., Emler, N., Jamieson, L. and Roberts, K. (1992) *Careers and Identities*, Buckingham: Open University Press.
Benefits Agency (1994) Income Support for all 16–17 year olds. For all staff dealing with 16–17 year old customers. Leeds, Benefit Agency.
Corbett, J. (1990) *Uneasy Transitions: Disaffection in Post-Compulsory Education and Training*, Basingstoke: Falmer Press.
Davies, P. (1999) 'Student retention in further education. A problem of quality or of student finance?' paper presented at the British Educational Research Association Annual Conference, University of Sussex, 2–5 September.
DfEE (1998) *Further Education for the New Millennium: A Response to the Kennedy Report*, London: DfEE.
DfEE/Employment Service (1997) *Operational Vision: New Deal*, London: DfEE.
Drury, J. and Dennison, C. (1999) 'Individual responsibility versus social category problems: benefit officers' perceptions of communication with young people', *Journal of Youth Studies*, 2(2): 171–92.
Employment Service (1998) *Design of the New Deal for 18–24 Year Olds*, London: DfEE, Welsh Office and Scottish Office.

Evans, K. and Furlong, A. (1997) 'Metaphors of youth transitions: niches, pathways, trajectories or navigations', in J. Bynner, L. Chisholm and A. Furlong (eds) *Youth, Citizenship and Social Change in a European Context*, Aldershot: Avebury.

Finn, D. (2000) 'Modernisation or workfare? New Labour's work-based welfare state', paper presented at an ESRC Labour Studies Seminar, Centre for Comparative Labour Studies, University of Warwick, 28–9 March.

Furlong, A. and Cartmel, F. (1997) *Young People and Social Change: Individualization and Risk in Late Modernity*, Buckingham: Open University Press.

Hales, J. and Collins, D. (1999) *New Deal for Young People: Leavers with Unknown Destinations*, ESR 21, Employment Service, June 1999.

Hasluck, C. (2000) *The New Deal for Young People, Two Years On*, ISER 41, Employment Service, February 2000.

Hayton, A. (ed.) (1999) *Tackling Disaffection and Social Exclusion Education Perspectives and Policies*, London: Kogan Page.

Hodgson, A. (1999) 'Analysing education and training policies for tackling social exclusion', in A. Hayton (ed.) *Tackling Disaffection and Social Inclusion*, London: Kogan Page.

Hodgson, A. and Spours, K. (eds) (1997) *Dearing and Beyond: 14–19 Qualifications Frameworks and Systems*, London: Kogan Page.

Istance, D., Rees, G. and Williamson, H. (1994) *Young People Not in Education, Training or Employment*, Report to South Glamorgan Training Enterprise Council, Cardiff: South Glamorgan TEC.

Jephcote, M. and Salisbury, J. (1996) 'Principals' responses to incorporation: a window on their culture', *Journal of Further and Higher Education*, 20(2): 33–48.

Kennedy, H. (1997) *Learning Works: Widening Participation in Further Education*, Coventry: FEFC.

Laarson, A. (1998) 'From Welfare to Work', UK Presidency Conference, Newcastle, 23 June.

Legard, R., Ritchie, J., Keegan, J. and Turner, R. (1998) *New Deal for Young People: The Gateway*, ESR8, Employment Service, December 1998.

Lucas, N. and Mace, J. (1999) 'Funding issues and social inclusion: reflections on the "marketization" of further education colleges', in A. Hayton (ed.) *Tackling Disaffection and Social Inclusion*, London: Kogan Page.

MacDonald, R. (1998) 'Youth, transition and social exclusion: some issues for youth research in the UK', *Journal of Youth Studies*, 1: 163–76.

Mackay, L. (1995) 'Troubled times: the context for interprofessional collaboration?' in K. Soothill *et al.* (eds) *Interprofessional Relations in Health Care*, London: Edward Arnold.

Marsh, K. (2000) 'New Deal and the colleges – forcing new wine into old bottles', paper presented at the London Region Post-16 Network Seminar on New Deal at the Institute of Education, London, 16 June.

Martinez, P. (1995) *Student Retention in Further and Adult Education: The Evidence*, Mendip Paper 084, Blagdon: FEDA.

Mathias, P., Prime, R. and Thompson, T. (1997) 'Preparation for interprofessional work: holism, integration and the purpose of training and education', in J. Ovretveit, P. Mathias and T. Thompson (eds) *Interprofessional Working for Health and Social Care*, London: Macmillan, pp. 116–30.

Moser, C. (1999) *Improvising Literacy and Numeracy: A Fresh Start*, London: HMSO.

NACETT (1998) *Fast Forward for Skills*, London: NACETT.

National Assembly of Wales (2000) *New Deal for Young People and Long-Term Unemployees: Statistics for Wales*, Cardiff: Government Statistical Service.

Parry, G. and Fry, H. (1999) 'Widening participation in pursuit of the learning age', in A. Hayton (ed.) *Tackling Disaffection and Social Inclusion*, London: Kogan Page.

Peck, J. (1998) 'Workfare, a geopolitical etymology', *Environment and Planning, Society and Space*, 16: 133–60.

Prime Minister (1997) Speech by the Right Honourable Mr Tony Blair MP at the Aylesbury Estate, Southwark, London, 2 June. London, PM press office.

Prince's Trust (1997) *What Works? Jobs for Young People*, London: Prince's Trust.

Rees, G., Fevre, R., Furlong, J. and Gorard, S. (1997) 'History, place and the learning society: towards a sociology of lifetime learning', *Journal of Education Policy*, 12(6): 485–97.

Rudd, P. and Evans, K. (1998) 'Structure and agency in youth transitions: student experiences of vocational further education', *Journal of Youth Studies*, 1: 39–62.

Select Committee (1998) *Disaffected Children*, vol. 1, London: HMSO.

Slater, J. (2000) 'Hardest nut yet to be cracked', *Times Educational Supplement*, 'Briefing', 31 March.

Social Exclusion Unit (1998) *Truancy and Social Exclusion*, London: HMSO.

Social Exclusion Unit (1999) *Bridging the Gap: New Opportunities for 16–19 Year Olds Not in Education, Employment or Training*, London: The Stationery Office.

Stokes, H. and Tyler, D. (1997) *Rethinking Inter-Agency Collaboration*, Melbourne: Language Australia.

Tight, M. (1998) 'Education, education, education! The vision of lifelong learning in the Kennedy, Dearing and Fryer reports', *Oxford Review of Education*, 24: 473–85.

Trickey, H. and Loedmel, I. (2000) *An Offer You Can't Refuse: Workfare in International Perspective?* London: Policy Press.

Walsh, K., Atkinson, J. and Barry, J. (1999) *The New Deal Gateway: A Labour Market Assessment*, ESR24, Employment Service, August 1999.

Welsh Office (1999) *New Deal for Young People and Long-Term Unemployed: Statistics for Wales. January 1998 to March 1999*, Cardiff: Government Statistical Service.

Yeomans, D. (1998) 'Constructing vocational education: from TVEI to GNVQ', *Journal of Education and Work*, 11(2): 127–34.

16 Disabled people, training and employment

Joined-up policy and its tensions

Sheila Riddell and Alastair Wilson

Introduction

Rethinking the role and function of the welfare state is central to the New Labour project. The Report of the Commission on Social Justice, published in 1994, set out key ideas on the development of a new 'intelligent' welfare state, designed as much to prevent as to alleviate poverty. The following points are among those identified as germane to the operation of the new welfare state:

- Wealth creation and wealth distribution are two sides of the same coin; wealth pays for welfare, but equity is efficient.
- Social justice cannot be achieved through the social security system alone; employment, education and housing are at least as important as tax and benefit policy in promoting financial independence.
- Paid work for a fair wage is the most secure route out of poverty. Welfare must be reformed to make work pay …
- The intelligent welfare state prevents poverty as well as relieving it, above all through public services which enable people to learn, earn and care.
- The welfare state must be shaped by the changing nature of people's lives, rather than people's lives being changed to fit in with the changing nature of the welfare state; the welfare state must be personalised and flexible, designed to promote individual choice and personal autonomy.

(Report of the Commission on Social Justice 1994: 223)

Elected to office in 1997, the Labour Party began to develop a swathe of policies to redesign welfare along these lines. Policy documents on health (*Independent Inquiry into Inequalities in Health*, Department of Health 1998), social security (*New Ambitions for Our Country: A New Contract for Welfare*, Department of Social Security 1998) and lifelong learning (*The Learning Age: A Renaissance for a New Britain*, DfEE 1998) all stressed the interconnectedness of education, training, employment, housing and health policies.

In all these documents, disabled people are identified as a key group for whom 'joined-up policy' is essential to enhance quality of life and challenge social exclusion, primarily through increased participation in employment.

There are almost certainly two reasons for this attention. First, the growing disability movement argued that the link between disability and poverty must be broken by eliminating all forms of discrimination, including those related to employment. Second, the Treasury was concerned at the growth in the number of people claiming Incapacity Benefit (1.6 million in May 1998, about three times the number receiving the benefit in 1980/1). DSS briefings issued at this time suggested that Incapacity Benefit had been used throughout the 1980s as an alternative to Unemployment Benefit, thus masking true levels of unemployment. The solution suggested by the government was to restrict access to Incapacity Benefit, but also to assist disabled people to retain and re-enter employment. While the disability movement was keen to defend existing levels of benefit, there was widespread support for active employment policies targeted at disabled people.

In this chapter, we begin by exploring tensions between employment and social security policy for disabled people in the post-war period. Subsequently, we describe the Labour government's attempts to develop unified welfare policy for disabled people, focusing in particular on the New Deal for Disabled People. Finally, we present four case studies of disabled people drawn from specific research projects (Wilson *et al.* 2000; Riddell *et al.* 2000), to illustrate the tensions between different aspects of policy which continue to be experienced by disabled people in their attempts to access the labour market.

Post-war training, employment and benefits policy for disabled people

During the Second World War, nearly half a million disabled workers were drafted into the labour force at various levels in support of the war effort (Lonsdale 1986; Humphries and Gordon 1992), and at the end of the war some effort was put into sustaining this employment as a result of what was regarded as a 'social obligation' (Thornton *et al.* 1995). The 1944 Disabled Person's (Employment) Act provided the first comprehensive employment enhancement provisions for disabled people and was in part a response to the labour market shortages that followed the Second World War. Aimed primarily at the war-injured (Barnes 1991: 68–9; Lonsdale 1990: 46–8), the 1944 Act provided for:

- the establishment of a quota scheme, whose aim was to ensure that at least 3 per cent of the workforce of all non-governmental organisations with more than twenty people were registered disabled people;
- the setting up of a national network of industrial rehabilitation units to rehabilitate disabled people, and the establishment of sheltered workshops and factories (termed at the time 'factories fit for heroes');
- the development of a service to help disabled people find employment.

Individual disability or deficit was seen as the main reason for high levels of unemployment among disabled people, and training for the individual to overcome or circumvent their problem was seen as the most immediate priority. However, rather more radically, direct intervention in the labour market was also seen as appropriate, so that disabled people were given some assistance in accessing employment rather than being expected to compete for jobs on exactly the same terms as the non-disabled population. This was done through the imposition of a quota system, requiring firms employing more than twenty people to ensure that 3 per cent of their employees were registered disabled. Although radical in its conception, the quota system in the UK was always limited in its application. For example, people with mental health problems were not included, and it was never enforced (there were only ever ten prosecutions for failure to comply). In the mid-1990s it was quietly dropped, to be replaced by the employment-related measures of the DDA and the Employment Service's 'Access to Work' programme. In other parts of Europe, most notably in Germany, far more rigorous quota systems were adopted and enforced.

The longer-term effects of post-war employment policy were influenced by the social security benefits measures which were put in place at the same time. Although at least some aspects of employment policy encouraged disabled people into the labour market, the creation of long-term 'out of work' benefits tended to reinforce exclusion from paid employment (Hyde 2000: 328). While these benefits were intended to offer support and security to disabled people (DSS 1990), they have been criticised from two quite separate perspectives. Treasury concerns with a rising social security bill led to criticisms that these benefits placed an undue burden on public finance (DSS 1998). Members of the disability movement argued that they failed to tackle poverty (Disability Alliance 1991) and justified the exclusion of disabled people from the labour market (Barnes 1991). Hyde (2000) and Barnes (1991) both concluded that the operation of post-war employment and social security policy was ultimately negative. The level of social security benefits failed to lift disabled people out of poverty, but the unskilled work which was often their only option in the labour market meant that they were worse off in employment than on benefits.

To summarise, in the immediate aftermath of the Second World War attempts were made to intervene directly in employment practice, but these efforts were undermined by adherence to an individual deficit view of disabled people, the instigation of segregated systems of training and the creation of perverse incentives to remain on benefits rather than enter employment. In the following section, we describe the development of social security policies and training and employment policies under New Labour, before turning to case studies which illustrate how these policies are experienced in practice.

Disability and welfare in the 1990s

Welfare policy for disabled people is currently influenced and delivered by a bewildering array of agencies, including the Benefits Agency, the Employment Service, further education colleges, adult and continuing education departments, Local

Enterprise Companies, social work departments, housing services, NHS Primary Care Trusts and voluntary organisations. The Employment Service and Benefits Agency are soon to merge into a Working Life Agency in an attempt to stream-line the system. Other agencies, such as the European Social Fund, are not involved in delivery but played a major role in funding and shaping innovations. Below, we focus on benefits and employment policies while recognising the wider interconnections with other social policy arenas.

Social security policy

As noted above, post-war social security policy existed in a state of tension with employment policy. Disabled people felt that its effect was to impose a poverty trap, while the Treasury disapproved of growing expenditure on Incapacity Benefit. The Green Paper *New Ambitions for Our Country: A New Contract for Welfare* (DSS 1998) expressed a commitment to tackling worklessness and removing barriers to employ-ment arising from the benefits system. Disabled people and those with a long-term illness were identified as being among the principal beneficiaries of 'rebuilding welfare around the work ethic' (DSS 1998: 3) In collaboration with the Employment Service and within the context of the New Deal for Disabled People, the Department of Social Security (DSS) acted as the lead agency in the introduc-tion of Personal Adviser schemes in pilot areas to advise and assist disabled people in obtaining employment. A number of new work incentive measures were also introduced to counter existing disincentives. One of the DSS's work incentive measures, referred to as the '52-week linking rule', was designed to ensure that indi-viduals who entered jobs but left them during the course of a year could return to their original benefits status. A study of Employment Service programmes (Wilson *et al.* 2000) suggested that people with learning difficulties and their families simply did not believe that the 52-week rule would be applied fairly and believed that entering employment was tantamount to giving up benefits entitlements.

Another work incentive measure having a particular impact on people with learning difficulties concerned 'therapeutic earnings'. This rule states that indi-viduals on income support with severe disablement allowance are allowed to work for sixteen hours a week without losing benefit. Any additional work under-taken may have devastating financial consequences and may threaten the individual's status as permanently disabled. In this way, what is billed as a work incentive measure may act as a powerful disincentive to greater economic activity (see Simons 1998 for further discussion of the complexities of the bene-fits system for people with learning difficulties). In a later section, we discuss in more detail the way in which individuals' benefits packages influence their will-ingness to participate in lifelong learning.

An important reform announced in the DSS Green Paper was the Reform of the All Work Test, identified as 'the key problem' with Incapacity Benefit. The following criticisms were made of it:

> It writes off as unfit for work people who might, with some assistance, be able to return to work, perhaps in a new occupation. It is an all or nothing

test, in the sense that it assesses people as either fit for work or unfit for any work. Thus many people who would be capable of some work with the right help and rehabilitation are spending their working lives on benefit. We want a new approach to IB which focuses on what people can do, not on what they cannot.

(DSS 1998: para 10, p. 54)

In addition to the All Work Test, a new personal capability assessment has been introduced in pilot areas. This is intended to identify people's abilities as well as their deficits and to pinpoint the type of work they might be capable of doing, given appropriate support. Clearly, this development might be seen in an optimistic light as challenging disabled people's exclusion from the labour market. Alternatively, it might be interpreted as an attempt to coerce disabled people into work, depriving them of the knowledge that Incapacity Benefits will continue to be paid.

Employment and training policy

Employment and training policy in the UK has a somewhat cumbersome structure. The Employment Service, an agency of the DfEE, has responsibility for employment programmes, whereas responsibility for training rests with Local Enterprise Companies (LECs) in Scotland and Training and Enterprise Councils (TECs) in England. Since the advent of the Scottish Parliament in 1999, the situation has become even more complex. Employment is a 'reserved' area of policy, with Westminster policy mediated through the Office for Scotland in Edinburgh, while Lifelong Learning and Enterprise is controlled by the Holyrood Parliament. There is some unease among MSPs about the division between enterprise and employment and the extent to which Westminster and Holyrood policies are aligned.

The Employment Service (ES) has a remit to assist disabled people, including those with learning difficulties, to access the labour market. Disability Employment Advisers, based in Disability Service Teams at Job Centres, assess the training needs of their disabled clients and place them on appropriate programmes, usually delivered by the voluntary sector and private training agencies. Such programmes include the New Deal for Disabled People, Access to Work, Job Introduction Schemes, Supported Employment (formerly known as wage subsidy) and Work Preparation (formerly known as job rehabilitation). Demand for such programmes is growing as more disabled people seek inclusion and support in the labour market. Annual expenditure on ES programmes is rising (e.g. government funding for Work Preparation was £8.7 million in 1998/9; for the year 1999/2000 £10.2 million was allocated). However, demand for support, for example through Access to Work, outstrips funding. The Employment Service is forced by the Treasury to report on the effectiveness of its programmes in moving disabled people into sustainable employment. Statistics on programme outcomes do not always support an economic case for expansion: for instance, in Scotland between 1997 and 1999, only 20 per cent of individuals participating in the Work Preparation Programme were working thirteen weeks after the end of their placement (Wilson *et al.* 2000).

Many ES programmes were not developed with people with learning difficulties in mind and may not offer enough support and flexibility to meet their needs. For example, as noted above, job rehabilitation, now known as Work Preparation, arose out of a recommendation of the Tomlinson Report and formed part of the Employment Act 1944. It was designed to meet the needs of disabled servicemen returning from the Second World War, offering a period of intensive training in Employment Rehabilitation Units. Although Work Preparation now tends to take place in workplace settings, it still only allows an individual six to eight weeks' training and is evaluated in relation to successful outcomes. Because of the lack of support available both during the training period and in subsequent employment, relatively few people with learning difficulties are included in Work Preparation programmes. For Incapacity Benefit claimants there is a constant fear that, if they demonstrate too much competence on a Work Preparation programme, they may have to 'retake' the All Work Test, thus compromising their former benefits status.

The New Deal for Disabled People (NDDP) outlined in the DSS White Paper (DSS 1998) was allocated £195 million from the government's 'windfall tax'. This was used to fund twenty innovative projects to test ways of helping people become more employable and move into work, an information campaign to raise awareness of existing provision, a pilot Personal Adviser Scheme in twelve locations, and research and evaluation. The Personal Adviser Scheme was targeted initially at people on Incapacity Benefit (IB), with the aim of moving long-term IB claimants back into the labour market. The DSS's work incentive measures, described above, were intended to lubricate the process. Letters were sent to IB claimants encouraging them to contact Personal Advisers at Job Centres to receive advice on the Single Gateway to Employment (now referred to as One, suggesting deification!). Although the letters emphasised that participation in the NDDP was voluntary, response by IB claimants was very low at 3.3 per cent (Arthur *et al.* 1999). Furthermore, despite the promises of novelty, people were directed towards existing and rather inflexible training such as the ES's Work Preparation Programme. Interim figures suggest that Personal Advisers carried out just over 11,000 interviews by the end of March 2000, resulting in about 2,755 job starts (DfEE 2000). At the time of writing, information was not available about the types of work gained, whether jobs were part-time or full-time, temporary or permanent, or the levels of remuneration.

Within the system as a whole, the Personal Adviser experiment appears to have had a wide impact. The government has announced its intention to merge the Benefits Agency and the Employment Service and to 'roll out' the Personal Adviser scheme. Every disabled person seeking employment will be allocated a PA, who will be charged with providing detailed information on labour market opportunities and support, and also the benefits system. Again, these developments may be regarded in a positive or negative light, since the Personal Adviser might act as a powerful adviser and advocate for the disabled person, but in a more punitive regime might act as an agent of coercion.

As noted earlier, in addition to ES programmes, training for disabled people is provided by Local Enterprise Companies (LECs) through Skillseekers and Training for Work Programmes. The principal task of LECs is to promote local economic development. Given this *raison d'être*, investment in people with learning difficulties may be contentious given that they may be, in perception or reality, less effective workers than their peers. There has been no planned development of LEC and ES training programmes, and as a result there is overlap in provision for people with less significant impairments, while very little provision is targeted at people with higher support needs.

The brief outline of the policy framework above indicates areas of tension within training, employment and benefits policy for disabled people. As in the rest of the public sector (Deakin 1994), quasi markets have been established within all service areas, but there is potential for power to remain with service purchasers and providers rather than service users, particularly when this group is likely to be poor, inarticulate and lacking powerful advocates. While genuflecting towards equal access, resource allocation policies tend to reflect the belief that investment in individuals' education and training must be in relation to their future ability to deliver added value to the economy.

Experiences of training, employment and benefits policies

In the following section, we present brief cameos of disabled people seeking to enter the labour market. The first three case studies (Jane, Gillian and Alan) are drawn from work funded by the DfEE as part of the National Disability Development Initiative. The research analysed outcomes for all participants in the ES's Work Preparation Programme in Scotland between 1997 and 1999, and also undertook twenty in-depth case studies of individuals during the course of their placement. A number of individuals were placed on the Work Preparation Programme by their Personal Adviser through one of the pilot NDDP schemes, and three of these case studies are presented here. Whereas the NDDP caters for relatively able people, many disabled individuals have much higher support needs and would not be regarded as suitable candidates for Work Preparation. These people, if they are fortunate, find their way on to a supported employment programme, often run by a voluntary agency contractor. As part of the ESRC's research programme entitled *The Learning Society: Knowledge and Skills for Employment*, a research project focused specifically on the meaning of the Learning Society for adults with learning difficulties. The final case study, that of Bobby, a young man with significant learning difficulties, is drawn from this research (see Riddell *et al.* 1999). The case studies are intended to illustrate the range of tensions between employment and benefits policies for individuals with different types of difficulty.

Jane

Background

Jane was a 21-year-old woman who lived with her parents in a small town. She attended the local secondary school and gained seven Standard grades at grade 4 or below. On leaving school, Jane completed a two-year extension course at the local FE college. As a result of a congenital condition leading to restricted growth, Jane tired easily and had a hearing impairment and a slight speech impediment. A training agency employee believed that she also had a slight learning difficulty. Although Jane completed several work placements at school and college, she had never had a job, and immediately prior to participating on the NDDP scheme she was working one day a week in a charity shop. While on her placement, Jane received Jobseeker's Allowance and Disability Living Allowance at the lower rate, which is not means-tested.

Placement process

After hearing about the NDDP through the careers service at the local college, Jane contacted her DEA, who subsequently took on the role of Personal Adviser. Following a series of interviews, she was referred to a training agency run by a voluntary organisation with a view to taking up an ES-supported employment wage subsidy scheme. Ultimately, it was decided to place Jane on an enhanced work preparation programme run by the voluntary organisation, with some job coaching. Jane's placement was in a large department store in the city centre. She felt confident about her ability to undertake paid employment despite recognising that she tended to get very tired: 'I need a wee bit of help at the start to get to know things, but once I get to know things, I'll be OK.'

Experience of placement

Jane began her placement in the lingerie department and described her first week as 'a nightmare'. She was unsure of her role and the colleague assigned to her often had to leave to work the till. She was confused by the boxes of bras, which all looked the same. Staff working with Jane had received no briefing about her difficulties and had to work out for themselves what support she needed. Her supervisor initially believed that she was 'stone deaf' and that she had difficulty distinguishing colours, commenting 'everything had just been a sea of white to her'. Other people thought she had difficulties reading the labels on boxes of goods.

As a result of these difficulties, the training agency was contacted and it was decided Jane would receive some job coaching. Jane already had a colleague acting as mentor, so the addition of the male job coach meant that there were two people shadowing Jane, which she felt drew attention to her difficulties rather than solving them. At this point, Jane was transferred to fashions, where she found the work much easier. She was given a small list of jobs to do in a defined area and the job coach was dispensed with. However, by the end of the six-week placement she was still working closely with other people and had not acquired important skills such as using the till.

Outcome

According to her supervisor, Jane was capable of independent work but would have required a much longer placement. At the end of this, mainstream employment would have been feasible. The possibility of an extended placement to move Jane into a period of training rather than assessment was not discussed with the Personal Adviser or the training agency. At the end of the placement, the plan was to seek a supported employment placement within the ES wage subsidy scheme, but demand outstrips supply within this scheme and there was no certainty that Jane would be successful. Another possible outcome would be a training placement in the Training for Work scheme. Alternatively, if Jane took the All Work Test and was found to be unfit for employment, she might claim benefit and undertake part-time work for less than sixteen hours a week under the therapeutic earnings regulations.

Gillian

Background

Gillian was a 19-year-old woman from a small town. She came from a large family (four sisters and one brother), all of whom lived at home. Gillian had epilepsy and was prone to attacks or seizures lasting for a few seconds and occurring three to four times a week; this was a dramatic reduction following a change in medication. Gillian was aware of the onset of seizures and dealt with them by sitting down and then relaxing afterwards. Although epilepsy is still a stigmatised condition, Gillian was confident in dealing with this situation and was not embarrassed or ashamed about it. She was capable of independent travel but wary of new routes or journeys, although her mother worried about her taking too many risks. Despite Gillian being seen as having learning difficulties, her assessments revealed nothing about the extent of these difficulties or their precise nature.

Gillian attended a special school until she was 16 and undertook several work placements. Since leaving school she had completed three short college courses and, having become bored at home, was now keen to find a job. In her profiling Gillian indicated that she would prefer to work with children or elderly people. Because of her impairment, neither of these was considered a suitable option and it was decided to seek a placement in retail.

Placement process

As a person on Incapacity Benefit, Gillian was invited by her local Job Centre to participate in an interview with a Personal Adviser. Prior to this, Gillian had been on a DEA's case load and had been assessed by an occupational psychologist. As a result of the interview with the PA, it was decided to place Gillian on the enhanced Work Preparation programme, and she was found a placement in a supermarket. The role of the Personal Adviser in this case was simply to act as a broker for Gillian in finding her a placement.

Experience of placement

The training agency told staff at the supermarket that Gillian had learning difficulties and gave them some briefing on how to help her. This was subsequently interpreted as 'short-term memory loss'. The store had previously worked with disabled people and were enthusiastic about 'giving her a chance'. Gillian was initially supported in her placement by a training agency worker, but this role was quickly taken over by the supermarket supervisor who felt that she needed to have tasks shown to her many times: 'She would have to repeat, repeat, repeat and repeat until she could do it with her eyes closed.'

Gillian was found to be a competent worker:

> This girl needs very little supervision and can work alone ... she is capable ... she only needs help to learn a new task ... she will get there in the end and achieve what you are looking for ... she doesn't require an Enable counsellor to be with her.

However, because of her difficulties, training took place slowly and staff felt that she would have needed several months before she was ready to use a till, a central part of retail work.

Outcome

At the end of her initial placement, Gillian commenced a Training for Work programme which would extend her time at the supermarket by six months and would enable her to commence SVQ levels 1 and 2 in retail. The staff were confident that she could progress to mainstream employment from this period of training, and there was likely to be a position available in the store. However, despite this optimistic assessment, the supervisor revealed that they actually expected Gillian to return to Incapacity Benefit at the end of her Training for Work placement and that her work would be restricted to sixteen hours a week, the period allowed under therapeutic earnings regulations.

Unfortunately, after a few months in the placement Gillian's medication gave problems and her seizures increased to the level of five to six per day. It was therefore decided that she should withdraw from Training for Work, return to her previous status as an IB claimant, and restart the placement when her condition improved.

Alan

Background

Alan was a 21-year-old man who had suffered brain damage in a road traffic accident when serving in the army. A large part of his rehabilitation was at a specialist head injuries unit. Subsequently, Alan was deemed unable to 'fulfil the high cognitive and physical demands of his trade' and was discharged from the army. This was a blow, because Alan had enjoyed his training and was looking forward to a career in the army. However, he was enthusiastic about finding a new area of work and was referred to a brain injury vocational centre run by a private training agency.

Alan's impairments consisted of poor attention capacity when completing more than one task, and some short-term memory loss. In conversation his speech was rather slow but there was no other immediate evidence of impairment. He was aware of his new limitations but felt that with enough time and training he would be able to return to work.

Placement process

As an Incapacity Benefit claimant, Alan was invited to attend an interview with a Personal Adviser. Although already involved in a training programme run by the voluntary organisation concerned with head injury, Alan was referred to another training agency by the Personal Adviser, causing some local tensions. Information was not sought from the original training agency and the assessment process started anew. Alan was allocated a work preparation placement as a trainee lifeguard at a leisure centre.

Placement experience

Having an interest in swimming, Alan was pleased with his placement and hoped to be trained as a lifeguard. Because of his impairment this was not possible, and Alan's placement job description was to assist in lifeguard duties and to work in the locker area, cleaning, helping customers and dealing with breakages and faults. Because of lack of contact between the two training agencies, Alan did not receive expert help and the pool staff were concerned that they had been asked to train Alan for a job which he would probably never be able to undertake for safety reasons.

Alan clearly enjoyed his placement (to the extent that he had to be sent home at the end of the allocated time, protesting that he wanted to work another few hours) and was very popular with other staff and management. He preferred the poolside work and dealing with the public and, although well aware that he was not a proper lifeguard, he was proud to wear the same uniform and work in the same area as colleagues. However, towards the end of the placement he became aware and felt aggrieved that other staff were being paid a wage while his work remained unpaid.

Outcome

At the end of the six-week placement, leisure centre staff felt that a further period of training was needed and that Alan's full potential had not yet been reached. However, a part-time job for twenty hours a week became available and Alan took this up. His case was reported in the press as a success story for the NDDP, although both voluntary organisations felt that their role had been down-played and the contribution of the NDDP had been minimal.

Bobby

Background

Bobby was a tall, heavily built man in his late thirties. He talked effusively and often cracked jokes, enjoying being the centre of attention. He had significant problems with time, dates and money, and anxieties about losing money or being defrauded. After special school, Bobby was placed at a resource centre catering for large numbers of people with learning difficulties. Group activities such as games took up most of the day. Bobby's key worker described it as very old-fashioned, and believed that Bobby's development as an adult was held back significantly by staying there for many years. He moved to a more progressive adult resource centre which attempted to place people in supported employ-ment. Bobby appeared to have been subjected to physical abuse at home by his alcoholic father and lived for some time in a hostel before moving into his present supported accommodation. Supported employment occupied a relatively small amount of his week, most of which was spent in leisure activities based in the day centre.

Placement process

Bobby was interviewed by the supported employment manager at the adult resource centre, and it was decided that he should attempt some limited work (not more than sixteen hours, classified as therapeutic earnings, giving him an additional £15 a week). His first placement was at a Church of Scotland café project which he did not enjoy, feeling that he was not treated with respect:

> The other job I had they were bossing me about, telling me I'm not doing my job. 'I cannae rush, I'm no machine,' I told her. She said, 'You get on with it, stop walking about.' I said, 'If you're gonna tell me what to do, I'll just walk out.' And I told the supervisor. She said, 'It's a good idea just to walk out if they boss you about.'

Bobby's second placement was at a café where he worked in the confined space of the basement kitchen.

Experiences of placement

Bobby's main task in his three-hour shift was to wash the used milk jugs, coffee pots and containers from the previous evening. The job had previously been done by an existing member of staff who felt that Bobby worked well and needed little help, although he was not convinced that Bobby was actually needed. Bobby appeared to have friendly interactions with the staff, and they made an effort to include him in banter and jokes. It was noticeable that he received more instructions than other members of staff.

Outcomes

Bobby was very keen to extend his involvement in the workplace by working more hours, but his present benefits arrangements made this very unlikely. He received the following amounts of money from a range of sources:

Disability Living Allowance	£12.90
Mobility component – lower scale	£12.90
Income Support – includes	
supported accommodation costs	
(£211.58) plus pocket money (£13.75)	£225.33

Earning more than £15 a week would jeopardise his housing benefit, used to pay for supported accommodation. Although he found this very restrictive in terms of personal freedom and clashed on a number of occasions with his housing key worker, he had no other living options. Moving on to Jobseeker's Allowance from income support with severe disablement allowance would have further consequences in terms of having to attend job training and interviews.

Although committed to the idea of working, Bobby spent so little time at his place of employment that it was almost an incidental part of his social life, which continued to centre round the adult resource centre and social clubs for people with learning difficulties. Although his life was now not entirely segregated, it was still by and large structured round 'special' services.

Discussion

The first three cases presented here were counted as successful outcomes for the NDDP programme, and they have some interesting common characteristics. The three individuals were all in the younger age group and had mild rather than significant disabilities. People with significant learning difficulties, mental health problems or physical impairments would be likely to have far greater problems in finding and keeping a work placement. Indeed, neither Alan, Jane nor Gillian required modifications of the workplace. It is also worth noting that, at the end of the thirteen-week post-placement period, none had found permanent full-time work and all, in the future, were likely to claim some form of benefit or remain on very low wages. Indeed, despite the 52-week rule, Personal

Advisers believe that people who move into full-time work for a period of time may find it difficult to return to their previous benefits package if the job does not work out in the long term. Even if full-time jobs were available, PAs suggested they would be cautious in advising people to take up full-time work.

Although the NDDP has claimed some early success in cases like those described above, training agencies tend to believe that some of this credit is misplaced. The NDDP has not initiated new training programmes, but buys into existing schemes, many of which have been pioneered by voluntary organisations struggling to survive in an area of the training market where finance is short-term and contingent on the attainment of strict targets. The imperfections of existing training programmes have thus been replicated within the NDDP. These include the very short time span allocated to Work Preparation and confusion about whether the purpose of this scheme is to assess or train individuals. In addition, as noted above, the perverse incentives of the existing benefits regime meant that many people felt they were subject to fewer risks if they remained on benefit. Some were simply 'going through the motions' in participating on the training programme, believing they had to demonstrate their inability to work in order to ensure that benefits would continue to be paid.

The fourth case study, Bobby, illustrates the wider problems experienced by people with more significant difficulties. It is evident that the articulation of employment, benefits and housing policy serves to ensure that people like Bobby are permitted only minimal participation in the labour market. Because Bobby is allowed to earn only £15 before losing his housing allowance, it is almost certain that he will be prevented from defining himself as a worker rather than a benefits recipient. This has clear implications for his identity, his financial status and his ability to enjoy other markers of adulthood such as living in a location and with people of his choice.

In conclusion, the government has stated clearly its resolve to reduce the number of new IB claimants, and, as Stone (1984) has argued, this anxiety may well be driven by fear that disability is an elastic category which readily justifies the distribution of resources to unemployed people in societies which regard employment as the basis for wealth distribution. The emphasis of the NDDP is clearly on tightening up the rules for gaining access to lifetime Incapacity Benefit. At the moment, there is relatively little coercion on disabled people to find work, but a system has been put in place which could be used to this effect. It appears that, because of the overt lack of coercion, the NDDP has attracted a group of disabled people who are very anxious to move into employment. However, for many of these people, existing schemes fail to offer them sufficient support to access the labour market. For those with more significant difficulties, the gap between employment aspirations and existing levels of support is even more striking. In addition, for disabled people with high or low support needs, the ongoing tensions between benefits and training and employment policies remain unresolved. The unemployment trap in which many disabled people find themselves (see for example, Simons 1998) has not yet been released.

Conclusion: joined-up policy, employment and the New Deal for disabled people

The NDDP exemplifies important features of the current labour market and the modernisation of welfare. Within the global economy, capital can be shifted round the world at great speed and industries rapidly relocated to cheaper production locations (Castells 2000). Ongoing employment in post-industrial countries depends increasingly on the ability to adapt to a constantly changing labour market. Secure employment is reserved for a relatively small elite, while most workers occupy insecure and poorly paid jobs. As secure jobs become increasingly rare, growing emphasis is placed on lifelong learning as the means for ensuring ongoing employability, if not employment. Participation in education and training, rather than being something which is entered into as a means of personal or career development, becomes a passport to benefits. In the future, it is clear that tighter links will be forged between education, training, employment and benefits agencies which in the past operated as autonomous entities. Professionals within these agencies will increasingly adopt the role of social entrepreneurs, working as free agents across previously sacrosanct departmental boundaries. On the one hand, this may be seen as a way of delivering individualised services focused upon the goal of social and economic independence for disabled people and others. On the other hand, it may reflect a retreat from a Keynsian economic perspective, in which government intervened to balance the interests of the free market and the common good. As the role of government diminishes to that of tinkering at the edges, individuals are increasingly expected to work out their own salvation, helped or sometimes coerced by the new professionals, social entrepreneurs working across 'outmoded' agency boundaries. Underpinning this strategy is the belief that individual entrepreneurialism, coupled with pressure on unemployed people to find work, will lead to job creation. Whether such policies will actually be successful for expanding labour market opportunities, particularly for those at the social margins and in times of economic recession as well as growth, remains to be seen.

References

Arthur, S., Corden, A., Green, A., Lewis, J., Loumidis, J., Sainsbury, R., Stafford, B., Thornton, P. and Walker, R. (1999) *New Deal for Disabled People: Early Implementation Social Security Research Report No. 106*, London: DfEE.

Barnes, C. (1991) *Disabled People in Britain and Discrimination: A Case for Anti-Discrimination Legislation*, London: Hurst Calgary.

Castells, M. (2000) 'Information technology and global capitalism', in W. Hutton and A. Giddens (eds) *On the Edge: Living with Global Capitalism*, London: Jonathan Cape.

Commission on Social Justice (1994) *Social Justice: Strategies for National Renewal* (The Borrie Report), London: Vintage.

Deakin, N. (1994) *The Politics of Welfare*, Brighton: Harvester Wheatsheaf.

Department for Education and Employment (1998) *The Learning Age: A Renaissance for a New Britain*, London: HMSO.

——(2000) *Interim Summary of the Consultation on Extension of the New Deal for Disabled People*, London: Department for Education and Employment.

Department of Health (1998) *Independent Inquiry into Inequalities in Health* (The Acheson Report), London: HMSO.

Department of Social Security (1990) *The Way Ahead: Benefits for Disabled People*, London: HMSO.

——(1998) *New Ambitions for Our Country: A New Contract for Welfare*, London: HMSO.

Disability Alliance (1991) *A Way Out of Poverty and Disability: Moving Towards a Comprehensive Disability Income*, London: Disability Alliance.

Humphries, S. and Gordon, P. (1992) *Out of Sight: The Experience of Disability 1900–1950*, Plymouth: Northcote House Publishers.

Hyde, M. (2000) 'From welfare to work: social policy for disabled people of working age in the United Kingdom', *Disability and Society*, 15(2): 327–41.

Lonsdale, S. (1986) *Work and Inequality*, Harlow: Longman.

——(1990) *Women and Disability: The Experience of Physical Disability amongst Women*, London: Macmillan.

Riddell, S., Wilson, A. and Baron, S. (1999) 'Supported employment in Scotland: theory and practice', *Journal of Vocational Rehabilitation*, 12(3): 181–95.

Riddell, S., Baron, S. and Wilson, A. (2000) 'The meaning of the Learning Society for adults with learning difficulties: bold rhetoric and limited opportunities', in F. Coffield (ed.) *Differing Visions of a Learning Society: Research Findings, volume 2*, Bristol: Policy Press.

Simons, K. (1998) *Home, Work and Inclusion: The Social Policy Implications of Supported Living and Employment for People with Learning Disabilities*, York: Joseph Rowntree Foundation.

Stone, D.A. (1984) *The Disabled State*, London: Macmillan.

Thornton, P., Sainsbury, R. and Barnes, H. (1995) *Helping Disabled People to Work: A Cross-National Study of Social Security. A Report for the Social Security Advisory Committee*, York: Social Policy Research Unit.

Wilson, A., Lightbody, P. and Riddell, S. (2000) *A Flexible Gateway to Employment? An Evaluation of Enable Services' Traditional and Innovative Forms of Work Preparation*, Glasgow: Strathclyde Centre for Disability Research.

Index